Demography of
The Dobe !Kung

POPULATION AND SOCIAL STRUCTURE

Advances in Historical Demography

Under the Editorship of

E. A. HAMMEL

Department of Anthropology
University of California, Berkeley

Kenneth W. Wachter with *Eugene A. Hammel* and *Peter Laslett*, Statistical Studies of Historical Social Structure

Nancy Howell, Demography of the Dobe !Kung

Demography of The Dobe !Kung

Nancy Howell

Department of Sociology
University of Toronto
Toronto, Ontario, Canada

ACADEMIC PRESS

New York   San Francisco   London   1979
A Subsidiary of Harcourt Brace Jovanovich, Publishers

ACADEMIC PRESS, INC.
111 Fifth Avenue, New York, New York 10003

United Kingdom Edition published by
ACADEMIC PRESS, INC. (LONDON) LTD.
24/28 Oval Road, London NW1 7DX

Library of Congress Cataloging in Publication Data

Howell, Nancy.
    Demography of the Dobe !Kung.

    (Population and Social Structure:
    Advances in Historical Demography)
    Bibliography: p.
    1. !Kung (African people) I. Title.
DT797.H68   301.32'968   79–10147
ISBN 0–12–357350–5

PRINTED IN THE UNITED STATES OF AMERICA

79 80 81 82   9 8 7 6 5 4 3 2 1

Contents

1

AN OVERVIEW OF THE POPULATION STUDY OF A HUNTING AND GATHERING PEOPLE

2

AGE ESTIMATION AND AGE STRUCTURE

3
CAUSES OF SICKNESS AND DEATH

4
THE MEASUREMENT OF MORTALITY

5
SIMULATING MORTALITY

6
AN OVERVIEW OF !KUNG WOMEN'S FERTILITY:
COMPLETED REPRODUCTIVE CAREERS

7
FERTILITY PERFORMANCE, 1963–1973

8
!KUNG FERTILITY PERFORMANCE IN COMPARATIVE PERSPECTIVE

9
PRIMARY AND SECONDARY STERILITY: NORMAL AND PATHOLOGICAL CAUSES

10
FATNESS AND FERTILITY

11
POPULATION SIZE, GROWTH RATES, AND THE AGE DISTRIBUTION: SIMULATIONS OF FERTILITY AND MORTALITY

12

MARRIAGE AND REMARRIAGE AMONG THE !KUNG

13

FERTILITY PERFORMANCE OF !KUNG MEN

14

THE SIMULATION OF FERTILITY WITHIN MARRIAGE

15

SOCIAL STRUCTURAL IMPLICATIONS OF DEMOGRAPHIC PARAMETERS: KINSHIP TIES AND KINSHIP GROUPS

16

GENETIC IMPLICATIONS OF !KUNG DEMOGRAPHY

17

THE DEMOGRAPHIC PROSPECTS FOR THE FUTURE OF THE DOBE !KUNG

Preface

The central demographic problem of the twentieth century is rapid population growth and its consequences. But we know that over the whole range of human history and prehistory, most groups had little or no growth and considered growth of population a blessing rather than a problem. And most groups, during most centuries, lived by hunting and gathering. In this study, we look closely at one of the small groups of hunter–gatherers who have persisted into the twentieth century, living at low densities in a quiet and remote area in the Kalahari desert, the Dobe !Kung.

This book presents the results of 2 years of demographic fieldwork with the Dobe !Kung and subsequent analyses that attempted to extract the meaning from what was observed there. Chapter 1 examines whether the Dobe !Kung of the 1960s and 1970s can be considered an example of the hunting and gathering way of life and reviews the history of contact in the area. Chapter 2 presents the method used to handle the crucially important problem of age estimation. Empirical results of the fieldwork are concentrated in a series of chapters organized by topic: mortality in Chapters 3 and 4, fertility in Chapters 6 and 7, and marriage and divorce data in Chapter 12. Readers who have encountered these topics in the reports of investigators of the !Kung (Lee 1972a, Marshall 1976, Howell 1976a) will note that the results presented here are much more detailed. With the increase in investigators, in observation time, and in topics explored, results can now be presented as frequency distributions and cross-tabulations, with attention to variance as well as central tendency.

In addition to concern with variability within the observed population, the small size of the !Kung populations leads to concern with variability over time. The method used to explore this problem is computer microsimulation. No special knowledge of computer simulation is expected from the reader, but those who are interested in exploring the method can consult Dyke and MacCluer (1973) for a general discussion of alternative methods, and Howell and Lehotay (1978) for a description of the particular method used here. Chapters 5, 11, and 14 show the results of simultion studies for particular variables in populations like the !Kung.

From the empirical studies, we find that !Kung fertility is low in comparison with other populations that do not use contraception. Chapter 8 examines !Kung fertility in comparative perspective, and Chapters 9 and 10 look at alternative hypotheses for the causes of low fertility. Chapter 13 reorganizes the data on fertility and compares the performance of men as fathers with that of women as mothers.

Finally, the results of the investigations on death, birth, and marriage are incorporated into a single model, and some of the implications of these rates on long-term population structure are explored. The rates described are seen as internally consistent with the persistence of a viable population with the age structure of the observed !Kung. In addition, the model extracts some of the "invisible" implications of the population structure for kinship and for genetic transmission across the generations. Finally, brief consideration is given to some future changes in the !Kung population.

One result of this detailed description and analysis is a large number of tables. Readers who are not trained in demography may be reassured to know in advance that there is nothing mathematically complex about this research, and no skills beyond arithmetic are needed to follow the arguments and reproduce the results. A second result is a lengthy study of a small population: It is embarrassing to admit that the book has nearly as many pages as the population has people!

Acknowledgments

The Botswana government provided research permission and cooperation in this research for all of the members of the multidisciplinary expedition, which was organized at Harvard University in 1967 and was led by I. DeVore and R. B. Lee. Field colleagues Irven DeVore, Patricia Draper, Henry Harpending, Richard Lee, and John Yellen shared in the logistics of the expedition as we each carried out our independent studies. From the !Kung perspective, the years 1967–1969 will probably be remembered as years when plagues of investigators descended upon them. The !Kung showed inexplicable patience with the investigators, teaching us their language, answering innumerable questions, agreeing to be measured and examined, and even giving their blood in the interest of science. The cooperation of !Kung informants made the fieldwork for this study relatively easy and often fun. The value of the research stems largely from their contributions.

Contact with the population from 1969 to 1972 was maintained through the friendly cooperation of scholars who were in the field—Polly Wiessner, Megan Biesele, Mel Konner, Marjorie Shostak, Ed Wilmsen, and especially Richard Lee, who made two additional field trips and provided essential data. Lee also contributed the photos reproduced in the text.

Preliminary data analysis was carried out at the Princeton University Office of Population Research, with invaluable contributions from Ansley J. Coale and Jane Menken.

In Toronto, I have benefited from the assistance and collaboration of Victor Lehotay, who wrote the computer simulation program, AMBUSH, to and beyond my specifications. Colleagues in the Departments of Sociology and Anthropology at the University of Toronto contributed friendly interest and stimulating questions. A first draft of the manuscript was improved by the methodological comments of Bonnie Erickson and Terry Nosanchuk.

The final version was written in the pleasant surroundings of Berkeley California, thanks to sabbatical leave from the University of Toronto. I appreciate the hospitality of members of the Department of Anthropology, especially E. A. Hammel, of the University of California, Berkeley.

List of Figures and Tables

Figures

Tables

1

An Overview of the Population Study of a Hunting and Gathering People

The !Kung "Bushman" people of the Kalahari desert in Africa occupy an anomalous position in the world of science. They have been selected for intensive study precisely because they are geographically, socially, and economically removed from modern, industrialized society, living in a sparsely settled and remote portion of an enormous semidesert. The !Kung maintain the language and culture of a fully developed hunting and gathering society with (until very recently) no dependence on cultivated plants, no domesticated animals other than the dog, no stratification system based on kinship or occupation, no power or authority structure extending further than the local bands composed of a few related families, no wage labor, no use of money, and no settled sites of occupation.

At the same time, the !Kung have become well-known figures to students—both undergraduate and professional—of Western social science. The faces of !Kung informants gaze from the covers and the illustrations of many texts in anthropology and sociology; students memorize and repeat generalities of !Kung ethnography and watch films of !Kung subsistence and curing behavior (J. Marshall 1956). There are over 100 publications of research on the !Kung of Botswana and Namibia stemming from the Marshall expeditions and the Lee-DeVore expeditions alone (Lee and DeVore 1976:377–394). It is probably true that more North American college students would recognize the names and faces of !Kung hunters than could recognize the heads of state of African countries.

1

Why has all this attention been developed around the !Kung people? Part of the answer lies in the people themselves. The !Kung are a physically attractive people, with slender, graceful bodies and open small-featured faces that are appealing and photogenic. Their culture is simple and has its striking features. The struggle for subsistence, the click language, the emphasis on sharing and humility, the drama of the curing dances in which individuals go into trance and speak directly to spirits to cure sickness, and the pervasive humor, teasing, and playfulness of the !Kung style are all features that are relatively easy to convey and interesting to learn about. Another portion of the answer lies in the characteristics of the people who have gone to live with and study them. The !Kung have been visited by scientists with a wide range of scientific interests, some of whom are in addition photographers of unusual skill (J. Marshall, R. Lee, I. DeVore, M. Shostak) and writers capable of conveying the experience (especially E. Marshall Thomas).

But the most important reasons for the attention paid to the !Kung people are due to what they represent in the history of the human species. Horticulture, agriculture, industry, and commerce are recent inventions from the perspective of human history as a whole. The hunting and gathering adaptation long preceded these innovations in human organization and has since coexisted with them. Hunting and gathering served as the sole basis for human life during the long period in which human groups evolved from prehominids to the fully sapient form of *Homo*, living in sparsely settled groups that flourished sufficiently to occupy the entire planet before the domestication of plants and animals. To understand the prehistory of our species, we must know a great deal about the hunting and gathering stage of our cultural evolution. For this reason, prehistorians of all kinds—archaeologists, physical anthropologists, geneticists, ecologists, and, most recently, sociobiologists—turn to the study of the hunting and gathering peoples of the past and present.

To develop knowledge of prehistoric conditions, the major target of study is actual prehistoric remains, since they provide information on the size and spatial organization of prehistoric groups, their food sources, duration of tenancy of sites, and the like. But the archaeological record is necessarily silent about the details that we need to understand the basic human range of adaptation, topics like the division of labor, sex roles, psychological reactions, social control, and social organization. For the study of aspects of life that leave no trace in the archaeological record, we are fortunate to have contemporary human groups that continue to live by hunting and gathering to serve as an "ethnographic analogy" of prehistoric people. The analogy is far from perfect: One cannot merely assume a straight-line projection into the past, since the modern hunter–gatherers are not biologically primitive or unevolved and there are no populations of hunter–gatherers entirely unaffected by the presence of complex societies. Nevertheless, surviving hunting and gathering peoples can still be found on every continent in

1. AN OVERVIEW OF THE POPULATION STUDY

the world (Murdock 1968). This collection of small-scale societies attracts considerable scientific and scholarly attention because they are the only remaining representatives of the way of life that was once basic to all humans.

The !Kung as an "Ethnographic Analogy": Problems of Valid Generalization

The !Kung people, then, some of whom are the subjects of the present demographic study, are one of the best-known examples of the contemporary hunter–gatherer societies. Before starting the discussion of the particular !Kung population that is the basis of this study, it might be useful to emphasize several points about the relationship of a detailed study of a particular small group of people at a particular point in time to the long-range goal of generalizing these observations to the universe of the hunting and gathering adaptation. These points might be summarized as problems of "sampling" from the target phenomena: In what ways are the people studied a "sample" from the universe of all contemporary hunting and gathering societies, from the universe of the !Kung adaptation to its particular ecological and cultural situation, and from the universe of the !Kung adaptation as it varies over time?

Once the first question is raised, that of the !Kung of the Dobe area in the 1960s and 1970s as a sample of the universe of contemporary hunter–gatherers, the answer and the necessary limitations of the generalizability of this study are obvious. The !Kung were chosen as the subjects of this study for reasons of convenience, not because they were felt to be the most promising subjects in the world for demographic study, not as a random sample of the hunter–gatherers, and not because they are in some way "typical" hunter–gatherers. The !Kung language, culture, and economic organization had been sufficiently studied and described prior to this study that it was believed demographic study could usefully be done (despite many impediments, such as lack of written records and absence of knowledge of age and measured duration) and the results of such a study could be understood in association with other known features of the society. But the fact that the !Kung are a well-studied people does not in the slightest indicate that they are in some way the *typical* hunting and gathering people. It is surely illegitimate to use them as though they are the *prototypical* hunter–gatherers, knowledge of whom tells us all we need to know in order to apply the ethnographic analogy to models of prehistoric life. To describe the population processes of the universe of contemporary hunter–gatherers, it will be necessary to conduct many more studies of the kind reported here for the !Kung.

The second kind of sampling problem, that of generalizing about the universe of the !Kung adaptation to its particular ecological and cultural situation from the information reported here, requires us to consider the relationship of the geographically based group of less than 1000 particular people who were studied to the much larger population of !Kung-speaking people, estimated to number about 13,000, who live today in the countries of Angola, Namibia, and Botswana (where the subjects of this study are living). The subpopulation chosen for study is not a random sample of the larger !Kung group, and indeed, the group was chosen in part because it is an atypical group, more remote and undisturbed by contact with Bantu and European herders and farmers than those in other areas.

To locate the subjects of this study in time and space, it may be useful to look at a map. Figure 1.1 shows the region in Southern Africa where the approximately 13,000 !Kung live, along with many thousands of people of other ethnic groups. The area is vast, approximately 250,000 km², and seems to be approximately coextensive with the traditional !Kung range. That a single language and culture, with only gradual differences of dialect and customs, is maintained over such a vast area is impressive testimony to the viability of the loosely organized social structure of the !Kung people. The !Kung are not a tribe, and there is no evidence that they have ever been one, because they have no centralized leadership, no chiefs or elders who have the power to influence people throughout the !Kung range.

The !Kung language group is only one of several groups speaking click

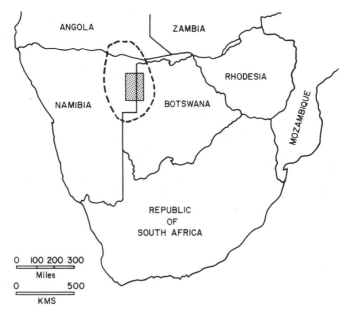

Figure 1.1. The location of the !Kung Peoples in Southern Africa. (See Figure 1.2 regarding shaded rectangle.)

1. AN OVERVIEW OF THE POPULATION STUDY

languages, all of whom have certain obvious physical features in common. All of these language groups together are the San (or Bushman) people.[1] Together with the Khoi (or Hottentot) people, they make up the Khoisan racial and linguistic group of Southern Africa.

The majority of the people of the !Kung linguistic group are "settled," living in dependency or symbiosis with European farmers and cattlemen in some areas, with Bantu farmers and cattlemen in other areas, and at a few governmentally or privately organized "settlement stations." Most of the !Kung people today speak several languages and are well acquainted with the rural versions of modern society, using cloth clothing, store-bought food, radios, innoculations, and sometimes schools. They are also acquainted, in most areas, with such disadvantages of modern society as poverty, the loss of status that comes with dependency and subordination to other ethnic groups, taxes, jails, and so on.

The process of "settlement" of the !Kung has occurred mostly within the past 50 to 100 years. Many of the settled !Kung still hunt and gather a portion of their food, but in most of these areas the population density of !Kung and other peoples, in addition to cattle and agricultural fields, has made it impossible for hunting and gathering to be a viable alternative to wage labor or dependence. No doubt hunting and gathering skills are being lost in many of these areas, as there is little or no opportunity to teach them to the young.

In the area selected for this study, the traditional !Kung way of life has been much less disrupted, in large part because the area was sufficiently dry and distant from other settled areas to discourage immigration by others in the early days. The isolation of the Dobe *area* long after !Kung in other areas were being settled did not imply, however, that the *people* of the Dobe area were similarly isolated. These people are well aware of the cultural and economic changes occurring throughout their territory and many of the individuals resident in the isolated Dobe area have, at some time in their lives, traveled to other areas and even in a few cases outside of the !Kung territory. When we study the culture, the social structure and the demographic processes of the Dobe area, we must accept the implication that they represent an adaptation to the conditions over a much larger area than simply the Dobe area.

The third and final "sampling" problem, then, is that of the time-bounded nature of the study, which was carried out by fieldwork during the period of 1967–1969, and which attempts to reconstruct demographic events during the lifetimes of the living people from the period of approximately 1910–1975. It is appropriate to study the demographic process of a hunting and gathering society over as long a period as possible in order to learn about the fluctuations over years and over generations as a small-scale group adjusts its numbers to its resources.

[1]The term *Bushmen* will not be used in this study to refer to the !Kung, since it has some derogatory connotations.

Unfortunately, it is unavoidably true that the long period of time studied involves substantial changes in the conditions of life of the !Kung people. Much of this chapter will be devoted to an account of the known features of contact and social change in the Dobe area during the past century, since we must know something of the degree and timing of external influences upon the !Kung in order to assess the generalizability of the results of the !Kung demographic study to the hunting and gathering way of life. The answer to the question of how much change has occurred to distort the observed demographic patterns of the !Kung does not have a clear-cut answer. Some of the sources of change, I argue below, could easily have operated for centuries before the present study was conducted. Other sources of change that were instituted during the lifetime of living people are observable through the data collected during the 1960s—it will be a large portion of the task in the chapters to follow to search for evidence of change in demographic parameters over time. For theoretical and methodological reasons, the data on the demographic processes of the !Kung will be organized and presented *as if* there is an unchanging set of probabilities of demographic events occurring over time, a set of probabilities that can be estimated by the study of the frequency of events to particular subgroups of people in particular observable periods. These assumptions are adopted for heuristic purposes and do not preclude the study of deviations from the assumptions. Later we will consider changes in diet and changes in the incidence of disease, particularly venereal disease, as possible sources of changes over time.

The Dobe Area

Dobe is the name of a small waterhole about 2 km east of the border between Botswana and Southwest Africa, or Namibia. Figure 1.2 shows the location of the nine year-round waterholes, some of the more important seasonal waterholes, and the hills and usually dry streambeds that determine the topography. Dobe is one of the smallest of the waterholes in the area, both in volume of water and in the number of people using the water. Its name has been adopted to refer to the whole area because it is easy to pronounce and because it is the one that R. B. Lee first lived at when he came in 1963 to begin this series of studies. The government of Botswana calls the same area the Xangwa district, named for another waterhole (spelled !Kangwa on the map of Figure 1.2).

The Dobe area as a whole is flat and dry and sandy, with bright sunlight and a vast open sky. Although the flatness makes it difficult to get a wide vista on the ground, one can often see the smoke of a grass fire burning many miles off in one direction, while seeing rain falling from an isolated cloud far off in another direction. The area is remarkably quiet to one whose ears are used to the din of city life. On the occasions when a truck comes to the Dobe area, one can hear

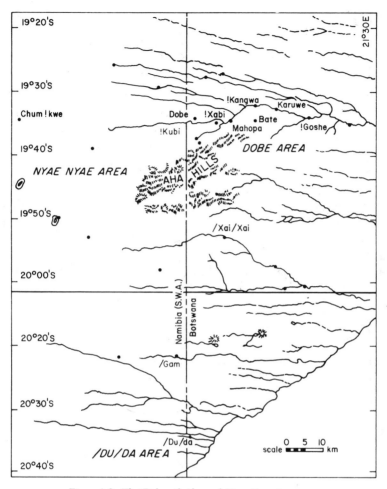

Figure 1.2. The Dobe, /du/da, and Nyae Nyae Areas.

the sound of the motor when it is still miles away, so that the people have the option of going out to intercept it when they choose or avoiding it. The sounds of a !Kung trance–dance can sometimes be heard from a camp miles away at night, when it seems almost that the purpose of the singing and clapping is to fill the vastness of the desert with the presence of people.

Most of the soil of the area is loose sand overlaying limestone. Where the limestone is exposed, water collects during the rains to provide temporary water supplies, ranging in size from a few cups to vast shallow pans that support water birds and swamp grass for a few months out of the year.

Following the rainy season of mid-December to April, there are several months of notably cooler weather. By June and July, temperatures reach the freezing point at night on a few occasions and the rhythm of !Kung life is modified to allow people to sit up around the fires at night and sleep in the sun during the day. The cold dry season is followed by the most difficult time of year, when daytime temperatures rise steadily, frequently reaching 43° C (110° F) in September to November. Vegetation is dry and brown, the temporary water sources have dried up, and the people are concentrated around the permanent water supplies, at nine points along the Xangwa and /Xai/xai valleys, living on short food supplies and often with equally short tempers. Late in November, the vegetation starts turning green again, usually some weeks in advance of the welcome first rains of the new year.

Scattered across the deep sandy soil are clumps of grass and other low vegetation distributed every few feet; groups of trees are more widely spaced. A detailed account of the geography, plant and animal life, and seasonal changes can be found in Lee (1965 and forthcoming).

The area as a whole is bounded by a waterless region of desert about 90 km wide to the east, between !Goshe in the Dobe area and Nokaneng, a substantial Tswana village on the margins of the water system of the Okavango swamps. People on foot or donkey prepare to cross this waterless area with some care, and consider the trip a major expedition. Careless travelers have died in the attempt. The boundary of the area to the north is a long waterless area between Dobe and N!aun!au, about 60 km to the north. This area is regularly used for hunting but is not permanently occupied. The southern boundary is less sharply drawn. The Aha hills divide the southern and northern sections of the Dobe area. There is one major waterhold, /Xai/xai, to the south of the Aha hills and a number of minor water sources, many of them on the Southwest African side of the border, stretching down almost to the Kuki fence north of the substantial European settlement area of Ghanzi. The Dobe area per se ends south of /Xai/xai. There is another area, /du/da, that was home for an additional 150 !Kung people in 1968 to the south. To the west the border of the study area is political rather than ecological. The Botswana–Southwest Africa border was fenced and provided with a dirt road for police patrols in 1967. Members of the expedition were not allowed to cross the border to follow the subjects of our research. Groups of !Kung move freely across the border, living first on one side and then on the other. Most of the research of the Marshall expedition that studied the !Kung during the 1950s was carried out on the Southwest African side of the border, and most of the places mentioned in their research, like the Nyae Nyae pans, are there. Early in the 1960s a settlement station called Chum!kwe, or Tsumkwe, was established about 50 km to the west of Dobe, in Southwest Africa, by the government and missionaries. The station provides medical care, education, wage work, training in agriculture and stockkeeping, and sometimes free food to the Nyae Nyae !Kung who have settled there.

The Dobe area as a whole includes nine permanent waterholes. Bantu pastoralists and their livestock have villages at all of these except the Dobe waterhole itself. The area also includes about 50 named places used for seasonal residence and hunting and gathering of wild foods when there are temporary water supplies following the rains. These seasonal water supplies are usually shallow pans where water collects in limestone depressions, or may be smaller water collections in holes in rocks, hollow tree stumps, and the like. Lee (1972b) has argued that the traditional pattern was to occupy the places with seasonal water during the rainy season, and to concentrate the villages around the permanent water sources only during the dry season. Today the permanent water sources are occupied throughout the year.

The Duration of the !Kung Adaptation: Refugees or Aborigines?

Alongside of the studies of the contemporary !Kung in the Dobe area, archaeological investigations of the occupancy of the past have been conducted. Yellen (1976) located prehistoric sites around waterholes in the Dobe area currently used by the !Kung, the earliest of which has been dated to approximately 11,000 years ago. The evidence suggests that people have managed to live in this desert area for at least 10 millennia. It is reasonable to assume that the prehistoric residents were hunters, and, given the current dates for the beginnings of agriculture in Africa, (approximately 10,000 B.P., see Clark 1976), we may see this ancient population as truly "hunters in a world of hunters."

It is naturally tempting to project a straight line of genetic and cultural descent from the makers of the ancient deposits to the contemporary !Kung, yet it is very unrealistic to hold such a model. Everything that is known about the history of ethnic groups over long periods of time suggests that it is far more likely that every group had periods of growth and splitting into segments, periods of decline and recombination, and a continuous process of intermarriage with members of other hunting and gathering peoples and influences from their culture. It is likely that the ancestors of the !Kung have made substantial migrations over the centuries, migrations that brought them into contact with other peoples. It is entirely possible that the ancestors of the contemporary !Kung may have tried other forms of economic organization, such as horticulture or domestication of animals, once or many times before "devolving" into a stable hunting and gathering adaptation in the Kalahari. The cultural history of the !Kung over a period of thousands of years has been lost through lack of records.

The earliest written records of the existence of Khoisan peoples were produced by Portugese explorers seeking a sea route to the Indies, just as Columbus documented the existence of North American peoples during the same period.

Southern Africa was "discovered" by Bartholomeu Dias in 1488 and by Vasco da Gama in 1497. Da Gama found hunting and gathering peoples in what is now St. Helena Bay, and cattle-keeping Khoikhoi (or "Hottentots") at Mossel Bay, initiating European–Khoisan relations by a combination of trading and fighting that was to continue, at an accelerated pace, over the next century. Elphick (1977) documents the decline of the Khoikhoi in the Cape from the establishment of a fort for restocking ships by the Dutch East India Company in 1652 under the command of van Riebeeck, until a smallpox epidemic in 1713 decimated the already weakened Khoikhoi. Elphick provides, incidentally to his main concern, tantalizing glimpses of the elusive "hunters." There is considerable historical evidence on the conflicts of San peoples with the invading settlers (Marks 1972) and much can be learned by "reconstruction" from later ethnographic observations (Bleek 1928; Schapera 1930). But much of this understanding is confined to the peoples south of the Orange River until the eighteenth century. Much of the northern interior of the continent, including the area now occupied by the !Kung, was terra incognita to literate observers until the nineteenth century.

Within the past few centuries, however, we do not need to rely entirely upon written records, as there is evidence from the collective knowledge of the !Kung themselves that their ancestors were living in isolation and relative ignorance of the continent-wide conflicts taking place between the Khoisan, the Bantu, and the European settlers. They were protected by the simple fact that none of the stronger peoples of southern Africa wanted to take their territory away from them, or even share it, until recently.

The major method the !Kung have for relating to the past is living memory. They believe that their parents and grandparents have told them everything they knew, and they have been told that they have always lived in this part of the world, in the Kalahari desert where the mongongo nuts grow, though not necessarily at these particular places in the vast area that the !Kung now occupy. It is interesting to note that the !Kung, at least those of the Dobe area, disclaim the rock paintings and cave art found in widely separated spots throughout their territory. Since contemporary people were not taught the techniques of rock painting and engraving by older people, they do not believe that their ancestors made the works of art. Similarly they do not claim to know who made the ancient deposits excavated by Yellen, since their ancestors told them nothing on the subject.

It is impossible to say exactly how much time depth is stored in the group's collective memories. When the !Kung claim that they have "always" lived in their present range, there is no way of knowing whether they mean for hundreds, or thousands, of years. We can, however, be confident that they have lived in their present range for at least several hundred years. The oldest people in the population were about 20-years old in 1900. They would have had ample opportunity to talk with and hear the stories of old people who had witnessed events from 1840, who in turn would have known people in their youth who were alive during the eighteenth century. If the !Kung of the eighteenth century had lived a radically different kind of life, surely the living people would know it.

What would life have been like for the !Kung in the eighteenth century, at the limits of traceable human memory? How much of the value of our studies for understanding the basic pattern of hunting and gathering life has been lost by arriving on the scene 200 years later?

The !Kung would not have been entirely unaffected by the presence of dense settlements, agriculture, and the territorial conflicts of outsiders to the Kalahari 200 years ago. Whether or not any !Kung person had ever met the outsiders face to face, the !Kung would inevitably be affected by the changes in game populations, animal migration routes, and more subtle ecological effects of the presence of outsiders. The !Kung were not "hunters in a world of hunters" 200 years ago—or even 2000 years ago—and recovery of the details of life in that period is hopeless.

In the eighteenth century, as now, it is likely that the !Kung were organized into small groups that moved frequently from one source of food to another. Had the !Kung of the eighteenth century been organized into tightly bounded small groups that maintained distinct gene pools, they could hardly have maintained a continuous language and culture over the enormous range that they claim today. The pattern of frequent long and short distance migrations, utilizing widespread kinship ties, must be an old pattern, with living groups forming and dissolving, coalescing and splitting to adjust group size to the resources available (Lee 1972b). While no or few individuals may ever have covered the whole !Kung range during a lifetime, nearly every individual can be expected to travel long distances, living in a number of places and encountering a wide range of other !Kung, even if always in relatively small groups.

In the eighteenth century, as now, it is likely that the !Kung population was not tightly bounded on its margins, just as it was freely mobile in its interior. At the points where the !Kung have frontiers with other peoples, one would expect the decentralized !Kung to be highly variable in their forms of interactions with others. The !Kung, being one of the larger groups of San, have frontiers with a number of other San peoples with distinct languages. It is likely that at least a small rate of intermarriage and blending of cultures has been going on with these groups for centuries, a process that is currently so advanced in the Ghanzi district, a place where a number of San groups are in contact, that !Kung are no longer always sure which customs, myths, and names were originally their own and which were adopted from others (M. Guenther personal communication 1975). Due to the wide mixing of the !Kung people overall, genes introduced into the !Kung population at the borders can be expected to find their way throughout the whole area. The same is true for customs, information, and material possessions: Items introduced at the borders would easily flow throughout the population. The institution of *hxaro*, giftgiving networks of !Kung that connect kin and kin of kin in complex chains (Wiessner 1977) was probably the means for diffusion of metal for arrowheads, for example, from the border regions throughout the territory long before there was any regular contact with non-!Kung in the interior of the region.

History of Contact in the Dobe Area

Around 1800, the Tswana people expanded their range northward into what is now called Ngamiland, the district of Botswana in which the Dobe area is located. The expansion occurred in the form of the creation of a new chieftainship, the Tawana from the Ngwato (Chirenje 1977). The new chief and his supporters established villages around Lake Ngami far to the east of the Dobe area. There were San and Kgalagadi peoples living in Ngamiland when the Tawana branch of the Tswanas arrived, but it was not necessary for the Tawanas to fight any organized group to obtain settlement rights. Apparently the settlement prospered from the start, since when David Livingstone visited in August 1849 (Livingstone 1851), he found an estimated 90,000 Tawanas and their cattle occupying a series of villages and cattleposts. Chirenje (1977:63) reports that the Tawana in Ngamiland had firearms by 1850. Introduction of guns led to an era of successful hunting, which had been followed by the decline of game populations in the more populous Tswana districts. In Ngamiland, on the "frontier" of settlement, plentiful supplies of game remained over a longer time. Additional observations of the Ngamiland Tawana are available from the visit of the trader James Chapman in 1862 (Chapman 1868).

Relations between the Tswanas and the previously resident San (or Sarwa, as they are called in the Tswana language) and Kgalagadi peoples seem to have been hierarchical in all cases and oppressive to the San and Kgalagadi in many instances. Chirenje (1977) describes the process of contact as follows.

> Initially the process of enticing serfs seems to have been a peaceful one, consisting mostly of placing some cattle under the care of a band or group of the Kgalahadi; in the case of the Sarwa, early contacts with the Ngwato were established during hunting trips, when the latter befriended them with presents of meat. This was probably the method adopted by other Tswana groups in bringing serfs under their control. On the other hand, the Tawana claim to have used witchcraft to bring serfs under their control. In all Tswana chiefdoms, overseers (*mong*) of serfs collected produce from them as tribute (*lekgetho*). This consisted of ivory, ostrich feathers, hides, and skins and as a reward for their service the Tswana master supplied them (through the overseer) with hunting dogs, allowed them to retain the meat of the animals they killed, and they were also free to milk the cows for their own consumption. Serfs remained attached to their master's family for the rest of their lives and they were inherited by his children and could be captured in war as booty. Serfs had no access to tribal courts [p. 260].

Chirenje goes on to cite historical records of the offer of San peoples for sale to early visitors by their Tswana "masters."

The Dobe area remained outside of this process of Tswana settlement until late in the nineteenth century. The earliest recorded impressions of the Dobe area come from 1875, when a European named Van Zyl came on a hunting party with some other European men to /Xai/xai (which he called "CaiCai"). Van Zyl found only !Kung living in the area. The !Kung recall the visit as a friendly one: One of the European men impregnated a !Kung woman, who had a son, the father of one of the current members of the population, a woman who claims special kinship ties with contemporary European visitors to the area. In the Nyae Nyae area to the west, where the Marshalls worked, it was a custom for European visitors to carve their initials and date of visit on a prominent baobab tree. The earliest date there is 1878 (Marshall 1976:55).

Around 1900 the Dobe area began to be visited irregularly during the rainy season by hunting parties of Tswana men who drove ox sledges across the wide band of waterless area to the east. The contemporary !Kung of Dobe say that these visits gradually became annual events, eagerly anticipated by the !Kung, since the Tswanas brought presents of tobacco, metal pots, wire for arrow points, and other objects in their empty sledges on the way in, leaving with the sledges loaded with dried meat and skins a few weeks later. !Kung–Tswana relations in the Dobe area, as described by the !Kung, seem to have followed the pattern described by Chirenje for an earlier period elsewhere, starting with hunting trips in which the !Kung had much to gain by cooperating with the armed Tswanas and leading to establishment of semifeudal relationships of a personal tie of loyalty and obligations between a particular relatively rich and powerful Tswana man and "his people." The !Kung have a word for the relationship in their own language, calling the Tswana their $k^{?}au$, or 'owner', which is clearly the relationship described elsewhere as "serfdom." The $k^{?}au$ is expected to supply contact with the outside world, protection from other non!Kung, adjudication of disputes, and an occasional share of food and goods to the !Kung person, in exchange for loyalty and work. Whatever the uses and abuses of this system outside of the Dobe area, within the area the people report that the relationship has usually been unoppressive and for many people had not been evoked by either side for years at a time. In an area like Dobe, it is obviously easy for a !Kung person to avoid the constraints of the relationship, if desired, by staying away from Tswanas.

During the period of the regular hunting trips, the Tswanas naturally noted that the grass of the Dobe area was rich and ungrazed and that their oxen grew fat on it. Gradually, and the chronology is vague, Tswanas started driving cattle with them on the rainy season trips, started taking Dobe !Kung people back with them to the east to help with the cattle year-round, and eventually established cattleposts in the Dobe area, staffed by a combination of Tswana immigrants and resident !Kung. The "pioneer" Tswanas were few and far between: Thomas (1959) reports that one of their informants in the Nyae Nyae area in the 1950s lived as a serf in childhood, around 1910, at /gam, a waterhole some 50 km south of the Dobe waterhole. The first Tswana families seem to have settled in the Dobe area itself in the 1920s, after which the Dobe area saw the development of two distinct ways of life side by side. For the first 20 years of Bantu presence in the Dobe area, however, the pace of change seems to have been slow. The numbers of Bantu and cattle in the area were small enough that they could not provide a major source of food or work for the !Kung people, so most of the people continued the pattern of hunting and gathering in small groups, occasionally visiting the cattlepost to ask for a gift of milk or tobacco. A few !Kung families seemed to have specialized in helping with cattle, often moving back and forth from the Dobe area into the Tswana-dominated regions to the east and back again.

In 1948 the Tswana tribal government appointed a "headman," Isaak Utuhile, to serve as judge and mayor of the Dobe area (designated the Xangwa area in official documents) and to administer the law to both the !Kung and the Tswana people. For the Dobe !Kung, this was the first formal authority structure that they had been involved in, as the traditional !Kung structure has no mechanism for adjudication of disputes or punishment of wrongdoers. It seems that bringing the Dobe area under "law and order" made it more attractive for cattle-keeping peoples in the overgrazed areas to the east. The establishment of the headman was soon followed by an increase in the immigration to the area. The migrations were probably triggered by an outbreak of tsetse flies into a previously fly-clear area around the borders of the Okavango swamp. The inability of cattle to coexist with tsetse fly increased crowding on the nearby range and cattle keepers actively sought new pasture lands for settlement while the Tsetse Fly Control Commission proceeded with the difficult task of driving the flies back into the swamps. The cattle keepers could not expand gradually into the lands between their settlements and the Dobe area because there is a long stretch of waterless land between them. Instead the cattle keepers, now under the protection of the new headman, crossed the waterless area and settled more or less permanently in the Dobe district. These cattle-keeping people consisted of members of several tribes: Tswana, Yei, and especially Hereros.

The Hereros are a Bantu-speaking pastoral people whose homeland is in Southwest Africa (Namibia). !Kung of the Dobe area recall stories of the forced migration of the Herero people across the Kalahari desert around 1905, when many were escaping from the Herero–German wars. Groups of these Hereros were met by !Kung groups, and in some cases saved by the helpful provision of water and food. Other stories tell of Herero groups that were refused help or even killed by !Kung. The Hereros settled far to the east of Dobe, in the better-watered areas of Botswana, and began building up their herds of cattle again after the wars. They have been so successful in rebuilding their herds that by 1950 Hereros were actively seeking new areas to settle. With the arrival of the head-man, the Hereros began settling in the Dobe area in the early 1950s, and by the mid-1960s about 70% of the approximately 200 Bantu residents of the area were Hereros. Many of these Hereros consider themselves only temporary residents of Botswana and are still hoping to return to their homeland in Namibia. In the meantime, they live with Tswanas and !Kung. Many speak the !Kung language and some Herero men have married !Kung women.

During the period of the Herero settlement in the Dobe area, the Marshall expedition was studying the !Kung living entirely by hunting and gathering 50 km away. After the completion of the Marshall research, the government set up a settlement station, which changed the lives of the Dobe neighbors to the west, and attracted some of the Dobe people into permanent residence.

In 1963, Lee arrived to study the people of the Dobe area during one of the periodic droughts to which the region is subject. The Bantu suffered more heavily from the drought than the !Kung did when many cattle died and crops failed for several years in succession. When Lee started his work, the "headman" was the only institutional force in the area and the border was unfenced. By 1967, when the fieldwork for this study was started, the fence and a parallel dirt road had already been constructed, and the !Kung area had been influenced and disturbed by the presence of the road construction gangs for some months. Later in 1967 a trading store was opened at Xangwa that, although oriented to the pastoralists who had cattle to sell and cash to buy goods, affected the whole area by bringing in more people, goods, and regular truck traffic. The store truck and the regular trips for supplying the expedition increased communication between the people of the Dobe area and the tribal capital in Maun. One result was pressure on the government to provide a primary school for the area, which, after a number of delays, opened in 1972 for both Bantu and !Kung children. By 1975 some 30 !Kung children had attended the school for at least part of a year, a European missionary had come to live permanently in the area, helping to organize development schemes, and the public health services of Botswana had made several trips to the area, surveying health needs and providing immuniza-tions. In the capital, Gaberones, the national government of Botswana has established a Basarwa Development Office to look into the economic problems and solutions for all of the San peoples of Botswana.

It is clear that the !Kung of the Dobe area and elsewhere have begun integra-tion into the national life of Botswana. The rapid social change of the past decade is in itself a fascinating topic of study (Lee 1975), but its effects were relatively slight up to 1973, when the data collection for the present study ended. Most !Kung people, on most days between 1963–1973, would have seen little impact of outsiders a few hundred yards beyond the scattered Bantu cattleposts or anthropological field camps.

The Status of the !Kung in the 1960s

In the 1960s the !Kung people were a long way from being a "pure" case of hunter–gatherers surviving unchanged from the Pleistocene. Even in the Dobe area, one of the most remote and isolated subpopulations, about 70% of the adult women and 90% of the men had some ability to speak one of the Bantu languages in addition to !Kung, the majority of the adults had been outside of the Dobe area at least once in their life, and about three-fourths of the women reported that they had lived with and been dependent on Bantus, either through their own work or that of family members, at one time or another. Nevertheless, the importance of contact and dependency on the Bantu and consequent distance from the traditional way of life should not be exaggerated. Almost all of the !Kung people of the Dobe area have the complex skills of hunting and gathering, the ability to recognize an enormous variety of plants, in all seasons, and to know their edible parts, and the ability to recognize animal tracks and to identify the desirable prey. Hunters find and kill animals with only spears and bows and arrows, and all !Kung can find water, and above all, survive with little equipment in the Kalahari. This knowledge is not (yet at least) at the stage of being merely theoretical: The people actually do leave the cattleposts and settlement stations, where life is easier in many ways, and go out into the bush, making their little villages, eating the wild animals and vegetables, and living for months at a time without recourse to the cattleposts. The time of arrival of the Bantu is recent: During much of the adult lives of the older members of the population there was no alternative to hunting and gathering as a way of life in the Dobe area. Even since the 1950s, when the pace of cultural change accelerated, the degree of contact has varied between individuals over time.

The Dobe area !Kung, then, are a population in which the demographic processes of a hunting and gathering people can be studied, as most of the constraints of their day to day life over the past 50 years or so have been formed by the requirements of hunting and gathering rather than a pastoral economic base. The process of contact that has been reviewed here only requires awareness of the degree and direction of the kinds of changes resulting from contact. The precontact period is not intended to refer to a mythical period when the !Kung were "hunters in a world of hunters," or even to the period in the eighteenth century when !Kung life would already have been influenced in subtle ways by the presence of outsiders. Precontact, for the purposes of this study, merely refers to the period before the Bantus had an effectively large presence in the area, before the 1950s.

The Definition of the Population of the Dobe Area !Kung

The population of interest in this study is that endogamous (inmarrying) group of people, including the !Kung observed in the Dobe area during the 1967–1969 period, that produces and maintains a gene pool, a language, and a culture from generation to generation. We must distinguish between the group that we have information on and the group that we would like to have information on. We have information about less than 1000 !Kung people during the 1963–1973 period, some information about their ancestors, and, for the older people, their descendents. We want to generalize from this information to the group of which these people are a part: the !Kung people over long periods of time.

The target population, then, is defined on *de jure* criteria: the members produced by the !Kung ethnic group population. We are little concerned with migration in and out of the Dobe area in this study, because members of the population remain in the *de jure* population no matter where they are. The *de jure* population of interest is not bounded by geographical limits. It is an empirical question how large it is; the answer depends on whether the !Kung people of the Dobe area intermarry with all !Kung-speakers, or whether they are a part of a subdivision of the total. Birth and death are the only means of entering and leaving the *de jure* population; marriage and migration merely form new links between descent groups in each generation, holding the whole together. Presumably subgroupings of the total !Kung language group can form and dissolve over time.

Difficulties of classification can arise when !Kung marry members of other ethnic groups. If the marriage partner lives with the !Kung, takes a !Kung name, and the couple raise their children as !Kung, we conclude that the population has gained a member, equivalent to the "birth" of an adult. If the outmarrying !Kung drops out of !Kung social relations, and if children are raised by the customs of the spouse, the person can be classified as leaving the population, equivalent to a death. Practically speaking, the !Kung of the Dobe area are a sufficiently distinct group that there is little difficulty in isolating the target population. Within the past 20 years, and occasionally before that time, !Kung women (but not men) have married Bantu, both Tswanas and Hereros. If this process continues over a long period of time, there will come a time when the Bantu and the !Kung in this area are a single population by the definition put forth above, reproducing a mutually influenced gene pool, culture, and languages over the generations.

The Demographic Data Collection

The assembly of information about the *de jure* population, however, has been necessarily *de facto*. Only people who were actually present in the study area were included: Even nuclear family members of studied people were excluded from the population list if they were consistently out of the area during the period of study and never seen by Lee or Howell. An attempt was made to catalogue 100% of the !Kung people who were ever physically present in the Dobe area, as shown in Figure 1.2, during the period 1963–1973. Non!Kung residents and visitors to the area, however, were not included, due to the difficulties entailed in learning two more languages and sets of customs in order to collect information. This study is not, therefore, equivalent to a census of a geographical area. !Kung women married to Bantu are included and counted as married women, but their husbands are not counted as members of the population. Their children are counted as !Kung only if they have !Kung names, therefore a few children of !Kung mothers who have Bantu names and who are being raised as Bantu are excluded from the study.

The sampling frame or master list of the population was started by Lee in 1963, when he assigned a unique identification number to each of the individuals he encountered in order to distinguish the many people who have the same names. Lee knew 466 people when he left the field in 1964 after his first field trip, 433 of whom had been entered on his "master list." By 1973, when he returned for a fourth field trip to the !Kung, the list had grown to 895 people, including about 200 who lived in the /du/da area, out of the Dobe district. The number of people who were members of the population fluctuates over time, as whole groups were added to the records when they were encountered, and as people were born, died, and entered the area as visitors. Census data will be presented for several points of time in more detail in Chapter 2.

In addition to the information of the master list, the data reported here were collected by observation and interviewing, in the !Kung language, during 22 months of fieldwork from June 1967 to April 1969. Information on the marital and fertility histories of women was collected by interviewing 165 women at the age of first menstruation or over, 100% of the women resident in the Dobe area at that time. Additional interviews were collected from adult women who came for temporary visits to the Dobe area during the fieldwork and reconstructions of the marital and reproductive histories of women who had died during recent decades were collected from surviving relations. But these interviews, which do not represent a complete collection, will not be used in the analysis.

The Dobe area !Kung population, then, has been observed during 1963–1964, during 1967–1969, and, by researchers who remained in the field after the demographic fieldwork was completed, from 1969 to 1973. By extrapolation and interviewing about missing observations, a full account of the events in the population during an 11-year period can be constructed, and this detailed knowledge of the most recent decade provides one important source of information on the flow of events. In a population as small as that of the Dobe area, however, it is entirely possible that the events during a 10-year period will not provide an adequate indication of the long-term levels of probabilistic events like birth and death, particularly since the most recent 10 years are precisely those in which the level of social change has accelerated and when our expedition may have influenced the events we came to study. The data from the recent past, then, is accurately collected but is likely to be atypical of the conditions in the Dobe area over a long period of time.

A second body of information is derived from the accounts provided by women who were past childbearing age in the 1960s. These 62 women and their experiences provide invaluable information on characteristics of completed reproductive careers. These events occurred sufficiently far in the past that they avoid the influences of recent cultural and economic change.

The third source of information is provided by women under age 45 in 1968, those who are reporting on lives in process. Much of the information provided by these women overlaps with that of the events of the past 10 years, but the bodies of data are not coextensive. The women at different stages of the reproductive process provide opportunities to test the hypothesis that women who have completed reproduction have undergone probabilistic processes very like those currently affecting younger women. The older women can be considered as a cohort, or group of cohorts, for comparison with the results of constructing "synthetic" cohorts based on combination of the events occurring to different groups of women *as though* a group of women were passing through that set of experiences during their lifetimes.

Each of these collections of data is, by demographic standards, small, and in each of them the absolute numbers of events available for analysis fluctuate over time in ways that make interpretation of the events difficult. While demographic processes have been found to be among the most regular and smoothly operating of human behavioral traits (in contrast to religious or political behavior, for example), the noise generated by random fluctuations of events in small populations continually threatens to drown out the regularities to be observed. To make the most of the data, we need a framework for interpretation, a model within which the shreds of evidence can be brought into alignment with one another, so that their implications and their interactions can be examined.

Models for Analysis of the !Kung Population

To maximize the usefulness of the available data, we shall assume that there is a basic set of parameters that characterize the !Kung people, with their particular set of genetic material, their particular set of customs and behaviors (including the crucial one of economic organization), living in the particular ecological setting of the Kalahari. We assume that events "on the ground" are a reflection, however dim, of certain probability schedules of those events, which might be thought to exist, as Plato suggests, "in the clouds," or merely abstractly. Events "on the ground" are the observable reality, and we shall examine the events known to us in considerable detail in this work. From the point of view of the people concerned, these events are the only reality that matters; from the point of view of understanding the realities and the problems of the contemporary Dobe area !Kung, for the purposes of administering social programs and the process of adjustment and adaptation to the newly instituted contact situation, the observed events represent "the facts of the case."

In demographic studies, however, we go beyond looking at particular events, such as births, marriages, and deaths, to consider those processes as the determinants, in the long run, of the numbers and proportions of people born, married, and dead, which in turn are the determinants of other aspects of population structure, such as the age–sex composition and the growth rate of the population. As in other demographic studies, here we will calculate not only the numbers of such events, but also the number of people who are at risk of that event, in order to estimate the probability of that event to people in those categories. We have confidence, on theoretical grounds, that all of the different probability schedules estimated for a particular group have to be internally consistent with one another in the long run, in the sense that the combination of schedules has predictable consequences for population structure and dynamics. If one combines estimated probability schedules and finds that the implications in the long run are internally inconsistent or would produce a population with very different features than the one observed, either the schedules have been estimated incorrectly or one or more features of the population has changed in the recent past, so that the population was not produced by the same processes that currently are seen.

The technique used to extract the probabilities from a collection of observed data and examine their implications is that of a life table. We start with a group of people of an arbitrarily large size (say 100,000 or 100) who are beginning to be at risk of the event. That cohort is subjected to the set of probabilities of having that event occur over successive segments of time, calculating by standardized techniques the frequency of the event by age in the cohort, the mean number of such events per unit of time, the probability of surviving from the beginning of the analysis to each point of time without having the event occur, and so on.

The technique used to examine the implications of a set of probability schedules estimated for a particular population is that of the stable population models. Stable population theory (Coale 1972; Lotka 1907) is a framework for determining the age–sex composition and the growth rate that would be produced by the long-term continuation of a particular mortality schedule and fertility schedule of a closed population. Stable population models are like "friction free" models in physics: Their usefulness is not restricted by the observations that no real human populations continue to operate under unchanging mortality and fertility schedules for long periods of time and few human popultions are clearly bounded (or "closed"). Stable population models show us what would happen, precisely, under given conditions, and tell us what to expect on the average in real populations that can be closely modeled. Demography has developed during a historical period in which rapid changes in probability schedules of mortality and fertility have characterized most of the world's population, so that rapid fluctuations in parameters in real populations are the expected rather than unusual case in analysis. One can argue a better case for expecting a population like the precontact !Kung to be well described by the stable population models than for most populations in the contemporary world. Tables showing the features of stable population models formed by the combinations of fertility and mortality schedules observed from a wide range of well-studied populations exist (Coale and Demeny 1966). Features of stable population models formed by mortality or fertility schedules that fall outside this known range can be calculated by computer programs (Shorter 1973; van de Walle and Knodel 1970).

Stable population models provide valuable indicators of the average population composition to be expected in a population produced by the fertility and mortality schedules estimated for the !Kung. They cannot, however, provide any indication of the variation in population features to be expected over time in so small a population as the !Kung. This variation may be extremely important in both the long and the short run, as, for example, fluctuations in the sex ratio and the probabilities of death to infants and children interact with the supply of available spouses and therefore the fertility performance of the population at a later date. We will investigate the variance observed from year to year and from group to group in the data on the actual !Kung population, but to interpret that variance we need a method of determining the theoretical variance expected from the probability schedules and the effects of the interaction of those variable processes.

To explore this aspect of "ideal" !Kung population functioning, we shall use Monte Carlo computer simulation of hypothetical populations modeled on the !Kung. A computer simulation program, called AMBUSH, has been written for the purposes of this research, with features tailored to the description of a population like the !Kung (Howell and Lehotay 1978). AMBUSH simulations combine the features of stable population models with the randomness or noise expected in a population like the !Kung when unchanging probability schedules of events are applied to individuals who do or do not have the event occur according to the draw of a random number. The AMBUSH simulations, like the real population, have a history and are subject to stochastic variation, the cumulative effects of random fluctuations over time. The outcome of AMBUSH simulations, unlike stable population models, is not determinant. To find the mean state of the population—comparable to stable population models with the same probability schedules—one must make a number of AMBUSH simulations and average them. The results of separate runs, then, provide information on the range of variability in population features to be expected.

Note that the observed !Kung population is comparable to just one of the AMBUSH simulation runs. It can be interpreted as just another of the possible outcomes of a single probability process, with two exceptions: The observed !Kung population may include observation error and certainly includes missing observations, so that ironically we know much more about the functioning of the simulated populations over time than we do about the real one; and the observed population is the source of the probability schedules that produce the simulation, so that it ought to be closer to the mean of the simulations than one chosen at random. Empirical studies of the !Kung will be presented apart from the simulation studies, which will be used (in Chapters 5, 11, and 14–16) to explore the implications of the parameters derived from empirical studies.

2

Age Estimation and Age Structure

In order to make a microdemographic study of a group of people, it is essential that time, in the form of age of individuals and of periods of time during which events occur, be available as the framework within which events are analyzed. Yet when one encounters a group of 20 or so !Kung, living in a bush camp quite isolated from events in the outside world, one necessarily doubts that the ages of these people can be determined accurately. The people themselves do not know their ages or dates of birth, nor do they use numbers over three in their own language. One can, of course, attempt to make a guess of their age from their appearance; this was done frequently in the field, as a part of the process of distinguishing individuals with the same name from one another. To complicate the process of age estimation, their way of life is so different from the people on whom we have constructed our standards of age appearance that we have to allow for the possibility that they age in an entirely different way from the familiar one.

Errors might run in either direction. We might guess them to be much younger than they in fact are: They are small and slightly built people, characteristically, with the type of facial features called pedomorphic (childlike). They live a healthy outdoor life, free of the aging effects of obesity and the stresses and strains of modern society, so that they might appear to us to be much younger than they actually are. Some observers have suggested that, on the contrary, they age much more rapidly than other people, due to the hardships of their life and their diet, the drying effects of sun and wind in the Kalahari on their skin, and so forth. Silberbauer, the official Bushman Survey Officer of the Bechuanaland Government (now Botswana), spoke of the difficulties of including the San people in the national census of 1964.

> Bushman age rapidly in their appearance and an individual who, one is quite certain, could not possibly be a day less than seventy years old, proves to be no more than 40. Bearing this in mind, it was decided to group all of the over-thirties together, as the enumerators' estimates of their ages would be so unreliable as to make the data useless [Silberbauer 1965].

Much of the potential value of this study depends on making adequate age estimates. For the purpose of looking closely at the vital population processes of death and reproduction, we cannot be satisfied with simply grouping the people into broad categories. Fortunately, the demographer working within an ethnographic context has time to develop knowledge of the interrelations of the people within the population and gains access to a considerable amount of information useful in making age estimates that census takers cannot easily obtain. Because the task of age estimation is so important to the value of the entire study, this chapter is devoted to an explication of how the estimates were made for the study population, along with some results of the study for the age structure, based on these estimates.

Demographic Techniques of Assessment and Correction of Age Estimates

By world standards the !Kung are extreme in their inability to provide information on their own ages, but problems of age estimation are present to some extent in many demographic surveys. Even highly sophisticated and literate populations have been found to have characteristic patterns of misreporting their own ages. These patterns, which can be seen in the single-year tabulations of age of "raw" census data from most countries of the world, commonly take the form of "age heaping" on numbers that end in five and zero, often combined with "heaping" on (or avoidance of) socially important ages (such as 18, the legal age of maturity, and 65, the legal age of retirement, in North America). "Age vanity," the tendency to report oneself as younger in middle age and older in old age than one actually is, has been rediscovered many times (Blacker 1965; van de Walle 1966).

In parts of the world where age estimates are made by the census taker from the appearance of the informant, different but also distorted age distributions are typically produced. A commonly observed pattern is to treat 5-year age groups as though they correspond exactly to socially recognized stages of the life cycle, so that infants and children who cling to their mother in the census taker's presence tend to be placed in the 0- to 4-year-old group, independent children who have no visible signs of sexual maturation are placed in the 5–9 age group, those who are sexually developing but not yet mature in the 10–14 category, postmenarchial but prefertile girls in the 15–19 category, and young parents are guessed as 20 and over. All over the world the raw age distributions of population where age is guessed by the census takers show a deficit of numbers at 0–4 years, an excess proportion at 5–9 years, and so on (United Nations 1967). The problem is not serious in national censuses, because techniques have been developed to make adjustments and corrections for age misestimation, smoothing the excess numbers at certain ages or age groups into those where there is a deficit, using statistical smoothing techniques or stable population theory models that relate the age structure to the recent history of fertility and mortality in the population. Uncorrected age misreporting could be extremely detrimental to the value of a demographic study, if, for instance, mothers who have their children at a young age are judged to be older than they really are. Age errors would then enter directly into misinterpretations of the age schedules of fertility. For another example, a deficit in a certain age category might be taken as evidence for an epidemic at the time those people were babies.

The techniques used to diagnose the problems and correct raw age distributions are derived from stable population theory. The central principle of stable population theory is that the proportion of the population in each age segment is determined by the fertility and mortality schedules that formed the population and does not depend upon an original age distribution or the fertility and mortality schedules of the remote past of the population. If the population is closed to migration, and if the fertility and mortality schedules are similar to the standards constructed from the study of many populations, and if those schedules have been unchanging over time, the age distribution will be that of one of the model stable populations. Many important features of the population are thereby known without further study. In fact, all particular populations known deviate from the models in some ways, not least in the sequence of historical changes of the fertility and mortality schedules. Nevertheless, the models are extremely useful as a series of standards against which to compare any particular population. Using the results of stable population theory, one can calculate the proper age distribution associated with any particular sequence of fertility and mortality schedules.

Rank Ordering the Population by Age

Probably the most powerful tool the anthropologist has to improve age estimates over those that can be produced by demographers is the wider study of the people and their interrelations that the anthropologist is likely to have made. Peoples who, like the !Kung, have no notion of absolute age often have a strong cultural concept of relative age, which in the !Kung case is incorporated into regularly used terms of address. The anthropologist, who observes the use of these terms over a period of time, knows that a person cannot be placed as older than his older brother or younger than his cousin who is called by a "younger" kin term.

F. G. G. Rose pioneered the systematic use of knowledge of relative age for improving age estimation (Rose 1960). After a substantial investment of time and energy on the job of age estimation, Rose discovered that he could produce a consistent age ranking for each of the two moieties of the Groote Eylandt tribe of Australian aborigines. He did this from the older–younger terms that people use not only for biological siblings, but for classificatory siblings as well. Rose's procedure was to arrange the aborigines first in the order of the ages he had guessed for them, then check those guesses by looking at the sibling term that a person used for each other person. The person he guessed as oldest should not call any other aborigine 'older brother' or 'older sister.' If he did, the other person was placed as the oldest and the original starting person as second. Each person was considered in turn on the criteria that they should not refer to anyone already placed by an "older" term and should call everyone not yet placed by a "younger" term. It is too much to hope that the ordering could be made completely without internal contradiction, but Rose found that the Groote Eylandt aborigines, at least, used their intramoiety terms consistently enough that he could produce an age ranking with considerable confidence. Figure 2.1 shows Rose's drawing of the age estimation procedure that he used, with age-ranked individuals across the bottom of the graph and the ages that they could be from 0 to 70-years old on the vertical axis.

Following Rose's procedure, the first step in making estimates of !Kung people's ages was to construct as accurate an age ranking of the people in the population as possible. Considerable data were collected on the kinship terms that people used for one another. The data were examined to find out whether the pairs of reciprocal terms were used consistently and to explore the patterns of real kin, fictive kin, and the lack of kin ties between pairs of people in the !Kung group. However, this procedure is inefficient as a means of age ranking: In order to know the kin terms used between each pair of 500 people, nearly 250,000 (N × N − 1) terms must be collected. To rank the !Kung by age, a special procedure was carried out in the field over a period of several months, combined with the program of physical measurements that was a regular part of the work of the expedition. Every few months for several years, the scale and height rod and a big bag of tobacco for gifts would be loaded on the truck and Lee and Howell would move to each village in turn to make measurements. These occasions were popular with the !Kung people, since they provided them with supplies of tobacco and a break in routine to sit in the shade for a few hours joking and

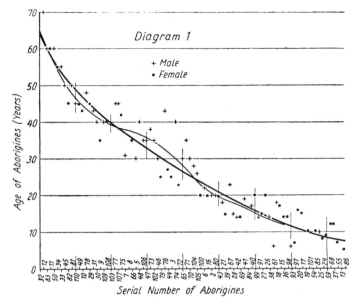

Figure 2.1. Estimation of age of aborigines (from Rose, F. G. G. *Kinship age structure and marriage of Groote Eylandt*, New York, Pegamon Press, 1960).

watching others being measured. They also provided a convenient opportunity to collect a great deal of casual information and news about the groups.

To construct an age ranking, a card listing identification on each individual was made as they came forward to be measured. The first person was not asked any questions. The second was asked whether he or she was younger or older than the first, and so on. It is important in making these age rankings to place the people who are best known in the area first. People who only came to the area as adults, whose placement may be difficult, should be placed later, since people rank themselves relative to those who have already joined the rank and the presence of ambiguous people may confuse the placement of those who come later.

Somewhat to my surprise, I found that people did not know their age relative to many of the others in the Dobe area and did not use any kin term, real or fictive, for people with whom they had never lived. The rank ordering, therefore, was confined to the members of living groups clustered around one or a few nearby waterholes in four areas. Within such a local area, all of the people are likely to know each other well. Exceptions might be temporary visitors to an area and people who married in or moved in as adults (who will have an opinion of their age relative to others, but this opinion is more likely to be wrong than among people who grew up together). Everyone, however, grew up somewhere, so on the second round of ranking the population, all of the people who could placed themselves in another list of rankings. About 10% of the adults were ultimately placed in more than one list. No attempt was made to place children born since 1963 into more than one list as their absolute year of birth is usually known.

Several hundred people did not place themselves into any of the rankings, because they were already deceased by 1968, they were out of the area, or they simply did not happen to appear for measurements at the time when I was constructing the age ranking. Most of these were placed by asking a close relative to place them. About 20 people were never placed by themselves or by their relatives. They have been inserted into the ranking by R. B. Lee, who saw all numbered people at least once.

The result of the age-ranking work, therefore, was four ranks, corresponding to four geographically clustered groups of waterholes, one combining the places !Goshe, !Kangwa, Karuwe, and Bate, consisting of 140 people; a second combining all of the groups that live around the Mahopa waterhole with those at !Xabi and Dobe, with 106 people; a third consisting of 64 !Kubi people, which includes many people classified as "marginal" who were only visitors to the area, most of whom were living at the settlement station at Chum!kwe in Southwest Africa; and finally 161 people at /Xai/xai and the southern bush camps.

These four rankings were later combined into one single ranking by matching the points at which an individual was included in two or more lists and mechanically interleaving the people between matching points, making one sequence of 841 cards ranked from youngest to oldest.

Fitting a Curve to the Ranked Ages

Assuming that the age ranking is correct, Rose saw that there has to be a line over the less than 100 years of human life span that represents the ages of the ranked individuals, sloping from oldest to youngest person, without reversals in slope. His procedure was to plot his guesses of people's ages based on their appearance (and those of another European who knew the people well), and find a line which minimized the deviations of the plotted points.

To begin the process of estimating actual ages of the !Kung, a graph like Rose's was drawn, with the identification numbers of individuals along the bottom and the years in which these people could possibly have been born along the vertical axis. The years of birth of the children born since 1963, when observation began, were plotted first, as these years of births were fairly certain. In order to use stable population models to assess the plausibility of various methods, a rough estimate of mortality was made by a preliminary calculation of the proportion of children born to postmenopausal women who had died in infancy. A preliminary estimate of the level of fertility was made through counting the mean number of children ever born to those same women. These preliminary calculations suggested that the model stable population relevant to the !Kung experience should be one with an expectation of life at birth around 30 years, with a small rate of population growth. This model stable population was then used as the criteria for judging the adequacy of a number of methods of estimating age on ranked individuals. Experiments were made plotting guesses of age based on appearance, or based on dates from event calendars of occurrences that could be dated outside of the study area (primarily murders and arrests by the police), and estimates based on typical differences in ages of close relatives, especially mothers and their children. Each of these methods produced a somewhat different estimated age for the individuals, with a somewhat different pattern of steep portions and plateaus in the slope of the curve. Since none of these methods that utilized information collected in the field seemed to be significantly more convincing than any other, it was decided to use the artificially smooth curve of the stable model population itself as the basis for making age estimates for individuals.

To refine the exact model to be used, however, it was decided not to rely upon the number of children born to postmenopausal women as the best indicator of fertility, since these births took place long ago and there were some preliminary indications that fertility among women currently in the childbearing period was not so high. Since, in stable population theory, fertility, mortality, and age structure are in a completely determinant relationship, knowing any two of the three features gives the third. The parameters used to isolate the stable population model used are (a) a life table with an expectation of life at birth of 30 years (MW5-F: Coale and Demeny 1966) and (b) the proportion under age 5 (known from direct observation) and under age 10. Determining which children were 10-years old and younger was done by collating the seasons of birth reported by mothers for the ranked children and grouping the seasons into years. Since ages for children 6 and under are nearly exact, the determination of the proportion 10 and under could be made without stretching the available information too thinly. These children were only 4-years old and younger when Lee arrived in the field in 1963 and there was not much time available in which confusion could be generated. Again, the determination of which child marked the boundary between the years was made from the mother's report on the season of birth. The boundary between years is the beginning of *bara*, the 'big rains', observed to occur during December or January.

Having selected the necessary two parameters, it is a simple matter to interpolate between columns of model stable populations to find the expected proportion at each 5-year age group for the standard population. Table 2.1 summarizes the features of the stable population model on which the age estimates were made.

The next step in the process is to decide on the target population to which the stable population age distribution is to be applied. There is no single point of

TABLE 2.1
Stable Population Model for Estimating !Kung Ages[a]

Age interval	Population in interval (%)	Exact age	Cumulative % at exact age x and under
0	2.84	1	2.84
1–4	8.93	5	11.77
5–9	10.11	10	21.87
10–14	9.61	15	31.49
15–19	9.14	20	40.63
20–24	8.59	25	49.22
25–29	7.97	30	57.19
30–34	7.35	35	64.54
35–39	6.70	40	71.24
40–44	6.07	45	77.31
45–49	5.45	50	82.76
50–54	4.81	55	87.57
55–59	4.08	60	91.65
60–64	3.26	65	94.91
65–69	2.39	70	97.30
70–74	1.53	75	98.83
75–79	.80	80	99.63
80+	.39		

[a] Interpolated from Coale and Demeny (1966:34); model "West" 5 (females) with 21.87% under 10-years old.

[b] Population parameters for this interpolated model on stable population: crude birth rate = 34.07; crude death rate = 33.33; average age = 28.6; dependency ratio = .663; growth rate (r) = .0074; gross reproduction rate (with mean age at childbearing = 27) = 2.124; total fertility rate (with mean age at childbearing = 27) = 4.375.

time at which all 841 ranked individuals were alive at the same time. The first decision, then, is to select a target date. Arbitrarily, the target date was made the end of 1968, near the end of my period of fieldwork, when there were 796 people alive. Use of any other date would change the exact composition of the population somewhat, as people enter and leave the population.

The next consideration is to eliminate the effects of migration into and out of the area as much as possible. Because there is probably some tendency for young adults to be more mobile and do more long-distance visiting than other members of the population, it was decided to eliminate all people classified as "marginal" in the census of late 1968, that is, people who were present in the Dobe area but had not settled and the residents of the southern bush camps (/du/da). This reduces the target population from 796 to 454. Finally, after a number of experiments that demonstrated that the males of the resident population were far more likely to be out of the area than females, it was decided to limit the target population to the female resident population present in the area during the census at the end of 1968. This target population is 244 individuals.

To assign individual ages, then, one orders only the target population in rank order, while retaining their place in the ranking for the whole population. For the target group only, then, we observe from Table 2.1 that the person at the 94.9th percentile should be the youngest person who is 65-years old. Calculating which individual that is, we place a point on the graph at 1903 (i.e., 1968 minus 65 years), as the estimate of her year of birth. Continuing to identify the person at 60-years old, 55, 50 and so on, we develop a series of points on the graph. Again using only the target population, we divide the women between those at 5-year points into each of the single years for birth dates, and plot those birth dates for the target population on the graph for the whole population. Connecting those points, one has an age estimate for the year of birth of each person, not only for the women alive and resident in 1968, but for all 841 people, the others being determined simply by their placement between those in the target population. Estimates for the few people over the age of 80 are simply guesses made by increasing the interval between surviving members of the population, on the assumption that most of the people at each of the single years are already dead. The estimates for extreme old age can only be very rough. Figure 2.2 shows the results of these procedures for the resident population.

Assessing the Age Estimates

Assessing the validity of these age estimates is a difficult task. Obviously, we cannot expect or hope that the use of a procedure that requires a number of arbitrary assumptions and that makes no provision for annual variations in fertility and mortality could produce age estimates that accurately express the exact year of birth for each individual. A reasonable goal is more modest: The procedure, to be judged successful, should produce estimated ages that are correct on the average, over the whole life cycle, even if individual ages are wrong by several years in either direction. The pattern of age misestimation should be random, rather than systematically distorting the results for certain groups. Perhaps the best single test of the plausibility of the age estimates is to look at the difference in age between mothers and their children over the life span, controlling for the order of the births. If our method of age estimation implies that the young women are approximately 20 years older than their first child, then mothers who are currently 60-years old and happen to have a first-born child in the age series should be approximately 20 years older than that child, too. At least, we would be sure that something was seriously wrong with the procedure if the older women were consistently 30 years (or 10 years) older than their first-born child. Figure 2.3 shows the mean age of mothers implied by the difference in age between themselves and their surviving children for each of their first five

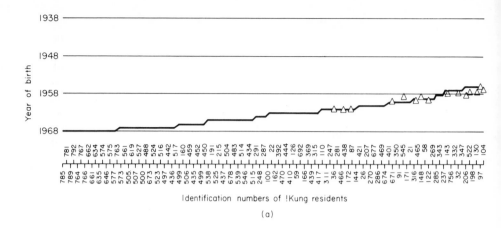

(a)

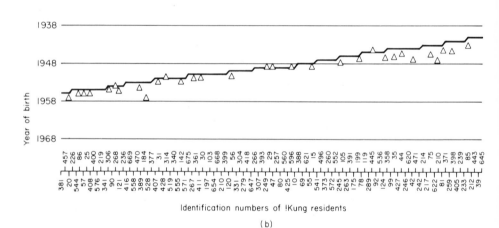

(b)

Figure 2.2. Estimation of age of !Kung residents. Solid lines show year of birth from stable population method discussed in the text. Triangles show independently guessed ages from event calendars and life events.

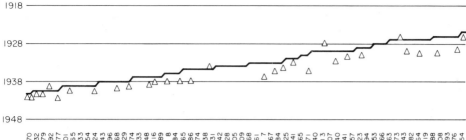

Identification numbers of !Kung residents

(c)

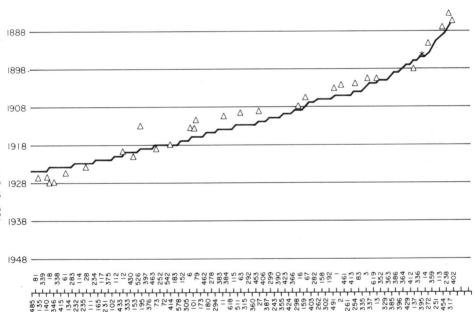

Identification numbers of !Kung residents

(d)

pregnancies and for 10-year age groupings of the mothers. Women in the last two cohorts, those born 1939–1948 and especially those born 1949–1958, have to be omitted because they have not yet had a chance to have their children, so we would be selecting for the youngest mothers at each birth order.

Let us consider the pattern we would expect to see on Figure 2.3 if the age estimates are correct and if births occurred in a completely time-standardized pattern: The lines for each pregnancy order should run straight across the graph. If, on the other hand, the timing of births has been regular but the age estimation procedure is consistently wrong, we would expect to see the lines parallel to one another and sloping either up or down toward the present, depending upon the direction of error in the estimation procedure. Instead, what we see in Figure 2.3 is a pattern of more or less parallel lines, varying as much as 5 years in the mean age at birth implied for a particular birth order. The first cohort, that of women born prior to 1898, has consistently higher ages at each pregnancy order, suggesting that the oldest women have been placed too old by the procedure. This cohort, however, contains only seven women, and the results are likely to be only a function of small number fluctuations. Over the rest of the age range, the differences in age at giving birth are not entirely consistent and seem to provide evidence that the age estimates are at least plausible.

Perhaps a better feel for the results of the age estimation can be derived from an examination of the results produced for an actual family, to consider whether the ages are believable in a group of people who are biologically related to one another.

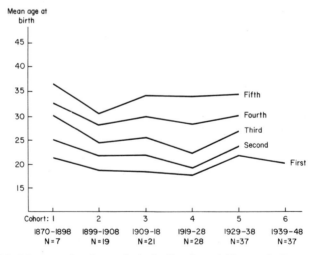

Figure 2.3. Mean age of mothers at the birth of live-born children implied by difference in age between mothers and surviving children in the age ranking, by cohort of mother's birth.

2. AGE ESTIMATION AND AGE STRUCTURE

The family selected for a closer look, in Figure 2.4, is one of the largest in the population, and also one of the best known to the members of the expedition. Most of them lived at the Dobe waterhole during much of the time that the study was conducted, often serving as prime informants on aspects of !Kung life. The central person in this group is /asa, a successful mother who had seven pregnancies with seven surviving children. Her year of birth, as estimated by the procedure described above, was 1923, making her 45 when photographed. Her husband Kasupe, was estimated as born in 1912, making him 11 years older than his wife, 56-years old when photographed. /asa is only 14 years older than her oldest child, according to the procedure, which is several years younger than the youngest mother we observed during the 1963–1973 period. Her birth year estimate, therefore, may be several years too young. The children of /asa and Kasupe are regularly spaced over the next 20 years according to the estimation procedure: N/ahka in 1937, Debi in 1939, N≠isa in 1944, N!uhka in 1949, ≠oma in 1951, Tin!ai in 1954 and finally Kase in 1957. This birth spacing is closer than we find in the general population, but of course that is to be expected of the most successful parents. By the time that /asa had her seventh child in 1957, her oldest daughter N/ahka had already had the first of her children, so the generations overlap. Since 1957, /asa and Kasupe have had many grandchildren not included in Figure 2.4, the diagram of the ages of this family, because their ages are not problematic.

The extraordinary feature of this family, which makes it so useful for consideration of the plausibility of the results of the age estimation technique over the whole life span, is that both /asa and Kasupe have one of their parents alive, or did in 1968. /asa's father, Kaše Tsi !xoi, is one of the oldest people in the population, with an estimated year of birth of 1886, 82 years old in 1968 when photographed. The old man still had the ability to walk long distances on group moves and collect much of his own food, although his hunting days are long past. In 1968, he was building his own hut when the group made a new village, and slept at his own fire alone at night, usually next to his youngest son, Bo, who is married and has a child. We see overlapping generations here too, as Bo (/asa's youngest brother) is younger than /asa's oldest children. If the age estimates are correct, the old man must have been over 30 at the birth of his first child, /asa's older brother who is now deceased. He would have been 37 when /asa was born and 54 when his last child, Bo, was born, which is at the limits of the observed range for contemporary ages at fatherhood. Unfortunately his own wife is dead so we do not have an estimate of her birth date to add to this sequence of events, but we do have some supporting evidence for the old man's age estimate from another woman in the population. Long ago, old Kaše married (or rather tried to arrange a marriage with) an old woman named Chu!o, whose date of birth is estimated at 1894. The attempt to arrange the marriage, which would have been a first marriage for both of them, occurred when Chu!o was premenarchial.

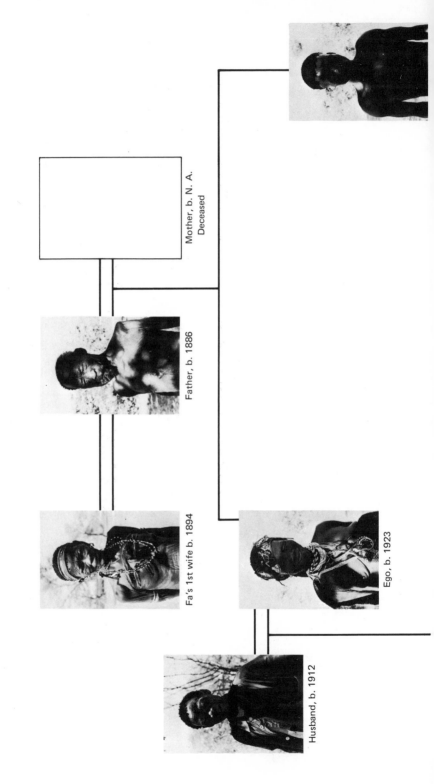

Mother, b. N. A.
Deceased

Father, b. 1886

Fa's 1st wife b. 1894

Ego, b. 1923

Husband, b. 1912

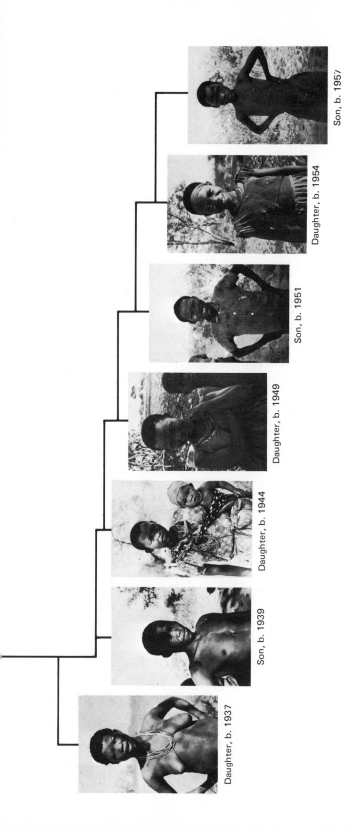

Figure 2.4. Estimated ages in a real family.

Figure 2.5. "Beautiful Unkha" in 1955 and 1968, and 1968 17-year olds. (Top left) Beautiful Unkha, "The lily of the field" in 1955—estimated age is 17, estimated year of birth is 1938; courtesy of E. M. Thomas. (Top right) The same woman in 1968, age 30. (Bottom left and right) Two more beautiful girls in 1968—estimated age is 17-years old.

Since the contemporary age at menarch is about 16, we estimate that this marriage must have occurred somewhere around 1910, which would make Kaše 24-years old at the time, the usual age for first marriages for men.

Kasupe is estimated to have been born in 1912, the oldest child of a mother who must have been around 75 in 1968. Unfortunately she lives across the border at the settlement station of Chum!kwe, and we have no photo of her. She is, however, the mother of one of the main informants of the Marshall family's studies of the !Kung Bushmen, called "old N/aoka" (Marshall 1976:xxii).

The Marshall family's expedition to a nearby area to study !Kung in the 1950s provides one more opportunity to test the plausibility of the estimation procedure. Elizabeth Marshall Thomas (1959:165) writes of the adventures of the imperious young woman, "beautiful Unkha, the lily of the field," who seemed in 1955 to be such a strange combination of a playful and rather silly child and a beautiful woman who could use her power over her husband and other men to tease and humiliate them. Although I had read The Harmless People before going to the field, I did not realize until I returned to my book collection that "beautiful Unkha" was the same person with whom I had shared a pleasant friendship at /Xai/xai in 1967–1968, trading gifts and favors and continually joking about trading husbands. She had been married for many years to a different husband than the one described in The Harmless People, had four healthy children and was a competent adult member of the community. Figure 2.5 permits us to look backward in time at the picture taken by John Marshall in 1955 to see if the aging process for at least this one woman is consistent with the ages we estimate people to be in 1968. Figure 2.5 shows the original picture from 1955, when she must have been 17 according to my age estimates, her picture in 1968 at the age of 30, and the pictures of some girls in the 1968 population who are estimated to be the same age in 1968 that "beautiful Unkha" was in 1955.

These kinds of "tests" of the plausibility of the method of estimation provide no solid basis for assessing the range of probable error in the estimates. The amount of error in estimation for any one person depends in part on the source of the error in the steps of the procedure. Wrong placement in the rank order, for instance, probably contributes to the largest errors for individual adults, although the ranking procedure itself seems to be the strongest feature of the procedure in reducing errors overall. If a person doesn't know his rank relative to the others in the area, or gives answers to the ranking placement which are obviously wrong (to him) due to "joking" relations with particular others, the individual error could be as large as 10 years for adults or old people. Another source of errors in the final estimates is problems with combining the four distinct age ranks into one: If the age structure of the four areas is actually rather different, combining them mechanically into one rank will introduce systematic errors. Finally, the choice of a curve-fitting technique can be a source of error. The technique used here assumes regular production (and maintenance) of people in each age group,

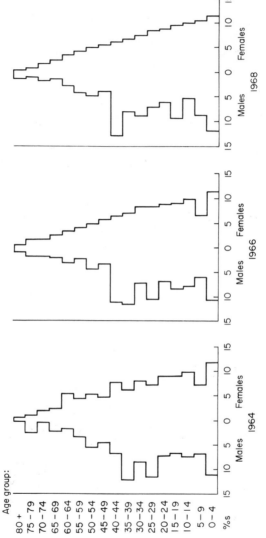

Figure 2.6. Age–sex pyramids, for resident populations of 1964, 1966, and 1968.

with no annual variation or annual variation that averages out into a smooth curve. Consider the effects of a run of good weather, good food supply, or simply good luck that produces twice as many surviving infants in one year as expected: Everyone older than those infants would be pushed up a year in age, and what is good luck from the !Kung perspective is disastrous for the age estimation procedure. Similarly, a run of bad luck that produced no surviving infants in a year would pull everyone older down a year in age. In a population so small that only about 15 infants are expected to be born each year, random or systematic fluctuations in births and deaths will be expected to introduce continuous errors of as much as several years in individual ages.

This problem is amenable to simulation. Later (in Chapter 11) we will calculate the number of years of error introduced into the ages of individuals by using the techniques of age estimation described here in comparison to simulated people's "real" ages as given by the program. These experiments will show us that we have to allow for a 2–3 year average error in estimation, but do not, unfortunately, provide a basis for correcting or further reducing the errors in age estimates in the real !Kung population.

Having produced this set of estimated ages, of course, we can proceed to analyze the available evidence on means and variability in the vital processes that produced the population over the period of the memories of living people. We will present the results of this analysis in the following chapters. With a more refined view of the fluctuations in vital processes, it is possible to return to the age estimation process and recalculate the age estimates, taking the history of vital processes into account. Extensive experimentation with this approach of making successive approximations to the probable age curve of the population based on the history of fertility and mortality schedule changes has shown that this does not improve the analysis, as different sources of errors are introduced. The strengths of the present procedure seem to lie primarily in basing the estimates on a rank order of the population, fitting a reasonably smooth curve to the whole population, and using these estimates of age consistently in all parts of the analysis so that interrelations between various aspects of population processes can be compared. The method requires that we tolerate uncertainty about the actual ages of the people: within a margin of up to 5 years for adults; surely more for people over sixty.

Age Structure of the Population

Having estimated the year of birth of each individual, let us now look at the implications of those estimates for the age and sex structure of the total population and various subunits within the population. Although we have used a procedure that artificially smooths the age distribution, the procedure is scarcely visible in the age–sex pyramids of Figure 2.6, except for the women resident in 1968, when the procedure was applied. Even for this group, some irregularities in the shape of the age distribution are produced by the small numbers to which the expected percentages must be applied: With only 244 people to allocate to 17 categories, it is not possible to match the expected percentages in each category exactly, as we cannot assign fractions of people to age categories. Figure 2.6 presents the age–sex pyramids of the census population, for residents only, at each of three points of time, approximately 2 years apart: 1964, during Lee's first field trip; 1966, when there were no observers in the field (the numbers were reconstructed back to 1966 during 1967); and at the end of 1968. Note that the shape of these distributions is basically pyramidial, as expected, but highly irregular. The distribution of men over the age groups is more irregular than the women's distribution, in part because the age estimates artificially spaced the women out over the age groups, and in part because men more often migrate into and out of the area. This migration is related to work characteristics and family status, both of which are associated with age. The dependency ratio, or burden of dependency (calculated as the number of persons 0–14 and 65+ divided by the number of persons 15–64) is a direct reflection of the age structure of the population, representing the number of adults who are available to provide food, shelter, water, and other necessities for the dependent members of the population, the children and old people who do not work.

Age Structure of Villages and Households

The age structure of the whole population is irrelevant to day-to-day life in the Kalahari, as the whole population never acts together or even meets together. People live with and act with the others who share their households, and the collection of households which make up a *chu/o*, a 'village' or living group. People change membership in households rather rarely, usually remaining in their parental household from birth to marriage. Sometimes older children will go to live with a grandparent or older relative, and adolescents will sometimes form a household with other adolescents before marriage, or live alone. Unmarried adults will usually maintain their own household, sleeping alone by their own fire and preparing much of their own food. At marriage the household will consist of the couple and will be increased by the birth of their children. A marital household will persist, losing members as the children grow up, until the marriage is ended by death or divorce. We will see later that the divorce rate is rather substantial in this population: A proportion of adults will be between marriages at any point of time. Households tend to be more stable than living groups, as whole households are usually the unit of change of residence. Villages are frequently moved en masse to another location, but the living group that makes up the village is somewhat more stable, with households more stable again. Since the living groups and the households are the basic units of life and work, let us look at their size and age–sex composition in more detail.

First consider the size of villages and the number of households in them. Data are available from a census taken in 1968, when 569 people were tabulated by household and village (data courtesy of R. B. Lee). There were 34 groups living and functioning as of that date (arranged in Table 2.2 in order of size). These villages were not randomly scattered throughout the bush, but are gathered around sources of water, especially since it was the hot and dry season of the year. Note that the 12 villages that have seven or fewer members are marked off from the others by a line in Table 2.2. Eleven of these 12 are closely associated with Bantu. Normally, !Kung living groups are not as small as these 12 villages, except temporarily perhaps in the process of forming or dissolving a group. These villages consist of men hired by Bantu to tend cattle somewhat away from settlements in order to take advantage of the best pasturage for the cattle. These men, and their dependents in some cases, are living in an "un-!Kung" manner. In some cases, these small living groups adjoin Bantu households, not counted here.

The minimum components of a village, normally, are 4 households and at least 10 members. The median group size, excluding the deviant small living groups shown in Table 2.2, is 20 members, divided into 6–8 households. The mean size of villages not closely associated with Bantu is 22.8 persons, and the mean number of households per village for the same group is 8.9, with the normal range from 6 to 12 households. As we will see later, the work demands of village life require multiple competent adults in a village to provide for the dependents, share the work load, and provide insurance for families in case of adult accident or illness. The dependency burden falls on individual villages more significantly than on the population as a whole, so the dependency ratio is presented in Table 2.2 for each village. Note that the mean dependency ratio for the 17 villages relatively independent of Bantu is .51 (there is approximately one dependent for every two adults), with a range from 1 to .2. The dependency ratio of "bush" villages has been eased by the presence of Bantu, who tend to attract families with difficulties in providing for their children or aged members. Note that the dependency ratio of the population as a whole in the model used to construct age estimates is .66.

Let us look at the age composition of households more closely, since it shows a clear pattern over the life cycle. As we saw in Table 2.2, household sizes are relatively small, the mean is only 2.5 persons per household, which is much smaller than household sizes in Botswana as a whole. A household consists of the people who eat and sleep together in intimate contact, sharing a hut, although rarely actually occupying it, since they sleep and eat at the fire just outside the door. Table 2.3, a cross-tabulation of the household sizes and the age structure of the population at the census, shows clearly that the larger households, those with

TABLE 2.2
Dobe Area !Kung Size of Households and Living Groups[a,b]

Living groups: (in order of size) Village number	Size	Household size (number of persons) 1	2	3	4	5	6	7	8	9	Number of households	Dependency ratio
9	1	1									1[b]	Inappropriate
33	1	1									1[b]	Inappropriate
34	1	1									1[b]	Inappropriate
14	2		1								1[b]	.00
28	3	1	1								2[b]	.00
12	4		2								2	.25
13	4				1						1[b]	.50
15	5					1					1[b]	.60
32	5		1	1							2[b]	4.00
17	6	2			1						3[b]	.20
8	6	1				1					2[b]	1.00
10	7	1					1				2[b]	.50
5	10	1	2			1					4[b]	1.00
6	10		2	2							4	.20
20	10	2	2		1						5	.43
11	14	1	3	1	1						6	.40
1	15	1	5		1						7	.50
16	15	1	2	2	1						6	.40
18	16	2	2	2	1						7	.45
27	16	2	1	1	1	1					6	.60
3	20	7	4	1		1					12[b]	.33
30	20		3	2	2						7	.25
31	20	2	4		1		1				8[b]	.42
22	21	3	4		1		1				9	.75
23	21	1	5	1				1			8[b]	.50
24	21	3		1	1	1	1				7	.50
29	24	2	5	2			1				10	1.00
4	28	2	1	3		3					9[b]	.55
25	30	1	5	3	1		1				11	.76
7	32	3	3		2	3					12	.77
2	33	1	4	3	1	1	1				11	.57
26	43	7	5		5		1				18	.65
21	45	6	7		4					1	18[b]	.66
19	62	6	6	6	1	2	2				23	.44
Total households		62	80	31	27	15	10	1	0	1	227	Mean = .51
Total persons		62	160	93	108	75	60	7	0	9	569	

Average household size = 2.5 persons

[a] From census of November 1968, includes Xangwa and /Xai/xai, not /du/da.
[b] Indicates close association with Bantu.

four or more persons, are composed of children and their parents. Almost 80% of children (under 15) live in households of four or more people, while only 4% of children live with only one other person, who would necessarily be their mother. The largest household in the population has nine members, a couple and their seven children. Fortunately for them, they live in a Bantu-style house and don't need to sleep on the ground next to their fire, as one can easily imagine that it would be cold being the ninth person out from the fire. In the absence of Bantu support, this family would probably encourage childless relations to take some of their older children into their household. But as we shall see in the section on fertility, without Bantu support it is less likely that this family would have so many children.

The second largest household, of seven members, is a polygamous household living in traditional !Kung style. The two mothers shelter their children on separate sleeping mats; the husband chooses his spot. All other households have six members or less, and those with six, five, and four members have a large component of children. Notice in Table 2.3 how membership in the largest households drops off after age 50, as the children grow up and leave the parental households.

TABLE 2.3
Size of Households and Age of Individuals, Dobe Area !Kung[a]

Age of individuals	Household size (number of members)									
	1	2	3	4	5	6	7	8	9	Total
0–4	0	2	15	17	16	17	1	0	2	70
5–9	1[b]	3	3	17	18	12	2	0	2	58
10–14	1[b]	2	7	13	6	7	1	0	1	38
15–19	10	15	9	11	4	2	1	0	2	54
20–24	4	12	13	6	2	1	0	0	0	38
25–29	10	13	9	7	8	2	0	0	0	49
30–34	8	13	9	11	4	9	1	0	1	56
35–39	8	14	8	4	4	3	0	0	0	39
40–44	2	14	5	8	9	6	1	0	1	46
45–49	1	12	4	10	1	0	0	0	0	28
50–54	1	19	3	1	2	1	0	0	0	27
55–59	2	11	6	2	1	0	0	0	0	22
60–64	5	14	0	1	0	0	0	0	0	20
65 +	9	16	2	0	0	0	0	0	0	27
Total persons	62	160	93	108	75	60	7	0	9	569
Total households	62	80	31	27	15	10	1	0	1	227

[a] From census of November 1968, includes Xangwa and /Xai/xai, not /du/da.

[b] These two children classified as living alone actually live with Bantu families that are not considered part of this population.

Note too that households of only one member have a distinct age pattern. Overall 27.3% of the households were occupied by only one person in 1968 and 10.9% of the population were living in such households. Children cannot do so, almost by definition, since they need care and warmth at night. As children approach sexual maturity, however, they leave their parental households for marriage, for households with other young people or grandparents, or begin to live alone. The proportion of single-person households is nearly 20% in the 15–19 year age group, and this rate of single-person households remains in the 10–20% range until about age 35, representing single and divorced adults, especially men. From 40–55 the rate of single-person households is extremely low, but increases again in old age when widowhood ends marriage for many: 25% of the people 60–65 and 33% of those over 65 live alone, although generally in the same living group '*chulo*' with offspring, siblings, or other close kin.

The modal household size over all age groups is two, primarily representing married couples without children.

3

Causes of Sickness and Death

I say, it is enough, if we know from the *Searchers* but the most predominant Symptoms; as that one died of the *Headach,* who were sorely tormented with it, though the *Physicians* were of Opinion, that the Disease was in the *Stomach.* Again, if one died *suddenly,* the matter is not great, whether it be reported in the Bills, *Suddenly, Apoplexy,* or *Planet-strucken,* &c.

[John Graunt, *Natural and Political Observations*
... Made Upon the Bills of Mortality, 1662]

Understanding the mortality conditions of the Dobe !Kung is an essential part of our task in this work, but the resources available for the analysis are, in many respects, inferior to those available to John Graunt in 1662, when he compiled "Bills of Mortality" from London death certificates, which included age and cause of death. Even in populations with excellent systems of medical care and careful record keeping, it is often difficult to determine the causes of death and disability.

Among the !Kung, who had no regular access to Western medical facilities for diagnosis and treatment during the period of this study, the difficulties are compounded. I had few opportunities to directly observe people "sick unto death," and in any case lack of medical training would likely render direct observation useless for any but the most blatant symptoms. !Kung people were interviewed about the condition before death of deceased family members, but (like me) they are untrained in classifying causes of death according to the medical model. While they do not describe deaths as "planet-strucken," their cultural view of the ultimate causes of death necessarily influences their value as informants. The single largest cause of death elicited from !Kung informants was "//ganwa [god] killed him" or "Heaven ate him," although they were in addition willing to provide naturalistic descriptions of that part of the body that seemed to be diseased and the behavior of the patient before death. Fortunately, physicians paid brief visits to the Dobe area on several occasions, Truswell and Hansen in particular making a systematic survey of the health of the population (Truswell and Hansen 1976). Their findings will not be repeated here, but will be exploited, where possible, to explore causes of death.

Information on cause of death has been systematically collected from three different groups at risk. The first of these is all of the deaths ($N = 94$) that occurred between 1963 and 1973 to the study population; the second is deaths to the children ever born to the 165 adult women interviewed during 1967–1969 ($N = 180$); and the third collection of information is on the husbands of these same women ($N = 68$). For each death reported, the living informants were asked "achede !ku a" (What killed him?). In this chapter, we will consider the information available on the answer to this question, admitting that much of the information is anecdotal and impressionistic. In the next chapter, we will construct life tables showing the probability of death by age and sex from all causes combined, taking care to determine the person-years at risk of death at each age as well as the number of deaths known. For this chapter, the procedure will be necessarily less precise.

Sanitary Conditions and Customs That Affect Mortality

A traditional hunting and gathering village is, of course, technologically very simple, but it has many advantages from a public health point of view. The houses are made of poles and thatched with grass, and not actually occupied very much of the time. People sleep outside, next to their fires, where the sunshine helps to disinfect the area. Most of the Kalahari is deep sand, which is convenient for kicking over bits of garbage, sputum, and babies' urine and feces. Older children and adults leave the village for elimination, again kicking a bit of sand over the results, depending upon the sun and the dung beetles to disinfect the rest. Flies and other insects are attracted to fresh meat and other food, which is rarely covered. Insects also infest the houses and the people, but villages are easily moved to another location. One woman told me that she likes to make a new house when insects become well-established in the old one, and another man said that the proper time to move to a new village is when the old one begins to smell.

When people move to a new village, they are likely to take their own supply of insects, body lice, with them. People relaxing in the shade will often combine quiet conversation with delousing of their clothes and each other's hair. Many people rarely wash themselves during the part of the year when water is scarce, but seem to enjoy splashing and washing when the seasonal pools are available. Some people rub oil into their skin, to which dust clings, apparently to provide some protection against sun and wind. !Kung babies and children are subject to sunburn, and mothers of infants are so conscientious about protecting infants from exposure to the sun under their leather capes that Hansen and Truswell, the physicians associated with the expedition, found craniotabes, caused by deficiency of vitamin D, among babies in the first months of life. The condition is easily reversed when they are exposed to the sun in older infancy. The suede clothing of the traditional !Kung is well-suited to the hard wear and difficulties of washing with which the people live.

The purity of water supplies is an important aspect of public health. There are only two flowing springs in the whole area, other water sources consisting of standing water from limestone wells within a few feet of ground level or temporary pools formed by rain. This standing water is easily contaminated by people and animals who come to drink. Traditional !Kung like to make their village far out of sight and hearing of the well, so as not to disturb animals who use the water. Water is collected at least once a day in ostrich eggshells for the families' use in the village. Some of this water is used in cooking, but the people do not systematically boil or otherwise purify their drinking water.

When !Kung settle with Bantu or imitate the Bantu style, many aspects of this pattern are changed. Villages tend to be larger, and remain in use for much longer periods of time, years rather than months. Bantu houses—made of plaster composed of termite-hill earth, cow dung, and water over a framework of sticks, with a thatched roof—are much larger than !Kung houses. Bantu-type houses typically have a fire inside, with the smoke escaping through the loosely made roof. The cattle, in a nearby kraal, encourage the breeding of thousands of flies, so that being covered with flies is a constant penalty of cattlepost life. Both !Kung and Bantu get so used to the presence of flies that they rarely bother to brush them off, even when flies settle on their eyes and mouths.

Because cattlepost villages are larger and longer lasting, disposal of human feces is more of a problem. The area in a large circle around the village becomes heavily trampled down by the movement of humans and cattle, and becomes foul-smelling from the accumulation of animal and human feces. The wells around cattleposts are usually enlarged and frequently muddy from the watering of cattle. The Bantu people are more likely than the !Kung to take their drinks in the form of tea or soured milk rather than straight from the waterhole, but they also drink the available water without boiling it. Neither the !Kung nor the Bantu accept the germ theory of disease, and both groups judge the quality of the water by its taste rather than its cleanliness. To the best of my knowledge, bacterial studies have not been made on the waterholes, but it is likely that they are a major source of infection in the area.

The !Kung who live on cattleposts are more likely than their more traditional neighbors to wear cloth clothing, but they are unlikely to have the soap and washing facilities necessary to keep such clothes clean. The clothes of !Kung on cattleposts are usually ragged and an undistinguished brown color, contributing to the impression that the cattlepost people are badly off compared to those who live in the bush. One must be careful in examining the differences between the two styles of life not to attribute causation to a simple association. Some of the obviously ill, crippled, or otherwise handicapped people seen at cattleposts may be there not because the cattleposts caused the conditions, but because life is easier or indeed only possible under the reduced pressure of cattlepost life.

A final important determinant of the conditions that affect the level of mortality and resistance to disease for the !Kung is diet. All observers agree that the traditional !Kung diet is made up of a large number of species of plants and animals, some of which are extremely attractive foods, good tasting, high in nutritional value, and easy to collect. Physicians Truswell and Hansen, who made several trips to the Dobe area for medical examinations of large numbers of !Kung people, stress the absence of nutritional deficiency diseases and confirm that the subjects studied seem to have optimal levels of proteins, vitamins, and minerals, falling below expected levels only in sodium chloride and cholesterols. Both of those deficiencies are probably advantageous rather than harmful to !Kung health. Observers disagree, however, about whether the traditional !Kung diet is deficient in calories: Truswell and Hansen point out the extreme thinness of members of the population and suggest that their small stature may be in part a function of undernutrition, while Lee agrees with the observations of thinness, but points to advantageous aspects of small stature. When !Kung move to cattleposts, they modify their diet by including quantities of cultured milk and grain porridge, in addition to hunted and gathered foods. Cattlepost foods tend to be high in calories and low in bulk compared to bush foods, particularly attractive for children and old people, and desirable foods for !Kung of all ages. Families who are burdened with sick or handicapped members, many children, or old people tended to congregate at cattle posts in the 1960s, and the healthy members of the groups tended to gain weight on the high-calorie diet available there.

The direct effects of caloric abundance or scarcity, apart from the effects of deprivation of particular dietary components like protein, vitamins, and minerals, is not entirely clear. In general we expect a well-fed population to offer more resistance to constant levels of infection than a marginally nourished population. Certainly it is true that among contemporary populations the lowest levels of morbidity and mortality tend to be associated with the most abundant food supplies. A number of physicians and nutritionists have suggested that these low levels of health problems might be lower still if, in addition to being well nourished, people would voluntarily restrict their caloric intake to maintain leanness. The extreme thinness of the !Kung people, which is one of the most striking physical features of the population, along with the documented nutritional quality of the diet in all aspects except calories, provides an opportunity to observe the processes of morbidity and mortality in a situation rarely observed in the modern world. This situation is likely to be closer to the norm for human populations during the long period of time prior to the development of reliance upon agriculture.

Social Costs of Morbidity and Mortality

Unlike many people of the world who have witchcraft theories of sickness and death, the !Kung tend not to blame themselves or each other when misfortune occurs, but blame their god or simply accept "that's the way things are." When a child dies, the parents are unhappy, but mourning is not extensive. The parents hope to have another child to whom they can give the same name. When an adult dies, he or she will be mourned by relatives and living mates, the person will be buried with some ceremony, and ordinarily the village will be moved to another place. The surviving spouse usually remarries quickly and life goes on. When an old person dies the acknowledgment is similar, although the surviving spouse is less likely to remarry. Death is a reoccurrent and unremarkable event in the lives of people of all ages, and most people will lose several relatives and friends to death during every year of their life.

Death is the extreme of the process of sickness and injury; for every person who dies from a given cause, there are likely to be more who suffer from the same affliction but do not die of it. In the small groups in which !Kung have traditionally lived, an acute illness or serious injury to a member of the group places a heavy burden on the ability of the group to function. The social costs involved come in several forms: the need to provide magical and practical treatment, nursing care, and provision of food to the sick person, and the loss to the group of the food usually produced by that person. These costs fall differentially upon group members and the adequacy of the care provided to patients may differ from person to person.

During a crisis of acute illness or serious injury, one of the responses of the group is to organize one or many sessions of trance curing, the traditional form of !Kung treatment. This requires that the people who are the *n/um kausis* "owners of magical medicine" go into a trance state to effect magical cures of the sick person. The whole living group is involved in curing, singing and dancing to provide the stimuli that put the *n/um kausis* into trance. These dance rituals usually last all night, and the people will be exhausted and may find it difficult to work the next day, when the ritual may have to be repeated, continuing until the patient dies or recovers (Katz 1976; Lee 1967, 1968). Trance dances are not pure drudgery for the !Kung; on the contrary, they are usually enjoyable high points of normal life. When combined with a crisis of serious illness in the group, however, trance curing demands enormous commitments of time and energy from the group.

Similarly, sick people need care, someone to bring them water and food while they rest by the fire at their hut. For each sick person, the question arises which person will have the primary responsibility for seeing that the patient's needs are met. Ordinarily this issue is handled through ties of close kinship. If one has a spouse, parent, or adult child within the living group, there is no problem about providing care, and there is only the question how the care shall be divided among those who want to help. It often happens, however, that sick people are among those who have no close kin within the living group.[1] When the closest tie with one of the productive adults in the group is a distant one, such as uncle, aunt, cousin, or in-law, the productive adult may value his or her relative leisure more than the welfare of the sick person and attempt to dodge the responsibility. Or it may happen that the closest link may run to an adult who is already heavily burdened and has little ability to take on more responsibility. This theme in !Kung life was elaborated in a song composed in 1967 by a middle-aged mother of four children. Her song, set in a complex musical form, repeats a refrain: "Why is it that people don't give me mongongo nuts, so that I could crack them and provide for my old uncle."

Differential provision of food and care to the sick are difficult to observe, in part because if the !Kung think that there is any reason to hope that the anthropologist will take over the provision of food and care for the sick, they tend to deny that they ever expected to help out. In most cases observed in the field, one is impressed by the quality and quantity of effort expended on the sick. In a few cases, however, where needed care was not forthcoming, one realizes that the care is not an automatic response to need.

One such case involved not sickness but pregnancy and the breakdown of a marriage. Although spouses are ordinarily treated as full kin for the purposes of distribution, "stinginess" is often mentioned as one of the causes of a divorce. In fact, refusal to share food and other resources may be a *result* of a decision not to continue the marriage rather than a cause. Lee has discussed a number of instances of people being "driven out" of a group by refusal to share food, which Lee describes as a process of "group fission by conflict" (Lee 1972a). In a situation that I observed closely, a young woman had married into a group where she

---

[1]For the probabilities of having one or more relatives in each category by age and sex, see Chapter 16.

had no ties except to her new husband and his family. They were married about a year before she became pregnant. During the pregnancy, her husband showed little interest in caring for her, and his family followed his example. The family apparently stopped providing food for her about midway through the pregnancy. Not being a particularly resourceful person, she was unable to gather sufficient food to meet her needs in the unfamiliar area, and subsisted on meals begged from a local Bantu family while passively waiting for her mother to come to get her. Late in pregnancy she was driven by hunger to steal food from my supplies while I was away from camp, an extremely unusual event among the !Kung. Her in-laws denounced her, apparently hoping I would take her off to jail and end the problem for them. Naturally, I was sympathetic with her predicament when I discovered that she had lost weight in the eighth month of pregnancy despite the theft. Both she and the baby survived the birth and the subsequent divorce, and have gone back to live near her own family.

In another case, observed by Wiessner, a recently widowed woman of 67 became ill and depressed and laid around her fire rather than keeping up her usual active gathering routines. For weeks the old lady wasted away, subsisting on occasional gifts of food, while Wiessner (who was also ill at the time) over-heard people in the village actively quarreling with one another about whose responsibility it was to take care of her, accusing one another of "killing" her, while she was still alive. Her son and his wife, who happened to be away doing wage work on a cattlepost, would surely have taken the responsibility of providing care had they been present. The woman died of unknown causes before the argument was settled. It is, of course, impossible to know whether she would have died in any case. The kinds of care that the !Kung can provide cannot prevent death from many causes. What these observations suggest is that the care ordinarily provided by the !Kung can and does prevent death from minor causes that would be very serious if they could not rely upon one another to help them through crises. The provision of care is not automatic.

An additional social cost of morbidity and mortality is the loss of income to the group that results from the inability of one of the productive adults to work. Even when everyone in a group is healthy, the work of providing the food, water, and other necessities of life tends to be very unequally distributed within the group, whereas consumption of these necessities tends to be quite equal, with the redistribution occurring primarily through close kinship links within the group. Productive adults take primary responsibility for providing for their own children and other close kin who need support, increasing their effort when they have many dependents to provide for and working at a more leisurely pace when they have few dependents. Each group needs to have some adult members who regularly produce more than their dependents consume in order to provide a cushion of security for the group in times of crisis, but the ability of a group to provide for nonproductive members is not unlimited. Given their limited economic base, it seems remarkable that the !Kung are able to support such a large proportion of dependent people.

These dependents include all of the young, healthy and sick, up to the age of about 15. People over the age of 60 may make regular contributions to the group, but these are likely to be less than their own needs for consumption. In addition to the dependency burden caused by the age distribution, the productive adults need to provide for the acutely ill, and for the permanently disabled and handicapped, including among the adults 5 people who are totally blind, 23 with vision handicaps, 11 who are partially crippled, several with chronic illnesses, and some with mental handicaps such as lack of intelligence or unstable emotional states that prevent a full contribution. Today we see these handicapped people and their families clustered around the cattleposts, where life is easier. In the precontact period, it seems likely that more of them would have failed to survive. When we examine the range of the composition of living groups, looking at the numbers of households, the age distribution of members, and the economic structure of the groups, we must keep in mind that group sizes not only have ceilings caused by the pressure of consumption of food resources, but also have floors, minimal viable group sizes, caused in part by the need to provide multiple adult providers to care for the whole group during the sickness or disability of any one of them.

Occupational Hazards of the Hunting and Gathering Way of Life

There are a range of risks associated with the hunting and gathering way of life per se. For instance, there are extremely dangerous animals in the Dobe area, including lions, leopards, elephants, buffalo, occasional rhino, and many species of poisonous snakes. None of these species represents food to the Dobe !Kung, and none of them hunt man systematically for food. A respectful avoidance seems to characterize the normal intraspecies relationships, each party attempting to avoid contact, but occasionally encounters occur. An old man who was said to have lagged behind a group on the move was killed by lions in the past, and two men in the current population had earned the nicknames "lion" and "leopard" respectively when they were injured in fights with these animals. Under traditional hunting procedures, hunters commonly find lions (or hyenas or vultures) eating a dead animal when the hunters track their quarry to the place of death. The !Kung men drive off scavengers, if there is any meat left, by shouting and swinging sticks. The hunters do not make any serious attempt to kill scavengers under these conditions. In recent years, however, lion and leopard hunts have been organized by Bantu when cattle have been killed, with the

!Kung acting as trackers, backing up the armed Bantu with their spears. There have been several injuries inflicted on !Kung men during these hunts.

The usual prey species of the !Kung are ungulates, wart hogs, porcupine, spring hare, and so forth (Lee 1972b), none of which are likely to attack the hunter. Hunters are occasionally injured by kicks or goring from dying large animals, and may be scratched or bitten by smaller ones. The !Kung say that an experienced hunter can prevent these kinds of injuries and that prevention is the best cure. When talk turned to "mad" dogs, one day, I asked the people if they had a treatment for them. "Yes," was the answer, "climb a tree."

Unprovoked attacks by animals are not common, but prevention of them is a common theme in !Kung life. By the ability to recognize tracks of animals and snakes, the people are aware of the presence of danger, and take steps to avoid it.

The !Kung believe that it is more dangerous to be in the bush, away from the village, at night than in the day, both because it is difficult to exercise care and because animals are believed to be more dangerous. The circle of fires in the village and the presence of other people permits a degree of relaxation of care, but even in the village danger can approach. A middle-aged woman was attacked by a badger while sleeping next to her fire in the daytime not long ago, and had many infected bites and scratches. Snakes are frequent unwelcome visitors to villages. They are usually detected by their characteristic tracks before hurting anyone and are killed and sometimes eaten. Puff adders are commonplace, primarily dangerous to children and old people. Black mambas are relatively uncommon but feared as a danger to people of any age. People are likely to move the whole village if a black mamba is in residence, rather than attempt to kill it. Thomas (1959) provides a poignant account of an amputation of the leg caused by a snakebite. Centipede and scorpion stings are a constant hazard of handling firewood, but, although painful, are not usually dangerous.

When care is momentarily relaxed, as when hunters run after an animal after wounding it, the risks rise sharply. Thorns deeply imbedded in the feet are a common result, and the consequences are occasionally very serious. A young hunter had to be taken into the hospital at Maun in order to cure a persistent infection in his foot resulting from such a thorn injury, which threatened to cripple him permanently. In a similar accident, a hunter injured himself with a poisoned arrow.

Probably the most serious cause of hunting accidents, in the sense of injuries leading to death, is not the animals themselves, but the weapons that the !Kung use to kill those animals. The !Kung hunting technique involves poison, derived from the grubs of a beetle, smeared on the shafts of their small arrows. The poison is extremely potent: The small amount carried on a few arrows can kill an animal as large as a giraffe or a buffalo in a few days. It can also kill people, deliberately or by accident. Although the !Kung are more cautious in the handling of the poison and arrows than in any other area of camp life, preparing arrows slowly and deliberately, hanging the finished arrows up on a tree well out of the reach of children, and keeping them in a carefully constructed quiver, accidents do happen, especially in the excitement of hunting. Even if the injury is only a scratch, when poison is involved it may be very serious.

The treatment for poison injuries, unlike many conditions, is more mechanical than magical. The injured person and others methodically make a number of cuts around the injury and on the injured arm or leg, and attempt to suck out as much of the poison as possible. These cuts leave vivid and easily identifiable scars, seen on 13 out of 126 adult men who were examined for scars. Only the least serious injuries show up in such a tabulation, since more serious injuries are fatal. One man in the Dobe area lost his foot and ankle to gangrene complications of arrow poison around 1960, and goes about on crutches.

When one of the best hunters of the Dobe area accidentally jabbed a fully poisoned arrow into the calf of his leg in 1968 during a hunt, we had an opportunity to observe the course of arrow poisoning close up. Apparently Kumsa dropped his arrows after successfully wounding a wildebeest, while he ran to see how much the animal was bleeding at the site of the shooting. Running quickly back to gather up his arrows before pursuing the animal, he knelt on a poisoned arrow that was sticking up in the sand, and received a deep cut in the calf of the leg. Pursuit of the animal was immediately forgotten, as this experienced hunter knew that the accident could easily be fatal. He quickly sucked as much of the poison as he could from the injury, and limped back to the village. There his family and fellow hunters started the traditional treatment for arrow poisoning, while another member of the group ran off to ask DeVore, who was camped a few miles away, for assistance.

Lee and I and some visitors came upon the scene by chance an hour or two later, while DeVore was administering first aid.[2] Kumsa, his wife, and his brother-in-law were loaded on the back of our truck for an emergency trip to the hospital in Maun, at least 16 hours away. Before we left, the !Kung told us that he wouldn't live through the night. Indeed, he was unconscious during most of the trip, but arrived alive at the Maun hospital, where the doctors treated him initially for shock, and then, in the weeks that followed, for a series of massive infections of the injured leg. Apparently this was the first case of successful treatment for arrow poisoning recorded in modern medicine. Six weeks later, Kumsa and his relatives returned to the village to find that his death had already been mourned and accepted by his other relatives, who were disconcerted to find him alive and walking again, apparently suspecting that he was not their old

[2] The visitors were my father, David Howell, and Jim Laughlin of Fort Meyers, Florida. Both responded heroically to the demands of the grueling all-night trip, doing more than their share of the driving and sitting on the roof of the truck, necessitated by turning the body of the truck into a makeshift ambulance.

3. CAUSES OF SICKNESS AND DEATH

friend Kumsa at all, but some kind of a ghost created by the doctors at the hospital. It took several months before Kumsa's social relations returned to normal.[3]

It is interesting to note that gathering, as opposed to hunting, does not seem to be a highly risky business. Perhaps this conclusion seems obvious, since plants don't bite, but observation of the women as they go about their gathering routines suggests that dangers are avoided rather than nonexistent. The dangerous animals and snakes of the area are just as much a risk to women as to men, perhaps more so because the women go about unarmed, taking no spears or bows and arrows to defend themselves.

It is a commonplace of speculators on the evolutionary processes of hunter–gatherers that "the men hunt while the women stay at home with the children," but this generalization is demonstrably untrue for the !Kung. Women work away from the camps on a regular basis, traveling widely, without weapons or guards to protect them. Lee (1972a) estimated that adult !Kung women travel 2400 km per year in the course of gathering, visiting, and moving camp. While some of this walking is done with husbands and other armed protectors, the majority of the walking is performed alone or in small groups of women. The women's defenses seems to be primarily preventative. They watch carefully for tracks of dangerous animals and snakes to avoid them, they may talk loudly while moving through the bush to warn animals of their presence (in contrast to the silence of stalking hunters), and they avoid running and sprinting, when prevention is difficult. Theories of the relations of the sexes that suggest that women are subordinate to men because the women need male protection are inconsistent with the frequency and distance that women travel through the bush, the fact that women use this freedom to meet husbands and lovers in the bush for sexual adventures, and that women typically give birth alone or with a few other women out in the bush, away from the village.

Other occupational hazards of hunting and gathering as a way of life are falls from trees (in the course of gathering honey or fruit) and burns from fires. Marshall (1976:70) reports that !Kung are sometimes killed by lightning striking a tree under which they seek shelter in a rainstorm, though I obtained no reports of this. The village fires are a constant source of danger to babies and small children, who are likely to fall in or near a fire sooner or later. Complications from burns may be a contributing factor in many deaths of small children. Adults are

[3]The !Kung have complex notions of gratitude and obligation, illustrated by the strains introduced into the relationships between Kumsa and the anthropologists, especially Lee, by intervention in the accident. Kumsa had long been an unusually cooperative informant, a central member of the small band at Dobe waterhole that had adopted Lee into the kinship system. Kumsa and his relatives apparently resented the intervention, complaining about aspects of the experience that were not to their liking, and refused to cooperate with routine aspects of the research after the accident. See Lee (1969a) for further discussion of this aspect of !Kung culture.

so often mildly burned from village fires in the course of putting in or taking out food and from sparks that fly out from burning wood, especially if the person is asleep next to the fire, that the danger is simply routine. Probably most !Kung have at least one substantial burn scar on their bodies. Another occupational hazard is grass or bush fires, set casually by the !Kung in the dry season to send a long-distance signal or simply to burn off the old grass to encourage the growth of new to attract animals. In 1968 we talked to the survivors of an accident from a bush fire. A group of five traveling through the bush lit the grass around them to send a signal to those they were approaching. The wind shifted and blew up the fire so that it engulfed them, killing a 54-year-old man and his 12-year-old daughter, and badly burning the other three. The three survived with care from their relatives, but were seriously ill for weeks and are badly scarred, as well as being deprived of two of their family members.

Childbirth is, of course, another routine but occasionally hazardous part of life. In 1975 P. Wiessner encountered a young woman who had contracted malaria during the second half of a pregnancy; she was very pale, weak, and had extremely low blood pressure. The young woman was taken by truck to a hospital, where she was diagnosed as toxemic. The baby miscarried but the mother survived. It seems likely that under normal circumstances in the bush the mother would have died as well. Another mother died from some complication 3 weeks after childbirth; the child died the following day. Death in childbirth is not a common event; the !Kung must have been rigorously selected against any genetic predisposition for difficult childbirth. The rate of death in childbirth is probably lower for the !Kung than for some other peoples of the world who give birth without medical assistance, due to the !Kung custom of noninterference in birth, which helps prevent puerpereal infections. Complications of childbirth are, however, likely to be fatal when they occur. Two of the men in the 1968 population had lost wives in childbirth some years earlier.

Another risk in !Kung life comes from the dangers of isolation and exposure in the bush; this risk too is minimized by prevention and planning. Several !Kung told of times when they found themselves isolated far from others due to some unusual combination of circumstances (returning from a trip late in the evening to find that the group had moved, getting lost on a trip, or finding that a needed source of water had dried up) when they felt that they were near to death. Naturally a child or an old person is much less likely to survive this kind of experience. In 1971 a 7-year-old boy attempted to follow his mother, who had gone out gathering, and got lost in the bush. Despite their justly famed tracking techniques, the searching family did not find him until the third day of the search; he was dead, according to the father, from "hunger, thirst and cold" (Wiessner personal communication 1976). Draper's (1976:207) accounts of the casual but effective supervision of children, who usually play within eye or ear contact distance from the village takes on added significance with this account.

3. CAUSES OF SICKNESS AND DEATH

In 1968 a young !Kung woman was caught having sexual intercourse in her hut by her much older Bantu husband. The lovers were so frightened that they burst right through the back walls of the hut and ran off into the night, naked. The story was told and retold with gales of laughter the next morning, much to the chagrin of both the lover and the husband, until it was realized that the young woman was nowhere to be found in the nearby villages. Hilarity turned to concern when her footprints were found heading in the direction of her mother's village, more than 50 km away, since she had no means of making fire or protecting herself during the long journey. A search party was organized (excluding both the husband and the lover). They caught up with her soon after she arrived at her mother's village, after she had spent two nights naked and alone in the bush. That she was unharmed must be in large part a matter of good luck.

Interpersonal Violence, Homicide, and Suicide

The !Kung have been called "the harmless people," by Elizabeth Marshall Thomas, and it is clearly true that much of the !Kung culture and ideology is focused around the issues of controlling arrogance and anger among people. Lorna Marshall (1961) and Lee (1972a) each considered aspects of the !Kung way of life that help keep interpersonal conflict under control. Nevertheless the !Kung are well aware that they have the power to kill one another by assault or, more efficiently, by the use of poisoned arrows. The adult women reported six cases of murder of husbands and two cases among their own children; all of these were murders of men rather than women, and all of the cases since 1948 lead to court cases where the murderer was prosecuted and sent to jail. There were no murders during the 1963–1973 period, but there was a case of a woman in her fifties who married a hot-tempered man in his twenties. People say that he beat her up and she died, but they do not seem to think that he actually killed her, and he was not tried in court for the assault. Since that time, his reputation for violence has made it difficult for him to find another wife, and as of 1968 he was one of the older unmarried men in the population. Another murder was probably prevented in 1968, when a man in his late twenties, who had been drinking "home-brew" beer near the store at Xangwa, attacked a man, hitting him over the head with a heavy stick of wood. The assailant was subdued and locked up in a Bantu-style house until he sobered up. H. Harpending cleaned the victim's enormous head wound, stopped the bleeding, and did his best to close the edges with tape.

Although the known murders are concentrated among men, women seem to be at least as likely to resort to violence in extreme anger as men are. I personally witnessed a fight between two women that alternated between shouting argument and blows, hairpulling, and scratching for several hours, while, incidentally, both women were carrying small babies on their backs. This particular argument started when one woman teased the other about her husband having sexual intercourse with other women. The insulted wife believed that the teasing woman was having an affair with her husband, although other people said that this was not true. People in the village intervened during the most violent parts of the fight to separate the two women, and sent a messenger to the mother of the insulted wife, who arrived late in the day and took her daughter (and the husband and children) away for a while. Another fight between women occurred a few months later at /Xai/xai; it too apparently involved sexual jealousy between the two women and resulted in bruises and scratches on the face and back, but no serious injury.

Violence between husband and wife, which is one of the most common areas for combat in some societies, occurs among the !Kung, but is likely to lead rapidly to divorce rather than a prolonged conflict. A husband who was leaving his wife to go live with another woman infuriated her by taking their only blanket with him when he packed up a donkey for the trip. She snatched it back, and he beat her with a donkey whip until her relatives stopped him, when he left as planned (but without the blanket). In another case, a wife who knew that her husband was having an affair with another woman hit him while he slept, apparently intending to kill him. The marriage ended in divorce soon after.

An effective method of marital social control was recounted in an amusing way by a !Kung man, who says that dutiful !Kung wives bring their husbands to heel by silently sinking their teeth into the man's arm while the whole village is peacefully sleeping at night. The man awakes and finds himself in the ridiculous position of being bitten by his wife, unable to cry out and disturb the village without making a fool of himself. The informant says the man pleads, in whispers: "Release me, I beg of you, what have I done that disturbs you? Shall I give you a present? Shall I do more hunting? Or is it knowing so-and-so that is bothering you? I beg of you, let go, and tell me what I must do." Without uttering a word of reproach, the wife extracts the promise she wanted (and perhaps many others besides). Our informant joked that teeth marks will be found in the arms of all of the apparently happily married men in the group, but I never saw any.

Another incident involving sexual jealousy occurred at /Xai/xai when a nearly blind man tracked his wife's footprints into the bush and found the signs that she had been having sexual intercourse with a man whose footprints unmistakably identified him as the husband's younger brother. The husband came to the brother's sleeping place that night and hit him over the head. The brother woke up and ran away, leaving the next day for the East, where he engaged in wage labor for a while, not returning for 6 months.

While this man's attack was ineffective, when men become murderously angry they are much more likely than women to actually kill, since they have regular access to the poison arrows that can easily kill a person. It may be that because men have effective means of homicide and are aware that other men have it too, they are somewhat less likely to physically attack another man. Lee (forthcoming) made a study of known murders in the area, and turned up some 23 cases in living memory among people known at least by name to the Dobe area !Kung. Most of these murders were committed by men, using poison arrows. The starting incident seems often to involve sexual jealousy, but the actual victim or victims of the angry party is as likely to be a relative who has taken the side of one of the combatants, or even a bystander, as one of the parties to the conflict. Several murders involved a chain of retribution for past murders, and at least a few seemed to be cases of righteous "execution" of a person believed by relatively disinterested parties to be a danger to the whole community through his bad temper. Another possible cause of murder in the past is the "execution" of a person whose behavior is viewed as so outrageous that it represents a threat to the entire community. A well-known case of brother–sister incest during the study period had not lead to any attacks on the guilty parties, but a number of people suggested that in the old days, before the presence of Tswana courts and police, someone would have killed the brother, rather than allow him to make the gods so angry that the whole community would suffer in some unspecified way. It is interesting to note that this liason was ended by the death of the sister in her early twenties, before she married or conceived a child, apparently from TB.

In cases of sexual jealousy, as we have seen, the angry party might attack the spouse or the other person, presumably depending upon whether he or she wanted the marriage to continue. The third possibility is that one may attack oneself, in the form of suicide. The !Kung say that suicide comes to a person's mind when they are in the emotional state of *dokum*, or shame. One feels like throwing oneself in the fire, people say, and some individuals have tried to kill themselves in this state. Women do not handle poison arrows or other weapons in the ordinary course of events. The taboo against women's use of weapons seems to be one of the cultural rules most rigidly observed among the !Kung, who tend to be easy-going about most restrictions. In the state of *dokum*, however, several women have been known to take poison arrows to injure themselves, as have several men. Others will attempt to prevent this if they can, and will treat the injury with the usual procedure of drawing off as much blood and poison as possible from the injured limb if the person succeeds. None of the suicide gestures reported during the 1963–1973 period resulted in death, and none of the deaths to children or husbands were reported to be from suicide. It is possible, however, that this form of death would not be reported by the usually cooperative !Kung.

Violence and murder between ethnic groups has also occurred during recent decades, but estimating its incidence is complicated by the strong belief, shared by the !Kung and the Tswana, that the Tswana can kill by magical means. Two of the six murders of husbands of !Kung women were committed, according to the women questioned, by Tswanas, one in anger and one as an "execution" for cattle theft by an apparently self-appointed Tswana judge. Three of the children of the adult women studied and two of their husbands are reported to have died from Tswana witchcraft, in addition to those classified as murdered. No one died from Tswana magic during the 1963–1973 period, but we observed people in a state of panic on several occasions, fearing that they had been bewitched. A 40-year-old father of a thriving family who believed that he was bewitched after killing a cow became suddenly and totally blind.

With all of this violence between adults, it is striking that the !Kung show great restraint in physical violence against children. All observers agree that !Kung parents are extremely nonpunitive with their children, and even tolerant when little children occasionally slap or insult their parents. People say that children have no wits and that they therefore are not responsible for their actions. Occasionally the same argument will be made of an adult: An old man slapped his aged wife when she angered him by failing to answer when he accused her of not getting water one day. Her son heard of the incident and came to reproach the old man (who is not his father). "She has no more wits than a baby," her son asserted, so that the old man had no right to hit her; others agreed.

Infanticide, of course, is the killing of children, but is not the result of aggression or anger. Six among the 180 deaths to the children of adult women were reported to be cases of infanticide.

Summary of Deaths by Violence

To summarize the incidence of deaths by trauma and violence, then, including accidents, death in childbirth, and murder (including those by magical means), 13 out of 180 deaths to children, 9 out of 68 deaths to husbands, and 6 out of 94 deaths to numbered people during 1963–1973 were recorded, approximately 5–10% of all deaths known.

Infectious and Communicable Diseases

Most of the causes of sickness and death reported by the !Kung are not so dramatic nor so easily described as those already discussed. The !Kung, like people everywhere, suffer from a range of minor and major illnesses that, in the absence of a physician's diagnosis, are difficult to pin down. Fortunately, physicians visited the !Kung population on several occasions during the study period, and have recorded their diagnoses of the conditions they saw, making it possible to extend knowledge of certain cases to larger numbers of conditions seen. Tentatively, then, the incidence of infectious diseases during the 1967–1969 period is summarized as follows.

The !Kung of the Dobe area seem to have been spared the devastating epidemics of contagious diseases that are relatively mild to most populations but have decimated small and remote groups like the !Kung in other parts of the world. Rubella (measles), mumps, and chicken pox were not seen in either children or adults during the 1967–1969 period, and the people do not report that they have been a severe problem in the past.[4] Smallpox was endemic in Botswana during the 1950s and even, according to Guenther (1976) during the mid-1960s, at Ghanzi. Sometime during this period a public health team visited the Dobe area (apparently the first to do so) and innoculated the people they found against smallpox: Vaccination scars are commonly seen in people over 15 in the Dobe area. As far as could be determined, however, there was no outbreak of smallpox in the Dobe area.

Truswell and Hansen (1976:169) report that tuberculosis appeared to be fairly common. In a series of tine tuberculin tests administered by Lee and Howell in December 1968, positive responses were found in 17% of the 12 children tested (under 15 years), in 56% of 59 persons 15–59, and in 87% of 15 persons over age 60. Acutely ill people from the Dobe area taken to the hospital at Maun or the clinic at Chum!kwe have been diagnosed and treated for pulmonary and other forms of TB. Tuberculosis is probably one of the most common causes of deaths, especially for adults and older children. Among deaths to the children of living women, 14 cases were attributed to "chest," as were 12 of the deaths to husbands and 9 of the deaths to numbered people between 1963 and 1973. Although some of these deaths may be due to pneumonia or bronchitis, tuberculosis is clearly a significant health problem in the population, one that the Botswana medical service has been taking steps to bring under control since 1974. The increase in positive tine tests with age suggests that exposure has been cumulative over many years. The likelihood that TB has increased from contact with other ethnic groups is not clear.

Lupus vulgaris, a form of TB that affects the skin and cartilage of the nose and face, "the flat-face disease," was reported to be present by Truswell and Hansen (1976:169) and was seen by Howell in seven adults. While this condition must be debilitating in some ways, most of the people who show it seem to carry out the normal range of activities for their age and sex, so that strictly speaking it is not handicapping. An exception is a man of about 50 with a large family who is going blind from involvement of the disease with his eyes, and who is, in addition, particularly grotesque in appearance.

[4]Wiessner, however, reports that both mumps and measles were seen at the /Xai/xai waterhole during 1973–1975 (personal communication 1976), causing acute illness but not death.

Venereal disease is unlikely to be fatal, but has as great a demographic impact as fatal diseases because it can lead to sterility among adults. The !Kung distinguish two diseases, *linono* and *besheba*, which they recognize as having some relation to sexual intercourse and to subsequent loss of fertility. Generally speaking, *linono* seems to be the label for gonorrhea while *besheba* corresponds to syphilis. Truswell and Hansen (1976) identified both gonorrhea and syphilis in the population. Few !Kung have had their self-diagnosis confirmed by a physician and among women it may be that the association between *linono* and infertility causes some infertile women to assume that they must have had the disease, even in the absence of symptoms, whereas others who have experienced symptoms may perceive themselves as free of the disease provided that they retain their childbearing ability. Overall, nearly a quarter of the 165 adult women report their belief that they have been infected with one or both diseases, with a heavy concentration of cases in certain age groups. Table 3.1 shows the reports of the women on their contact with venereal disease.

The age pattern in Table 3.1 is an odd one, with low proportions reporting VD at the young ages and at the old ages and high proportions in the middle. When we examine trends in births per decade later, we will see a relative absence of births in the period of 1948 to about 1960, due to the failure of the same women who report VD to have as many offspring as expected. As noted in Chapter 1, 1948 is the date of the assimilation of the Dobe area into the tribal administrative structure of Botswana (then the Bechuanaland Protectorate). A "headman" was appointed and his administration encouraged migration of Bantus into the Dobe area. Some of the migrants brought families, but many were single men, some of whom eventually married !Kung women and many of whom had sexual relations with !Kung women. Some of these migrants, it is

TABLE 3.1
Women's Reports on Venereal Disease, by Age

Age	N	VD status			VD cases, by type		
		Don't know	None	VD	Gonorrhea	Syphillis	Both
15–19	25	15	7	3	2	1	0
20–24	21	1	14	6	6	0	0
25–29	16	0	13	3	3	0	0
30–34	18	1	11	6	4	2	0
35–39	19	3	4	12	5	4	3
40–44	13	3	7	3	2	0	1
45–49	15	0	13	2	2	0	0
50+	47	1	44	2	1	1	0
Total	174			37	25	8	4

likely, were infected with venereal disease, and the relatively free sexual practices of the !Kung insured that the disease spread widely through the population, including many people who have had no sexual contact with Bantu.

Table 3.1 shows that the women born about 1930, those 35–39 in 1968, had the highest percentage reporting VD, 66%. That group also has the lowest rate of achieved fertility, as we will see later. The age pattern of the reported incidence of disease and the timing of infertility presumably caused by the disease suggest that gonorrhea occurred in the form of an epidemic in the Dobe population during the early 1950s, and has been gradually decreasing in frequency and severity since that time. The decrease in severity in recent years is likely due to treatment facilities, which are effective for new cases, although there is rarely anything to be done for women who have already been sterile for some years. The !Kung, who up to 1976 had no regular medical facilities in the Dobe area, may also be benefiting from the better overall medical care in the country as a whole, as visitors to the area are less likely to bring in gonorrhea during the recent past.

Other illnesses seen in the Dobe area include colds, influenza, pneumonia, chronic bronchitis, and emphysema (which Hansen and Truswell suggest is related to the !Kung fondness for tobacco as well as the irritation of the smoke from fires), tonsillitis, rheumatic fever, and mitral valve disease of the heart. Diarrhea and diseases of the digestive tract are observed, and deaths caused by "stomach" accounted for nine of the children's deaths and two of the deaths during 1963–1973, but none of those to husbands.

In addition to diseases caused by bacteria and viruses, the !Kung are subject to parasitic infestations. !Kung of all ages commonly have lice (*Pediculus*) and the more fastidious among them can be seen finding and killing lice in their hair and in the folds of their clothing. People who are not observed "grooming" should not be assumed to be free of lice, but are more likely simply tolerant of them.

External parasites seem to cause relatively little distress, but internal parasites are more serious. Malaria is probably the most common form of parasitic disease. Hansen and Truswell found active cases of malaria in 1967 and 1968, and palpable spleens, a sign of malaria, in many others. They suggest from their observations that malaria is particularly frequent during the rainy season, when ponds of standing water encourage mosquito transmission. Although the anopheles mosquito is common in the area, the mosquito has to bite an infected person in order to transmit the malaria parasite. It is likely that the incidence of transmission varies widely from one year to the next, depending upon the extent of standing water and the presence of infected persons in the area. It seems possible that in the precontact period that interregional migration was too infrequent to permit endemic malaria. Bilharziasis, the extremely serious disease caused by infestation with schistosomes, found over much of southern Africa, is unusual or unknown in this desert area. Hookworm (*Necator americanus*) was found by Hansen and Truswell in 3 out of 18 fecal samples examined, but the anemia characteristic of infestation with hookworm was not detected. Amoebic dysentery has been contracted by anthropologists in the area, probably by water contamination. It was not detected in any !Kung people, but it is a likely candidate for the true cause of some of the deaths by "stomach."

Overall, the viruses, bacteria, and internal parasites are the greatest threat to human life and health among the !Kung, far greater than the risks from dangerous animals, poisonous snakes, or hostile people. While it is difficult to be sure of the precise cause of death in any particular case, it is likely that 70–80% of deaths to the !Kung are due to these infectious and parasitic causes. Since these are causes of death that modern medical practice is best able to cure and prevent, it is likely that the !Kung mortality conditions in the Dobe area will improve strikingly in the near future.

Degenerative Disease

Three of the major causes of death in most modern societies—cardiovascular disease, cancer, and motor vehicle accidents—are nonexistent or minor problems for the !Kung. The absence of motor vehicle accidents is merely due to the lack of motor vehicles, but the rarity of deaths due to cardiovascular disease and cancer is more interesting. Some of the lack of such cases is merely due to the fact that mortality overall is quite high: People die from infectious diseases before they have an opportunity for exposure to the risk of degenerative disease. But Truswell and Hansen (1976) and Kennelly, Truswell, and Schrire (1972) provide some basis for believing that !Kung probabilities of deaths from these causes may be lower than others, even controling for the age structure of deaths and competing risks. Truswell and Hansen found no evidence of coronary heart disease, which they note is associated with the extremely low levels of serum cholesterol observed, one of the lowest levels in the world. They also note no evidence of hypertension and no evidence of increases in blood pressure with age, which they relate to the low salt diet and the extreme thinness of the people. No doubt the combination of diet, frequent exercise, low levels of contact with chemical pollutants of some kinds, and the genetic constitution of the !Kung people are all involved. It is striking to note among the Dobe area !Kung that people who manage to survive illness into old age are frequently strong and vigorous (Biesele and Howell forthcoming).

Certain kinds of physical degeneration over the years are regularly seen among older !Kung. For instance, while tooth decay (caries) is rare, teeth gradually wear down over a lifetime so that the oldest people may have no teeth at all over the gum line and are forced to pound their food in a mortar before eating. Teeth do not seen to have evolved to last throughout a long human lifetime, at least under the level of abrasion caused by the typical !Kung diet.

Eyes, too, seem often to give out in old people, as a combination of the effects of infection (conjunctivitis and tracoma), injuries, and cataracts. Truswell and Hansen found that some degree of lens opacity is the rule in older San. The survey of handicaps in December 1968 revealed that 3 of the 104 children examined had serious permanent eye problems, though none of them were totally blind; many more children had conjunctivitis; 28 of the 241 adults had severe eye problems, including 5 who were totally blind; and 16 of the 40 old people (40%) had severe vision handicaps, including 4 blind people. The relative rarity of blindness among children is interesting in a population in which syphilis is said to be prevalent: Only one woman who believes that she has had syphilis has a child with severe vision problems, a boy who is blind in one eye.

Truswell and Hansen note that mild osteoarthritis is seen in elderly !Kung, often in the knees. The survey of handicaps revealed that about one-third of the !Kung over 60 walk with difficulty, often using a walking stick.

Hearing, on the other hand, seems usually to be well preserved into old age, and Truswell and Hansen remark on the good condition of ears of even very old !Kung. No doubt this well preserved hearing plays some role in the mental alertness and social awareness frequently noticeable in old people among the !Kung. That sensory deprivation is usually isolating is underscored by the unusual vivacity of one old blind man. His wife leads him everywhere on a stick, and she keeps up a steady stream of communication to him, letting him know who is present, what they are doing, and so on, in a process he calls "borrowing her eyes." He has developed an unusual interpersonal style emphasizing enthusiasm and humorous exaggeration, which is quite in contrast to the style of other blind people, who tend to be withdrawn and hesitant in interaction.

Deaths due to degenerative disease can occur at any age, since genetic defects in children could be classified as degenerative causes of death (even though the mechanism of death is likely to be infanticide if the defect is one that can be observed by the mother). A young man died in 1970 with abdominal pain that suggested a ruptured appendix; a woman in her forties died of painful breast growths that were probably due to cancer (but which may have been a form of TB); and one of the old men who died probably had a heart attack or a stroke (people said, "he wasn't sick, he just fell down"). The process of natural selection, however, is most effective in eliminating degenerative disease that occurs before the end of the reproductive period; conditions that develop later in life are difficult to select out. In modern societies, most people die of degenerative disease in old age. Old people, among the !Kung, seem to die primarily from infectious diseases that they may have been better able to resist earlier in life. If the !Kung are truely less subject to degenerative disease than other people, due to some features of their environment, their habits, or their genetic composition, the anticipated reduction in infectious diseases with the introduction of modern medicine in the years to come may reveal that superiority more clearly than it can now be seen (provided, of course, that the unique features of the !Kung life that produce it are not changed by the introduction of medical care).

Causes of Death in Comparative Perspective

Preston, Keyfitz, and Schoen (1972) and Preston (1976) have continued the task begun by John Graunt in 1662 of examination of the implications of death certificates containing age and cause of death for a wide range of populations around the world and at various times. Although there are difficult problems of classification of death certificates into groups of causes (discussed in the works cited), Preston has revealed remarkably robust trends in changes in cause of death as mortality levels improve across populations, and remarkable regularities in cause of death within populations at a similar level of mortality. Although our information on !Kung causes of death is only partial and impressionistic, it may be useful to compare our guesses as to the proportion of deaths from the three major types of causes—violence, degenerative disease, and infectious and parasitic disease—to Preston's results for population at a roughly similar level of mortality, even though the economic organization of these populations (such as

TABLE 3.2
Percentage of Newborn !Kung Who Will Ultimately Succumb to Various Causes of Death, by Age and Sex

Age group	Survivors to start of age group	Deaths to group	Cause of death		
			Infectious	Degenerative	Violence
Females only					
0–14	100	47	41	2	4
15–59	53	36	32	1	3
60+	17	17	9	7	1
Total		100	82	10	8
Males only					
0–14	100	49	43	2	4
15–59	51	38	27	1	10
60+	13	13	7	5	1
Total		100	77	8	15

Chile 1909, 1920; England and Wales 1861; Italy 1881; and Portugal 1920) is far more complex than anything known to the !Kung.

For the !Kung, we can anticipate the results of the next chapter to specify the *level* of mortality as one with an expectation of life at birth of about 30 years for both sexes. We would expect to see about 34 deaths per 1000 people per year.

Almost half of the deaths will be persons under age 15. I have guessed that four of these deaths, for both sexes, might be due to violence, including two cases of infanticide and two from childhood accidents such as fire, falls, exposure, and the like. A few deaths for both sexes might be due to degenerative diseases of childhood, genetic abnormality, and so forth. The major category of cause of death for children must be infectious diseases.

TABLE 3.3
Average Percentage of Newborns Who Would Ultimately Succumb to Particular Causes of Death at Life Expectancies under 40 Compared with !Kung[a,b]

	Percentage of deaths			
	Males		Females	
Causes of death	Others[c]	!Kung	Others[d]	!Kung
Infectious and parasitic diseases	80	77	80	82
Respiratory TB	8		7	
Influenza, pneumonia, bronchitis	22		21	
Diarrheal diseases	6		7	
Other infectious and parasitic diseases	12		12	
Certain diseases of infancy	6		6	
Other and unknown causes	26		27	
Degenerative diseases	14	8	17	10
Neoplasms	2		3	
Cardiovascular disease	10		12	
Other degenerative	2		1	
Violent causes of death	6	15	3	8
Maternal causes	—		2	
Violence	6		1	
Totals	100	100	100	100

[a] Adapted from Preston, *et al.*, *Causes of death: Life tables for national populations*, 1972, Tables I-1a and I-1b.
[b] See Table 3.2.
[c] "Others" consist of the average for six populations with male expectation of life of less than 40 years. See Preston *et al.*
[d] "Others" consist of the average for eight populations with female expectation of life of less than 40 years. See Preston *et al.*

Slightly more than a third of the deaths will occur among persons 15–59. For women, three of the deaths are tabulated as due to violent causes; two in childbirth and one other. Men in the same age group have many more violent deaths, due to occupational hazards, hunting accidents, murder, and so on. Over the lifespan, men are about twice as likely as women to die of violent causes. Degenerative diseases are insignificant for both sexes during the adult years, and again the infectious and parasitic diseases must be causing most of the deaths.

Even in old age, when a minority of deaths occur, infectious and parasitic diseases are strong competitors with the degenerative diseases as a cause of death. Table 3.2 summarizes these guesses.

Preston, Keyfitz, and Schoen (1972) present a table showing the percentage who will ultimately die from various causes for all of the available populations with mortality levels roughly comparable to that of the !Kung. The deaths are subdivided into finer categories than can be managed for the !Kung, and these categories are grouped into the three types—infectious, degenerative, and violent causes—that have been used to describe the !Kung. Table 3.3 shows the comparison of the !Kung with the average for the populations with life expectancies of less than 40 years for the major types and the breakdown of causes within types for the other populations. The table suggests that the !Kung have somewhat higher rates of death by violence, and somewhat lower rates of deaths from degenerative causes, than populations in more developed economies but with roughly comparable levels of mortality, whereas deaths from infectious and parasitic disease are the major component in all of the populations. It must be admitted, however, that this tabulation is highly speculative, especially for the !Kung, but in part for the other populations as well.

Recent Changes in Cause of Death

Again anticipating the results of the next chapter, there is some evidence that mortality levels have declined in the most recent decades, so that the !Kung have a somewhat better chance of surviving all causes of death combined than they did in the past. Yet there is also evidence that some pathogenic agents, notably venereal disease and tuberculosis, have increased during the same period. These observations imply that some causes of death prevalent during the precontact period have declined, so that we obtain a distorted view of the mortality conditions that would characterize undisturbed hunter–gatherer !Kung.

What would people have died of under undisturbed hunting–gathering conditions? We cannot know with any certainty, of course, but we can probably guess at least the direction of changes.

It is unlikely that degenerative disease would be more prevalent in the pre-contact period, which narrows the choice to the remaining alternatives of violence and infectious disease. Infectious disease, we have noted, might be smaller as a category if the diseases introduced by contact with outsiders had been avoided. On the other hand, the category might be equally high or even higher, with somewhat different diseases taking their toll.

Violence may have been a somewhat higher cause of death in the past, when large game animals were more frequent and adjudication of disputes was absent. But it seems likely that the addition of the cattlepost alternative to bush living may have changed !Kung mortality primarily through the incidence of death as a consequence of more or less equal rates of serious injury and sickness. Cattleposts seem to be used by the !Kung as a way of avoiding the crises of food provision for sick and injured persons, and their families, so that fewer individuals succumb to the complications (such as pneumonia) that follow accidents or illness and are aggravated by inadequate diet during convalescence. I would guess, therefore, that there has not been a major shift between the categories of violence, degenerative causes, and infectious disease, but rather that there has been a shift within the category of infectious disease so that we now see a somewhat larger proportion of illness from highly contagious causes and a lessening of mortality from illnesses that are strongly influenced by physical condition, particularly short-term dietary shortages.

4

The Measurement of Mortality

Although it is very difficult to determine the causes of death, the fact of death itself is a sufficiently clearcut and memorable event that deaths can be tabulated with some confidence. Indeed, it is generally more difficult to count the living population who were at risk of death at the time than to count the deaths themselves. With allowance for these difficulties, it is possible to measure the probability of death in definable groups with some accuracy, even if the interpretation of those measures is problematic. This chapter is an account of that process, first establishing the conceptual framework of life-table analysis, discussing the ways in which human mortality varies in general among populations, then looking at data from the !Kung, to place the !Kung experience in comparative perspective.

The Conceptual Framework of Life-Table Analysis

The methods used here for life-table analysis are conventional and will be familiar to demographers. Since some of the readers of this study may not be familiar with these techniques, and since the methods are used extensively in this work, not only for the analysis of mortality in this chapter, but later for the analysis of entrance to the postmenarchial state, for entrance to marriage, divorce, and widowhood, for childbearing, and for moving from one birth interval to the next, we will briefly outline the method and define the terms of life-table analysis here. A fuller discussion of the methods, treating special problems that can arise in data analysis, can be found in Barclay (1958).

Life-table analysis provides a way of linking observable events to the consequences those events would have in an "ideal" population, free of the effects of the size of the population, the recent history of disturbances in the population, and odd features of the resulting age distribution. The analysis begins by an estimation of the probability of the given event during a segment of time to those at risk of the event. For illustration let us say the event is death, the period of time is a year, and the population at risk has been exhaustively enumerated and all ages (and other relevant characteristics) of individuals, both those who live through the year and those who die, are known. We calculate the age-specific death rate by dividing the number of deaths to persons in the age group by the number of person-years lived in the age group.

Person-years lived is a calculation of the amount of time spent by persons in the group at risk of the event, combining the periods spent by different people to a common base. For example, in a group of 10 persons, of whom 2 die in the year, the person-years lived consist of 8 (from those who survived the full year) plus the sum of the parts of the year lived by those who died. If each lived 6 months, the person-years lived by the 10 would be 9 years. Over the age of 5 years, after which the probability of death is approximately equal throughout the year, it is conventional to assume that all those who died lived half a year. In infancy, and less so during childhood, adjustments are made to take account of the observed fact that the probability of death is highest at the beginning of the year and declines throughout the interval. When detailed data are available, one sums the actual periods of time lived by those who died, but Barclay (1958) provides adjustment factors for the years of childhood for cases where the exact period is not known.

The age-specific mortality rate (M_x) is calculated by dividing the number of deaths to persons in the age group by the number of person-years lived in the age group. For the example given above of 2 deaths in 9 person-years, M_x, would be .22. To estimate the probability of dying within the interval to those who start the interval (rather than the proportion of deaths to the midyear population), we adjust M_x by a simple formula to obtain q_x, the life table mortality rate ($q_x = M_x / 1 + \frac{1}{2} M_x$). For our example, q_x is .22/1.11 = .20. When we know the number of events that occur to a group of people who have already passed through the age interval, we calculate q_x directly.

With a set of q_x values, one for each age interval, we are ready to examine the implications of that set of probabilities for the functioning of an ideal population formed by those rates. The life table is made up of a number of columns, with one entry in each for each age group. The first row, that of age 0 (birth to

4. THE MEASUREMENT OF MORTALITY

the first birthday) has an initial starting group (a cohort) of constant size, conventionally 100,000, (or, if the absurdity of applying probabilities derived from a small number of cases to such a large cohort is bothersome, 1000 or even 100). This column, l_x, represents the survivors to age x: All survive to birth, some smaller proportion survive to age 1, 2, 3, . . . until the advanced age at which none of the original group are still alive. To find the proportion surviving to each age, we multiply the l_x (those who start the interval) by the q_x (the probability of dying in the interval) to obtain d_x (the number of deaths in the interval in the artificial population). Subtracting d_x from l_x gives the number of survivors to the beginning of the next age interval. The variable d_x is an abbreviation of "deaths during age x" in a life table analyzing mortality; in other contexts it may mean the number of menarches, marriages, divorces, births, or other types of events, but we will call it d_x in all of these analyses in order to be clear that we are talking about the concept of "events generated by $l_x \times q_x$, which are to be subtracted from the current l_x to give the next l_x." This procedure is continued through the age groups until we reach the highest age to which any survive, or the highest at which it is reasonable to continue the analysis: There is some small probability of surviving to over 100 years, but typically the life table ends earlier. At some advanced age, such as 85, we simply assume that the probability of death in the interval is 1.0, so that all the people who start the interval die in it.

The second group of columns of a life table operates on somewhat different principles, and it is not always necessary to carry out the full analysis. The variable L_x is an estimate of the number of person-years lived in the artificial population, roughly speaking, all of those who survive the interval plus half of those who die in it. If the interval is more than 1 year, L_x includes a count for each year survived, not simply each person. This variable corresponds to the census count for each age group that would be obtained if one could observe the ideal population. The term T_x is calculated by summing the L_x counts from the oldest age to the youngest, and represents the person-years left to live by the survivors at each age. It is an intermediate step for the calculation of the final column of the life table, e^0_x the expectation of life at age x, which is calculated as T_x/l_x, the average number of years remaining to the survivors at age x. The first entry in the e^0_x column, the expectation of life at birth, can be used as the "name" of a life table, representing the average number of years lived by the people born into the population.

Model Life Tables

Hundreds of empirical life tables from diverse human groups have been calculated, and many methods have been attempted to accurately sum up the regularities found again and again in these tables. Human mortality probabilities over the life span have not been found to have a simple form that can be fit by a single mathematical function, but more complex summary methods have been found to express the regularities.

Several series of model life tables have been constructed by demographers (Carrier and Hobcraft 1971; Coale and Demeny 1966; United Nations 1955; Weiss 1973) using somewhat different methods. All of these model life tables series distinguish at least two parameters, that of the *level* of mortality, which can be indexed by the expectation of life at birth, and that of age *pattern* of mortality within each level. The age pattern of mortality probabilities reveals striking similarities in life tables that are at the same level of mortality. The pattern of q_x is always U- or J-shaped, with relatively high probabilities of death in infancy, declining throughout childhood, until they reach their lowest point in the life span around the age of 10. Characteristically, the probability of death is quite flat throughout adolescence and adulthood, rising only slightly from one year to the next. Around age 45, the probabilities start to increase from one year to the next at a higher rate, increasingly rapidly throughout the fifties, and continuing to rise

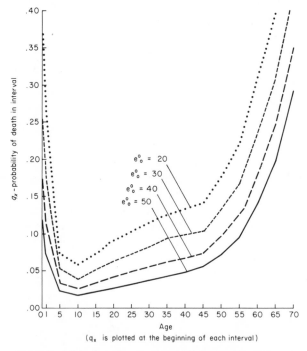

Figure 4.1. Probability of death (q_x) per age interval, for Coale and Demeny "West" model life-tables for females with expectation of life at birth of 20, 30, 40, and 50 years. (Note: the length of the first interval is 1 year; the second is 4 years; all others are 5 years.)

4. THE MEASUREMENT OF MORTALITY

at a slower rate throughout the older years of life, until they reach totality at some advanced age. Figure 4.1 shows the values of q_x in the Coale and Demeny (1966) "West" series of model life tables for women spaced 10 years apart in expectation of life at birth. The corresponding male models look very similar, but have a slightly lower expectation of life than that of women at the same level, caused by a slightly higher probability of death at each age.

The reasons for these regularities in human mortality schedules are presumably biological in nature: There must be a regular process of changing susceptibility or resistance to stresses (causes of death) over the life span. While the process necessarily has a genetic basis, it is not a genetic difference between individuals we are observing in the regularities of life tables, but a difference seen within the same individuals over the course of their lives. If this relative susceptibility and resistance by age is uniform from one person to another, and if we imagine an experiment in which the same "dosage" of a constant group of stressors is applied to each person in the population, we would expect to see that the only differences in mortality over the life span would be those of the underlying resistance. The constant features of mortality schedules, then, are reflections of this biological parameter of the species as a whole. Thus variable aspects of the age pattern of mortality schedules among populations can be attributed to: (a) the failure of populations to have a constant package of stresses, or causes of death, impinging on the group. Some groups are subjected to more TB, while others have higher incidence of diarrheal agents in their drinking water, and so on; (b) the failure of the existing causes of death to impinge upon members of the population equally, for each person to be subjected to a constant "dose" of the stressor. Aspects of the culture and customs may expose certain age groups in the population to more (or less) of the stressor than others, thereby influencing their rates of mortality, even though the biological ability to resist the stress may be the same at that age as it is in other populations.

The differences among groups in mortality probability by age, then, are likely due to different mixes of cause of death and different degrees of protection and support given to various age groups. Differences between series of model life tables, similarily, such as Coale and Demeny's "East," "West," "North," and "South" models (the names refer to areas of Europe), reflect the different mixes of cause of death and care provided. Until the influences of each particular cause of death can be specified, it will not be possible to isolate the constant feature precisely (Preston *et al.* 1972; Preston 1976).

No particular human population ever fits the model life tables exactly, and each of the series of model life tables expresses the central tendencies in life tables slightly differently, extracting somewhat different conclusions, based on somewhat different methods of summation. Figure 4.2 shows the age pattern of q_x for females in a number of model life tables with the same expectation of life at birth, 30 years. The sources are the four Coale-Demeny regional models, the

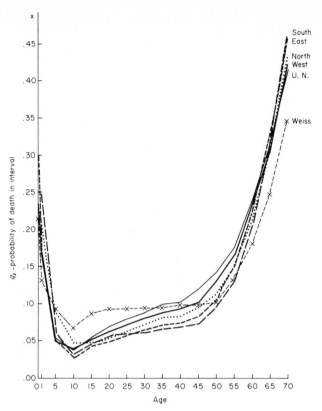

Figure 4.2. Probability of death (q_x) per age interval, for 6 model life-tables with the same expectation of life at birth (30 years). From: Coale & Demeny (1966) for North, South, East, West; Level 5, U.N. (1955); Level 3, Weiss (1973).

United Nations model, and one of Weiss's. Each is a kind of an average and would not be expected to agree with any particular population extremely closely. Nevertheless, the agreement between the different models is significant, and it is this general agreement that is important for the study of the !Kung and other hunter–gatherers.

For the purposes of this work, I will consistently use Coale and Demeny's "West" series of models, not because they have been found to fit the !Kung experience better than others only slightly different, but because they are based on the largest and most cosmopolitan data collection from empirical populations (not only populations in Western Europe, but some in Asia as well, populations that, at the time when they had levels of mortality comparable to the !Kung levels, were keeping the best records). Weiss' series of model life tables, which were constructed for the purposes of modeling small-scale population like the

!Kung, have not been used here because Weiss has chosen to incorporate features of small-scale populations that might easily be due to observational error rather than features of their probability schedules. In any case, the Coale and Demeny series, in the form of their *Regional Model Life Tables and Stable Populations,* have certain convenient features that Weiss' tables lack.

It is difficult and possibly pointless to construct the life-table experiences of hunter–gatherer populations as a purely empirical–inductive problem. Instead, the fragmentary data is better used to test the null hypothesis that the mortality experience of these people is the same as that of people in general, as expressed in the model life tables. The alternative hypothesis, that the !Kung have a mortality experience that is significantly different from that embodied in the model life tables, is easier to test and assess than attempting to build up an inductive view of !Kung mortality. If the age pattern of susceptibility to death were significantly different for the !Kung than for other people, if, for instance, the shape of the curve of probability of death by age were not J-shaped, but constantly increasing (or decreasing) with age, bimodal, or some other pattern, the deviation will become apparent when we compare the observed pattern of death with the expected pattern derived from the model life tables. Similarly, if the shape of curve of probability of death is J-shaped, but the ages at which the curves pivot are very different from those expressed in the model life tables (for instance if mortality continues to decrease to a much younger age or a much older age before starting the adult increases), or if the increases in older years begin at a much younger age (say age 30 rather than the usual age 45–50) or a much older age (say 60), these patterns will be discernible in even a relatively small collection of data, although small deviations from the expected (say a minimum probability of death at age 15 rather than 10) are likely to be undetectable.

A central question of this study of !Kung mortality, then, is the extent to which the data fits the model life tables. For the level of mortality estimated for the !Kung experience, does the age pattern of mortality conform to the panhuman models, or on the contrary does the !Kung experience suggest that there is a wider range of variability in human populations than that expressed in the model life tables? The models, after all, have been constructed by summarizing the experience of well-studied populations of agricultural and industrialized societies, people who live under very different conditions than those of hunter–gatherers. Most of these populations have far better conditions of public health and treatment medicine than the !Kung, and indeed the range of the model life tables of mortality comparable to the !Kung are based upon relatively few populations, most of which are historical rather than contemporary data collections, and some of which are simply extrapolations of the trends of the model life tables based on better mortality levels to the worse mortality levels, which have not actually been observed. If the !Kung experience fits the model life tables, we can tentatively conclude that the general features of the model life tables express general features of human biological processes that are sensitive to environmental fluctuations in level but not in age patterns of mortality. This is a useful conclusion, because if it is reconfirmed in the study of other isolated hunting and gathering societies, it means that we can use model life tables as a surrogate for empirical study of mortality in situations when the data base is lacking. If the !Kung data were not well fit by the models, it would represent a warning that the model life tables should not legitimately be used for these purposes.

!Kung Mortality

To analyze mortality, we need to find collections of observations with particular properties. The population observed must be *closed*, that is, we must have a criterion on which to set boundaries of the group, such that we have complete information about those in the group and events outside the group cannot creep in to distort the results. In addition, we need to know the age of members of the population when they die and the ages to which others survive, so that we can calculate the population at risk of death at each age and the frequency of deaths during each interval. Fortunately, it is not necessary that this carefully observed closed population of people with known ages have a typical age structure for the population, and it is not necessary that all of the deaths and years lived have been at the same time.

Deaths to the Children of Interviewed Women

The best source of data available for analysis comes from the closed population of children ever born to the 165 adult women who were interviewed about their life histories. These women, who range in age from 17 to over 75, have reported on the birth of 500 children born to them by the end of 1968. (The round number of 500 is a coincidence.) The women reported 555 pregnancies rather than 500, but those that ended with the birth of a child who never showed any sign of life (i.e., miscarriages) are eliminated from this analysis. Babies who died within minutes of birth, even if they never received a name, are included. Some of these births occurred very recently (one on the last day of 1968), so that the babies have not been at risk of death very long, whereas others were born long ago (in the extreme case, in 1907, making the "child" 61-years old in 1968). Later we will analyze these same births to learn about the childbearing process. Here we are not concerned about where these children came from, but only what happens to them after birth. From their experience, we will estimate the probability of dying during successive age groups.

Before we look at the data, we should explicitly consider the possibility that the answer to this question has been already subtly built in by the process of age estimation discussed in Chapter 2. It was necessary to assume a typical schedule of mortality (and fertility) in the past in order to fit a curve to the rank-ordered ages of the living population. The question naturally arises whether we are caught up in a process of circular reasoning, assuming a level of mortality to assign ages, and then extracting the assumption as if it were an empirical finding from the same data. Fortunately, there is no danger of that happening here, since the ages of deceased children were not (and could not be) assigned by the same age estimation procedure used for living people. When the women were interviewed about their children, considerable effort was expended to determine all of the available facts about when the birth occurred, such as the season of the year, where the mother was living at the time, who else was living there who would recall the birth, and so on. In the analysis phase, the estimated year of birth for surviving children (numbered) was the year of birth derived from the age estimation procedure. The years of birth for deceased children and for surviving children who are not members of the numbered population were guessed at by their placement between numbered siblings and by their mother's accounts of which members of the numbered population were born around the same time. The birth years of these offspring, therefore, are more uncertain than those of the surviving numbered children.

Similarly the ages at death of deceased children (as opposed to the year of birth) are guesses rather than estimates arrived at in a systematic way. Mothers were asked for each deceased child about the developmental markers that had been reached by the child before death (could the child sit up, walk, was he or she weaned, old enough to go off to play with the other children, sexually mature, and so on) and whether other events such as the birth of younger siblings had already occurred. Mothers were also asked to identify someone in the living

TABLE 4.1
Mortality Measures on Ever-Born Children of 165 Women

Exact age[a]	Started interval	Currently in interval	Completed interval	Deaths	q_x	l_x	d_x
0	500	25	475	96	.202	100,000	20,200
1	379	42	337	59	.175	79,800	13,965
5	278	46	232	17	.073	65,835	4,824
10	215	32	183	8	.044	61,011	2,685
15	175	36	139	5	.036	58,326	2,098
20	134	58	76	7	.092	56,228	5,179
30	69	47	22	5	.227	51,049	11,588
40+	17	16		1	—	39,461	

[a]Note that the length of each interval is determined by the difference between age x and $x + 1$, hence the first interval is 1 year in length; the second is 4-years long; 3–5 are 5-years long; 6–7 are 10-years long; and the final interval is open-ended.

population who is about as old now as that child was at death. The ages at death, then, are only approximate, but have not been produced by the assumptions of the age-estimation procedure.

Table 4.1 shows the calculation of the mortality rates from the raw data. Since the same procedure will be used in many calculations, let us look at the numbers closely to be sure it is clear how they are made. Five hundred children born to these women started the first year of life, but 25 of these children were born during 1968 and hence were still *in* the first interval. All of these babies, including three who had died before the end of 1968, are excluded from the computation of the probability of death in the first year of life, because we have no way of knowing how many of the 25 will eventually die before the end of the first year. Including those who died among the deaths but not including those who were surviving at the cutoff point would overestimate the death rates. Four hundred and seventy-five children therefore started and ended the first interval, among whom 96 died. The probability of dying in the first year of life (age zero) is $q_x = 96/475 = .202$.[1] The number who start the second interval, which is 4 years long, is $475 - 96 = 379$. Again we remove those who are still in the interval (42) before making the calculation of q_x. In this way we obtain a q_x measure for each of the age intervals, stopping when the number of people who have passed through the interval is too small to serve as a reasonable base for the calculation.

The partial life table based on these deaths consists of an application of the q_x measures to an artificial cohort of 100,000, showing the number of deaths that would be produced for each age group in the artificial population. Since we run out of data for estimating q_x before we reach the highest age to which anyone can survive, we cannot calculate the L_x, T_x, and $e^0{}_x$ columns of the life table. We can, however, compare the l_x column to that of the model life tables, as shown in Figure 4.3. We see that the l_x calculated from the !Kung children born to interviewed women seems to fall between Coale and Demeny's "West" models with expectation of life at birth of 30 and 35 years. There is no evidence here that the data require us to reject the null hypothesis that the !Kung have an age pattern of mortality more or less like everyone else.

When we look closer at this collection of data for what it can tell us about subsidiary patterns in !Kung mortality, we must consider the possibility that the numbers are so small that the results are extremely unstable,[2] so that obtaining significant differences between subgroups of the population means nothing but the presence of a high noise-to-signal ratio. To explore this possibility, the body of data was divided into halves on a random basis and the life tables were

[1]Note that this estimate does not need to be adjusted by the $M_x - q_x$ conversion factor, because we have isolated the number who started the interval rather than using the midyear population as an estimate.

[2]The small number problem and the standard errors of the estimates derived from these bodies of data will be considered in more detail in Chapter 5.

4. THE MEASUREMENT OF MORTALITY

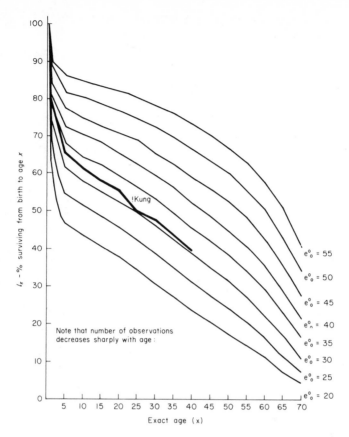

Figure 4.3. Survivorship to children born to 165 interviewed women. (Note: the regularly spaced l_x times are from Coale and Demeny (1966) "West" models, for females.

recomputed for the two random groups. No important differences between the groups in the calculation of q_x appeared under the age of 20, where the number of cases in both groups were substantial. Similarly a rather arbitrary geographic division of cases into two groups on the basis of the place of residence in 1968 showed no significant differences between the groups under the age of 20. Dividing the cases into the two sexes shows small differences in survivorship to age 20, in the expected direction of females having a slightly greater chance of survival at each age, as shown in Figure 4.4.

When we divide the available cases by the date of birth of the child, however, to look for trends over time, rather large differences in the mortality experiences of the different birth cohorts emerge. Table 4.2 shows the survivorship to age 15 of the children born in five successive 10-year periods. The first two cohorts are incomplete, but they seem to be surviving at a higher rate than children born in

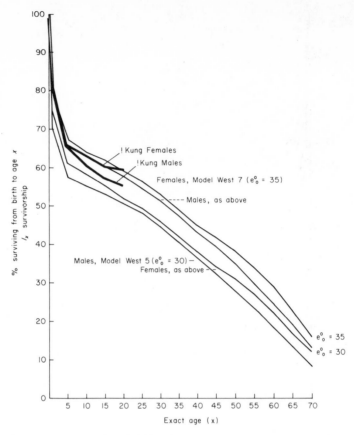

Figure 4.4. Survivorship of children born to 165 women, male and female.

earlier periods. The third cohort, those born between 1939 and 1948, seem to have been characterized by a substantially higher infant mortality rate than other cohorts, but reasonably good survivorship in early childhood. The children in the last two cohorts seem to have remarkably high rates of mortality in the age groups 1–5 and 5–10. It is possible that these differences between the cohorts are more apparent than real, as older women may have exaggerated the age of their children at death; the groups are also small, which tends to inflate the importance of small differences between the groups. If, however, we recombine the data into halves, distinguishing the children born before from those born after 1950, a date that seems to have marked an acceleration in the rate of social change and increase in contact with and dependency upon Bantu and their cattle in the Dobe area, and plot the survivorship curve (l_x) that cumulates the effects of mortality for a cohort to each age, the differences between the two groups,

TABLE 4.2
**Mortality Rates (q_x) and Survivorship (l_x) to Children of 165 Women,
by Decade of Birth of Child**

Age x	N	Deaths	q_x	l_x	d_x
Children born 1959–1968, average age (in 1968) 5 years[a]					
0	138	22	.159	100,000	15,900
1	116	6	.052	84,100	4343
5				79,757	
Children born 1949–1958, average age 15[a]					
0	93	20	.215	100,000	21,500
1	73	5	.068	78,500	5338
5	68	3	.044	73,162	3219
10	65			69,943	
Children born 1939–1948, average age 25					
0	106	32	.302	100,000	30,200
1	76	11	.149	69,800	10,400
5	63	2	.032	59,400	1901
10	61	1	.016	57,499	920
15	60	0	.000	56,579	0
Children born 1929–1938, average age 35					
0	97	16	.165	100,000	16,500
1	81	19	.234	83,500	19,539
5	62	6	.097	63,961	6204
10	56	4	.071	57,757	4101
15	52	0	.000	53,656	0
Children born 1919–1928, average age 45					
0	55	9	.163	100,000	16,300
1	46	15	.326	83,700	27,286
5	31	6	.193	55,414	10,695
10	25	2	.080	44,819	3586
15	23	0	.000	41,233	0

[a]Table is incomplete.

plotted in Figure 4.5, appears to be highly significant, greatly exceeding the differences between groups formed on other criteria (such as residence and sex). Note that the age patterns of mortality shown in the graph are each roughly consistent with the expectations of the model life tables, but that the level of mortality for the groups is very different. The mortality experience of the group born since 1950 has to be truncated at age 20, but seems to fall between the

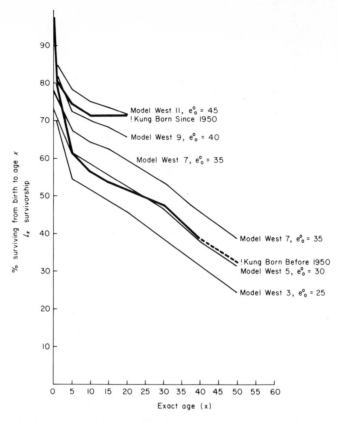

Figure 4.5. Survivorship of !Kung children born prior to 1950 and those born since 1950.

Coale and Demeny models with expectation of life at birth of 40 and 45, whereas the group born before 1950 (which is plotted to age 50 since the members of this group include those born long ago) is quite closely matched to the model with expectation of life at birth of 30 years.

The evidence from the mothers, then, tells us that mortality conditions have changed in the recent past, improving so that children, and presumably persons of all ages, have a higher probability of surviving from one age to the next than formerly. In a sense, this is unfortunate, since the best data (in the sense of the most complete and fully documented events) exists in the recent past, the 10 years surrounding the fieldwork period, after the change in mortality has already occurred. While this is certainly good from the point of view of the !Kung, it means that we must modify our impressions of !Kung life derived from the most recent observations when our goal is to understand the traditional adaptation.

4. THE MEASUREMENT OF MORTALITY

With these strictures in mind, let us examine the data collection during the recent past, using it as another set of pieces of the puzzle to fit into our developing picture of the !Kung population dynamics.

Current Mortality: Deaths in the 1963–1973 Period

Ninety-four of the 841 people registered as members of the population had died by 1973. Table 4.3 presents the numbers of deaths in each age and sex category. Overall there are more deaths to women than to men during the period. Even when we divide the deaths into three broad age groups, childhood (0–14), adulthood (15–59) and old age (60+), there are significant differences

TABLE 4.3
Deaths by Age and Sex, for 94 People (Among 841 Numbered People) Who Died Between 1963 and 1974

Age group (at death)	Male	Female	Total
Zero–infants	14	6	20
1–4	5	6	11
5–9	3	3	6
10–14	0	1	1
Age zero to 14	22 (53.7%)	16 (30.2%)	38 (40.4%)
15–19	0	0	0
20–24	0	4	4
25–29	0	1	1
30–34	1	2	3
35–39	2	1	3
40–44	2	2	4
45–49	1	2	3
50–54	1	3	4
55–59	0	1	1
Age 15 to 59	7 (17.1%)	16 (30.2%)	23 (24.5%)
60–64	2	8	10
65–69	1	6	7
70–74	2	4	6
75–79	5	1	6
80–84	1	1	2
85+	1	1	2
Age 60+	12 (29.3%)	21 (39.6%)	33 (35.1%)
Total	41	53	94

between men and women in proportions of death by age. This result could be due to real differences in the probability of death for !Kung men and women in the period, to differences in the numbers of persons of each sex in the age groups who were at risk of death during that time, or to chance fluctuations in small numbers. To make the !Kung experience comparable to deaths in other populations, we need to transform the crude numbers of deaths shown in Table 4.3 into rates.

The 94 people who died during the period were, according to !Kung custom, buried near their place of death, and their skeletons would be difficult to locate by archaeological techniques. Imagine for a moment, however, that the !Kung had established a graveyard in 1963, and that all of the people who died between then and 1974 were placed in that graveyard, when a new location was established, a situation comparable to the best data sources from prehistoric populations. On the basis of these 94 completed lives, supplemented by no information on the living population from which they were drawn, what conclusions would be drawn about the mortality conditions of the !Kung population?

TABLE 4.4
Life Table Based on 94 Deaths 1963–1974[a]

Age (x)	N deaths	N lived to x and over	q_x	l_x	d_x	L_x	T_x	e^0_x
0	20	94	21	1000	210	853	34,569	34.57
1	11	74	15	790	118.5	2923	33,716	42.68
5	6	63	10	671.5	67	3190	30,793	45.86
10	1	57	2	604.5	12	2993	27,603	45.66
15	0	56	0	592.5	0	2963	24,610	41.54
20	4	56	7	592.5	41.5	2859	21,647	36.54
25	1	52	2	551	11	2728	18,788	34.10
30	3	51	6	540	32	2620	16,060	29.74
35	3	48	6	508	30.5	2390	13,440	26.46
40	4	45	9	447.5	43	2130	11,050	24.69
45	3	41	7	404.5	28	1953	8920	22.05
50	4	38	11	376.5	41.5	1779	6967	18.50
55	1	34	3	335	10	1650	5188	15.49
60	10	33	30	325	97.5	1381	3538	10.89
65	7	23	30	227.5	68	968	2157	9.50
70	6	16	38	159.5	60.5	646	1189	7.45
75	6	10	60	99	60	345	543	5.48
80	2	4	50	39	20	148	198	3.96
85+	2	2	100	20	20	50	50	2.50
Total	94							

[a] Sexes combined.

4. THE MEASUREMENT OF MORTALITY

Table 4.4 shows the life table computed on the experience of only these 94 people, assuming that each person who died at a higher age was at risk of death at all lower ages. The two sexes are combined in order to strengthen the numerical base and to average the obvious differences between the sexes seen in Table 4.3. All 94 people who died were (at one time) at risk of death at age 0; 20 of them actually died during this period. The probability of death (q_0) therefore is 20/94 = .213. The q_x terms for each age are computed by dividing the number of deaths to people in the age group by the number who survived to the beginning of that interval and over, up to age 85+, when two people died out of two who survived to 85, a rate of 1.0. The expectation of life at birth computed from this data is 34.57 years. Figure 4.6 shows the survivorship curve (l_x) computed on the deaths, which is close to the Coale-Demeny model with expectation of life at 35 years across the life span.

Demographers are generally wary of the validity of computing mortality schedules from a collection of deaths only, not only because of problems of underreporting deaths, but because the denominator of the q_x measures, conceptually, is the number of people at risk of dying in the living population.[3] Although it is true under any mortality conditions that all the people will die eventually, survivorship consists of putting that eventuality off into the distant future. Particularly during a period of improving mortality, the analysis of only those who died during a period, excluding a measure of those who survived throughout the period, will exaggerate the level of mortality, making it appear worse than it really is at that period of time.

To calculate rates of deaths based upon those who died relative to all of those at risk, however, we cannot use all of the information on deaths, due to difficulties in linking the deaths to the larger group of people at risk from which they were drawn.

The numbered people have spent varying periods of time at risk of death on our records. There is always a certain amount of ambiguity about the status of people during the year they are entered on our registration system: Were we completely consistent about including or excluding persons who had died in the preceding months? Were we any more likely or less likely to register a family with a recent death, perhaps because families with a dying member are unlikely to

---

[3]A life table based only on deaths must assume that the deaths were drawn from a stationary population, or make some assumption about the rate of growth in the living population at the time of the deaths. An examination of the age distribution of the dead associated with various life tables and rates of growth (Coale and Demeny 1966) shows that the growth assumption is extremely powerful in the interpretation of results. This is a chronic and probably unsolvable problem in paleodemography, where empirical work must rest on skeletal collections. For a discussion of this problem, see the "review symposium" for Acsádi and Neméskèri's *History of human life span and mortality* in *Current Anthropology*, 1974.

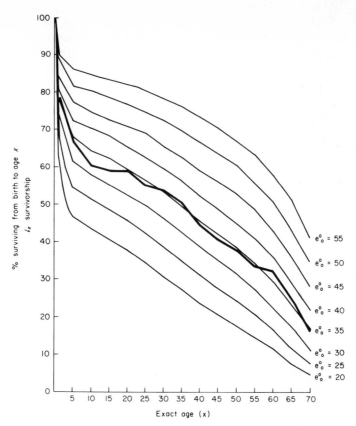

Figure 4.6. Survivorship of 94 persons (both sexes) who died between 1963–1973. (For data, see Table 4.4.) Models are from Coale and Demeny (1966) "West" models for females.

come to visit our camp and be registered, or more likely to come in the hope of obtaining medical care? Similarly, there are problems with recording the number of people at risk of death among the "marginal" members of the population, those who came as visitors and were recorded at one time, but who may have left the area again later. News of deaths to particular people travels widely in the Kalahari and would eventually be carried to the kinsmen whom the visitors had come to see, but there could easily be a time lag of up to 6 months before the news of a death is received and recorded.

To construct life-table estimates of the probability of death per year at each age, it is better to confine the analysis to the best known segment of the population: the residents and those people who have been under observation for a substantial period of time. These requirements lead us to concentrate on the people who were registered during the first phase of the expedition, that is, during Lee's first field trip in 1963 and 1964. Lee registered 466 people at that time (Lee 1969b). Eliminating 48 people who moved out of the area and were lost to close observation, we have a population of 418 people observed for more than 10 years. Due to the problems of interpretation of the first year of observation, both deaths and exposure to the risk of death in 1963 are dropped from the analysis. To count the number of people at risk of death at each age, we simply tabulate the people by their age during each year from 1964 to 1973 (or up to the year of their death). Forty-nine of these 418 people died during the 10-year period, so their deaths are allocated to the year of age the person was at that time. Following this procedure we obtain a count of the number of person-years spent at each age and the number of deaths at that age.

At the end of the period of observation, all of the survivors from the original group of 418 are 10-years older than they were at the beginning. This is fine for

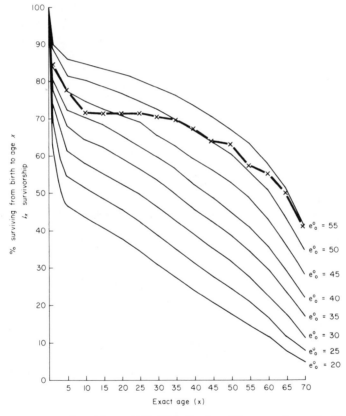

Figure 4.7. Survivorship of !Kung, 1964–1973. (Based on 418 persons observed for 10 years and 164 children born 1973–1972.)

observation of adults and old people, but it means that the only observations for infancy are the survivors of the children born in 1964; at age one, those born in 1964 and 1965, and so on. The numbers of cases at the early ages are too small to be comparable to observations at older ages, so we need to supplement the observations for the young ages. Again, the criterion of a base population is a closed group of carefully observed people. The infants born between 1963–1973, who will be analyzed later for their implications for fertility, form the base for mortality estimates in infancy and childhood, using the 164 (out of 179) who had completed the first year of life by the end of 1973 to estimate infant mortality, the 151 who had completed the second year of life for mortality at age 1, and so on. Only 52 children among those born during 1963–1973 had reached age 7 by 1973, and there are slightly more cases in the analysis of the people registered during 1963 and 1964, so we shift to the larger body of data at age 7. Table 4.5 presents the calculation of the life table by single years of age for these people.

Note that the data upon which Table 4.5 is based has some peculiarities. The number of person-years at risk of death at each age, for instance, differs from the age structure of the population in the censuses shown in Chapter 2, both because the entire population is a year older at each year of observation and because the base population happens to have irregularities from one age to the next. This should not matter, since we only want to use these numbers to estimate the probability of death at each age, but it is a reminder that we are dealing with very small numbers. The problem of small numbers is more acute when we relate the numbers of deaths at each age to the numbers of persons observed at each age. With only 49 deaths, and 88 single years of age to which they can be allocated, it is necessarily true that many single years of age will have no deaths in them, and consequently we estimate a zero probability of death at that age. We know that this cannot be literally true, as there is no age segment of the human life span in any population in which the probability of death is zero. Similarly, by chance alone two or more deaths may fall into a single year of age and the estimate for probability of death suddenly takes a large jump. We have to assume that if we had many more observations, the rates of probability of death for age groups would average out to form some kind of a smooth curve, with positive rates at all ages.

Although we want to consider the question of the kind of smooth curve of rates that seems to underlie the !Kung mortality experience, we do not want to smooth the rates so drastically that we are left with a completely fictional model of !Kung mortality. We can increase the stability of the !Kung results somewhat by abridging the single-year life table shown in Table 4.5 into a life table with 5-year age groups over age 5, which will both average results for 5-year groups and automatically cumulate results through the computation of l_x. Following the conventional procedure, infant mortality (q_0) is kept separate from mortality from early childhood, ages 1–4. Note in Table 4.6 that the survivorship curve

4. THE MEASUREMENT OF MORTALITY

TABLE 4.5
Probabilities of Death and Survival to Each Age, 1964–1973

Age x	Persons observed at age x	Deaths at age x	q_x	l_x	d_x
	Part I: From survivorship of children born 1963–1973				
0	164	25	.152	100,000	15,200
1	151	3	.020	84,800	1696
2	135	4	.030	83,104	2493
3	115	3	.026	80,611	2096
4	97	1	.010	78,515	785
5	78	1	.013	77,730	1010
6	60	1	.017	76,720	1304
	Part II: From survivorship of 418 people observed over 10 years				
7	52	1	.019	75,416	1433
8	59	2	.034	73,983	2515
9	66	0	.000	71,468	—
10	64	0			
11	63	0			
12	59	0			
13	64	0			
14	64	0			
15	71	0			
16	72	0			
17	68	0			
18	68	0			
19	65	0			
20	66	0			
21	67	0			
22	71	0			
23	68	0			
24	67	0			
25	66	0			
26	71	0			
27	77	0			
28	75	0			
29	80	1	.013	71,468	929
30	78	0		70,539	
31	84	0			
32	78	0			
33	75	0			
34	74	1	.014	70,539	988

(*continued*)

TABLE 4.5 (*cont.*)

Age x	Persons observed at age x	Deaths at age x	q_x	l_x	d_x
35	67	0		69,551	
36	64	1	.016	69,551	1113
37	67	0		68,438	
38	70	0			
39	69	1	.014	68,438	958
40	69	0		67,480	
41	66	1	.015	67,480	1012
42	70	0		66,468	
43	69	0			
44	66	1	.023	66,468	1529
45	64	0		64,939	
46	64	0			
47	57	0			
48	51	0			
49	48	1	.021	64,939	1364
50	44	2	.045	63,575	2861
51	39	1	.026	60,714	1579
52	35	0		59,135	
53	37	0			
54	39	1	.026	59,135	1538
55	39	0			
56	34	0			
57	31	1	.032	57,597	1843
58	36	0		55,754	
59	34	0			
60	37	0			
61	36	1	.028	55,754	1561
62	35	0			
63	33	1	.030	54,193	1626
64	31	1	.032	52,567	1682
65	27	2	.074	50,885	3765
66	25	0			
67	27	0			
68	25	2	.080	47,120	3770
69	21	1	.048	43,350	2080
70	17	0		41,270	
71	17	0			
72	17	1	.059	41,270	2435
73	13	2	.154	38,835	5981
74	11	2	.182	32,854	5979

(continued)

4. THE MEASUREMENT OF MORTALITY

TABLE 4.5 (*cont.*)

Age x	Persons observed at age x	Deaths at age x	q_x	l_x	d_x
75	12	1	.083	26,875	2231
76	10	1	.100	24,644	2464
77	9	1	.111	22,180	2464
78	9	1	.111	19,718	2189
79	8	1	.125	17,529	2191
80	6	2	.333	15,338	5108
81	4	0		10,230	
82	4	0			
83	4	0			
84	4	0			
85	3	1	.333	10,230	3407
86	2	0			
87	2	0			
88	1	1	1.000	6823	6823

(l_x) of the single-year life table is preserved in the abridged life table, and the q_x terms are computed by dividing d_x by l_x rather than either summing or averaging the q_x terms of the single-year life table. The abridged life table goes beyond computation of the q_x, l_x, and d_x terms to calculate the L_x column, the number of person-years lived in the interval for a stationary population with the mortality experience described, the T_x terms, the number of years left to live by the survivors to age x, and e^0_x, the expectation of life (average number of years left to live) at each age to the survivors to that age. The expectation of life at birth calculated from the data is over 50 years, a figure which I find difficult to accept as an accurate indicator of typical !Kung mortality in the period. An expectation of life at birth of 50 years implies that !Kung mortality conditions are as good as would have been found in England and Wales in 1900, or in the United States in 1910 (Preston *et al.* 1972). Even the region of Southern Africa in which the !Kung live has probably not attained such a high expectation of life at birth as yet. While there are no accurate life tables for Botswana, educated estimates by demographers suggest an expectation of life at birth of around 40 for the country as a whole (Derek Hudson personal communication 1976; Population Reference Bureau 1972). It is unlikely that the !Kung, who are the segment of the population most removed from medical care, would have mortality conditions significantly better than the average. Doubt of the acceptability of the conclusion is increased when we look at particular features of the life table computed. Table 4.5 shows that there were no deaths at all between the ages of 10 and 29 in the observed population, and only 7 between the ages of 30 and 49. In the next

TABLE 4.6
Abridged Life Table, !Kung 1964–1973, from Table 4.5

Age x	q_x	$l_x{}^a$	d_x	$L_x{}^b$	T_x	$e^0{}_x$
				From single-year life table		
0	.152	100,000	15,200	89,360	5,009,944	50.10
1	.083	84,800	7070	323,325	4,920,584	58.03
5	.081	77,730	6262	372,995	4,597,259	59.14
10	.000	71,468	0	357,340	4,224,264	59.11
15	.000	71,468	0	357,340	3,866,924	54.11
20	.000	71,468	0	357,340	3,509,584	49.11
25	.013	71,468	929	355,017	3,152,244	44.11
30	.014	70,539	988	350,225	2,797,227	42.24
35	.030	69,551	2071	342,577	2,447,002	35.18
40	.038	67,480	2541	331,048	2,104,425	31.19
45	.021	64,939	1364	321,285	1,773,377	27.31
50	.094	63,575	5978	302,930	1,452,092	22.84
55	.032	57,597	1843	283,378	1,149,162	19.95
60	.087	55,754	4869	266,597	865,784	15.53
65	.189	50,885	9617	230,386	599,187	11.78
70	.349	41,270	14,395	170,362	368,801	8.94
75	.429	26,875	11,539	105,532	198,439	7.38
80	.333	15,338	5108	63,920	92,907	6.06
85+	1.000	10,230	10,230	28,987	28,987	2.83

[a] l_x is taken directly from Table 4.5. d_x is $l_x - l_{x+5}$. q_x is d_x/l_x.

[b] L_x is an estimate of person-years lived in the interval in the stationary population. $L_0 = .3l_0 + .7l_1$ (to take account of the fact that deaths tend to occur early in the interval); $L_{1-4} = (.4l_1 + .6l_2) + \frac{3}{2}(l_2 + l_4)$. Otherwise $_5L_x = \frac{5}{2}(l_x + l_{x+5})$ and $L_{85} = \frac{3}{2}(l_{85} + l_{88}) + \frac{1}{2}l_{88}$. T_x is the person-years to live by the survivors to age x, computed by summing the L_x terms from the bottom. The expectation of life at age x, $e^0{}_x = T_x/l_x$.

chapter we will consider the probability that such unlikely events as a "death dearth" will occur by chance in populations of a given size, observed over a given period of years. Here let us consider the possibility that there is some particular kind of bias in the selection of the people observed that would produce this result.

Two possibilities arise. The first is that the group of young adults who remained to be observed in the Dobe area are unusually healthy, not a random sample of people of that age at all. We have noted before that people who are ill tend to go to a cattlepost rather than continue the strenuous life in the bush. Moving to one of the local cattleposts would not remove such people from observation, but moving to one of the numerous cattleposts out of the area would. Migration of unhealthy people might be encouraged by the easier access to hospitals and Western medicine in "the East" or on the Chum!kwe settlement station in Namibia.

On the other hand, it is entirely possible that this outcome is the result of our own expedition's interference in the natural course of events in the area. When I recall the cases where members of our expedition took strenuous measures to save the life of a sick or injured person, as in the case of Kumsa (the poison arrow victim), it does seem that most of these cases involved adults, especially men. Of course we had no conscious policy to attempt to help adult men and not others, but the kinds of dangers to men (arrow poison, mauling by a lion, septicemia from being accidentally caught in a Bantu's animal trap, an infected thorn in the foot) elicited our intervention in a way that disease did not. It may be due not so much to our unconscious preference for adult men as the !Kung's: They may be less fatalistic about deaths of adult men and may have solicited our help more actively for such people.

Unfortunately, we have evidence from outside of this carefully delimited body of data that the probability of death to young adults is not unusually low for the !Kung, either for the past (from the analysis of the mothers' data) or for the present. Among the 94 deaths examined above, there was, in fact, a run of deaths to young adults, including several of young women in the /du/da population to the south of the Dobe area, during the 1964–1973 period, which indicates that we can not support the hypothesis that the !Kung have an unusual genetic disposition to resist death during young adulthood.

In the next chapter, we will attempt to increase our understanding of the implications of this empirical data through considerations of the expected degree of sampling variation and error in data collections of this kind.

5

Simulating Mortality

In the last chapter we asked what level of mortality the !Kung of Dobe have experienced; we answered on the basis of empirical data drawn from several sources. Each of these sources provided a perilously small data base and we postponed asking what degree of confidence could be based upon the results.

The subjects of sampling error and degrees of confidence in estimates are often neglected in demographic studies, because both the nature of the data (vital statistics records and census) and the universe about which conclusions are drawn make a poor fit to the assumptions of statistical processes. Birth and death records are usually collected in a way that is designed to incorporate all such events over a period of time and in a defined locality, just as the census is by definition a complete inventory of the people living and their characteristics. Demographers have developed elaborate techniques for the detection and correction of systematic error within nearly complete data collections, but less often find it useful to sample from the data base or to treat the data base as a sample from some larger universe. The Ns (numbers of cases) analyzed in most demographic studies are, in any case, so large that the sampling distribution of statistics is closely approximated by the theoretical values that apply when the population is infinitely large.

The !Kung study, of course, is very different. The number of cases available for analysis is so small that there is a continual danger of missing even the major trends in the results due to small number fluctuations and error. The strategy for carrying out studies in which the data is scarce may justifiably be different from that of large-scale demographic studies. Of course one should attempt to make the data collection as large as possible by including cases over as large an area and as long a time as possible, but this is a counsel of perfection that does not help in the interpretation of the small data base that represents the best the present investigator could do.

The universe about which one wishes to generalize is also different in the case of a small study of a population like the Dobe !Kung than it would likely be in a national population study. To make the most of the Dobe !Kung study, we want to view it as a case drawn from a larger category of populations of its type.

The Universe of !Kung-like Populations

We would like to be able to generalize about the mortality conditions in a universe of populations with the environment, the technology, the cultural practices, and the genetic composition of the precontact !Kung, unaffected by the changes in diet and medical practices introduced recently by Bantus and Europeans. As an empirical problem, we can imagine how to approach this question, even if we cannot carry it out. If we had access to a workable "time machine," we would locate a number of such environments occupied by peoples with the characteristics of the !Kung and observe the incidence of mortality by age and sex over long periods of time. With an effective and cheap time machine, we might sample both populations and periods of time in order to explore the components of differences in mortality from one observation to another. We would allocate observed differences to (a) random "meaningless" variations caused by the applications of constant probabilities to small numbers of discrete individuals at various ages and the resulting irregularities in the age distribution produced by those random fluctuations; and (b) changes in the underlying probabilities of death by age, caused by variations in climate, the food supply, the populations of microorganisms and predators, genetic and cultural variation, and so on. This second kind of variation is of great importance in understanding the population dynamics of prehistoric populations, but in the absence of a real time machine it is difficult to attach meaningful values to the consequences of environmental variations. Research (on rainfall variability, measuring tree rings, etc.) may ultimately provide a secure basis for modeling environmental variation in prehistoric populations (see Jorde and Harpending 1976), but since we have no basis for assessing this for the !Kung, we will concentrate on the assessment of the first sort of variability, stochastic random fluctuation, and assume (while not believing) that environmental fluctuation is nonexistent.

Simulating !Kung-like Populations

The exploration of random fluctuations in mortality caused by applying constant probabilities of death by age and sex to stochastically fluctuating populations can be explored, using a computer microsimulation program in lieu of a time machine. Starting with the actual !Kung population of 1968, hypothetical populations are created in the computer of "people" who are born, marry, have children, sometimes divorce and remarry, and die according to the probability schedules and cultural rules observed among the !Kung. AMBUSH, the computer program designed to carry out these simulations of populations based on the !Kung observations (Howell and Lehotay 1978), operates by retaining the individuality of a set of hypothetical persons, generating events for these individuals by a Monte-Carlo process. In the case of death events, we instruct the computer to create a random number between 1 and 100,000 each time a new baby is born, such that each number in the range is equally likely to be drawn. To determine the ultimate age at death, the computer compares the random number to the distribution of the age at death (the d_x column) given for the life table for that sex that characterizes the !Kung. Since in the life table 29,546 out of each 100,000 newborn males will die during the first year of life, a "boy" is given an age at death of zero if the random number drawn falls between 1 and 29,546. Each single year of age has the area of its probability of death in the life table, up to age 79. All of the people who would be expected to die at ages of 80 and over (less than 3%) are grouped together to die at age 80 to close out the table.

The number of people who are at risk of death in each age group and at each period of time depends upon the history of events in the population. In other words, it is a stochastic outcome of a number of processes, only one of which is death itself. The year of death of individuals is determined at their birth, and stored along with other information about the person. During the period of life, he or she has the same probabilities of everyone else who is alive (and of that age and sex) of marriage, childbirth, and so forth. The year of death of each person is determined independently, but the number of deaths in any particular year is a function of a number of variables, such as the absolute number of people alive at that time, the age distribution of the population at that time, the number of births produced in that year (because the probability of death is very high in the first year of life), and simple random fluctuations. In a population that averages only 500 persons alive in each year and has an intrinsic crude death rate of about 34 (for the two sexes combined) when it is not growing, we only expect about 17 deaths per year to people of all ages. The fluctuations in deaths over a short period of time like a year, then, will be considerable, and our ability to detect the underlying mortality probabilities that form a population are very much a function of the length of time we observe events in the population and cumulate the results.

To illustrate this point, we examine a series of experiments on mortality using the AMBUSH program. All of the simulations used here have exactly the same underlying probabilities of events, specifically the mortality schedules of Coale and Demeny's MW5 for the two sexes, and a fertility regime (to be described in greater detail later) modeled on the observed !Kung fertility performance, one that is sufficient to keep the population stationary or slightly growing, on the average, though particular populations may decline or grow for random reasons.

Observations of the Simulated Populations

Simulations are a valuable adjunct to empirical study in small populations like the !Kung because they demonstrate very graphically some of the pitfalls of generalizations from small data collections. To explore this point, we will present results from three series of simulations of mortality. The first series consists of the accumulation of mortality indicators in runs that start with the 1968 !Kung population and begin tabulation after 50 years of simulation (in order to avoid tabulating features of simulations that are derived from peculiarities of the starting population). The group of "long runs" allows the population to go on until either the population reaches an absolute limit of about 750 people, or it reaches a time limit of 350 years of tabulated simulation. The size limit is imposed by the costs of increased computer storage and does not correspond to events that would terminate a population in the real world. The time limit of 350 years is equally arbitrary, imposed on the assumption that we will not learn anything additional for the present purposes by continuing the simulation for a longer period of time.

The group of long runs represents the ideal harvest of the observational time machine we have posited. The results are free from errors of age estimation and from omissions of lost data and they each represent a substantially large body of data. As we see in Table 5.1, the long runs continued from 130 years to the maximum of 350 years and provide data on 2612 to 6857 deaths during the period of simulation.

If we reduce the period of time observed, however, in order to create hypothetical data collections closer to the realities of observations that can be made on contemporary hunting and gathering groups, or which might be produced from historical records of observation of a group during the early period of contact, we clearly note some of the difficulties of assessing the underlying probabilities of death from the empirical data. To compare with the long runs of AMBUSH simulations, a series of runs of 20 years and 10 years have been prepared, in both cases tabulating the features of deaths in the population during the period, after an untabulated period of 50 years of simulation, again to avoid the features of the initial population.

TABLE 5.1
Crude Deaths Rates (CDR) in the Simulated Populations

	Years	N deaths	Mean CDR	Variance	Lowest	Highest
			I. Long simulations			
1.	209	4005	34.92	50.02	21.78	47.00
2.	132	2719	35.15	79.48	17.51	55.73
3.	130	2612	36.31	94.26	20.15	55.55
4.	181	3948	33.69	52.77	19.86	48.96
5.	351	6857	36.13	49.91	22.05	50.08
			II. 20-year runs			
1.	20	311	38.75	57.00	19.95	51.34
2.	20	351	41.12	155.40	9.25	73.73
3.	20	362	36.76	81.20	21.91	49.79
4.	20	323	31.29	62.90	15.38	44.25
5.	20	370	36.21	57.20	19.64	47.24
			III. 10-year runs			
1.	10	170	35.89	67.10	19.23	46.41
2.	10	182	36.29	40.30	23.90	45.54
3.	10	186	39.09	71.90	25.52	54.50
4.	10	202	38.25	51.80	24.76	52.14
5.	10	140	30.64	148.60	8.86	48.24

Crude Death Rates in the Simulated Populations

Crude death rates are calculated by dividing the number of deaths during a single year by the midyear population alive at that time and multiplying by 1000 to express the number of deaths per 1000 persons. Crude death rates have not been presented for the !Kung population due to difficulties in the accurate determination of the number of persons at risk per year (but see Howell 1976a:142).

Table 5.1 shows the crude death rates for the simulated populations, summarized from calculations made on single years. It shows that the mean crude death rates observed in the runs varies by as much as 3 deaths per thousand in the long runs, and by as much as 10 deaths per thousand in the short runs. The final columns show that the crude death rate in any single year is an extremely unreliable indicator of the underlying mortality probabilities in a small population, since values as low as 9 and as high as 74 might be produced by chance alone from an invariant mortality schedule.

Life-Table Indicators of Mortality

The crude death rate is a poor choice as an indicator of mortality, as its annual nature exacerbates our chronic problem of small numbers and it fails to make any use of the valuable information we have on the age and sex of those who die. Much better indicators of mortality can be found by combining observations over the available period of time into information on the age and sex categories of those who die, parallel to the life-table categories of d_x (proportions of deaths in the cohort in each age category) and l_x (proportions who survive to each age and beyond).

AMBUSH presents the outcome of the mortality process during the period of simulation in the form of a percentage distribution of deaths in each age group, for the two sexes separately. In effect, this distribution is the stochastically produced reflection of the d_x column of the life table that formed the population, and the outputs can be compared with the input d_x schedule to observe random fluctuations.

Figure 5.1 shows the proportion of deaths in each age group, for the females only, in the life table that formed the population (plotted by bar graph conventions) and the distributions produced as output in each of the five long runs of simulation (plotted as connected points, for contrast). We see in Figure 5.1 that

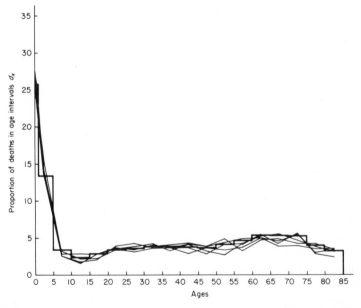

Figure 5.1. Age at death (d_x): proportion of deaths in each age interval, long runs. (For values, see Table 5.1.)

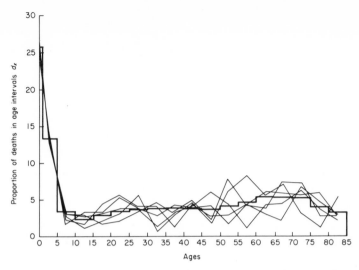

Figure 5.2. Age at death (d_x): proportion of deaths in each age interval, 20-year runs.

the simulations consistently reveal the underlying input probabilities with relatively little variability between simulations, since we are basing the estimates on a considerable amount of information in each simulation. Figures 5.2 and 5.3 show, however, that simulations vary considerably among themselves and in comparison with the identical input schedule when produced by the analysis of a smaller number of deaths, numbers that are realistic estimates of the amount of information that might be gathered from real small populations, observed over what is a substantial period of time from the point of view of a human researcher's life span.

Intuitively, looking at Figures 5.2 and 5.3, we may feel uneasy about the possibility of determining the true underlying probabilities of mortality by induction from the study of realistic data collections comparable to those of the !Kung. Statistically, we can show more precisely that the uneasiness is justified.

The hypothesis to be tested is that the observed distribution of deaths by age was produced from the Coale and Demeny "West" model life table with expectation of life at birth of 30 years. We know from the way that the simulations were produced that the hypothesis is true for the simulated populations (although we can never know this for a real data collection). The alternative hypothesis is that the underlying mortality is higher or lower than that of the model. We can test this hypothesis from simulated or real data by 18 independent tests, corresponding to the proportion of deaths in each of the age segments, and we can test it independently for the two sexes or combine the sexes if that is more convenient. Here we will test it only for females.

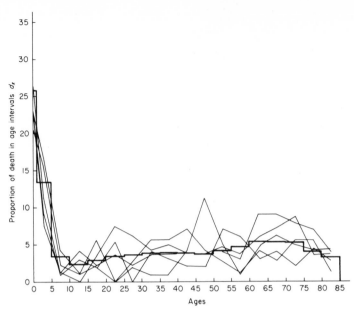

Figure 5.3. Age at death (d_x): proportion of deaths in each age interval, 10-year runs.

Let us take the first age segment, birth to exact age one, and consider the case where the number of deaths observed is 1000 and another case where the number of deaths is 100. The expected number of deaths at age zero is $N \cdot p$, where N is the total number of deaths to persons of all ages and p is the probability that a death that occurs will fall into that age interval (d_x). We expect 295.46 deaths to occur at age zero, on the average, in a large number of runs with 1000 deaths, and we expect 29.546 to occur, on the average, in runs of 100 deaths. In any particular run, of course, the number of deaths at age zero has to be a whole rather than a fractional number. The standard error for those proportions will be $\sqrt{N \cdot p \cdot (1-p)}$, 16.8 for the case with 1000 deaths and 4.3 for the case with 100 deaths. We accept the hypothesis when the observed d_0 falls within the range of 1.96 times the standard error around the expected value, and reject the hypothesis if it falls outside that range. Clearly the proportion of the whole within the permissible range is much wider with the small number of deaths than with the larger number, and we are in danger of accepting the hypothesis with only 100 deaths even when the true probability is different.

This is not an impossible situation for testing the d_0 age segment, since at least p, the probability of death at that age, is fairly substantial. The dilemma of statistical testing of the hypothesis by the d_x values is demonstrated more clearly if we look at another of those independent age segments into which deaths may fall.

5. SIMULATING MORTALITY

Let us look at deaths in the interval of age 20–24. The probability of a death falling into that age segment is .03386, so the expected number of deaths in a collection of 1000 is 33.86 with a standard error of 5.82, and the expected number in a collection of 100 deaths is 3.386 with a standard error of 1.84. For the small data collection, then, our 95% confidence intervals include from 0 to 7 deaths in the age group, and we have virtually no possibility of rejecting the hypothesis because the confidence intervals are so wide. Certainly we could not devise a statistical test that would allow us to discriminate between hypotheses that the underlying mortality schedule was that of any close alternative schedule, such as those with expectation of life at birth of 20 or 40 years, by testing the individual d_x entries for any of the ages past childhood.

The d_x life-table measure, then, has the statistical advantage that each segment is independent of the others and we can make up to 18 distinct tests of the hypothesis that the population was formed by a particular life table, but it simultaneously has the disadvantage that it makes stiff demands on the data available. Each segment requires a substantial number of deaths in order to discriminate between hypotheses, and it is sensitive to errors in age estimation that shift even a few deaths into the wrong age segment. Conceptually, d_x is not the most convenient or enlightening measure of mortality, since its L-shaped curve fails to distinguish clearly between mortality differences after childhood and makes it very sensitive to the commonly observed underreporting of infant and childhood mortality. When testing alternative hypotheses, d_x also has the disadvantage that because it must sum to a constant total, the curves of alternative hypotheses cross and recross each other.

Rather than group the d_x measures into wider age categories, it may be most sensible to abandon the use of d_x altogether, shifting to the related measure of l_x, which cumulates d_x from birth to each age. The use of l_x costs us the independence of the various age segments: Falling below the expected survivorship at one age increases the probability that the population will also fall below the expected level at the next age, even if the number of deaths in the interval is the expected. We can calculate standard errors and confidence limits for l_x, but it is unclear how to interpret more than one point in the l_x curve. It may happen that the empirical curve will cross and recross the theoretical curve over the life span, a property that can be used to identify the relevant probability schedule. If the observed l_x falls into the calculated confidence interval at each point in the age span, one can be more than 95% sure that the hypothesis should not be rejected. The use of l_x has the additional advantage over d_x that the theoretical curves for alternative hypotheses do not cross each other, and the importance of any errors in age estimation in the empirical population are minimized by cumulation.

Figure 5.4 shows the l_x curves for the range of Coale and Demeny "West" models for females and the results of the five AMBUSH long run simulations

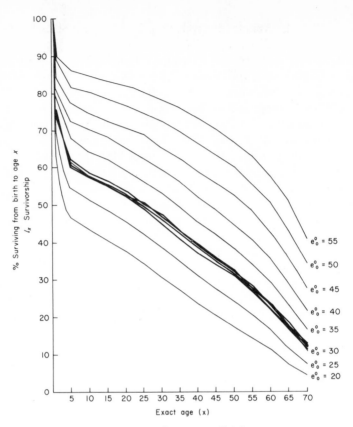

Figure 5.4. Survivorship to age x (l_x), long runs.

generated with the use of Model "West" Five, with expectation of life at birth of 30 years, plotted over the theoretical curve. To plot l_x from AMBUSH simulations, we start with 100,000 persons at birth and subtract the successive d_x terms to determine the proportion surviving to each age. We see from Figure 5.4 that the randomly generated long-run populations are in close agreement with each other and with the theoretical value of l_x for the life table from which they were generated, not exceeding 3% difference in the percentage surviving to any age over the life span. Although none of the simulated populations exactly match the probability schedule that produced them, there would be very little danger of mistaking the correct model life table from the results of any one simulation, and virtually no danger of doing so with five simulations to compare, provided that one knows in advance that they were all produced by the same probability schedule.

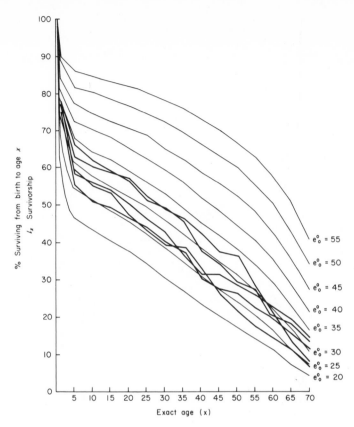

Figure 5.5. Survivorship to age x (l_x), 20-year runs.

When we look at the comparable distributions from short runs of 20 and 10 years, however, we see that the use of l_x rather than d_x has improved but not solved our problem of generalizing from small numbers. Figure 5.5 shows that the l_x terms in the 20-year runs bracket the theoretical values that produced them, but the results of single runs, as anticipated, tend to stay above or below the theoretical values due to the cumulation of the mortality trends. If we had information comparable to these five distinct runs, we would have no difficulty in selecting Model "West" 5 as the underlying probability, but from any one run we might erroneously select a higher or lower level (specifically models with expectation of life at birth 5 years higher or lower) as our best bet.

When the data collection is smaller yet, because the period of time observed is shorter, we see in Figure 5.6 that the variance of the observed survivorship curve is wider yet. One of those simulations, as it happens, rather resembles the

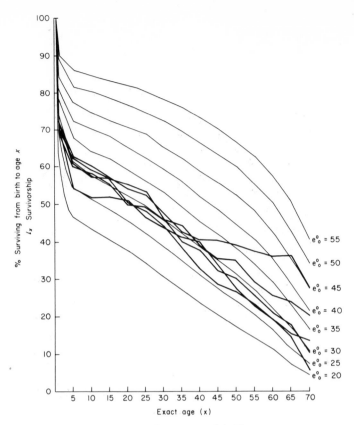

Figure 5.6. Survivorship to age x (l_x), 10-year runs.

puzzling pattern we observed in the !Kung data for the living population of 1963–1973 in that there are few deaths to persons in the adult ages, so that a large proportion of the total survive to old age. Naturally we expect such unlikely patterns to be more frequently found in very small data collections such as these 10-year runs.

We can calculate standard errors and hence confidence intervals for l_x terms for collections of deaths of varying size, even though the lack of independence of l_x to various ages prevents us from carrying out a rigorous statistical test of the hypothesis that a particular data collection was drawn from a population with a given mortality schedule. Nevertheless, these standard errors and confidence intervals are useful in allowing us to estimate in advance the value of a mortality data collection of a particular size, or conversely to plan how long we would have to observe a particular society in order to collect enough information on deaths to estimate the underlying mortality schedule. Table 5.2 shows the standard errors

5. SIMULATING MORTALITY

TABLE 5.2
Standard Errors of l_x[a]

			N = Number of deaths observed						
Age	l_x	$p(1-p)$	50	100	150	200	250	500	1000	2000
1	.7443	.1903	.0617	.0436	.0356	.0308	.0278	.0195	.0138	.0098
5	.6121	.2374	.0689	.0487	.0398	.0345	.0308	.0218	.0154	.0109
10	.5814	.2434	.0698	.0493	.0403	.0349	.0312	.0221	.0156	0110
15	.5586	.2466	.0702	.0497	.0405	.0351	.0314	.0222	.0157	.0111
20	.5300	.2491	.0706	.0499	.0408	.0353	.0316	.0223	.0158	.0112
25	.4961	.2500	.0707	.0500	.0408	.0354	.0316	.0224	.0158	.0112
30	.4604	.2584	.0719	.0508	.0415	.0359	.0321	.0227	.0163	.0114
35	.4234	.2441	.0699	.0493	.0403	.0349	.0312	.0221	.0156	.0110
40	.3860	.2370	.0688	.0487	.0397	.0344	.0308	.0218	.0154	.0109
45	.3494	.2273	.0674	.0477	.0398	.0337	.0302	.0213	.0151	.0107
50	.3138	.2079	.0645	.0456	.0372	.0322	.0288	.0204	.0144	.0102
55	.2738	.1983	.0630	.0445	.0364	.0315	.0282	.0199	.0141	.0100
60	.2274	.1757	.0593	.0419	.0342	.0296	.0265	.0187	.0133	.0094
65	.1736	.1435	.0536	.0379	.0309	.0268	.0240	.0167	.0120	.0085
70	.1201	.1057	.0460	.0325	.0265	.0230	.0206	.0096	.0103	.0073
75	.0692	.0644	.0359	.0254	.0207	.0179	.0160	.0085	.0080	.0057
80	.0307	.0295	.0243	.0172	.0140	.0121	.0109	.0077	.0054	.0038

[a] Coale and Demeny (1966), Model "West" Five.

for l_x for data collections of various sizes, and Figure 5.7 plots the confidence intervals for l_x over the theoretical values from the model life tables, showing how wide a range of error might be expected. We see in Table 5.2 that 50 deaths have a standard error of about .06 (or 6%) in proportion surviving to each age over the life span; for 500 deaths we have a standard error of about .02; for 2000 deaths the standard error is reduced to about .01. If we want to achieve 95% confidence that any observed l_x will fall within 6% of the expected value, so that they will not cross or overlap the l_x lines for life tables with expectation of life at birth 5 years higher or lower, for example, we will need about 250 deaths. In a population of 1000 living persons, with a crude death rate of 35, one would accumulate 250 deaths for analysis in 15 years, if the sexes are being tabulated separately, in about 7.5 years if the sexes are combined.

Effects of Errors in Data Collections on Mortality

This consideration of expected fluctuations in mortality indicators in small populations only includes random sources of variation, such as those that enter into the AMBUSH simulations. In real populations, the fluctuations in indicators of mortality derived from observed events will always be the result of at least

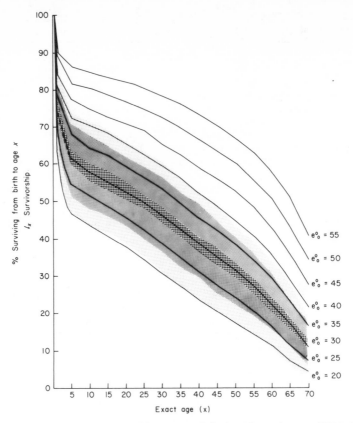

Figure 5.7. Ninety-five percent confidence intervals for l_x with sample sizes of 2000, 500, 100, and 50 deaths. (Confidence intervals are 1.96 × standard error of l_x.

the following factors: the true underlying probabilities of death by age, the random occurrence of events of low probability, and errors in observation and age estimation. I believe that the !Kung data collection is as free from observation error as careful fieldwork and a cooperative population can make it, but I would second Carroll's (1975) assertion that all data collections contain error, it is only the rate of that error that varies.

Consider the effects of some of the common errors found in demographic data collections on the subject of mortality. Infant deaths are frequently, if not invariably, underreported, in part due to subtle distinctions between live births that end in death during the first minutes of life and miscarriages that are counted neither as births nor deaths, in part due to the inability or unwillingness of informants to recall and report on events that may have occurred long ago and leave no reminding consequences.

In assessing the probable degree of underreporting of infant deaths in particular data collections, we should look for the general pattern that the earlier in life the child died the less likely its death is to be reported, so that the quality of the data improves over the course of childhood. The implication is that if estimates of mortality from infancy and childhood differ, the estimate from childhood is more likely to be correct because it is less likely to be influenced by underreporting.

Similarly, the longer ago an event occurred, the less likely it is to be reported. Data collections that are equal in the number of observations but that differ on the period of time over which that data was collected should differ in the degree of underreporting of deaths, particularly infant deaths. The pattern can be explored empirically, if it is reasonable to assume that mortality conditions have not changed over the period of the data collection. If deaths in the past are more often underreported, mortality should appear to be lowest in the distant past, becoming worse as the present is approached. Brass (1975) has some ingenious techniques for correcting this kind of underreporting of events, but these techniques cannot be useful in a situation, like the !Kung's, where mortality seems to be improving over time. These considerations do suggest that estimates of mortality for the past are likely to err in the direction of overestimating the level of survivorship.

A second form of common error in data collections on mortality is caused by age misestimation or misreporting. These errors are not serious if they merely occur in the form of "age heaping" on round numbers or preferred ages, since there are smoothing techniques available and the calculation of the l_x column automatically cumulates the survivorship curve, averaging out these errors. The problem is a systematic one, however, at more advanced ages. In many societies older people exaggerate their chronological age for purposes of prestige. If these exaggerated advanced ages are used in the construction of the life table, the survivorship of the whole population will be exaggerated and mortality conditions will appear to be more favorable than they really are. This problem is not likely to enter into the current estimates of !Kung mortality, given the age estimation procedure, which assigned individual ages as a product of a single age distribution, and can hardly enter into the interpretation of retrospective mortality, since few of the "children" of the adult women had reached middle age, never mind very advanced ages. These problems should, however, be taken into account in the assessment of mortality estimates made by various procedures in comparative populations.

The implications of errors of underreporting of deaths and/or errors in estimation of age of death are serious. The life-table analysis is a way of cumulating effects from birth to each higher age (via the l_x and d_x columns) and cumulating from the oldest ages to the youngest (in T_x and e^0_x). When the data cannot be trusted at the extremes, the value of the whole analysis is threatened. What we need is an indicator that is computed independently for each age segment, so that we can put more trust in the indicators for those age segments that seem likely to be accurately reported. For small scale data collections from living populations, q_x (or M_x) serves adequately as an indicator of mortality and can be computed directly from the data for that age interval. If the data is adequate for ages 5–65, for instance, but early childhood and old age data is suspect, one can compute the middle indices of q_x, find a model life table with a best fit for the 5–65 years, and use the q_x terms for childhood and old age from a model life table. It is extremely useful to have some trustworthy indicators at the ages below 10 and above 45, because those segments will provide more sensitive indicators of q_x than the middle years, during which we expect to find little change from one interval to the next, and in which the probability of death per interval is relatively low, so that number of deaths observed per interval in small groups is likely to fluctuate widely. As a rule of thumb, when the addition of one death to an observed group causes the estimate of the probability of death to change dramatically, the small number problem is acute.

When the data collection is based on a skeletal collection, even the computation of q_x fails to be independent of errors of underreporting and age misestimation, as the denominator of q_x requires cumulation from other ages. Underreporting at any age will throw off the q_x terms at all ages, moving them to a higher or lower level than they should be. In a case where the completeness of the skeletal collection is believed to be good for the middle years, say ages 10 to 60, perhaps the best method of estimating the probability schedule of mortality from which the deaths were drawn is to compute the q_x terms in the usual way, assuming that the levels of q_x are probably in error but that the ratio of q_x to q_{x+5} for the middle age categories should be correct, and try to fit those ratios to the ratios of the model life tables. It is unfortunate for this procedure that q_x terms tend to be constantly increasing in model life tables at all levels of mortality precisely in the range where the data is likely to be best (i.e., ages 10 to 50). The larger the skeletal collection, and the further at each end the adequate data extend, the better the chances of success with this technique. The N used to calculate the standard error of the distributions in this case would be based on the number of deaths within the range of the good data, not the total skeletal collection.

AMBUSH Perspectives on Assessment of the !Kung Mortality Data

In Chapter 4 we asked what level of mortality the !Kung have experienced, according to the fragmentary data available to us, and we came up with different answers from different groups of data. From the mothers who gave birth before

1950, we concluded there was an expectation of life at birth of 30; from deaths in the 1963–1973 period we calculated 35; from survivorship of children born since 1950 we estimated 40–45; and from lives in progress between 1963 and 1973 we obtained an estimate of 50. If there were only one set of probabilities underlying the events studied in these various collections of data, so that these results were all estimates of the same quantity, we would have to conclude that the methods used are unacceptably loose, producing widely varying indicators of the same process. The framework provided by AMBUSH permits us to go beyond this discouraging conclusion to place our confidence in the indicators differentially.

One criterion for differential assessment of the various methods used is the size of the data collections. If we divide the data collections into those derived from (a) the mothers, (b) the deaths, and (c) current observations, we see that the number of relevant events in the three collections are very different. The mothers provide information on 274 deaths in a population of 475 people, with a total of about 9500 person-years lived among them. The analysis of deaths is based on 94 deaths to 94 persons, with over 3290 person-years lived. The current observations are based on 583 persons observed for 4980 person-years, with only 49 deaths among them. Clearly the data from the mothers is the largest data collection, and on those grounds alone must be accorded heavy weight.

A second consideration is that of the age structure of the three collections. The mothers provide data primarily on the first 15 years of life, a period when the probability of death is high and rapidly changing by age, a period of life when data is relatively valuable. The mothers' data represents a larger N for the purposes of calculating the standard error of the measurement, because all of the deaths are concentrated within the first portion of life. Since the probability of death in the first 15 years of life is approximately .5 for mortality conditions like the !Kung, the mothers have provided part of the data on a collection of deaths that would be approximately size 500 over the life span. The l_x measures calculated from the life table of mothers' data (Table 4.1) falls within the 95% confidence intervals for MW5 with $N = 500$ as far as the l_x measures go, except at age 5, when l_x is slightly above the confidence interval.

The collection of deaths to 94 persons includes a substantial proportion of observations in infancy and old age, when the probability of death is high and information is relatively valuable. The l_x measures for this life table (shown in Table 4.3) fall into the 95% confidence interval for MW5 with $N = 100$ up to age 60, but of course these measures would also fall into the confidence intervals, wide as they are, for model life tables with considerably higher expectation of life at birth.

The collection of data on current lives, however, is a much smaller data collection. Even though the person-years lived observed is very high, a large proportion of those fall into the adult ages, where the probability of death is low and the patterns of mortality are difficult to detect. The number N, for the purposes of calculating the standard error of measurement of l_x, is only equal to the number of deaths, 49. The confidence interval around the hypothetical survivorship curve is extremely wide with such a small number of deaths, as we saw in Figure 5.4, but the l_x measures computed in Table 4.6 do not fall into the confidence interval shown in Figure 5.4 for MW5 with $N = 50$. We can reject the hypothesis that the expectation of life at birth for the current population is as low as 30 years, but the data does fall into the confidence intervals for the hypothesis that the expectation of life at birth was in the range of 37.5 to as high as 50 years, without matching any of the expected curves in shape very closely. It seems reasonable to conclude that the data indicates that mortality was in the range of expectation of life at birth around 30 years in the past, and has improved somewhat in recent years.

A final implication of the AMBUSH simulations lies in the issue of internal consistency of results. Mortality does not exist in isolation in the simulations, and cannot in the real population either. When we collect our best information on fertility (shown in the chapters to follow), we derive an overall picture of the !Kung fertility functioning. When this typical fertility is combined with mortality modeled by a life table with expectation of life at birth of 30, we find that the simulations produced grow or decline in size rather slowly, depending upon random and stochastic processes. In the long run, over the average of a number of simulations, the populations produced are nearly stationary, balancing mortality and fertility in a way consistent with long run persistence of the population and producing age distributions that are consistent with the age structure of the current population. Mortality levels that are much higher than $e^0_0 = 30$ produce on the average a growing population and a younger age distribution than is consistent with either the observed population characteristics (such as the age distribution) or the long-run theoretical expectations based on hunter–gatherers in a difficult environment.

6

An Overview of
!Kung Women's Fertility:
Completed Reproductive Careers

The !Kung recognize that pregnancy is the result of sexual intercourse and that every conception involves a father as well as a mother. Conception may be the impetus to marital rearrangements if the woman is not currently married to the father, but in the vast majority of cases the woman is married to the father of her unborn child.

!Kung women tend to put off acknowledging pregnancy to others until it is obvious, but they are aware that the first indication of pregnancy is a missed menstrual period. Women commonly anticipate their menstrual periods by the phases of the moon. One woman told me: "When you first expect a period and don't see it, you smile to yourself and say nothing. When the moon comes again and you don't see it, you know there is a baby growing, and your heart is happy."

Menstruation is *tsausi chisi*—'women's business'—and is not usually discussed with men, even between husband and wife. The !Kung have a belief that intercourse during menstruation is harmful to men, so that husbands come to expect their wives to avoid intercourse during a certain phase of the moon. Some husbands guess at pregnancy in the first months, when their wives do not avoid intercourse at the expected time. In any case, the pregnancy is noticeable rather earlier among these people, who do not cover their breasts and abdomens, than it would be among fully clothed people. Sometime during the third or fourth month the pregnancy becomes public knowledge; after that the woman will speak freely about the anticipated child with people who hope that she will name the child after them and others. It is not entirely clear whether the reluctance to announce pregnancy before it is obvious is due to knowledge that many conceptions end in spontaneous abortion during the first weeks or months and hence are unimportant, whether it is considered "bad luck" to "count your chickens before they are hatched" (as we, not they, say), or whether it is part of the !Kung cultural complex that discourages anyone from pointing out his or her own accomplishments to others, in the same way that hunters do not mention their successes unless asked (see Lee 1969a).

If the pregnant woman has a child still nursing, the child will be weaned when the pregnancy is acknowledged. The weaning is not done harshly—the child is not slapped or scolded for demanding the breast—but the mothers firmly refuse, telling the child that "this is now the food of your sibling." Some of the !Kung expressed the belief that the milk of a pregnant woman will harm a child, although they do not seem to worry about this during the early months of pregnancy. It is expected that children will cry and be sad or angry when they are abruptly weaned during pregnancy. Considerable sympathy was expressed for a 2-year-old being weaned, who cried, refused other food and distractions for several weeks, and actually lost weight. People observed that the child was unusually young to be weaned and did not yet have sufficient "wits" to understand why it was necessary. Shostak (1976:251) presents vivid and still resentful memories from a middle-aged woman of her own weaning. Wiessner (personal communication 1976) reports that a child who was something of a behavior problem, given to temper tantrums and aggression against other children and her mother, behavior that is rarely seen among !Kung children, was understood by adults to have been deeply affected by her early weaning: "Her heart is still angry about milk," the child's aunt told Wiessner. Often a relative will take over the job of carrying the weaning child for most of the time during the days or weeks that weaning is in process, in order to remove the presence of the attractive breasts from the child's immediate attention.

Women continue their usual routines during pregnancy, receiving and apparently expecting little solicitude from other members of the group. Nausea in early pregnancy is known but is not taken very seriously. Mothers with other children to care for may be hard-pressed to meet their family's needs for food and water, especially during late pregnancy; the assistance of other women, usually their own kin, may be accepted and appreciated. Women expecting their first child typically do not have much work to do before the baby is born, and, in two cases that I observed, sat around the village during the last weeks in evident discomfort and anxiety. Pregnancy seemed to be often a time of drawing closer to the woman's own kin, especially women, and away from the husband. In both cases the young women, who were expecting their first child, had married into the local group and were apart from their own mothers, sisters, and other kin who might have provided some comfort. The anxiety and depression expressed is not altogether unrealistic. In the absence of medical facilities, complications of birth may well lead to death. On the basis of the few cases known, deaths in childbirth tend to occur during first pregnancies. In both of the cases, the birth was successful in the sense that the mother and child both survived, but in both cases the women have since returned to live with their own families, one after divorce and the other with her husband.

Birth, like menstruation, is *tsausi chisi*, 'women's business', and men are excluded from the scene of birth. Often, in fact, it seems that the husband "just happens" to be away from the village for a few days at the time of birth. When labor contractions begin, the cultural ideal is that the woman says nothing, but goes alone to a spot in the bush out of the sight and hearing of the village, to bear the child alone. After the baby has been delivered, people say that the mother should clean up the baby, dispose of the afterbirth, place the baby in a sling under her suede *kaross* ('cape') and return to the village to sit by her cooking fire, until the baby is noticed by others. In the cases observed, however, this cultural ideal was not met. Often, one or more adult women go with the mother into the bush to keep her company and offer what assistance can be given, at least building a fire, offering the mother tobacco between contractions, and so on. There are a number of magical means of hastening or easing a difficult birth (the one I saw involved pulling a loosely tied cord downward over the abdomen). To my knowledge no such practices as turning the baby around in the case of a breech delivery are attempted. There are no "specialists" in childbirth, no "midwifery," and the *n/um kausi*, 'medicine owners' are not summoned to go into trance and use their magical powers to aid in a normal birth. They may be called in a case where the mother had some complications of childbirth that made her ill but well enough to go back to the village.

The custom that women should or can give birth alone gives the mother the unquestioned right to control infanticide. At the scene of the birth, usually before the baby is named and certainly before bringing the baby back to the village, it is the mother's responsibility to examine the baby carefully for birth defects. If it is deformed, it is the mother's duty to smother it. Many !Kung informants told me that this examination and decision is a regular and necessary part of the process of giving birth, although no one named any particular case in which infanticide was done for reasons of deformity. The conspicuous case in the population is one in which it was not done; a severely deformed little girl happened to be born at one of the major cattleposts in the late 1950s. As the story is retold, 10 years after the event, some Bantu women were present at the scene of birth along with !Kung women. When the child was seen to have six toes and an extremely small head, the !Kung women, including the mother, wanted to smother it, but the Bantu women found this unacceptable. One of the Bantu women went to tell the governmentally appointed Bantu headman who had recently taken up residence in the village. He sent back word that infanticide would be considered murder and the responsible parties would be taken to the district capital to stand trial, so the women permitted the child to live. Under cattlepost conditions, the severely retarded child has survived, although she is not accepted as a *zun/wa* ('a real person,' their name for themselves) by people outside of her own family. The family is tied to dependence on the cattlepost, since this child could hardly survive under bush conditions.

!Kung infanticide is not equivalent to murder in their eyes, since they do not consider birth to be the beginning of life of a *zun/wa*. Life begins with the giving of a name and the acceptance of the baby as a social person back in the village after the birth. Before that time, infanticide is part of the mother's prerogatives and responsibilities, culturally prescribed for birth defects and for one of each set of twins born. There are no pairs of twins surviving in the population, although it is not entirely clear in each case of twin birth whether one or both died naturally or was killed. People cannot distinguish between normal infant death and infanticide in any particular case, unless the mother is willing to talk about it or there were witnesses to the birth. Six cases of infanticide were acknowledged among the 500 live births to the living women reported in 1968. In one case the father died during the pregnancy, in another an older mother had seen her two previous babies die from her failure to produce sufficient milk, and in a third the baby probably had the "wrong" father. It is difficult to estimate the incidence of infanticide, since it is not necessary for mothers to admit it unless they choose to do so, but the incidence of reported fetal wastage and infant mortality are approximately the expected rates, so it is likely that the rate does not exceed a small percentage of live births. Infanticide of the deformed, twins, and "unlucky" births has little demographic effect on the population in any case, since the people are selecting children who would probably die anyway. The primary effect is likely to be that of reducing postpartum infertility and thereby increasing the mother's chance of reconceiving quickly. Infant mortality is high—about 20% of live births—so that returning to the village after a birth without a baby to show is a fairly common event. No doubt the custom of silence about birth spares the feelings of the mother.

After the birth, the parents are not supposed to have sexual intercourse until after the woman has had a menstrual period. The couple are, however, expected to continue their pattern of sleeping on the same mat within the village at night, now with the baby at the mother's breast so that it can suck whenever it wakes at night. People insist that sexual intercourse should be avoided during this period, but laughingly admit that the rule is not always followed. It is probably true that sexual intercourse is at least less frequent during the year following the birth, when the mother carries the baby continually, permitting it to take breast milk whenever it wishes. Some babies get extremely fat during this period before walking starts.

All mothers supplement their infant's diet of breast milk with other foods after a few months, by premasticating or pounding foods in a mortar to soften them. The bush-living diet of nuts, roots, berries, and meat, however, is much less palatable to infants than the milk and grains available at cattleposts. No !Kung woman has the equipment to bottle feed a baby, but supplementary feeding of cows' milk to infants from a cup or gourd is now commonly observed on cattleposts. Even usually bush-living mothers, when they make an occasional visit to a cattlepost, will take the opportunity to provide a meal of cows' milk to their babies and children. Lactational demands on the mothers, then, must have declined during the time since the cattleposts were established, especially for the !Kung women who live there. Mothers continue to breast-feed their children on demand, and carry the child on the back, continuously at first, later only when the child is tired or the pace of movement is too rapid for the child to maintain, until the next pregnancy intervenes. Fuller accounts of the behavior of infants, children, and parents, and the pace of development of children, can be found in reports by Draper (1972, 1975, 1976) and Konner (1972, 1973, 1976).

The !Kung women report that menstruation may resume any time after a surviving child has started to walk, which places the event in the last part of the first year of the child's life, at the earliest, while menstruation will resume much sooner, within a few months, following a child who dies at birth. The mean length of the period of postpartum amenorrhea, however, is likely to be much longer than the minimum. In a rural district of Bangladesh, for example, Menken (1975) reports that only a quarter of the women have resumed menstrual periods 12 months following the birth of a surviving child and Huffman *et al.* (1978:1155) assert that average duration of postpartum amenorrhea is 18–24 months in developing countries where prolonged breast-feeding is practiced. Since I did not actually visit the postpartum women each month to ask whether menstrual functions had resumed, it is difficult to interpret the women's generalizations about the resumption of menstruation. This fact was impressed upon me during an interview with an older mother whom I had just met. When I asked her whether she thought that the current baby, asleep under the leather cape on her back, would be the last or whether she expected to have more children, she said she would have more, and that her current state of amenorrhea would end "when my baby can walk." Around that time, the "baby" stirred and stretched out her long arm, silently climbed out of the back of the cape without assistance, and ran off to join some children at play. The baby in question was about 4-years old!

!Kung women do not use contraceptives or abortifacient techniques, as far as could be determined. A few spoke vaguely of herbal concoctions that prevent pregnancy or cause abortions, but only one woman claimed to have taken such medicine, after the sudden death of her two children. Her ensuing sterility could easily have been caused by her advanced age. Attempts to track down the actual herbs used led to people saying that "only the Bantu know how to make it" or that the person who knows how to do it happened to be away. Demographically, such potions probably have no effect. The !Kung marry early and do not attempt to limit their births. We naturally expect to see a high level of fertility as a result. The !Kung, however, complain that they do not have enough births, explaining the scarcity by the perverse selfishness of the god of the !Kung, who likes children and keeps them to himself in "heaven" rather than allowing them to go to earth and bring joy to their parents. Rather than accept the !Kung's subjective impression of the frequency of childbearing, in this chapter we will look at the levels of fertility achieved by the !Kung women who have completed their childbearing period.

The Measurement of Fertility

Fertility is generally easier to measure than mortality, but just as in the case of mortality it is essential that we relate the events to a clearly defined population "at risk." In this section we will consider only the women's fertility (men's fertility will be discussed later) and we only need to focus on their behavior during the age range 15–49. When we look at a group of completed reproductive careers, we can say that the women were "at risk" for each of those 35 years. If each woman at risk has a baby in a given year, we compute the age-specific fertility rate for that year as 1.0; if half have a birth, the rate is .5, and so on.

Fertility differs from mortality and many other processes that we will study in that it can occur repeatedly while the person to whom it occurs remains at risk of its reoccurrence. To summarize birth probabilities over the whole reproductive career, therefore, we can sum the probabilities over each age segment to obtain the average number of children who would be born to a cohort experiencing those rates; this summation is called the total fertility rate. Age-specific fertility rates can be computed for single years of age, or for 5-year age groups. When we sum 5-year rates, we must multiply them by five in order to obtain the total fertility rate, as each woman spends 5 years at risk of birth at those rates.[1]

Completed Reproductive Careers

We have several sources of information on !Kung womens' reproductive careers and we wish to make maximal use of all of them to understand typical

---

[1]More precisely, an age-specific fertility is equivalent to an M_x term in the life table, representing the proportion of people in an age group who experience an event. Since the women observed here have passed through the childbearing years, the proportion who have a live birth is the best indicator of the probability of doing so, and does not need to be corrected for the effects of those who have not yet been at risk over the whole period. The $M_x - q_x$ conversion is discussed in Chapter 4.

and special patterns in !Kung fertility. One important source is that of the women aged 45 and over. These women provide the only information on questions that require looking at completed reproductive performance, such as age at menopause, and they provide valuable sources of information on the context of changes in fertility performance during the recent decades of accelerated social change. While we cannot afford to be uncritical of any of the evidence available, the histories provided by the usually cooperative 62 women past childbearing age provide our clearest window into the fertility of the !Kung.

Production of Live Births

The 62 women who were 45 years and older in 1968 reported having given birth to 291 children born alive (excluding miscarriages and spontaneous abortions), an average of 4.69 apiece. These are all of the births these women will ever have, a statement of which I can be confident, since the births in the population were monitored during the following 5 years by other observers. The women had between one and nine live births apiece over the course of their lives. The mother's age at each of these births has been estimated by subtracting her year of birth from the child's estimated year of birth for those children who were found in the master list of the population and hence had their ages estimated by the procedure discussed in Chapter 2, and from a year of birth estimated by an *ad hoc* procedure based on questioning the mother about the circumstances of the birth, the identity of other children born the same year, and placement between siblings with regular birth year estimates for those children who were not in the master list of the population because they have died or moved away. It is unavoidable that age estimates, both for the mothers and for the children, are more insecure when the births occurred in the distant past.

Using these estimates we tabulate the estimated age of the mother at the birth of each of her children to construct age-specific fertility rates. Table 6.1 shows the number of women who gave birth to a child in the age classes 15–19, 20–24, 25–29, and so on. The one birth estimated to have occurred to a woman at age 14 is included with the 15–19 age group, since it seems very likely that the mother's age has been underestimated (see Chapter 2) and that she was actually a few years older at the birth.

When we look at the age-specific fertility rates for these women, several features stand out. The main feature is that these rates are low at all ages for a population without contraception. The total fertility rate computed in Table 6.1 is only 4.69, which can be interpreted as the average number of children who would be born to a group of women who experienced these rates as they pass through the age groups, all of whom survive to the end of the childbearing period. For the population as a whole, in the long run, the average number of

TABLE 6.1
Age-Specific Fertility Rates and Parity for 62 Women Age 45 Years and Older

	Parity									Total	At risk[a]	Age-specific fertility
	1	2	3	4	5	6	7	8	9			
15–19	1	0	5	3	12	7	8	6	0	42	310	.135
20–24	5	7	10	7	14	10	11	10	1	75	310	.242
25–29	0	5	2	11	8	10	14	10	3	63	310	.203
30–34	0	1	3	1	13	9	8	9	3	47	310	.152
35–39	0	1	1	2	11	5	8	8	1	37	310	.119
40–44	0	0	0	0	6	6	5	4	1	22	310	.071
45–49	0	0	0	0	1	1	2	1	0	5	310	.016
Number of children	6	14	21	24	65	48	56	48	9	291		.938[b]
Number of mothers	6	7	7	6	13	8	8	6	1	62		
Mean parity										4.691		

[a]The number of person-years at risk of birth during each interval is 62 women × 5 years.

[b]The total fertility rate of 4.691 is computed by summing the age-specific fertility rates for the 5-year intervals and multiplying by five.

children to the women who start their childbearing careers must be less, as we have seen that a substantial proportion of the women who are alive at age 15 will die before age 50. A second distinctive feature of the age-specific fertility rates is that the rates seem to be somewhat lower for the age groups 35–39 and 40–44 than we would expect to see on the basis of the rates at the earlier portion of the reproductive period.

Since the low overall level of age-specific fertility is consistent with all the results of this study, there is no reason to doubt that it is a real property of the population. The minor decline in fertility at the older ages is a more subtle feature of the population; we cannot be sure that it is not the result of sampling error in the small numbers studied. If sampling error has produced an underestimation of the level of fertility at these ages, the effect of correcting that error would be to increase the age-specific rates at those ages and consequently the total fertility rate by a small margin, to approximately 4.8.

When we look more closely at the parity distribution shown in Table 6.1, we notice different features about the fertility experience of this group of women. The modal number of children ever born is five, with a remarkably symmetrical distribution around the mode. Studies of parity distributions in populations without contraception have revealed that such distributions are typically skewed, with a tail toward the higher parities. Cavalli-Sforza and Bodmer (1971:310) have suggested that such distributions can best be modeled by a negative binomial distribution, with the variance more than double the mean, rather than the more obvious Poisson family of distributions, which has a variance equal to the mean.

6. AN OVERVIEW OF !KUNG WOMEN'S FERTILITY

The variance for the parity distribution of the !Kung women is 4.88, which is a good fit to the Poisson distribution.

If we break down the parity data into the age cohorts that make it up, as seen in Table 6.2, we can see that the symmetry of the parity distribution is a regular feature of the data for all of the women past childbearing age, but that there seems to be a historical trend toward declining fertility as we approach the present, with the oldest women reporting the highest number of children ever born.

Experience with data collections in other populations, particularly nonliterate populations, has led to the opposite expectations: Ordinarily we find that older women increasingly underreport the number of children ever born to them, presumably through "forgetting" to mention children who died young and even those who have moved away. Brass (in Brass *et al.* 1968) has developed a useful technique for assessing and correcting the degree of underreporting of the older women, but this technique cannot be used when we find evidence of fertility decline over time.

A third striking feature of the parity distribution in Tables 6.1 and 6.2 is the complete absence of women at parity zero, women who never had a child. This is an unexpected observation, as we expect to find a certain minimal incidence of complete sterility in every population, based on the theoretical grounds that the reproductive system is sufficiently complex that it has a certain probability of failure, and upon the observational grounds that some 3–10% of married post-reproductive women in other populations without contraception have zero children.

These three features of the parity distribution—the symmetry and low variance of the distributions, the apparent declining parity over time, and the absence of zero parity—require some explanation. Are we observing important and distinctive features of the !Kung population, are the results merely produced

TABLE 6.2
Parity Distributions for 5-Year Cohorts of Women 45 and Over

Age group	Number of live births										$\bar{X}$	Variance
	0	1	2	3	4	5	6	7	8	9		
45–49 (15)	0	3	2	2	2	2	1	1	1	1	4.1	6.64
50–54 (12)	0	2	0	2	3	2	2	0	1	0	4.2	4.15
55–59 (9)	0	0	2	0	0	4	1	1	1	0	5.0	4.00
60–64 (12)	0	1	2	1	0	3	0	2	3	0	5.0	8.45
65 and over (14)	0	0	1	2	1	2	4	4	0	0	5.3	2.86
Total 45 and over	0	6	7	7	6	13	8	8	6	1	4.6	4.87

PRODUCTION OF LIVE BIRTHS

by the low signal-to-noise ratio in a small number of observations, or is there some explanation in the way the data were collected or in the historical events in the area that have produced these findings?

The most obvious explanation is the null hypothesis: Sampling variation produces unusual results in small populations. Certainly the number of women involved is small, but the null hypothesis is nevertheless unconvincing. We see the Poisson distribution of parity approximated in each of the age groups, largely because the maximum number of births observed to any woman, nine, is not high enough to allow the variance to increase much in excess of the mean (assuming a unimodal distribution). As we will see in subsequent chapters, everything we learn about the length of the reproductive period and the birth intervals suggests that the maximum parity of nine is a real and special feature of this population.

The null hypothesis is not convincing on the question of trends of declining mean parity over time because the order of the decline over the age groups is regular, not moving up and down from group to group. On the observation of a lack of women at zero parity, the null hypothesis is clear-cut and more difficult to reject. We ask what is the probability of observing zero "successes" in 62 trials when the probability of a "success" is in the range .03 to .10 for a discrete binomial distribution. If the probability is as low as .03, random fluctuations could readily produce the observation, but if the probability is really as high as .10 we can reject the null hypothesis. Since we don't know what the real probability is, we have to remain uncertain about the explanation.

An alternative hypothesis, that the decline of mean parity over time and the absence of zero parity women has been produced by the systematic removal of certain segments of the initial population, may be more plausible. Consider the effects of differential mortality for women depending upon their reproductive success. If women who fail to achieve the status of a reproductive member of the population (those with zero parity at advanced ages) were badly treated, the probability of death for such women might be increased sufficiently that, in a group of women past childbearing age, the sterile might have been removed from observation by an earlier death. Such an explanation might be extended to explain the apparent increasing success of the older women: Those who had more children have presumably more surviving children to contribute to their welfare in their old age, so that they would be more likely to survive to advanced ages to report their parity. This hypothesis loses much of its appeal, however, when we question the !Kung and when we observe the fate of sterile women in the contemporary population. There is no evidence that the !Kung mistreat infertile women or those who have no surviving children.

A more promising mechanism for the absence of zero parity women is selective migration. Perhaps the infertile women, prior to 1950, unsuccessful by the standards of hunting and gathering life, found it easy and attractive to migrate into surrounding districts, where Bantu and European farmers and cattle herders offered employment, while adults who had the responsibilities of caring for small children may have found it difficult or less attractive to shift into another way of life.

We are fortunate in having a basis to check this hypothesis, by comparing the older women in the Dobe area with the older women in the much larger data collection made by Harpending (1976) in connection with his genetic studies. The study covered !Kung people throughout Ngamiland, the district of Botswana of which the Dobe area is only a rather sparsely populated part. Areas to the east and south of the Dobe area include large numbers of !Kung, some of whom migrated from the Dobe area, especially during the period 1920–1950. Harpending collected reproductive histories from 145 postreproductive women across Ngamiland (including the 62 in the Dobe area). Overall, he found that about 10% of the women surveyed never had a child, distributed as 15% of those in the areas dominated by cattle culture since the 1920s and 0% of those in the Dobe area, where cattle keeping and employment for infertile women has been possible on a large scale only since the 1950s. It seems likely, therefore, that differential migration of infertile women has occurred. Differential mortality and sampling variation may also play a part.

Although we cannot be sure that women with zero parity have been removed from the observed population, and we cannot be sure how many such cases there have been, if any, the possibility of primary sterility is sufficiently likely to make it worthwhile to consider what would happen if some such women were added to our collection of histories of older women.

One consequence is that the average parity, the age-specific fertility rates, and the total fertility rate, as shown in Table 6.1, would all be lower if a few women of zero parity were added to the observed population. If we guess that the number of missing women with zero parity is 6 (in addition to the 62 observed), the mean parity and the total fertility rate would be 4.3 rather than 4.6, and the age-specific fertility rates would be reduced at each age by 9%, as we are in effect adding 30 years of exposure to risk of birth in each 5-year age group without increasing the number of births.

If, on the other hand, we take the implications of the higher parities of the women past age 55 seriously, we might want to adjust our estimate of the past parities of the !Kung upward rather than downward. We see in Table 6.2 that the mean parity for the women past 55 is 5.14 (with a variance of 4.20). But if we add 3 hypothetical women with zero parity to that group of 35, the mean parity would have been 4.74 (with a variance of 5.06), close to the average for all women past age 45.

A close examination of the reproductive histories provided by the 62 women past childbearing age, therefore, has not led us to a single satisfactory estimate of their performance, but to a relatively narrow range of total fertility and mean parity that seems to have characterized them. This range has a minimum of 4.30 and a maximum not exceeding 5.00. In the work to follow we will use the observed results, with a total fertility rate of 4.69, as the single best indicator of the reproductive performance of the women past age 45.

In Table 6.1 we considered all women to be at risk of giving birth from their fifteenth birthday to the end of the forty-ninth year, a total of 35 years. We can refine our understanding of the fertility performance of the !Kung women by looking more closely at the evidence on the ages at which they begin and end their childbearing careers, so that we can separate out the reductions in fertility that are due to the supply of available mothers from those due to variations in fertility performance among women who are actively involved in the childbearing process.

Entrance into the Childbearing Population: Age at First Birth

Each of the 62 women have had a first birth, an event that is convincing evidence that they had achieved reproductive ability by that age. From the

TABLE 6.3
Age at First Birth for 62 Women Age 45 and Over

Age	Number	At risk of first birth	q_x	l_x	$1000 - l_x$	d_x
14	1	62	.016	1000	0	16
15	2	61	.033	984	16	32
16	4	59	.068	952	48	65
17	10	55	.182	887	113	161
18	6	45	.133	726	274	97
19	13	39	.333	629	371	209
20	12	26	.462	420	580	194
21	6	14	.429	226	774	97
22	4	8	.500	129	871	65
23	2	4	.500	64	936	32
24	1	2	.500	32	968	16
32	1	1	1.000	16	984	16
33	0	0		0	1000	

Totals   62   1000

Mean age (observed) = 18.79
SD = 2.46
Median age = 19.23
Modal age = 19

fifteenth birthday until the first birth, however, we cannot be sure that the young women are really at risk of pregnancy, since they may not yet be having sexual relations or they may not yet be producing viable ova. Our best evidence for exploring the relationship between age at marriage and age at menarche in connection with the first birth comes from the younger women, in whom the events are more recent and hence more reliably dated. For the older women, we will simply ask how much of the maximal reproductive period (age 15–49) is not used because the women have not started their childbearing careers as yet.

Table 6.3 shows the distribution of age at first birth for the 62 women. Since first birth is a unique event, we analyze the experience for the cohort by computing a life table in the usual way. Note that the mean age at first birth is 18.8, the median is 19.2, and the mode is 19.0. First births are tightly clustered in the ages 17–20, when two-thirds of the women have them. We can obtain a minimum estimate of the percentage fecund by age x by looking at the cumulative percentage who have had their first birth at year $x + 1$, since they must have been fecund the preceding year to allow for the 9 months of pregnancy and a few months for tries at conception. The proportion of the childbearing period (15–49) occupied by prefecund states among women who will eventually bear a child, then, is estimated at 14%.

Secondary Sterility

Primary sterility is the "not yet" state; secondary sterility refers to women who have had a child in the past but who have stopped reproduction before age 50. As in the analysis of primary sterility, we cannot always be sure what causes lack of childbearing, whether the woman has passed menopause, is still having menstruation but is not producing viable ova, is not having sexual relations, is sick, or is simply unlucky.

Although virtually all !Kung women cease childbearing activity before age 50, early menopause does not seem to be a large part of the explanation for that phenomenon. It is difficult to date menopause, since there is no striking event to mark it. Many of the women in their thirties and forties are amenorrheic at any point of time due to postpartum states or illnesses. They have no way of knowing whether their menstrual cycle will reappear. The !Kung women tend to be optimistic; they only report themselves as postmenopausal when they have had long periods of lack of menstruation that they cannot otherwise explain. In crosssection, 66% of the 12 women 45–49 report themselves as premenopausal, 17% of the 12 women 50–54, and one of the 9 women 55–59. All women 60 and over are unquestionably postmenopausal.

We can estimate the womens' ages at final birth by the same method as age at first birth. The distribution and its analysis is shown in Table 6.4. Note that a few women cease childbearing at extremely young ages; these tend to be the women

TABLE 6.4

Age at Final Birth and Proportion Fecund (Past First Birth, not yet at Final Birth) by Age

Age	First birth in year	At risk of final	Number of final births	q_x	Percentage fecund $(1000 - l_x)$	d_x
19	36	36	2	.056	580	32
20	12	46	4	.087	742	65
21	6	48	1	.021	774	16
22	4	51	1	.020	823	16
23	2	52	2	.038	839	32
24	1	51	1	.020	823	16
25		50	2	.040	807	32
26		48	0	.000	775	0
27		48	2	.042	775	33
28		46	3	.065	742	48
29		43	1	.023	694	16
30		42	0	.000	678	0
31		42	1	.024	678	16
32	1	42	0	.000	678	0
33		42	1	.024	678	16
34		41	6	.146	662	97
35		35	2	.057	565	32
36		33	2	.061	533	33
37		31	5	.161	500	81
38		26	3	.115	419	48
39		23	5	.217	371	81
40		18	2	.111	290	32
41		16	1	.063	258	16
42		15	3	.200	242	48
43		12	4	.333	194	65
44		8	3	.375	129	48
45		5	3	.600	81	49
46		2	2	1.000	32	32
47					0	

Mean age at final birth = 34.35
SD = 8.2
Median age = 37
Mode = 34

who have only one or a few births. The probability of having the final birth by age x is remarkably flat until the early thirties, when the probability (q_x) rises and continues to rise until the end of the childbearing years. The oldest birth observed was at age 46. Mean age at final birth is 34.35, the median is 37.00, and the mode 34.00. Many women report that they never resumed menstruation after the birth and lactational amenorrhea of the final child, which is one of the reasons why menopause is so difficult to date exactly. Others, especially those who had the final child early, menstruated for many years afterward.

The life-table analysis for the incidence of the final birth, shown in Table 6.4, is a special and rather complicated one. In the analysis of age at first birth, we started a cohort at age 14, moving them across the dividing line of the first birth until all are entered at age 32. In the case of final births, we can't start with a fixed cohort because women are not at risk of the final birth until the year they have the first one. Some of the women will have left the childbearing state before others have even entered it. To calculate the number of people at risk of having a final birth at each age, the l_x column of Table 6.4 is composed of the cumulative d_x column of Table 6.3 (those who have had their first birth by age x). The q_x for final births is computed from the number at risk as usual. The number of persons to whom that probability will be applied, however, will first grow, as the women have their first child, will simultaneously grow and decline during the period when women are having both first and final children, and will decline after all of the first births have been produced. The interpretation of the l_x column of Table 6.4 is not the conventional one of proportion of a cohort who survive to be at risk of having that event, but is rather an indicator of the proportion of the cohort who are past the first birth and have not yet had their final birth, the active childbearing population by age.

Figure 6.1 shows that the !Kung women had concentrated their childbearing within a fraction of the time available to them between ages 15 and 49. The limits of the childbearing years suggest a 35-year duration of childbearing, but the difference between the mean age at first birth (18.79) and the mean age at final birth (34.35) is only 15.56 years. The area under the curve of active childbearing years (shown in Figure 6.1) is 43.9% of all years between 15 and 49. If we add 1 year for each first birth, to allow for pregnancy and a few months of tries at conception, and add 4 years to allow for postpartum infertility following each final birth (equivalent to the interval between births), the percentage of the

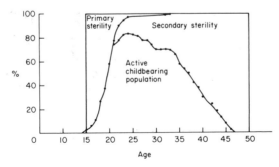

Figure 6.1. Childbearing status of women by age, for women 45+ in 1968 (from Tables 6.3 and 6.4).

time between ages 15 and 49 occupied by fecund women comes to 58.2% of the total.

Primary sterility accounts for 14% of the total when calculated on the observed data. The balance, 27.8% is accounted for by secondary sterility, the loss of reproductive capacity prior to age 50.

Parity and the Length of the Reproductive Span

Figure 6.2 shows the scattergram of the length of the reproductive period, measured as time from first to final birth, by the number of children the woman ultimately had. The relationship between these two variables is clearly a strong one: The more successful women go on bearing children over a longer period of time, rather than simply crowding more children into a similar length of time. The Pearson product–moment correlation coefficient for this relationship is .885, indicating that 78% of the variance in these two variables can be understood by their relationship, leaving only 22% of the variance in parity to be

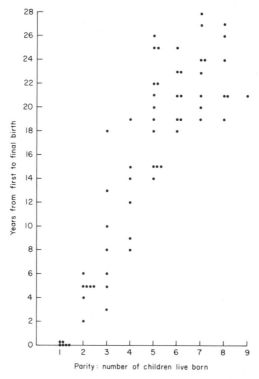

Figure 6.2. Years from first to final birth by parity, women 45+.

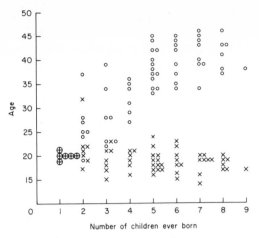

Figure 6.3. Age at first and final birth, by number of children ever born, women 45+. (X shows age at first birth; O shows age at final birth.)

attributed to the length of birth intervals and other causes of variability in fertility performance within the childbearing period. When we compare the !Kung fertility performance with that of other populations, which is a different question, we see that the length of birth intervals is more important than other factors in accounting for interpopulation variance.

The duration of the childbearing period is clearly an important factor in understanding differences between women in reproductive success. Figure 6.3 shows the age at beginning and ending childbearing for the same 62 women. Note that there is a slight negative correlation between the age at first birth and parity: The most successful mothers start their childbearing slightly earlier than the less successful, on the average. A much stronger positive correlation exists between age at final birth and number of children ever born: The successful women continue childbearing longer. Age at first birth is not highly correlated with age at final birth (not shown) because there is so little variability in age at first.

Birth Intervals and
Their Evidence for Fertility Limitation

The age estimation procedure and the reconstruction of fertility histories for these women past age 45 provides some information on the length of the birth intervals of these women. The data is far from precise, merely expressing in whole years the differences between the mothers' ages at successive live births.

We will look at more accurate and detailed information on the length of birth intervals later (from recent events). Nevertheless the data from the older women permits us to examine the question of whether these older !Kung women were deliberately restricting their fertility.

Henry (1961) noted that a regular feature of populations in which deliberate fertility restriction is not used is the regularity in the length of birth intervals from the first interval to the second from the final interval, the penultimate. Final intervals tend to be substantially longer than other intervals in all populations, as fertility declines with age.

Table 6.5 presents the data on length of birth intervals from these older women. For the total of 229 intervals between births, the mean length is 4.12 years. When we compare the first and penultimate intervals, to look for evidence of deliberate fertility limitation, we see some increase in mean length, from 3.90 years for first intervals to 4.55 for penultimate intervals. This observation is consistent with a suspicion that the women are deliberately restricting their fertility at higher parities. When we compare the two distributions carefully, however, the evidence is weaker. There is a skewed but smooth distribution of cases in years 1 to 7 for both first and penultimate intervals. The main difference

TABLE 6.5
Length of Birth Intervals (in Whole Years) for Women of Completed Reproduction[a]

Years	All intervals		First intervals		Penultimate intervals	
	N	%	N	%	N	%
1	9	3.9	0	0.0	1	2.4
2	38	16.6	7	16.7	4	9.5
3	49	21.4	10	23.8	10	23.8
4	71	31.0	16	38.1	13	31.0
5	22	9.6	5	11.9	5	11.9
6	18	7.8	2	4.8	2	4.8
7	3	1.3	1	2.4	1	2.4
8	7	3.1	0	0.0	2	4.8
9	4	1.7	0	0.0	2	4.8
10	1	.4	0	0.0	0	0.0
11	2	.9	0	0.0	2	4.8
12	3	1.3	1	2.4	0	0.0
13+	2	.9	0	0.0	0	0.0
Total	229		42		42	
$\overline{X}$	4.12 years		3.90 years		4.55 years	
SD	4.00 years		1.74 years		2.34 years	

[a]For 42 women who had four or more births.

between the two distributions is the proportion of cases that fall beyond 7 years. There is one case of a 12-year birth interval among the first intervals, and six long intervals among the penultimate intervals. If we compute the mean and standard deviations on the smooth portion of the curve only, the statistics are almost identical (they are 3.71 and 3.75 for the means; 1.17 and 1.25 for the standard deviations.) In such a small collection of cases, we can look at the exceptions for their special features: The long first interval was a surviving son to a marriage that was thereafter infertile. When the husband died, the mother remarried and had three more children. Among the penultimate intervals, two cases involved widowhood and remarriage; several of the others involved miscarriage or abortion during the interval.

The evidence from our crude data on the length of birth intervals, therefore, does not indicate the older !Kung women practiced deliberate fertility limitation.

Causes of Low Parity

!Kung women seem to concur that having children is a good thing and perceive themselves as anxious to have more children. They say they do not practice contraception, and, among this older group, none of the women expressed any dissatisfaction with having too many children, only with not having enough or having too many die in childhood. We will look at causes of infertility in more detail later, when we examine the evidence from the lives in progress of women in the childbearing period in 1968. Here we can only point to some factors which do *not* explain the high proportion of women who have fewer children than they wish.

The cause is rarely pathological sterility caused by venereal disease. The !Kung know what venereal disease is (as discussed in Chapter 3) and know that it can cause sterility. Among these older women, only four reported that they thought that they had contracted it. Gonorrhea seems to have occurred as an epidemic during the 1950s, at a time when most of these women had completed or were at least well into their prime childbearing years, so that little reproductive capacity was lost.

Nor is the low fertility performance a result of failure to marry, or to remarry when a woman is widowed or divorced. We will look at the probabilities of these events later; here it is sufficient to assert that these processes could not account for a large portion of the low fertility.

In the chapters that follow, we will look at the fertility performance of the !Kung women in greater detail, searching for the causes of low fertility performance among the younger women, those under age 45 in 1968, for whom the timing of reproductive events can be more accurately dated.

7

Fertility Performance, 1963-1973

For data on fertility among women who were in the childbearing age groups during fieldwork, there are two sources of information, retrospective cumulative accounts provided by the women about their own experience, and direct observation of events. This chapter will be based upon the direct observations of births to the defined population of resident women over an 11-year period.

Lee laid the basis for this analysis when he constructed the population register on his first field trip, during 1963 and 1964. Lee recorded the details of each birth that he observed while he was in the field and at least estimated the season and the year for those births that occurred out of observation. Most important for this work, he noted in addition the people who definitely did not have a new birth during the period of observation. During my fieldwork, 1967-1969, I collected data on current fertility performance for each woman (and man) in the target population and confirmed through retrospective studies that Lee had done a thorough and accurate job during the earlier period. Births between 1964 and 1967 were dated by questioning the mother and other observers of the birth regarding the season of the year and other events of the year in which the births occurred, being particularly careful to include infants who had not survived as well as those who had. Attention was focused on each potential parent in turn in order to make negative information as firm as positive information. People who were lost to observation because they moved outside of the area were removed from the denominator of the fertility performance measures, the population at risk of giving birth. Konner sent details of births that occurred in 1969–1971 while he was in the field. In mid-1973, Lee returned to the field and brought fertility records up to date for the period 1969–1973, and Polly Wiessner, in the beginning of 1974, corroborated Lee's account and brought the data collection to the end of 1973. Although I have information on a substantial number of new births since 1973, I do not have any positive indication that they represent all of the births that occurred, so they will be disregarded here.

The direct observations include a total of 1434 person-years over the 11-year period, to a total of 166 women. These women overlap with the group of 165 women who have been the major informants of this study, but all women over age 50 in 1963 are excluded from this group. There are 47 younger women who are like the major informants in being residents of the Dobe area, well observed over the 11-year period, who are included here though they were too young in 1968 to be included in the group of 165 interviewed women.

The advantage of this body of data is that it has been carefully collected and double-checked by several investigators so that we can have some confidence that we have not failed to observe any births that took place among this group of women during the period and, equally important, we know that the others did not have live births during the period. I would not make the same claim about pregnancies that ended in spontaneous abortion or miscarriage. Although some cases of fetal wastage have been reported in this group, I am not confident that I heard about all such cases, so they will not be tabulated here.[1]

The basic data on this 11-year period is a matrix consisting of 35 single years of age (from 15 to 49) and 11 years of observed birth events. As an example of the cells in this matrix, there are five girls 15 years old in 1963 and none of them have a live birth, forming an entry of 0/5. In 1964 the same girls are 16 and one has a birth, so the entry is 1/5, and so on. The entries in single cells are too small for statistical analysis, but we can sum the cells for more stable results for age-specific fertility rates for the whole period and for information on annual variations in fertility.

Age Patterns of Current Fertility

When we sum across the years in the matrix, we obtain observation on about 50 teenagers in each single year of age, with declining numbers for older ages, reaching about 30 for the oldest women (exact numbers shown in Table 7.1).

[1]The known incidence of fetal wastage is about 10% of the number of live births, both for the 1963–1973 period and among the pregnancies reported by the women in their reproductive histories. Although the !Kung women do not seem to have a great reluctance to discuss fetal wastage, they consider it unimportant, especially if it occurs early in pregnancy, and I have no doubt that the actual incidence is much higher.

TABLE 7.1
Age-Specific Fertility Rates for Women (Based on 1963–1973 Experience)

Age	Births to women age x	Woman–years at age x	Single-year, age-specific fertility rates	5-year, age-specific fertility rates
15	0	53	.000	
16	1	54	.019	
17	2	56	.036	
18	3	50	.060	
19	10	49	.204	
15–19	16	262		.063
20	7	46	.152	
21	16	44	.364	
22	9	45	.200	
23	4	41	.098	
24	9	40	.225	
20–24	45	216		.208
25	10	42	.238	
26	12	41	.293	
27	9	40	.225	
28	8	38	.211	
29	9	41	.220	
25–29	48	202		.238
30	11	41	.268	
31	10	41	.244	
32	7	42	.167	
33	5	41	.122	
34	5	43	.116	
30–34	38	208		.183
35	6	42	.143	
36	1	39	.026	
37	8	40	.200	
38	4	42	.095	
39	3	42	.071	
35–39	22	205		.107
40	2	40	.050	
41	1	38	.026	
42	4	38	.105	
43	0	36	.000	

(*continued*)

TABLE 7.1 (*cont.*)

Age	Births to women age x	Woman–years at age x	Single-year, age-specific fertility rates	5-year, age-specific fertility rates
44	1	34	.029	
40–44	8	186		.043
45	1	34	.029	
46	1	33	.030	
47	0	32	.000	
48	0	30	.000	
49	0	26	.000	
45–49	2	155		.013
Totals	179	1434	4.275	.855 × 5 = 4.275

Each woman observed at a single year of age is a unique individual, but the women observed at the next age are a largely overlapping group, so that the observations at adjacent ages are not independent. The effects of this are most clearly seen in the age-specific fertility rates during the early twenties. At age 21 it happens that a large proportion of the group, 16 out of 44 women, have a baby

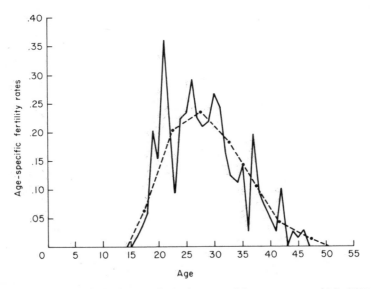

Figure 7.1. Age-specific fertility rates for single years and 5-year age groups, births 1963–1973. (Solid line shows single-year rates; dashed line shows 5-year rates.)

7. FERTILITY PERFORMANCE, 1963–1973

TABLE 7.2
Women's Age at Childbirth for Birth Orders (1963–1973 Data)

Age of mother	First	Second	Third	Fourth	Fifth	Sixth	Seventh	Eighth	Total
				Live birth order					
15									0
16	1								1
17	2								2
18	3								3
19	9	1							10
20	6	1							7
21	9	6	1						16
22	1	7	1						9
23	1	2	1						4
24		4	3	2					9
25	1	5	4						10
26	1	2	7	2					12
27			4	4	1				9
28		1	3	4					8
29		1	2	4	2				9
30	1	1		4	4	1			11
31	1		6	1	2				10
32	1			1	3	2			7
33			1	1	1	2			5
34				1		1	3		5
35				4	1	1			6
36								1	1
37		1	2	1	2	2			8
38					1	2	1		4
39	1			1		1			3
40					1		1		2
41					1				1
42		2					1	1	4
43									0
44							1		1
45						1			1
46								1	1
Totals	38	34	35	30	19	13	7	3	179
Mean age	21.4	24.9	27.5	30.1	32.8	35.6	38.0	41.3	27.9
SD	4.63	5.52	3.68	3.81	4.00	3.77	4.16	5.03	6.58
Median age	19.6	24.0	27.1	28.8	32.2	35.5	38.5	42.5	

TABLE 7.3
Annual Variations in Fertility, 1963–1973

	1963	1964	1965	1966	1967	1968
Age 15–19						
Number of births	0	1	0	3	1	1
Number of women	20	20	23	23	23	23
ASF	.000	.150	.000	.130	.043	.043
Age 20–24						
Number of births	5	2	4	5	6	6
Number of women	17	16	17	17	18	20
ASF	.313	.125	.235	.294	.333	.300
Age 25–29						
Number of births	4	3	3	4	7	3
Number of women	21	20	18	20	19	16
ASF	.190	.150	.167	.200	.368	.188
Age 30–34						
Number of births	4	1	4	2	1	6
Number of women	18	20	19	18	19	21
ASF	.222	.050	.211	.111	.053	.286
Age 35–39						
Number of births	5	0	3	1	1	3
Number of women	19	19	18	17	17	18
ASF	.263	.000	.167	.059	.059	.167
Age 40–44						
Number of births	1	0	0	2	1	0
Number of women	12	13	16	18	19	19
ASF	.083	.000	.000	.111	.053	.000
Age 45–49						
Number of births	0	0	1	0	1	0
Number of women	12	12	11	12	12	12
ASF	.000	.000	.091	.000	.083	.000
Total births	19	9	15	17	18	19
Total women	118	120	122	125	127	129
Total fertility	5.36	2.38	4.36	4.53	4.96	4.92
General fertility rate	.161	.078	.123	.136	.142	.147

7. FERTILITY PERFORMANCE, 1963–1973

1969	1970	1971	1972	1973	Total
1	2	0	2	3	16
25	25	26	27	25	262
.040	.080	.000	.074	.120	.063
5	6	1	3	2	45
20	23	23	23	23	216
.250	.261	.043	.130	.087	.208
5	2	5	3	9	48
16	17	19	18	20	202
.313	.118	.263	.167	.450	.238
3	6	6	5	0	38
20	18	20	19	16	208
.150	.333	.300	.263	.000	.183
3	3	3	0	0	22
20	19	18	19	21	205
.150	.158	.176	.000	.000	.107
1	1	1	0	1	8
19	18	17	17	18	186
.053	.056	.059	.000	.056	.043
0	0	0	0	0	2
12	16	18	19	19	155
.000	.000	.000	.000	.000	.013
18	20	16	13	15	179
32	136	141	142	142	1,434
4.78	5.03	4.16	3.17	3.56	4.28
.137	.150	.110	.092	.106	.125

during that year. At ages 22 and 23, the age-specific fertility rates drop sharply, in large part because the 16 women who had a birth at 21 are still in states of postpartum infertility caused by that birth, although they are counted as being at risk of a birth at the next age. Plotting the age-specific fertility rates shown in Table 7.1 by single years of age, as shown in Figure 7.1, produces a saw-toothed pattern that is an artifact of this method of data collection. The data is accurate, but needs to be smoothed into 5-year age groups, as is shown in the last column of Table 7.1, and is also shown in Figure 7.1. We note that the youngest age at childbearing during the 1963–1973 period was 16; the oldest was 46; and the mean age of women at childbearing was 27.93 years (with a standard deviation of 6.58 years). The sum of the age-specific fertility rates, representing the number of children who would be born to a woman who passed through these series of rates, is 4.25, a figure very close to the total fertility rate that we calculated for the women over age 45 (after we had made an adjustment for the absence of zero parity women). As we will see in the sections to follow, however, there are certain differences between the way the total fertility rates of the older women and the younger women are achieved.

The age of women at childbearing is naturally associated with the birth order of the child that is being born. Table 7.2 shows a cross-tabulation of age of mother in single years of age by the birth order of the child. Preceding pregnancies that ended in pregnancy wastage are not counted here, but those that ended with the death of a liveborn infant are included (even if the preceding births occurred prior to 1963).

Annual Variations in Fertility

If we count up the births and the person-years at risk for years rather than ages, we obtain some information about annual variations in fertility during the period of observation. As in the case of single years of age, we see that the results are unstable, leading to widely differing indicators of fertility performance from one year to the next, as shown in Table 7.3. Table 7.3 directs our attention to the dangers of obtaining longrun indicators of fertility in a small population from observations over so short a period of time as a year or a few years.

Some of the explanation of annual fluctuations may derive from the artifact of observation of the performance of a largely overlapping group from one year to the next, as was noted when looking at performance at single years of age. Nineteen women, for example, had a live birth in 1963, out of 118 women at risk. In 1964, when the indicators of fertility shown in Table 7.3 drop sharply, those 19 women are still counted as being at risk of birth, but actually most of them will be temporarily infertile due to birth and lactation. The problem is not so acute for annual variations as we are dividing our information into only eleven categories, rather than the 35 categories used for single years of age. Another cause of annual variations, undoubtedly, is not an artifact of measurement, but represents the response of the population to real environmental fluctuations, from one year to another, in elements such as rainfall and the food supply.

The annual variations are rather dramatic. Between 1963 and 1964, for example, when Lee observed and recorded the population during a record-breaking drought in Botswana, the decline in fertility is sharp. During 1963, when Lee observed that the hunting and gathering !Kung were relatively well off, depending on their drought-resistent wild food sources when the cattle-keeping Bantu were suffering, the fertility of the !Kung was above average. However, the fertility for 1964 declined precipitously, showing the least annual rate yet recorded. Even if the number of births in 1964 has been somewhat underestimated by difficulties of assigning births to years when we returned in 1967, there seem to have been fewer births than expected during the 1964–1966 period. We note another decline in fertility during 1972 and 1973.

Numbers of Children Born Per Woman

We have seen that there were 179 births during the 1963–1973 period to the women in the study group. Another dimension of those births is the number born to the most successful mothers and to the less successful mothers, and how many women failed to have any children at all during the period. Table 7.4 presents this information. Each woman observed has been classified by her age in 1963, including the 118 women who were 15–49 in 1963 plus 47 more who were

TABLE 7.4
Number of Children Born in 1963–1973 by Age of Women in 1963

Age in 1963	Number of women	Number of live-born children					
		0	1	2	3	4	5
5–9	25	21	4				
10–14	22	13	4	3	2		
15–19	20	3	3	3	7	3	1
20–24	17	3	2	2	6	3	1
25–29	21	8	2	1	7	3	
30–34	18	9	4	2	1	2	
35–39	19	10	6	3			
40–44	12	10	1	1			
45–49	12	12					
Totals	166	89	26	15	23	11	2
Number of children	179	0	26	30	69	44	10

younger than 15 in 1963 but entered the childbearing years during the 11-year period. Each woman is cross-tabulated by the number of live births during the period. The maximum number of births observed was five; the average was slightly more than one birth apiece to the women. Many (89) of the women, however, had zero births. Some of these failures to bear children should not surprise us, as the woman may have been just entering or just leaving the childbearing period of life during the fixed period of time. But others, those in the maximal childbearing years, are apparently sterile, and require attention to the causes of their sterility.

The infertile women will be considered in detail in a later chapter. In the balance of this chapter we will concentrate on the most fertile women, those who had two or more children during the 1963–1973 period, looking at the intervals between their births.

The Length of Birth Intervals

The level of fertility achieved by fertile women is determined by the spacing between one birth and the next, the birth interval. These birth intervals determine the number of children that can be "packed" into a reproductive career. The length of these intervals has important consequences for the health and activities of both mothers and their children, as well as being a major determinant of the overall level of reproduction for the population as a whole.

Conceptually, each birth interval can be divided into three segments. The first segment is the "idle" period following a live birth. During this period there is no probability of conception, because the mother is not ovulating, because she is not having sexual relations, or both. The second segment begins when both ovulation and sexual relations are present and lasts until the next conception. The woman is "at risk" of pregnancy during each of the months of this segment; it is the base from which probabilities of conception per month ("fecundability") should be calculated. The third segment of the birth interval consists of pregnancy, the period from conception to the next live birth. It is the most invariant segment in duration for the pregnancies that end in live birth. The actual length of !Kung pregnancies has not been measured, but there is no evidence to suggest that they differ from the universal duration of 9 months. When the pregnancy ends in fetal wastage, the three time-consuming states of birth intervals must be gone through again, although the duration of at least the "idle" period is likely to be relatively short. See Henry (1972), Perrin and Sheps (1964), and Sheps and Menken (1973) for more precise conceptual and mathematical formulation of birth interval analysis.

Observationally, it is often not possible to tell which of these three segments a particular woman is in during a particular month in a birth interval. In order to date conception for the !Kung, we simply count backwards 9 months from a live birth. The "idle" period is marked by an absence of menstrual periods or sexual relations. In order to divide the months in the birth intervals into the three components, it would have been necessary to collect information monthly from the women in the fertile years on whether they had a menstrual period and sexual relations within the previous month. This information was not collected from the !Kung women, so we cannot perform any statistical analysis on the length of components of birth intervals. We can, however, measure the total length of the birth intervals during the 1963–1973 period and use these concepts to explore the determinants of the timing of births.

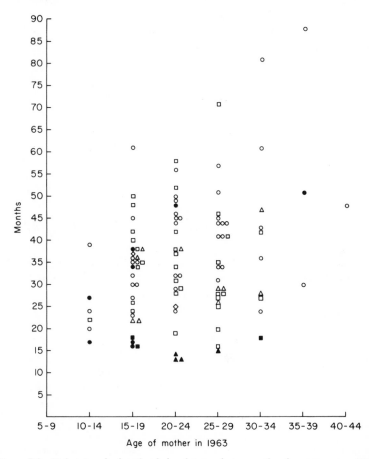

Figure 7.2. Birth intervals, length of closed intervals in months, for age groups. (○ = first interval; □ = second interval; △ = third interval; ◇ = fourth interval.) Black symbols indicate that first infant died.

THE LENGTH OF BIRTH INTERVALS

The data base for the birth interval analysis consists of the same births and women at risk of birth that were used to compute age-specific fertility: the births between 1963–1973 to 166 resident women. We have 21,912 months of observation (132 months apiece on 166 women), but 4632 of these months (21% of the total) occur to women who are under age 15 or over age 49 and are irrelevant to the analysis of fertility performance. A substantial proportion of women between ages 15 and 49, as we have already seen, are not fertile and make no contribution to the analysis of birth intervals. After removing these infertile women's contribution to the months observed, there are 9600 months remaining.

The degree of precision in the measurement of number of months from one birth to the next is not uniform in these observations of birth intervals. Some dates of birth are known to the day, but others are only known to the season and year, in which case the middle month of that season is taken as the date of birth. An allowance of 3 months is probably sufficient for all of these measurements, and the average error must be less. Note that pregnancy wastage is disregarded in counting the months from one live birth to the next, so that the time absorbed by the pregnancy and recovery from fetal wastage is included in live birth intervals. Figure 7.2 presents the scattergram of the raw data from which we will work, showing the length of closed birth intervals observed for women classified by their age in 1963, with symbols differentiating the order of the birth interval for the woman and whether or not the first of the pair of children died before the birth of the second.

Birth Intervals as a Property of Mothers

Individual mothers had between zero and five births during the 11-year period of observations, as shown in Table 7.4. There is a strong age pattern in the number of births within a fixed period of time, as the youngest and oldest women are constrained both by not having a full 11 years in which to have births and have a lower rate of age-specific fertility during each of the years, as we have already seen. This is not a peculiarity of the !Kung, but would be true of any group subdivided by age. The distinctively !Kung feature is the relatively small proportions of women who have higher numbers of births during the period, which is a function of their relatively long birth intervals.

To examine the pattern of birth intervals as a feature of the mother's reproductive ability, we look only at the woman's experience in the months following her first birth during the period of observation. Seventy-seven women have a first birth; we count for each the number of months that elapse before she either has a second birth or reaches the end of the period of observation and is withdrawn. Note that since the first birth a woman has in the period of observation can occur at any time, women may be withdrawn from observation after relatively few months. The youngest woman who had a child, for instance, was 7 years old in 1963, had her first child at 17 and was withdrawn from observation 12 months later, while a woman who had her first child in 1963 would remain at risk of having a second for another 10 years. From this tabulation, we cumulate the number of women still at risk of having a second child at each month, and from that calculate the probability of closing the interval by having a second child at each month. This probability can be used in a life-table analysis (as a q_x) to calculate the probability of having had an additional child within x months (l_x). Note that the cumulative probability of closing the interval will not reach 1.0, as not all women will ultimately have an additional child—there is some probability that each child is the last.

A striking feature of the raw data on birth intervals in Figure 7.2 is the clustering of birth intervals in which the first of the pair of children died in infancy at the bottom of the graph, at intervals of less than 20 months. When an infant dies and the mother is not lactating, ovulation may resume within a month or so of the birth. Adding 9 months for the next pregnancy, the minimum possible birth spacing is about 11 months. Thirteen months is the shortest interval observed and 16 months is the median length of the 11 notably brief intervals that follow an infant death, implying 7 months from the birth of a nonsurviving infant to reconception. These few cases provide some evidence for the belief that the cause of the relatively long birth intervals observed is not difficulty in reconception after ovulation and sexual relations resume (i.e., low fecundability).

Figure 7.3 presents the probabilities of having had a second child x months after a first, including only one interval per woman, both including and exclud-

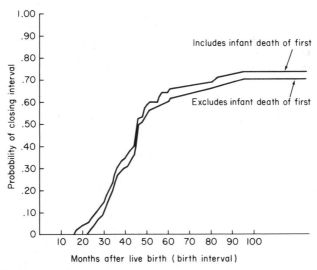

Figure 7.3. Probabilities of birth intervals within x months. First interval per woman only. (Mean length of 50 intervals = 39.7 months; SD = 14.1. In 42 intervals in which first child survived, mean = 41.3 months and S.D. = 14.2.)

ing the cases in which the first of the pair of infants died. Figure 7.3 shows that half of the women will have had the next birth 46 months after the first, and a quarter of the women will have had their next birth by 36 months after the first. By 96 months (8 years) after the first, only about 70% of the women had followed up the earlier birth by another. For more than a quarter of the women, then, the first birth observed is also their last. This is a maximum estimate of the proportion of women ending fertility, as it is possible that some may yet go on to have an additional birth later than 96 months following the earlier one. In the population as a whole, the longest birth interval observed was about 17 years, to a woman who had several children in her early twenties, and who found herself pregnant again at the age of 42, much to her delight and surprise. Such a long interval would not be detected in this analysis, but they are very rare.

Birth Intervals for the Population as a Whole and as an Event in the Life of Children

When we consider the role of the length of birth intervals in producing the level of fertility for the population as a whole and the effects of spacing on the fate of the children, we broaden our attention from only the first interval for each woman to all intervals. The higher order intervals tend to be shorter, as only the women who have relatively short intervals can produce multiple births within the set period of observation.

To compute the probability of closing the intervals by months for all intervals, we again tabulate the birth intervals and the month during which the woman was withdrawn from observation by reaching the end of the period of observation. This time we have 102 closed birth intervals to work with and 77 "withdrawals." Each woman is counted from the birth of her first child during the period. We record the number of months to the next birth, and then move the woman back to the start of the counting frame, considering the month of birth of the second child to be the beginning of the second interval, continuing until her last child born during the period of observation. After the birth of the last, we count the number of months to the end of the period of observation and withdraw her from observation at that time, in order to take into account that she was at risk of having an additional child during the period.

Dividing the number of births by the number of women at risk of having a birth in each month, we obtain the q_x terms and calculate a life table. The results of this analysis, showing the probability of having an additional child x months after the birth of the previous one, is shown in Figure 7.4 for the intervals, including ones in which the previous infant died.

In Figure 7.4 we also classify the women by their age at the first of the two births in an interval, showing the age pattern of probability of having an additional child by x months after the first. It is clear that the youngest women,

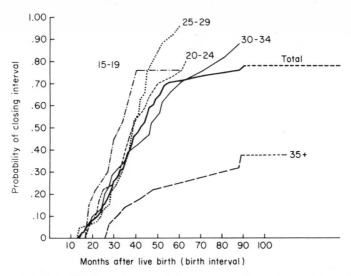

Figure 7.4. Probability of an additional birth within x months of a birth, all intervals, and age groups. (Mean length of 102 intervals = 35.4 months, S.D. = 13.9.)

those who had the first of the pair of births when they are 15–19, have significantly shorter intervals than others. Women over 35 at the first of the two births have extremely long intervals if they complete the interval at all. Among women having a child between the ages of 20 and 34, however, and this includes about 75% of the births (according to the age-specific fertility rates), the differences by age are not very great. About 40% of the birth intervals are 36 months or less overall, including the intervals in which the previous child died.

Summary of Fertility Performance, 1963–1973

We have seen, in Chapter 6, data on fertility performance of women over 45 in 1968 and data on the fertility performance of younger women in this chapter. There are many questions yet to be explored, for example, rates of entrance and exit from the childbearing state, incidence and causes of infertility over the life cycle, and the role of marriage in fertility. In order to focus on the distinctive features of !Kung fertility, it is useful at this point to look at data from some other populations in order to develop a comparative perspective on the !Kung. We will return to a detailed consideration of the !Kung data in later chapters.

8

!Kung Fertility Performance in Comparative Perspective

Comparison Populations

Most of the population data that can conveniently serve as a comparative framework for looking at !Kung fertility are from large populations of industrialized or agricultural peoples. Anthropologists have prepared reports on the demographic functioning of some peoples who are closer to the !Kung in societal complexity and economic organization, but unfortunately many of these studies involve complex problems in data and conceptual organization that would require considerable methodological discussion prior to comparisons. For our purposes, the literature from demography, which uses the conceptual framework adopted in the !Kung study, and especially from historical demography, provides a convenient comparative framework to identify the features of !Kung fertility performance that are distinctive. The many ways in which the !Kung are simply like all other people studied, conforming to the general human pattern, can also be recognized.

In comparing the !Kung with other groups it is essential to distinguish among the kinds of populations formed by groups that use various methods for restricting fertility below their biological maximum. One of these methods is the restriction of marriage to only a portion of the women in the childbearing age groups. We will find it necessary to adjust observed data for the proportion married (or engaged in sexual relations) at each age group. A second method of fertility restriction is modern contraception, or the traditional methods of fertility control which resemble contraception in their effects.

Louis Henry has led the study of fertility in populations without contraception, historical and contemporary. Henry (1961) defined *natural fertility* as the behavior affecting fertility that is unchanging no matter how many children have already been born, in contrast to *controlled fertility*, where women or couples modify their behavior depending on the number of children already born, attempting (with various degrees of success) to cease childbearing when they reach the desired number of children. Controlled fertility uses modern contraception methods, but may also include other kinds of behavior (such as abstinence within marriage). Natural fertility, although never including contraception techniques, may include behaviors such as long lactation, postpartum sex taboos, or ritualized separations of the couple, as long as the same practices are carried out after any birth.

Since contraceptive use is so widespread in the modern world, and increasing all the time, it is somewhat unusual to find natural fertility regimes functioning today. Therefore much of the population data available for comparison with the !Kung comes from studies in historical demography. An exceptional natural fertility population in the modern world is the Hutterites, the people of a series of interconnected religious communities in the western United States and Canada. The Hutterites (Eaton and Mayer 1953) provide a useful model of maximal fertility, as these healthy and well-nourished people desire large families for religious and practical reasons. They do not practice any form of contraception, postpartum sex taboos, or long lactation that might depress their fertility. Among the natural fertility populations known, the Hutterites have the highest level of achieved fertility, with an average of 12.4 births per woman married continuously during the reproductive years, 15–49, for a group studied in the 1950s (Eaton and Mayer 1953). The Hutterites are useful as a standard of comparison for fertility achieved by other populations—a calibrated yardstick—against which we can measure the ways in which other populations fail to achieve maximal levels of fertility.

Coale (1965) developed a series of measures of fertility performance designed to indicate how closely a given population approaches the maximum fertility it might attain and to what extent the failure to achieve maximum fertility is due to the proportion of women in the fertile years who are unmarried, as opposed to low levels of fertility achieved within marriage. Coale uses the Hutterites' age-specific marital fertility rates as a series of weights to adjust for the relative importance of the various age segments of the reproductive years: Low rates of proportion married in the 15–19 age group, for instance, have relatively little effect on fertility compared to low rates in the 20–24 group, when fertility is normally much higher. These weights adjust various populations to a common base. The computation of Coale's fertility indices requires knowing the number

TABLE 8.1
Fertility Indices for the !Kung and Other Populations[a]

	Index of overall fertility (I_f)	Index of marital fertility (I_g)	Index of proportion married (I_m)
Natural fertility populations			
Hutterites (1925)	.70	1.00	.70
Taiwan (1930)	.54	.66	.78
Bulgaria (1900)	.52	.70	.73
India (1945)	.50	.57	.88
Chinese farmers (1930)	.45	.51	.87
!Kung (1968)	.34	.40	.86
Norway (1900)	.33	.73	.42
Controlled fertility populations			
France (1870)	.28	.48	.54
U.S. (1900)	.29	.49	.58
U.S. (1960)	.28	.36	.75

$I_f = \Sigma f_i w_i / \Sigma F_i w_i$
$I_g = \Sigma g_i m_i / \Sigma F_i m_i$
$I_m = \Sigma F_i m_i / \Sigma F_i w_i$

where
f_i = births per woman in the ith age interval
g_i = births per married woman in the ith age interval
w_i = number of women in the ith age interval
m_i = number of married women in the ith age interval
F_i = births per woman in the ith age interval in the standard population of married Hutterites, 1921–1930. These are

15–19	.300
20–24	.550
25–29	.502
30–34	.447
35–39	.406
40–44	.222
45–49	.061

[a]*Sources:* Coale, A. J. Factors associated with the development of low fertility: a historic summary, United Nations World Population Conference, Belgrade, Yugoslavia, 1965; Barclay *et al.,* Indices for the Chinese farmers, 1976.

of women and the number married in each 5-year age group from 15–49 and the number of births occuring to these women. Table 8.1 presents the fertility indices for the !Kung and a number of other populations, both controlled and natural.

COMPARISON POPULATIONS

Table 8.1 shows a number of distinctive patterns in the ways that populations regulate their fertility performance. The three highest fertility populations, those of the Hutterites, Taiwan, and Bulgaria, are alike in that they have a relatively high proportion of the women in the fertile years married and a relatively high level of fertility within marriages.

The next three populations, those of India, the Chinese farmers and the !Kung, have substantially higher proportions of the women in the fertile years married compared to the first group. These populations can be characterized as "early and universal" marriage for women, even if the Index of Proportion Married shows that marriage is not quite universal. Within marriages, however, these three populations show low levels of fertility performance without the use of modern contraceptive techniques. Populations like these are good candidates for explanation by Frisch's fatness hypotheses on control of ovulation (to be discussed later).

A third type of population functioning is represented only by Norway in 1900 in Table 8.1, but has been commonly observed. Low overall fertility is achieved by an extremely low proportion married and high fertility within those marriages. This is the typical "European fertility pattern" observed in historical demography. The Irish case is the classical one, persisting into the middle of the twentieth century in a pattern of late marriage and relatively high proportions never married, but extremely high marital fertility.

The controlled fertility populations show two patterns as well. France in 1870 and the United States in 1900 had quite low proportions married *and* relatively low levels of marital fertility, which in combination produce an Index of Overall Fertility lower than any of the natural fertility populations. With the development of highly effective contraception techniques, populations like the United States in 1960 can achieve the same very low levels of overall fertility with a higher proportion of women married. Most of the industrialized nations since 1950 have patterns like that of the United States in 1960.

Parity Progression Ratios

Parity progression ratios are calculated from reports on parity, the number of children ever born to women past reproductive age. The ratios take advantage of the time-dependent nature of parity: The first ratio shows the proportion of all women who ever had a first live birth, whether or not they went on to have additional births. The second ratio shows—for the women who had at least one child—what proportion progressed to having two or more, and so on. Very high fertility populations may have parity progression ratios that are very nearly constant over a wide range of parities; roughly the same proportion of women cease further childbearing after each birth. The women of Quebec who were over

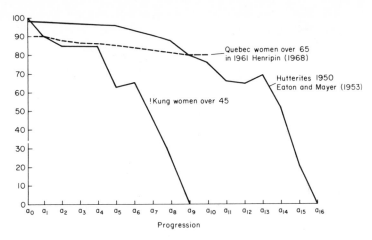

Figure 8.1. Parity progression ratios of high fertility groups and !Kung.

65-years old in 1961, for instance, had parity progression ratios between .9 and .8 from the first progression (from 0 to 1 child) to the tenth (from 9 to 10 children). Henripin (1968:57) notes, "This means that about nine-tenths of the women who have had a child, whatever the birth order of that child, have had another later." Eventually, of course, the women reach the end of the childbearing years, by arriving at menopause or by an earlier loss of fertility, and the parity progression ratios decline to zero.

Figure 8.1 shows the parity progression ratios for the !Kung, for the Quebec women studied by Henripin (1968), and for the Hutterite women (Eaton and Mayer 1953). The striking feature of the !Kung pattern in parity progression ratios is the sharp decline in ratios after the fifth child, whereas the high-fertility populations show a slower decline at higher parities. Note that the !Kung decline, like that of the higher natural fertility populations, is convex in shape, while a population practicing contraception would show a concave shape as couples cease childbearing after reaching their desired number.

Parity progression ratios are a useful tool for isolating the sources of differences in reproductive performance between populations. Figure 8.2 shows hypothetical parity progression ratios for the types of populations discussed above. Populations like the Hutterites, which have high proportions married and high natural fertility, have a parity progression ratio curve that is high and declines at high parities only. Populations like the !Kung and the Chinese farmers start high and decline in the same convex pattern but at considerably lower parities, as they take longer to have each child and arrive at the limits of their reproductive span at lower parities. Populations that follow the "European fertility pattern" of late marriage and low proportions ever marrying but high

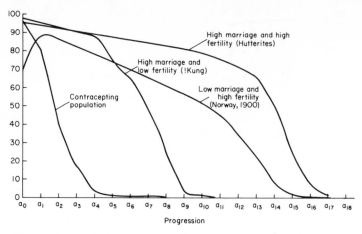

Figure 8.2. Hypothetical parity progression ratios for types of populations.

marital fertility will have parity progression ratios that start low and decline slowly. Populations practicing contraception, on the other hand, can have patterns where the ratios start high but decline swiftly, in the concave shape.

Age-Specific Marital Fertility Rates and Patterns

To compare fertility performance between populations, we want to distinguish among differences due to the proportion of women married (and hence exposed to the risk of pregnancy), differences due to use of contraceptive techniques or other changes in behavior after the birth of a desired number of children, and differences that persist after controlling for these sources of variation. We can do this by looking at marital age-specific fertility rates, calculated only upon the married women in each age group, and by distinguishing between natural fertility and controlled fertility populations.

Henry's (1961) studies of natural fertility populations led him to conclude that although the *level* of natural fertility varies between groups, the age pattern of natural fertility is relatively invariant. This conclusion, which is strikingly parallel to the discussion on the regularities in age patterns of mortality for populations at a similar level of mortality (discussed in Chapter 4), suggests that biological limitations to fertility form an important component of natural fertility regimes. Whatever the factors are that contribute to high fertility performance at one age group, the same influences result in high fertility at other ages.

Figure 8.3 illustrates Henry's point. It presents the marital age-specific fertility rates for the Hutterites, for the average of 13 high-fertility natural fertility

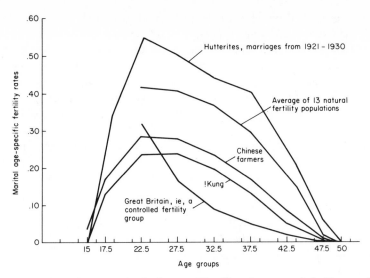

Figure 8.3. Marital age-specific fertility rates for Hutterites, natural fertility populations, Chinese farmers, the !Kung, and controlled fertility populations.

populations compiled by Henry (including the Hutterites), for the Chinese farmers studied by Barclay (Barclay *et al.* 1976), and, for contrast, the rates given by Henry for a controlled fertility population. The !Kung rates shown are calculated from the age-specific fertility of the current population (Table 7.1), adjusted by the proportion married in age group (Table 12.1, given later). We see that all of the natural fertility populations are generally similar in the shape of their marital age-specific fertility schedules over the span, with rates near zero at age 15 and age 50, maximum fertility in the age group 20–29, and declining fertility at older ages in a pattern that forms a convex curve. The controlled fertility population stands out in sharp contrast by the concavity of the shape at older ages, reflecting the changes in the probability of birth for couples who have achieved their desired family size. Henry does not present data on the age group 15–19, since the populations he studied varied widely in the proportions married and the percentage of brides who were pregnant at marriage.

The *level* of marital fertility shown by the natural fertility populations, however, varies widely. The Hutterite case has been chosen as the extreme, but we see from Henry's 13 populations that levels near the Hutterite one have been observed. Indeed, some demographers have speculated that natural fertility would always be high when accurately measured on cohabiting women.

The evidence for the existence of the very different level—exemplified among natural fertility populations by the !Kung—has been strengthened recently by the completion of the analysis of a large survey on Chinese farmers and their families made during the 1929–1931 period (Buck 1937). For decades the fertility data from this study was stored and ignored following preliminary analysis that revealed very low fertility. Since this pattern was thought to be impossible without modern contraceptive techniques, it was attributed to incomplete and inadequate data collection. With the development of sophisticated techniques for testing the adequacy of the data base (Barclay *et al.* 1976; Brass 1975), the data was reanalyzed, revealing that it was in fact well collected (from a group of 46,601 families). With the use of necessary adjustment techniques, the patterns of high mortality, low natural fertility, and early and universal marriage for men and women make up a picture of the population that is internally consistent and congruent with other sources of information on the population collected at the time. (For details of this fascinating incident in the history of science, see Barclay *et al.* 1976.)

The !Kung fertility patterns that we have explored in preceding chapters seem to be very similar to those of the Chinese farmers, resulting in a somewhat lower level of age-specific fertility at each age for the !Kung.

Declining Fertility with Age

Henry (1961) suggested that the age pattern of decline in age-specific fertility rates, using the rate for age 20–24 as a base, may be the most invariant compo-

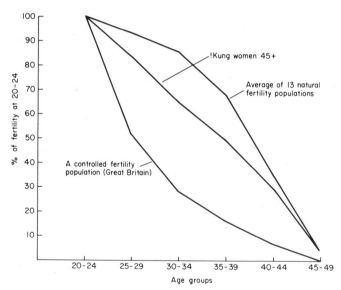

Figure 8.4. Age pattern of decline in age-specific fertility, using rate for 20–24 as a base. (Data from Henry, 1961.)

TABLE 8.2
Age-Specific Percentages of Sterility in Married Women

Populations[a]	Age groups				
	20–24	25–29	30–34	35–39	40–44
Five European populations[b]	3	6	10	16	31
Rural Japan[b]	4	10	19	33	53
!Kung women over 45 in 1968	12	23	32	54	78
!Kung women by age in 1963—percentage having 0 births in subsequent 11 years	18	38	50	53	83

[a] All are natural fertility populations.
[b] From Henry 1961.

nent of the shape of natural fertility populations. Figure 8.4 shows the decline for the !Kung, for the average of 13 natural fertility populations computed by Henry, and for a controlled fertility population. Note that the !Kung decline with age is nearly flat, declining more swiftly than the high fertility natural populations, but less swiftly than the population practicing contraception. The reason for the sharper decline is presumably that a higher proportion of !Kung women at each age have reached the end of their reproductive span than the women in the other natural fertility populations.

We can explore the decline in age-specific fertility rates further by comparing it with the decline in the proportion of surviving women who are past childbearing by age. Henry was able to determine the age-specific percentages of sterility (lack of childbearing from that age on) for married women in 6 of the 13 natural fertility populations that he investigated. Table 8.2 shows Henry's data, rearranged to group the 5 populations of European origin together. The data on rural Japanese women, his only nonEuropean case, is presented separately, as it has a distinctively higher rate of sterility by age. The percentage of the !Kung women

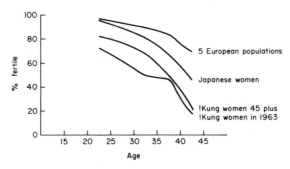

Figure 8.5. Percentage capable of childbearing by age.

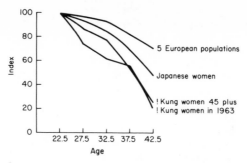

Figure 8.6. Index of proportion capable of childbearing, by age. (Data from Henry, 1961.)

who had completed childbearing at each age was computed for the women past age 45 in Table 6.4 (graphed in Figure 6.3). We use the percentage who have had the final child by the midpoint of the interval for comparison with Henry's data. For the younger women, we use the percentage of the age group who have no children in the following 11 years as the indicator for percentage who are sterile.

Table 8.2 shows that both the younger and the older !Kung women have much higher rates of sterility by age throughout the childbearing years than the populations studied by Henry. Figure 8.5 plots the inverse of the numbers in Table 8.2 ($100 - N$) to show the percentage who are not sterile by age for the same populations. Clearly the !Kung levels are substantially lower than the other populations, not only for the younger women, who have had problems with venereal disease during recent decades, but for older women as well. Recall that the older women were under suspicion of underreporting sterility because none of them had had zero children, although we see here that in comparative perspective their rate of sterility at each age is extremely high.

Figure 8.6 adjusts the same data to show the curve of percentage sterile by age, using the percentage capable of childbearing at age 20–24 as a base (equal to 100). The graph confirms that the decline of the fecund population by age is steeper for the !Kung than for Henry's populations, and shows especially clearly the effects of the excess proportion sterile among the younger women, which is caused by venereal disease.

Duration of the Reproductive Span and the Length of Birth Intervals

!Kung fertility is lower than that of other natural fertility groups, in part, as we have seen, because the !Kung women cease childbearing (become sterile) at higher proportions in each age group, which makes the duration of the reproduc-

TABLE 8.3
Length of the Reproductive Span and the Length of Birth Intervals (!Kung and Comparison Populations)

	Mean age at first birth (1)	Mean age at final birth (2)	Length of reproductive span (years) (3) = (2)−(1)	Observed mean birth interval (months) (4)	Total fertility (5)	Implied mean birth interval (months) (6) = $\frac{(3) \cdot 12}{(5) - 1}$
Hutterites	22.2	40.9	18.7	25.5	10.2	24.4
Punjab villages	20.0	37.0	17.0	32.6	7.5	31.4
!Kung						
Women 45 and over	18.8	34.4	15.6	49.4	4.7	50.6
Current fertility	19.9	34.4[a]	14.4	35.4	4.3	52.4

[a] These women have not had a final birth, so this figure is an estimate.

tive span shorter, on the average, than that of other groups. It is not clear, from these data, whether the length of the reproductive span accounts for the entire difference in total fertility between groups, or whether the length of the birth intervals adds an independent component to the differences in fertility between groups.

To investigate this question, we need data that provide the mean age at first and final birth and data on the mean length of observed birth intervals. Table 8.3 shows this data for the Hutterites (Tietze 1957), for 11 Punjab villages (Potter *et al.* 1965), and for the !Kung. The table shows clearly that the length of the reproductive span alone does not account for the differences in total fertility between the groups.

By a simple arithmetic manipulation, we can compute a measure of implied birth interval lengths from the length of the reproductive span and the total fertility rate, to compare with observed birth intervals. We do not expect identity of the implied and observed measures of birth intervals, as they are calculated by different methods and from different observations. Nevertheless, agreement between the measures is close for three of the four groups show in Table 8.3. The high fertility Hutterites show an implied birth interval length of 24.4 months and observed intervals of 25.5 months. The intermediate Punjabi women have implied birth intervals of 31.4 months and observed intervals averaging 32.6 months. The low fertility !Kung women past age 45 have a mean implied interval of 50.6 months and crudely measured observed intervals (from Table 6.5) of 49.4 months.

The !Kung women who are currently in the fertile years, however, show no such agreement between their implied birth intervals of 52.4 months and the observed mean birth intervals of 35.4 months. Part of the problem may be that we do not know their mean age at final birth, since they are still in the reproductive period, and we used the parameter from the older women to estimate this quantity. From their age at first birth, total fertility rate, and mean observed length of birth intervals we infer that the mean age at final birth will be only 29.8 years. This seems unlikely. Instead it is probable that we are seeing the effects of an increase in sterility and, perhaps, the result of oversampling short birth intervals in a fixed period of observation. We will explore issues related to these possibilities in Chapters 9 and 10.

For present purposes, we can conclude from the data in Table 8.3 that both the length of the reproductive span and the length of birth intervals are involved in producing differences in total fertility rates between populations, and of the two, the length of the birth intervals is the more important variable. The data also suggest the hypothesis that the two variables tend to be positively correlated in natural fertility populations, rather than equilibrating. We will see some of the reasons why this might be true in Chapter 10.

The !Kung and the Hutterites: Accounting for the Differences

The Hutterites have the highest and the !Kung the lowest natural fertility schedules known. Starting with the high marital age-specific fertility schedule of the Hutterites, we can allocate the difference between their fertility performance and the !Kung's to three sources: the proportion married at each age, the supply of fertile women to bear children, and the speed at which fertile women have their children. Figure 8.7 diagrams the results of the calculations.

The top curve in Figure 8.7 shows the marital age-specific fertility rates of the Hutterites, the rates used by Coale in constructing the fertility indices. The marital total fertility rate is 12.4.

The next highest curve in Figure 8.7 shows the age-specific fertility rates that would have been found among the Hutterite women if they had the same proportions married at each age as the !Kung women did in 1968. The total fertility rate for the Hutterites declines to 10.92. (In fact, the Hutterites had a lower rate of proportion married than the !Kung, as we saw in Table 8.1 from their I_m index.)

The third line in Figure 8.7 represents the age-specific fertility rates for Hutterite women, married and unmarried, if they had the same percentage infertile in each age group as the !Kung women 45 and over had. In fact, we don't know the percentage sterile by age for the Hutterite women, so the rates

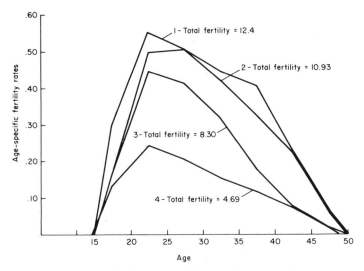

Figure 8.7. Hutterite and !Kung fertility compared.

given by Henry for the average of five high natural fertility European populations have been used in the intermediate calculations. With the percentage sterile of the !Kung, assuming that this variable is independent of the percentage married, the total fertility rate for the Hutterites would have dropped to 8.30, implying that the Hutterites would have lost an average of 2.6 children per woman surviving to the end of the reproductive period to sterility, accounting for 34% of the difference between the !Kung and the Hutterites' performance.

If the Hutterites had not only the marriage and sterility distributions of the !Kung, but the !Kung birth intervals as well, presumably they would have the age-specific fertility rates of the !Kung. The difference between the Hutterite total fertility rate reduced by !Kung sterility and proportion married (8.30) and the Hutterites' rate reduced by all factors (4.69) amounts to a loss of an average of 3.60 children per woman who survives to the end of the childbearing period, 47% of the difference between the !Kung and the Hutterites.

To investigate the roots of these differences in fertility performance, the following two chapters will focus on the evidence for two hypotheses that might explain why the !Kung fertility is so low. Chapter 9 will look at the evidence on causes of the high rate of sterility and the effects of venereal disease on the !Kung women. Chapter 10 will focus on the possible impact of the !Kung diet and activity patterns on fertility.

9

Primary and Secondary Sterility: Normal and Pathological Causes

We have found that the !Kung population, in comparison to others, has a scarcity in the supply of potential mothers. Reproductive opportunities are lost in primary sterility, before fecundity is established, and secondary sterility, following childbearing but prior to the usual age of menopause. In this chapter we will explore the evidence for the various determinants of primary and secondary sterility for the women in the childbearing years of life during the 1963–1973 period of observation.

Some of these determinants are results of normal biological processes, the pace of maturation and aging as indicated by the markers of menarche and menopause. Other determinants, such as marriage rates, are social in origin and more easily controlled by the people. The sterility caused by venereal disease is of quite another nature. Since there is no reason to believe that it was characteristic of the !Kung traditionally, it is important to assess its impact and understand the extent to which the present population dynamics are unrepresentative of hunting and gathering groups.

Primary Sterility

Primary sterility declines with age, from 100% at some young age at which none of the members of a cohort are yet fertile to a minimum when the process of maturation is complete.

167

Age 8

Age 9

Age 10

Age 11

Figure 9.1. !Kung women, ages 8–23.

9. PRIMARY AND SECONDARY STERILITY

Age 12

Age 13

Age 14

Age 15

Age 16

Age 17

Age 18

Age 19

Figure 9.1. (continued) !Kung women, ages 8–23.

9. PRIMARY AND SECONDARY STERILITY

Age 20

Age 21

Age 22

Age 23

PRIMARY STERILITY 171

Our analysis focuses on events such as marriage, menarche, and first birth by the absolute age of the individuals. To understand these analyses, it is helpful to have an idea of the degree of development of the girls at each age.

Figure 9.1 shows photographs, taken by Lee in 1968, of several young women at each single year of age from 8 to 23 to illustrate the appearance of the young women by age. Photographs are not quantifiable evidence of the pace of maturation, but they do provide a basis for interpretation of the quantifiable data. The photographs show that while there is individual variation in the stages of maturation reached by girls of the same age, in general the physical changes accompanying growth are conspicuously related to absolute age. It is also clear from the photographs that the growth process is relatively slow among the !Kung, so that !Kung girls might easily be guessed on the basis of their appearance to be younger than they really are.

Incidence of Primary Sterility by Age

The best indicator of the end of primary sterility is the birth of the first child. Table 9.1 presents the age at the first birth for the 166 women who were closely observed during 1963–1973. The computation of q_x (the probability of having a first birth at age x) is complicated by the fact that 48 of the women have not yet had a first birth (as of the end of 1973). Most of these are young girls whom we started observing after age 5 in 1963, but some of them are fully mature, indeed three were past age 46 at the end of the observation time. To compute q_x we have to keep track of the number exposed to the risk of having a first birth in the age group. At age 14, there are 166 women exposed to risk. One has a first birth and is removed from the group at risk at age 15, when 5 more have a first birth. At age 16, 160 are exposed to risk, 9 have a first birth and 3 are withdrawn from observation without having the first birth. Only 148, therefore, are at risk at age 17. The probability, q_x, is computed in the usual way: number of first births divided by the number of persons at risk. The number of first births in the artificial population, d_x, sums only to 861 out of an initial cohort of 1000 because not all the women will have a first birth. The final column $(1000 - l_{x+1})$ gives the proportion of the initial cohort who have entered the childbearing population.

The proportion of women past primary sterility is plotted in Figure 9.2 from the final column of Table 9.1 by single years of age. For comparison, the similar computation for the older women is also shown. The women in the current population are, on the average, having their first birth somewhat later (mean 19.96 years) than the older women (mean 18.78). The mode is 19 years in both data collections, but the women in the current population show a larger proportion of first births past age 24 (9% as opposed to 2% for the older women), in the "tail" of the distribution.

TABLE 9.1
Age at First Birth and Proportion Past Primary Sterility, by Age[a]

Age	At risk of first birth	First birth at age x	Withdrawn from observation	q_x	l_x	d_x	Proportion past primary sterility $1000 - l_{x+1}$
14	166	1	0	.006	1000	6	6
15	165	5	0	.030	994	30	36
16	160	9	3	.056	964	54	90
17	148	13	3	.088	910	80	170
18	132	13	7	.098	830	81	251
19	112	21	4	.188	749	141	392
20	87	17	4	.195	608	119	511
21	66	14	4	.212	489	104	615
22	48	7	3	.146	385	56	671
23	38	5	3	.132	329	43	714
24	30	2	2	.067	286	19	733
25	26	3	1	.115	267	31	764
26	22	2	0	.091	236	21	785
27	20	0	1	.000	236	0	785
28	19	1	0	.053	215	11	796
29	18	0	1	.000	204	0	796
30	17	2	1	.118	204	24	820
31	14	1	0	.071	180	13	833
32	13	1	1	.077	167	13	846
33	13	0	0	.000	154	0	846
34	11	0	1	.000	154	0	846
35	10	0	1	.000	154	0	846
36	9	0	1	.000	154	0	846
37	8	0	0	.000	154	0	846
38	8	0	0	.000	154	0	846
39	8	1	2	.125	154	19	865
40	5	0	0	.000	135	0	865
41	5	0	0	.000	135	0	865
42	5	0	0	.000	135	0	865
43	5	0	1	.000	135	0	865
44	4	0	0	.000	135	0	865
45	4	0	1	.000	135	0	865
46	3	0	3	.000	135	0	865

[a]N = 166 women under age 50 in 1963; includes first births that occurred prior to 1963.
Mean age at first birth = 19.96.
SD = 3.76.
Median = 18.14.
Mode = 19.

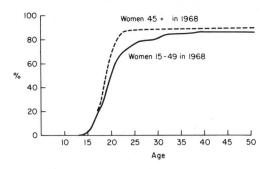

Figure 9.2. Percentage past primary sterility by age.

Causes of Primary Sterility

Between age 15 and the time of the first birth, an individual woman might be infertile because she has not yet had sexual relations, because she is not yet reproductively mature, because she cannot produce viable ova (even if mature), or some combination of these factors with chance rates of conception. Societies differ in the age at which women typically reach these reproductive states, and hence differ in the supply of available mothers.

The Timing of First Marriage for Women

The first of the milestones typically reached by !Kung women is entrance into sexual relations via marriage: 65% of the 165 adult women report that they were married before their menarche; 98% were married before their first pregnancy.

Marriage is a complex subject. Later we will discuss !Kung marriage customs and some of their structural implications for the organization of the !Kung society in more detail. Here we are only concerned with the timing of exposure to the risk of pregnancy through sexual intercourse. Marriage need not be equated with the first experience of sexual intercourse, since the !Kung do not seem to place any value on virginity and sex play among children is said to be common. Marriage is a useful indicator of exposure to sexual intercourse because sexual contact is likely to be regular within marriage, because the husband (unlike the playmates) is likely to be sufficiently mature that he is producing viable sperm, and because the event of marriage and the status of a married person is clear-cut in the culture. It is true that first marriages often end in divorce after a few weeks or months, but after that time the young woman is likely to be sexually active and to remarry quickly, so that she will continue to be exposed to the risk of pregnancy, even if the probability of conception for a previously married woman may be somewhat lower in each month than that of currently married women.

9. PRIMARY AND SECONDARY STERILITY

First marriages for !Kung women are generally arranged by the parents of the couple and may be discussed and negotiated for years before the marriage is consummated. !Kung marriage ceremonies are not elaborate (Marshall 1976), but the event is clearly marked by the construction of a hut for the newly married couple and by a change in kinship terms that the parties to the marriage use. In 1968 only one woman over the age of 20 had never been married, a disabled woman. Among the 25 15- to 19-year-old women, 14 were married, 2 were divorced, and 9 were single. At that time, none of the women under age 15 had been married. To study entrance into marriage, then, we concentrate on the teenage girls again.

For accuracy, we calculate the curve of first marriage frequencies by age only on the marriages that occurred between 1963 and 1969, since these can be dated accurately. Although colleagues cooperated to provide information on date of menarche during the time after I left the field, I failed to ask them to do this for first marriages, so the collection of cases is smaller. There were 18 girls whose first marriage was observed in the period of 1963 to 1969 and could be dated to within a few months. Subtracting the woman's estimated year of birth from the year of marriage gives the age at first marriage shown in Table 9.2, which gives the frequency distribution and the life-table analysis for those marriages.

Coale (1971) discovered that there are three variables that account for most of the differences between populations in the distribution of first marriage frequencies by age for women, which allows a wide range of populations to be described by a curve of first marriage frequencies with a constant shape. What differs from

TABLE 9.2
First Marriage Frequencies by Age

Age x	N^a	% of total	N at risk at age x	Probability of marriage at age x (q_x)	At risk of marriage at age x (l_x)	Number of marriages at age x (d_x)	Proportion already married at exact age x
14	0	0	18	.000	100,000	0	
15	3	16.7	18	.167	100,000	16,700	0.00
16	3	16.7	15	.200	83,300	16,660	16.70
17	8	44.4	12	.667	66,640	44,449	33.36
18	1	5.6	4	.250	22,191	5,548	77.81
19	2	11.1	3	.667	16,643	11,101	83.36
20	1	5.6	1	1.000	5,542	5,542	94.46
21	0	0	0			0	100.00

$^a N$ = 18 women married for the first time between 1963 and 1969.
Mean age at first marriage = 16.9 years.
SD = 1.39 years.
Median age = 17.4 years.

one population to another, Coale found, is (a) the age at which first marriages begin to be contracted, (b) the speed with which marriages occur in the population, and (c) the proportion of people who have ever been married by some advanced age. In keeping with our goal of presenting data on the !Kung in a form that is useful for comparison with other populations, the data on the cumulative proportion married at least once will be described in terms of these variables.

It is striking that the third variable, the proportion who ever marry by the latest age of first marriage, is close to 100% for both men and women among the !Kung. It seems to be true that under hunting and gathering conditions all normal adults eventually marry (Marshall 1976:270).

On the basis of only 18 cases of first marriage that can be dated, we cannot expect a close fit to Coale's standard curve of first marriage frequencies. The standard curve is plotted in Figure 9.3 over the observed data points as a hypothesis of the true population curve of cumulative first marriage frequencies for women. The origin of the curve of first marriage frequencies in Figure 9.3 lies at 14.5 years; at that age, the risk of marriage for women begins. The proportion ultimately married is 100%, which is reached by Coale's curve at the age of 22, virtually reached at 20. The value of Coale's parameter k, the speed at which the curve is completed, is .2, a rapid rate of progression into first marriage. The observed data points do not provide a basis for rejecting the hypothesis that Coale's standard curve is a good description of the population, as they would, for

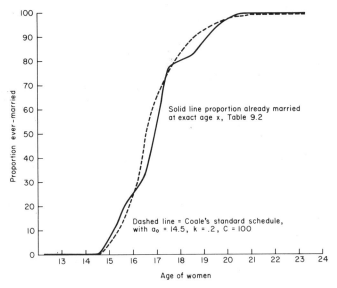

Figure 9.3. Proportion of women ever-married by age, compared with Coale's (1971) standard scedule of proportion ever-married.

9. PRIMARY AND SECONDARY STERILITY

instance, if the proportion married by age 18 were 50%, say, rather than the 78% observed. We can hypothesize, therefore, that if we had many more observations, with increased accuracy and precision, that the observed points would correspond closely to the standard schedule drawn in Figure 9.3. We cannot be confident, however, that even if the hypothesis is true at the present time, the distribution of first marriage frequencies by age in the past or in the future would have the same starting or ending points. While there is no clear evidence from the women of the Dobe area that the age at marriage has shifted radically over the decades covered by their lives, Lorna Marshall (1976:271–279) reports in detail on the marriage of a girl whom she first guessed to be 8-years old, later estimated to be about 10, in the Nyae Nyae area in 1953, and she indicates that marriages of girls this young were not uncommon. The bride in question had her menarche 6 years after the marriage, which tends to support the age estimate of about 10 years, as do the photos and height measurements given by Marshall. The distribution of first marriage frequencies by age, then, may have a considerably younger starting age among some !Kung groups, varying by regions or by time and presumably related to the available supply of wives.

What is the effect of the timing of marriage on the achievement of reproductive ability by age? Practically speaking, there is probably no or very little loss of reproductive capacity through failure to marry by the age of maturity. In 65% of the cases marriage precedes menarche; in another 30% or so of cases marriage follows menarche closely, and typically there is still a wait of some years before the first conception. Only 4 women out of the 165 informants had a premarital pregnancy; each of these women was involved with Bantu at cattleposts and had failed to marry at the usual young age. When a premarital pregnancy does occur it demonstrates that the young women need not have waited for marriage before starting to have sexual relations. Traditionally the mother would have married during the pregnancy so that by the time of birth of the child it would be legitimate (Marshall 1976:282–283).

Changes in the age at marriage in the direction of a younger distribution, which may have been characteristic of the !Kung in the past, therefore, would not increase the reproductive capacity of the population. Changes that would reduce reproductive capacity would be increases in the age at marriage exceeding two years; in addition sexual relations would have to be restricted to married couples. Such changes are unlikely to occur under the current cultural and economic organization of !Kung life.

The Timing of Menarche

Menarche represents an important stage in sexual maturation, one that the !Kung people mark with a ceremony and can report on and remember as a significant event. It is relatively easy to record the date of menarche of girls when it occurs, since the people have no reluctance to report it. Dates of menarche have been recorded by members of the expedition for 51 girls in the period 1963 to 1973 and are accurate to within a few months at worst. Subtracting the estimated year of birth for each young woman from the year in which menarche occurred provides an indication of the age of the women at menarche. Table 9.3 provides the distribution. An analysis of the age at menarche cross-tabulated by the year of menarche over the 11 years of data collection (not shown) indicates that there is no systematic time trend in the data, although the mean age per year fluctuates between 16 and 18 as a result of the small number of observations in any one year. This finding suggests that the age estimates used in this study are not systematically in error for the young women.

Table 9.3 indicates that there is an essentially normal distribution of age at menarche for the !Kung women, with the majority at ages 16 and 17. The mean age at menarche is among the oldest observed in known populations, but is within the known range. Ages as high as 16.5 have been found in historical data for European populations from several hundred years ago and are seen in under-developed countries at the present time. The mean age at menarche is much younger now in European populations, having declined by 3 or 4 months per decade in Europe in the last 100 years (Tanner 1962).

TABLE 9.3
Age at Menarche, for 51 Women Whose Date of Menarche is Known

Age	N	% of total	N at risk at age x	Probability of menarche at age x (q_x)	At risk of menarche at age x (l_x)	Number having menarche at age x (d_x)	Proportion already had menarche by exact age x
13	1	2.0	51	.020	100,000	2,000	0.00
14	1	2.0	50	.020	98,000	1,960	2.00
15	6	11.8	49	.122	96,040	11,717	3.96
16	16	31.4	43	.372	84,323	31,368	15.68
17	18	35.3	27	.667	52,955	35,321	47.05
18	6	11.8	9	.667	17,634	11,762	82.37
19	1	2.0	3	.333	5,872	1,955	94.13
20	2	3.9	2	1.000	3,917	3,917	96.08
21	0	0.0	0		0		100.00
Total	51						

Mean age at menarche = 16.6 years.
SD = 1.3 years.
Median age = 17.1 years.

Table 9.3 also gives a life table of menarche for the cohorts of young women passing through the adolescent years. The probabilities of the event (q_x) are computed by dividing the frequency of menarche at that age by the number who were at risk of menarche (in that they had not already had it) at the same age. By the time the group reaches the twenty-first birthday, all will have had menarche. (I found no report from !Kung informants of a woman who had never reached menarche by some advanced age, although many girls die before reaching it and amenorrhea—cessation of menstrual periods, sometimes for long periods—is common.)

Adolescent Sterility

It is normal that fertility does not immediately follow menarche, even in societies where marriage is early. Montagu (1957) collated extensive data from populations around the world to show that there is usually an interval of several years between menarche and first pregnancy, a period he called adolescent sterility. Due to late ages at marriage in European societies, scientists were slow to recognize that menarche marks an important stage in reproductive maturation, but not the final stage. The !Kung, who are accustomed to observing married menarchial girls, are aware that it is rare for conception to occur immediately after menarche, when, they say, a girl is "still an infant" (for reproductive purposes) and her husband should be "growing her up" by his hunting successes. People do not express concern about infertility for some 4 or 5 years after marriage and menarche, unless the young woman is believed to have contracted venereal disease.

Primary Sterility at Advanced Ages: Normal and Pathological Causes

We saw in Chapter 6 that the women over age 45 were remarkable in that all had at least one child. In other words, none of those women had primary sterility that continued throughout life. We noted there that sterility rates of 3–10% of women surviving to age 50 are commonly observed around the world, even in populations where medical treatment is excellent.

Among the younger women included in the present analysis, we see no such dearth of primary sterility. In the synthetic cohort shown in Table 9.1, based upon probabilities for these younger women, almost 14% reach age 46 without having had a child. By age 22, about 70% of the women have had a first child. Among those who have not, about half will eventually have one and about half will not, generalizing from the experiences of the current generation. Around this age, young women and their husbands and families tend to become concerned and seek the cause of the infertility.

One effective cause of infertility is celibacy, lack of sexual relations. Although virtually all !Kung women have married by this time, periods of celibacy seem to occur among the !Kung within marriage at least as often as outside marriage. Some husbands leave their wives for substantial periods of time, in recent years to go to the mines in Johannesberg in a few cases or to do wage labor. In other cases the sickness of the husband or the wife or the postpartum taboo might lead to a period of celibacy in marriage. The ease of divorce in the society makes it unlikely that personal disagreements would lead to long periods of time without sexual intercourse.

Marriage to an infertile man is a possible cause of a woman's infertility, but one which probably plays a small role among the !Kung. When a marriage fails to be fertile, both parties to the marriage are likely to try sexual contact with other people, divorcing the spouse and marrying the person with whom pregnancy has been achieved, if successful. There is one apparently infertile man in the population, 50-years old in 1968, who had been married to five of the women in the interviewed group. Four of these women had children before or after being married to him, but none conceived while married to him. His infertility probably accounts for the sterility of his current wife, a young girl.

Sterility induced by venereal disease is a more important cause of infertility in recent decades. When the gonorrheal infection enters the woman's reproductive tract, the Fallopian tubes may suffer infection and consequent scarring that can block pregnancy. Few of the women of the Dobe area had their sickness diagnosed by a physician, so determining exactly which women have been affected by venereal disease is difficult. The first indication a woman is likely to have of venereal sterility is the failure to conceive when she expects to do so. Conception can be delayed for many reasons, so that the women is likely to be unsure for some period of time whether she has been infected. When the fear becomes acute, the woman often tries conception with another partner, thereby ensuring the transmission of the disease to others. Many of the women of the Dobe area have sought medical treatment for VD and defined themselves as victims of it at that time. Unfortunately, many of them sought help long after the damage had been done.

Table 3.1 showed the women's reports of their experience with venereal disease, both gonorrhea and syphilis, by age. We saw there that most of the cases were concentrated among the women 30–39 in 1968. Older women reported very little experience of VD; women under 30 reported a substantial number of cases, but less than those 30–39. Some of the women under 30 are among those who are in primary sterility. In attempting to allocate individual women to various causes of primary sterility, we assume that those who report that they have had VD really did have it, and assume that the VD has caused the primary

TABLE 9.4
Causes of Primary Sterility, by Age in 1963

| Age in 1963 | N | Infertile 1963–1973 | Primary sterility | Causes | | |
				Immaturity	VD	Other
5–9	25	21	21	21		
10–14	22	13	13	13		
15–19	20	3	3		2	1
20–24	17	3	3		2	1
25–29	21	8	3		3	
30–34	18	9	3		2	1
35–39	19	10	3		2	1
40–44	12	10	0			
45–49	12	12	0			
Totals	166	89	49	34	11	4

sterility. Eleven of the 49 women who had no child during the 1963–1973 period (and who had no live births prior to 1963) can be accounted for by VD, as shown in Table 9.4. All of these women were at least 25 years old by 1973, so that it is likely that they will not have any children. If these women had been spared VD and had produced the mean number of children found in the population as a whole, they might have contributed an additional 50 members to the population by the time they reached the end of their reproductive lives, a not inconsiderable loss of population.

Four other mature women, we see in Table 9.4, have had no children for some reason, although they do not report contact with V.D. Most of the cases of primary sterility available to us, 34 out of the 49, are women who were only in their teens or early twenties by 1973, when observation ended. No doubt many of these are cases of adolescent sterility and the women will go on to have families in the future.

Since all of these women are still in the childbearing years, it is of course impossible to know whether they will eventually have a child. Even among women who report VD and have been sterile for many years, a pregnancy occasionally occurs. Presumably these women have experienced spontaneous remission of whatever the cause of the infertility had been.

Secondary Sterility

The second type of sterility that causes the !Kung to lose reproductive opportunities is secondary sterility, the premature loss of reproductive ability. As we

Figure 9.4. !Kung women, ages 25–29 to 60–64.

9. PRIMARY AND SECONDARY STERILITY

Ages
45–49

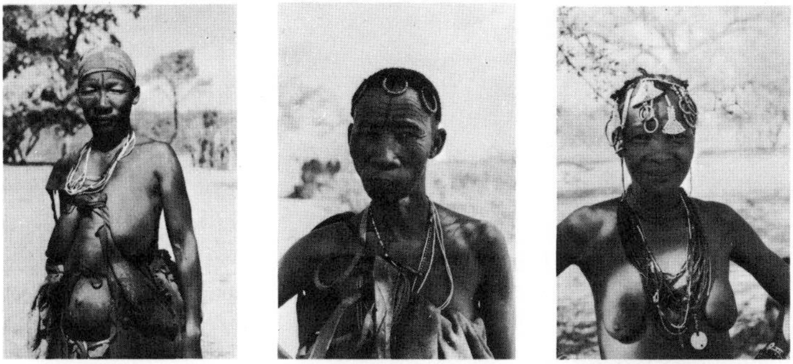

Ages
50–54

Ages
55–59

Ages
60–64

SECONDARY STERILITY 183

did in the case of primary sterility, we will attempt to quantify the incidence and the causes of secondary sterility. But in this case also, it is useful to have an idea of the appearance of the women as affected by the normal aging process. Figure 9.4 shows photographs of several women in each of the 5-year age groups from 25–29 to 60–64 to illustrate the appearance of women as they pass through and beyond the childbearing years. In general these photographs seem to show women who retain a youthful and attractive appearance well into the mature years. Reproductive ability seems generally to be lost prior to the change of appearance marking "old age."

Incidence of Secondary Sterility by Age

We cannot be sure that women will not have additional births in the years after 1973, but we do know the percentage of each age group who had no births during the 11-year period that started in 1963. Figure 9.5 shows the percentage of each group that had no births during 1963–1973 (from Table 9.4), plotted over the percentage past primary sterility. The percentage of secondary sterility in Figure 9.5 is an underestimation of the true proportion, as some of these women may have had their final birth some years prior to 1963.

Causes of Secondary Sterility

It is probably meaningless to seek the causes of secondary sterility for women over age 35, since so many women have completed their childbearing careers by that age, whether or not there are special causes of secondary sterility present. For younger women, however, we can classify the women who had once had a child but who had no children during 1963–1973 by whether they reported VD or not. Table 9.5 shows this tabulation.

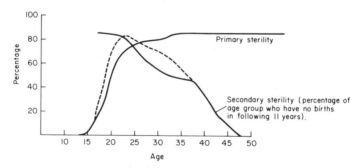

Figure 9.5. Curves of primary and secondary sterility by age. (Note: solid line based on 166 women 15–49 in 1973. Curve for women 45+ (in 1968) plotted by dashed line for comparison.)

9. PRIMARY AND SECONDARY STERILITY

TABLE 9.5
Causes of Secondary Sterility, by Age in 1963

Age in 1963	N	Infertile 1963-1973	Secondary sterility	Causes		
				Advanced age	VD	Other
5–9	25	21	0			
10–14	22	13	0			
15–19	20	3	0			
20–24	17	3	0			
25–29	21	8	5		3	2
30–34	18	9	6		4	2
35–39	19	10	7	5	2	
40–44	12	10	10	10		
45–49	12	12	12	12		
Totals	166	89	40	27	9	4

The Costs of Venereal Disease to the !Kung

During the 1963–1973 period, levels of infertility in excess of those observed for older women were costing the !Kung about 3% of their reproductive capacity per year. The older women were occupying about 53.5% of the years in ages 15–49 with fecundity (allowing 1 year prior to each first birth and 4 years following each final birth in addition to the years between the births of the first and final children). The comparable figure for the current women is 50.6% at most, a figure that may be exaggerated due to the difficulties of estimating secondary sterility in a population that has not yet completed childbearing. This is a decline of nearly 6%. If we adjust the total fertility rates calculated in Table 7.1 for this excess infertility, we would expect a total fertility rate of 4.5 at a minimum.

In addition, there is evidence that the losses to the !Kung population have been more severe in the past, during the 1950s and early 1960s, than they were during the 1963–1973 period. Figure 9.6 shows the number of births expected for the women in the group of 165 who were interviewed, if they had had the age-specific fertility rates of the current period (those of Table 7.1) during each year of their life. The numbers "expected" in Figure 9.6 do not refer to the whole population, but merely to this particular group of women, for whom we can determine how many there were in each age group during each year. Note that the expected numbers are fractions, even though a real population cannot produce fractional children.

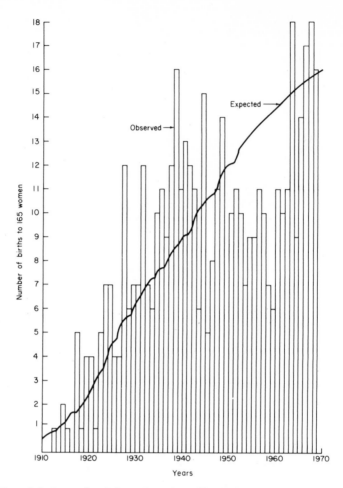

Figure 9.6. Expected and observed numbers of live births per year, for 165 women.

Plotted over the expected numbers of births are the numbers reported by the women in the study group. We would expect some variation from one year to another simply on the basis of the small numbers at risk. But Figure 9.6 shows that there were runs of years when fertility achieved was somewhat higher than expected (primarily 1935–1945) and, more importantly for the current population, a run of years from 1950 to 1962 when the number of children born were consistently fewer than expected on the basis of the present rates. These were the years when the women currently 35–44 were in their peak childbearing years. The loss of fertility to that group, primarily through venereal disease, was very striking. Over the 60 years represented in Figure 9.6, the age-specific fertility rates of the current population seem to be about average. The worst of the epidemic of gonorrhea seems to have passed, although the loss of reproductive opportunity to particular men and women cannot be reversed.

The costs of gonorrhea to particular women who were left sterile have been very heavy. Among the !Kung, women's lives are geared to childbearing and rearing; the childless woman is unemployed in the most serious business of life. DeVore once quipped that you can always tell the infertile women when you enter a new village because they are ones with the clean faces: Infertile women tend to be better dressed and more careful of their appearance than heavily burdened mothers. Some of the infertile women specialize in beautiful bead-work, some become involved in the new women's drum dance, a ritual of curing in which women rather than men go into trance states, some are active in *hxaro* (gift giving) relations, and others may carry on their sexual liaisons and romances with style and enthusiasm. The infertile women, on the average, have been more active than other women in assimilating to the new culture that the Bantu settlers have brought into the Dobe area. Many of them live on cattleposts and some do regular jobs for Bantu families. Some are married to Bantu men, forming links between their bush-living relatives and the new forms of culture.

The extent of infertility has not been catastrophic for the population as a whole. During the same period that fertility was at a minimum, mortality conditions were improving in the population as a whole; the balance between births and deaths in the current population is generally positive, leading to a moderate growth rate. Sufficient reproductive capacity has remained to carry on the population.

While VD has created heavy burdens for the population as a whole and for individual women, it does not entirely explain the low fertility performance of the !Kung. Even among unaffected women, reproductive ability appears relatively slowly, leaves at a relatively early age, and birth intervals are long. In the next chapter we shall consider why this should be true of the !Kung, when there are so many peoples in the world who have the opposite problem—more fertility than they can comfortably accommodate.

10

Fatness and Fertility

The fertility of the !Kung appears, from all the information available, to be low. It is not low in relation to the needs of the people to compensate for their mortality (a subject to be considered in more detail later), but low in comparison with the fertility achieved by other peoples of the world who do not practice contraception. We have sought an explanation of the low fertility, in the last chapter, in the epidemic of venereally induced sterility, but failed to find this factor an adequate explanation. There must be additional factors in the special conditions of life of the !Kung that lead to their distinctively low pattern of natural fertility.

There are a number of possible explanations for the observed low fertility. One hypothesis is that the !Kung actually do practice controlled fertility, changing their coital behavior when they have had all of the children they wish to have, but the evidence for this is unconvincing. Another hypothesis is that the presence of the nursing child inhibits intercourse by the parents, but this hypothesis fails to account for observed variation in birth spacing. A promising hypothesis entertained by Lee (forthcoming) is that the suppression of ovulation by lactation is more effective and more prolonged among the !Kung than among other peoples, because the !Kung offer the breast far more frequently than other people and children take a larger proportion of their food in this form. Research currently underway on the control of ovulation and reproductive spacing may yet suggest additional hypotheses on the mechanisms that produce low fertility in the !Kung.

In 1974, long after returning from the !Kung fieldwork and in the midst of struggling with the explanation of their low fertility, I heard a paper presented by Rose Frisch at the annual meeting of the Population Association of America on the "critical fatness hypothesis." Frisch's formulation of the relationship between fatness and fertility suggested an entirely new line of interpretation of the !Kung results and initiated a reexamination and reconsideration of much of the data, incorporating facts on diet and weight that had been collected for other purposes.

This chapter reviews Frisch's work, considers its application to the understanding of population dynamics in hunting and gathering populations, and looks at the available evidence from the !Kung on some of the relevant variables.

Frisch's Critical Fatness Hypothesis

Frisch began the series of studies that led to the critical fatness hypothesis with the question of the determinants of menarche in young women, a subject that has attracted considerable attention in biostatistics because of the dramatic changes in the age of menarche during the past century. Age itself is a good predictor of menarche within particular societies, but it cannot be the causal determinant of the maturation process because of the differences in age between populations and differences in age within the same population at different periods of time. Frisch and Revelle (1969) reported that although the mean age at menarche and at "peak weight velocity" (another identifiable point in the adolescent growth process) is older in undernourished populations than in well-nourished groups, the maturational events seem to occur at approximately the same mean weight within particular racial groups. Turning to longitudinal growth data from the United States, Frisch and Revelle found that height was related to age of maturation, as was already well known: Late maturing girls were taller, on the average, than early maturing girls. In contrast, the mean weight for early and late maturing girls differed little (Frisch 1972, 1974a).

Body composition of maturing girls changes in predictable ways. Increases in lean body weight (associated with height) make up one component of body composition; the deposition of fat on the body makes up a distinct component. Lean body weight increased by 44% from initiation of the adolescent growth spurt to menarche in the girls Frisch (1974b) studied, whereas fat typically increased 120% during the same period. Estimating the body composition of the girls at each point of the maturation process allowed Frisch and McArthur (1974) to refine the hypothesis. Since changes in fatness are the major component of changes in weight during female adolescence and since reproduction is an energy-consuming process, Frisch and McArthur (1974) hypothesized that a critical factor in starting and maintaining menstrual cycles is the possession of a minimal amount of fat stored on the body, the critical amount being determined as a proportion of total body weight or lean body mass.

Extending these studies, Frisch *et al.* (1973) estimated the body composition of menarchial girls, identifying the distribution of fatness at menarche. The tenth percentile, about 17% of body weight in fat, has been called the critical ratio for these women, although the authors note that other racial and ethnic groups might be found to have a different critical ratio. Frisch *et al.* (1973) also studied the process of height and weight changes after menarche, and found that young women continue to gain weight through fat deposition after menarche, a process that leads eventually to regular menstrual cycles with ovulation, which Frisch calls stable reproductive ability. The minimum of fat needed for stable reproductive ability is higher than that for menarche, about 22% of body weight in fat in the women studied. The period between reaching the critical level for menarche and that for stable reproductive ability seems to correspond to the period of adolescent sterility. Even after ovulation cycles have been established, Frisch and McArthur (1974) found evidence for a relationship between fatness and the menstrual cycle, as dropping below the higher stable reproductive ability level of fatness results in amenorrhea. A study of nonanorexic and anorexic women who became thin due to self-imposed starvation showed that those women stopped menstrual functions when their weight went below the critical proportion of fat for mature women. Menstrual periods resumed when they regained body weight to that level (Frisch and McArthur 1974; McArthur *et al.* 1976).

The essence of Frisch's hypothesis, then, is that women have a *minimum* weight (according to height) for the onset of menstrual cycles and a higher minimum for regular ovulation within those menstrual cycles. The mechanism proposed is a basic biological one, which may operate through effects on the metabolic rate or on the metabolism or storage of lipid-soluble hormones like estrogen (Frisch 1978). The hypothesis has wide-ranging implications through effects on what we called "the supply of potential mothers." The proportion of women in the age group 15–49 who are capable of childbearing is influenced by the age at menarche, the age of the end of adolescent sterility, and the temporary or permanent loss of fecundity to women whose fat deposits decline below the critical level. However, the hypothesis does not deny the role of other determinants of fertility performance, such as culturally defined rules of marriage, desired family size, and contraceptive effectiveness.

Frisch's hypothesis has been developed and applied to empirical studies within a society in which most women have been well fed (some would say overfed) all of their lives. In the contemporary United States, most women pass the critical fatness level for stable reproductive ability very early in life, even if they do not test that ability by bearing children for another decade or more, and they may remain well over that critical level of fatness throughout the rest of their lives, not even approaching it when dieting. Having 20% of one's body weight in fat may sound like a lot, but it represents a very slender body type. When one seeks examples in North America of women near or below the critical fatness levels, one finds them primarily among fashion models, ballet dancers, or in hospitals. Poorly nourished Americans tend to be fat rather than thin.

In the world as a whole, we see a wider range of diets, of fatness levels, and of fertility performance. If we used the inappropriate method of geographical correlation, we would have to conclude that high fertility is associated with poor diets and thinness in the contemporary world. That conclusion is irrelevant to the validity of the critical fatness hypothesis, which merely asserts that there is some minimum level of fatness below which fertility is not possible. If the results of diet, activity patterns, physiological stress such as high altitude, and burden of infectious and parasitic disease are such that women cannot remain above the critical level, then fertility performance will be reduced. Frisch (1975, 1978) is aware that although the critical fatness hypothesis may not account for much of the variation in fertility in industrial societies, it offers a promising means to advance our understanding of the determinants of fertility control in hunting and gathering societies.

Application to the !Kung

If we assume that Frisch and McArthur are correct in positing two critical levels of fatness associated with menarche and with ovulation, two lines of research are suggested. The first is an analysis of the diet and activity patterns of women in the various reproductive states. Lee (1965, forthcoming) has argued that most of the activities and organization of the !Kung can be understood as a minimax solution to the problem of obtaining the maximum amount of desirable foods at the least cost of effort to the workers. Variables like the division of labor within the group, the frequency of group moves and the distance and duration of hunting and gathering trips are therefore predictable once the constraints and strategy of the !Kung are understood. Some activities that would seem to increase food production for the !Kung can be shown by careful analysis to involve greater costs in caloric expenditure than would be justified by the increased production. Lee's ecological analysis can be read profitably with the question of the maintenance of necessary fat deposits in reproductive women in mind.

Here we will explore an alternative research question, focusing on the size and weights of !Kung women, looking for evidence that the low fertility achieved by the !Kung may be understood in part by the failure of some women, some of the time, to achieve and maintain critical fatness levels. We start by presenting data on the distribution of height and weight by age among the !Kung women, and go on to look at changes in weight for individual women at particular points in the reproductive process and differences in weight between groups of women. The small size and slenderness found among all !Kung, throughout their lives, is a distinctive feature of the !Kung population.

Data Collection on Height and Weight

Members of the population were measured frequently between 1967 and 1969, by Lee, myself, and occasionally other members of the expedition. On four occasions during the fieldwork period, Lee and I devoted a week or so to moving the scales and height rods to each village in turn, combining physical measurements of all members of the population with census surveys and work on age estimation. In addition we weighed the local people sporadically, wherever we happened to be, throughout the 22 months of fieldwork. The coverage of measurements is not uniform: Some people were weighed as often as 20 times whereas many others were weighed only during the weight campaigns or not at all. The measurements are not a random sample of the population, so frequencies of characteristics such as the age distribution, the proportions in various reproductive categories, and the proportions dependent upon one kind of diet rather than another should not be interpreted as the best indicators of those proportions for the entire population. The data is most useful for examining the relationships between variables, such as height or weight with age.

Weights were taken on a heavy-duty balance scale, at all times of day. People were asked to remove heavy clothing and bundles; remaining clothing was noted and samples of similar clothing were weighed and subtracted from weight measurements in the analysis. Where this adjustment was not made, the data was labeled "clothed weights." Small children were weighed by being held by an adult. The child was then handed to someone else and the adult was immediately reweighed, with the child's weight arrived at by subtraction.

Heights were measured on a wood and metal height rod with a platform floor to avoid the problems of people sinking into the loose sand as the measurements were taken. People wore thin-soled sandals or (usually) had bare feet. Children who could stand were measured if they were willing to cooperate, but excused if they were frightened. Few children over the age of about 3 hesitated to come forward for measurement, but our sample may be biased toward the braver (and perhaps larger) children among the very young. Virtually everyone else was measured, in most cases several times over the years of observation, so that we have verification of height measurements in the case of adults and measures of growth over time for children.

The purpose of the program of physical measurements was primarily to study seasonal changes in nutritional status and growth in children; this data will be presented elsewhere (Lee forthcoming). For the present purposes, it is sufficient to establish an overall picture of the typical size by age in the !Kung population.

To do this, I have selected one of the "height–weight campaigns," that of late December 1968 and early January 1969, to provide a single observation of both height and weight for 234 girls and women, combined into a cross-sectional view of size by age.

During the years of growth, we naturally expect younger children to be smaller than older children. In a cross-sectional view, they may not be, so we simply attribute the irregularities in the growth pattern implied to the results of individual variation. When the means for age groups do not make a smooth curve, we attribute that finding also to the fluctuations in numbers caused by the small sizes of the groups, which does not permit grouping enough cases to average out extremes. An advantage of the small number of cases is that we can look at the scattergrams of the data, showing individual measurements crossclassified by age and other characteristics.

Height and Weight of the !Kung Girls and Women by Age

Figure 10.1 shows the computer-produced scattergram of the height by age for 234 !Kung women and girls. (A "1" on the graph indicates an observation of a woman at that height and age, a "2" indicates that two women were observed at the intersection of that height and age, and so on.) As we would expect, there is a

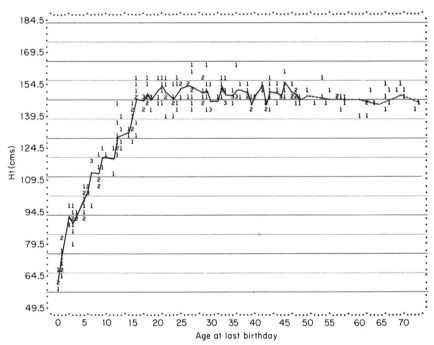

Figure 10.1. Scattergram and mean height by age, 234 girls and women.

steep climb in heights year by year for the first 15 years of life as the girls grow. By age 15, the mean height for the group has reached the adult level, but the variance in height is greater than that observed for the adult ages, indicating that some of the 15-year-old girls have "shot up," but others have not yet completed their growth. At ages 16, 17, and 18, the mean does not change much but the variance is reduced, as the girls become more alike in height. The mean height for single years of age varies between 142 and 154 cm—a function of the small number of cases at each year of age and the range of variability in normal adult height. Truswell and Hansen (1976) found a mean height of 150.12 cm (4 ft, 11 in) among the 74 women they measured, a figure close to the average (148 cm) for the adult women measured here.

The shortest adult women are slightly less than 140 cm (4 ft, 7 in): Such women are likely to be conscious of their shortness and may be teased about it by others. The folk explanation of shortness (and thinness) in adulthood is sickness or hunger in childhood. The tallest women are about 165 cm (5 ft, 6 in). Lorna Marshall reports that tallness is considered unattractive in women (1976:267): Several women had "tall" as a nickname attached to their given name. None of

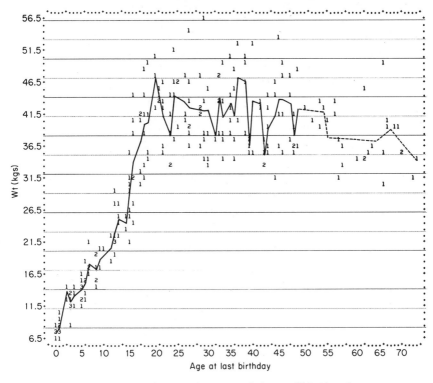

Figure 10.2. Scattergram and mean weight by age, 234 girls and women.

the women over 155 cm is over 50-years old, which may reflect increases in height for women who lived with Bantu and supplemented their diet with milk during childhood. There would have been few such opportunities 50 years ago and none prior to that time. Mean height seems to be somewhat less for women over 50, which may reflect changes in the vertebrae that occur with age (Friedlander and Oliver 1976).

Figure 10.2 shows the weight by age for women. Data for the 0-year olds (infants) misrepresents typical weights, since we included only infants who could and were willing to stand up to have a height measurement taken, that is, older infants. The mean weight of five female infants measured during the first month of life was 2.85 kg (about 6.25 lb), with a standard deviation of .459 kg. Only one of these babies falls below the World Health Organization standards for low birth weight (2500 gm or less) (World Health Organization 1961).

Like the height curve, the weight by age curve is fairly narrow in range and steadily increasing until age 15. Around 15, when the girls have attained most of their adult height, the range of variability in weight at the same age increases enormously. Some of the 15-year-olds are well into the range of adult weight, but other girls 15, 16, and even 17 are still in the immature range, under 30 kg. Over the age of 20, weight observations form a cloud of points little related to age, except that women over 50 tend to be somewhat lighter. The variability in weight of adult females is associated not only with height and with diet, as for men, but also with their reproductive status. Pregnant women gain 7–9 kg during their pregnancy, so that their weight is not an indication of their lean body weight or fatness. If we look at the 10 women with weights over 50 kg in Figure 10.2 for example, we see that 3 of these women were pregnant and gave birth within the following months, while 6 of the 7 others are "fat" women who regularly live at Bantu cattleposts and supplement their diet with milk. Even the heaviest of these women would not be judged obese by European standards: 50 kg (110 lb) is in the low range for North American women, even controlling for height.

Figure 10.3 shows the scattergram of height and weight measurements for the girls and women. As one would expect, the association between height and weight is strong among the immature women, as a function of the growth process, and is weakly positive among the fully grown women, among whom the taller women tend to be somewhat heavier but among whom reproductive status and fatness vary.

Weight, Fatness, and Source of Diet

Frisch and Revelle (1969) first used weight measurements as the primary data, but estimates of body composition were used as the critical fatness hypothesis was developed (Frisch and McArthur 1974). Frisch does not find it meaning-

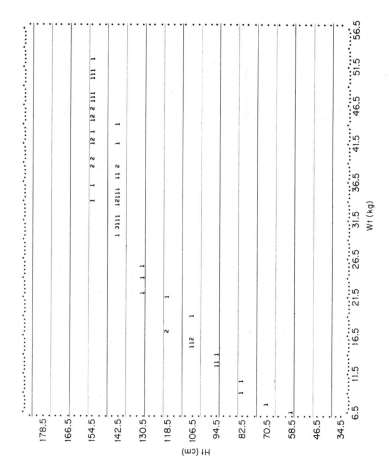

Figure 10.3. Scattergram and mean height by weight, 234 girls and women. ($r = 0.93$.)

ful to use weight measurements alone for the purposes of looking for evidence of the critical fatness phenomena (personal communication 1977).

There are several difficulties, however, about using body composition indicators to report on the !Kung data. The first is that height measurements were made only occasionally, but weight measurements were collected continuously, so that detailed longitudinal data is available on weight but not height. The second problem is that the regression equations relating height and weight to Total Body Water, and hence to percentage of fatness, were constructed by intravenous injection of deuterium oxide (Moore *et al.* 1963) and measuring its dilution in blood serum after measured periods of time, in a clinical population of North American women. !Kung women are sufficiently different from North American women in size, way of life, diet, activity patterns, and perhaps genetic potential that the regression equation should be recalculated before "plugging in" the heights and weights of !Kung women to obtain what could otherwise be spurious indicators. Although it is no doubt true that a single weight measurement tells very little about fatness, changes in weight within individual women— and differences in weight between groups of women—give some idea of relative fatness. We noted before the mean height of adult women in this collection of data is about 148 cm. The mean weight for adult women (including pregnant and lactating women) is about 42 kg. Applying the somewhat questionable procedure of using the Mellits and Cheek (1970) regression formulas on height and weight, the mean fatness of adult women in this data comes out to 23.7%, very close to the minimal level for ovulation in North American women (Frisch and McArthur 1974). Truswell and Hansen (1976:171–172), who performed physical examinations on a group of 74 !Kung women, found a mean height of 150.15 cm and mean weight of 40.08 kg, which gives a mean fatness of only 20.6% using the same equations.

That the !Kung women are very slender and have low fertility is undeniable. The association of these two observations, however, gives us no ability to explore the relationship between them. However, the arrival of Bantu cattleposts and the changes in diet and activity patterns for the !Kung women who have lived there in recent years gives us some opportunity to compare the weights and reproductive status of women with diets based on the traditional hunting and gathering way of life (even if they occasionally have meals derived from the cattleposts) with women whose diets are based primarily on milk and grain (even if these women continue to include collected wild foods as a part of their diet). The cattle-dependent women include all of those who live in certain villages (!Kangwa, !Goshe, and Bate) and some of those in other villages if they actually live with Bantu or if their family members have regular work taking care of cattle. The women classified as bush-dependent are all the others. I do not want to make excessive claims for the precision of this classification: It is entirely possible that the distribution of the percentage of food obtained from cattle overlaps somewhat between the two groups and there may be changes over time in the sources of food for some women which have not been taken into account here. But this rough classification does seem to partition the data on weights into meaningful categories, revealing patterns that cannot be seen when the data are pooled.

Fatness and Menarche

We have seen the age distribution of menarche (in Table 9.3) and the age distribution of growth in height and weight (in Figures 10.1 and 10.2). Frisch's hypothesis suggests that weight changes in adolescence are most sensibly examined not by age, but by relationship to menarche. Hence, for the 51 young women for whom I know the data of menarche (those in Table 9.3) weight records have been plotted, in Figure 10.4, by the time of the weight observation relative to menarche. Eleven of the young women had to be eliminated from this analysis for lack of useful weight records. Since weights were collected over a 2-year period, at most, none of the weight observations extend throughout the whole adolescent period. Multiple observations for the same young woman are connected by a line, solid for the ones who were primarily living on a cattlepost diet and dashed for those living in more traditional bush camps. Weight at first

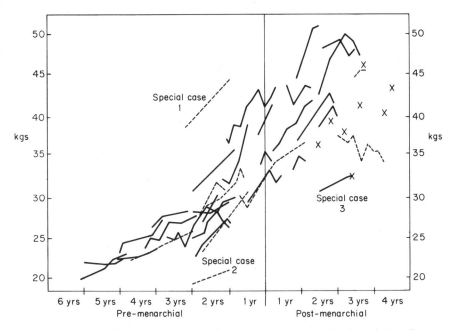

Figure 10.4. Weights during adolescence for young women, arranged by time relative to known data of menarche. Solid lines for cattlepost girls; dashed for bush girls.

birth is plotted by an "x" for 8 women, along with the period of time after menarche when that birth occurred. In general, this combination of a cross-sectional and a longitudinal view of weight gain during adolescence shows tightly clustered weights in the period up to 2 years before menarche, spreading out during the adolescent growth spurt as menarche is approached, and continuing to spread out after menarche as stable reproductive ability is attained.

Only five young women actually experienced menarche during the time that the weight observations were being made. At least for these few women, it is interesting to look at their body composition as implied by the regression equation to see the estimated percentage of fat at menarche, to compare with Frisch's

TABLE 10.1
Physical Measurements Surrounding Menarche for Five Young Women

I.D. number	Time relative to menarche	Height (cm)	Weight (kg)	Fat (%)[a]
48[b]	− 5 months	144.8	28.8	7
	+ 4 months	145.4	34.8	17
	+ 16 months	148.6	37.2	18
647[c]	− 1 month	146.0	34.5	16
	+ 1 month	146.0	35.7	18
	+ 3 months	146.0	34.3	15.8
675	− 3 months	None	37.9	—
	+ 1 month	148.6	39.3	20.6
	+ 3 months	148.6	41.4	23
340	− 12 months	None	37.8	—
	− 8 months	153.0	38.9	18
	− 2 months	None	43.4	—
	+ 6 days	157.5	41.0	17.8
	+ 4 months	158.0	43.4	22.0
267[d]	− 5 months	None	29.5	—
	+ 1 month	142.0	33.5	17
	+ 4 months	142.0	31.8	14
	+ 7 months	143.5	32.2	14

[a]Percentage of fat calculated by formulas from Mellits and Cheek (1970), where total body water (T.B.W.) = −10.313 + 0.252 (weight in kg) + 0.154 (height in cm); index of fatness = T.B.W. ÷ weight in kg; fat percentage = 1.00 − 1.39 (index of fatness).

[b]Pre-fertile.

[c]Age 18 at menarche; died at age 22, probably of TB.

[d]Was treated for venereal disease 4 months after menarche. Her first child was conceived 25 months after menarche.

10. FATNESS AND FERTILITY

reports for European women. Table 10.1 summarizes the data for the five cases. Although there are problems in observation arising from the fact that girls were measured at variable times before and after menarche, the data certainly suggest that the minimum figure of 17% fat found by Frisch to characterize European women at menarche is very close to the mean for !Kung women.

The fit of these five cases to the expectations generated by the Frisch results for European women is so close that in all fairness we should look also at a few cases that seem to be strikingly different from the others in the population. The atypical cases are easily recognizable on Figure 10.4, as they stand out from the other observations. Photos of these young women are shown in Figure 10.5. One of these, marked "special case 1" on Figure 10.4, is simply atypically heavy (44.5 kg, 1 year before menarche). She does not have a Bantu father, which might account for a different body type; she does not live at a cattlepost (her parents are among the most conservative Dobe families); and in fact her father is not even a successful hunter, as he has poor eyesight. There are other good hunters in her group, however, her mother is a very competent woman, and this young woman is clearly well nourished. Her menarche occurred at 18 years (Lee personal communication 1974), and her first child was born at age 21 (Wiessner personal communication 1975).

Two other women are atypical by being extremely small and thin. The one marked "special case 2" on Figure 10.4 weighed only 20 kg 2 years prior to menarche, and by 10 months before menarche she was only up to 21 kg (46 lb). Although she was unusually short for both her weight and her age, it is hard to imagine how she could have gained sufficient weight within 10 months to be anywhere near 17% of weight in fat by menarche. Her age at menarche was below the mean, age 15, and her first pregnancy occurred at age 18, but ended in miscarriage.

The other unusually small and thin woman (marked "special case 3") was observed 2 years after her menarche, which had also occurred at age 15. At this time she weighed 31 kg and was 142.9 cm in height. A year and a half later she measured 32.2 kg (71 lb) and was 145.4 cm in height. The Mellits and Cheek formula suggests that she had only 12.9% of her weight in fat at that time, even though she must have been 2-months pregnant.

Probably the only useful conclusion we can draw from these atypical cases is that there is variation within the !Kung population on the relationship of physical growth and sexual maturation, just as there is in North American populations. Frisch expects about 10% to be below the critical fatness level at menarche (which is, statistically, a tenth percentile measure), and offers no explanation of why many women are over the critical level at menarche in her study populations, stressing that the hypothesis is one of "necessary but not sufficient" conditions (Frisch 1978b). Indeed, we might find from a comparison of the !Kung to

Figure 10.5. "Special cases" on relationships of weight and age at menarche. (Top left) Special case 1 (see Figure 10.4). At age 16, 1 year prior to menarche she was unusually heavy. (Note the

10. FATNESS AND FERTILITY

other groups that the !Kung are distinctive in having relatively little variation in size during adolescence, so that a few unusual cases stand out in great contrast.

To summarize the data, then, we have seen that the !Kung girls grow rapidly, like girls everywhere, in the period immediately prior to menarche. It is therefore entirely reasonable to believe that the age at menarche cannot decline to younger ages in the !Kung population unless the girls grow more swiftly, reaching larger sizes at younger ages. Dividing the menarchial girls into those dependent upon food from cattleposts and those dependent on bush villages has not been of great help in understanding the relation of diet to menarche, primarily because only 9 of the menarchial girls are classified as living on bush foods. The cattlepost girls tend to be slightly heavier and taller at each phase of the developmental process, but the mean age of girls at menarche does not differ significantly between the two groups.

Fatness and Adult Sterility

In Chapter 9 we looked closely at 89 women who had no child during the period 1963–1973. Of these 34 were so young in 1973 that their primary sterility was attributed simply to immaturity; the other 55 were classified by whether they reported venereal disease, a cause of sterility that would presumably be effective no matter what degree of fatness the women possessed. To investigate whether any or all of these women are so thin that they may be below critical fatness levels, the weight records for these individual women have been plotted in Figures 10.6 and 10.7, classified by whether the woman was primarily living on cattlepost foods or bush foods. Thirty infertile women, all of those for whom I had at least three weight observations, have been included. Since there are no events in the reproductive cycle around which to organize this data, weights are plotted simply by the date of the observation, with a line connecting observations for particular women.

Let us look first at the weights for the infertile women living primarily on cattlepost foods, shown in Figure 10.6. Weights range from 34 to 54 kg. It is striking to note that the fattest women, those over 50 kg, are the women who have married Bantu rather than being simply workers or dependents, and, in one case, a woman who has planted fields and taken considerable responsibility for

Figure 10.5 (continued)

steatopygia). (Top right) Special case 2 (see Figure 10.4). At age 13, 1 year prior to menarche, she is unusually slender and undeveloped. First pregnancy occurred 5 years after this photograph was taken. (Bottom left) Special case 3. At age 18, 2 years after menarche, this young woman is remarkably short and thin. She conceived her first child a few months after this photograph was taken. (Bottom right) This young woman is close to the mean in age (17 years), in height (145 cm), and in weight (35 kg) at menarche. Percentage of fat calculated by the Mellits and Check formula, 4 months after menarche, was 17%.

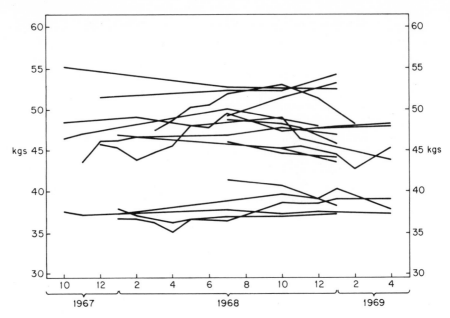

Figure 10.6. Weights of infertile women, living primarily on cattlepost foods.

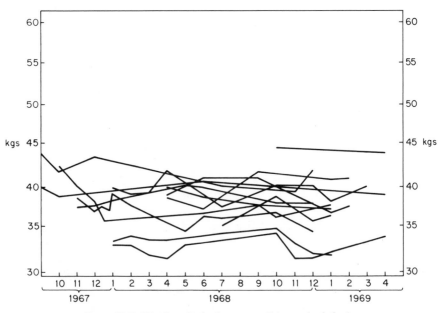

Figure 10.7. Weights of infertile women, living on bush foods.

cattle (along with her !Kung husband) and has been active in making and selling beer in recent years.

Note that the weights of infertile cattlepost women fall readily into two groups; one with weights consistently above 42 kg (slightly more than the mean weight for all adult women) and a nonoverlapping "thin" group with weights under about 41 kg. This pattern in the data is convenient, because it points our attention to rather different life situations in the two groups.

Among the "fat" cattlepost women, 7 of the 12 are among those who felt that venereal disease had made them infertile. Among the remaining 5 "fat" women, one is a young woman whose husband was acutely ill with tuberculosis during the period of the measurements. This woman may find that her fertility improves if her husband recovers his health, so that he is able both to work and to impregnate her. Another of the "fat" non-VD cases may be explained by the absence of her husband on wage work out of the area. Although gossip informs us that she is not celibate in his absence, her frequency of intercourse may be low. The remaining 3 "fat" women are past 35 and have had children in the past.

Among the 5 "thin" cattlepost women, only 1 reports herself a victim of VD. This finding of thinness associated with infertility in women who have not had VD does not necessarily imply that all these 4 women need in order to conceive is to gain a few kg. There may be reasons for the thinness, such as illness or widowhood, that would prevent conception even if the diet were improved. It is at least possible that thinness is the immediate cause of the infertility, even if other factors are the ultimate causes.

When we turn to Figure 10.7, to look at the weights of the infertile bush-living women, we see only the rudiments of a division into "fat" and "thin" groups. One woman is about 44 kg in weight, whereas the others show a tangle of overlapping lines of measurement, most of which are below 39 kg. The woman who stands out in Figure 10.6 by her heaviness suggests that the association between fatness and cattleposts is not accidental: She was brought as a bride for a 40-year-old son of a Dobe family directly from a cattlepost. Her presence also suggests that the association between cattleposts and venereal disease is not accidental: She is one of the two infertile women among those who live in bush camps who admits to having had VD.

These findings of low weight in infertile bush-living women suggest that the normal fatness levels of the !Kung may often be close to the critical level and that thinness may be playing some role in preventing or delaying conception. If so, it represents an automatic control over excessive population growth in isolated hunting and gathering groups when resources are scarce and life is hard: It eliminates a portion of the potential childbearing population. Presumably those eliminated from childbearing would tend to include those who have handicaps in life, such as poor food-gathering ability, a husband who is a poor hunter, or an absence of kinship ties to central people in successful groups.

Fatness of Fertile Women

We have seen a substantial difference in weight between bush-living and cattlepost-living women who are infertile. The following graphs, Figures 10.8 and 10.9, show the weights of women who are fertile within 1 or 2 years of the weight observations. In order to extract the information on weight by phases of the reproductive cycle, all of the observations have been classified by the number of months before or after the birth closest to the observations, so that measurements taken over a period of 22 months are displayed over a 50-month time frame, consisting of up to 30 months prior to the conception of the next child, the month of pregnancy during which the measurement was made (counting backwards from the known date of birth of the child), and up to 12 months after the birth. Again, comparing the graphs for bush-living and cattlepost-living women, we see striking differences in the levels and patterns of weight change over the reproductive cycle.

Looking first at Figure 10.8, the weights of fertile women living primarily on cattlepost foods, we see that fertile women overlap both the "fat" and the "thin" groups that we distinguished among sterile women in their nonpregnant weights. The fact that four women with nonpregnant weights of less than 36 kg conceived, and three of these had live births, helps us resist an overly simple conception of

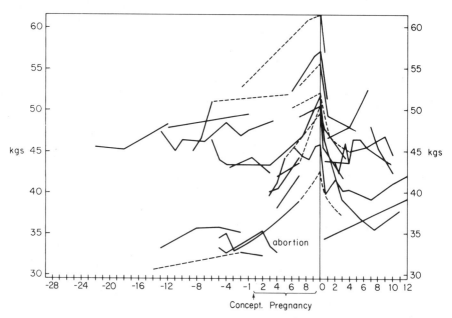

Figure 10.8. Weights of fertile women living on cattlepost foods, arranged by months before and after a live birth. Dashed lines connect data points more than 3 months apart.

the relation of weight and fertility. The women gain about 7–9 kg from conception to live birth and lose about 5 kg at birth. Among the women living on cattleposts—but strikingly not among the women living on bush foods—weight gains are sometimes substantial in the year after childbirth, when the bush-living woman typically increases her activity level through lactation and additional work with little increase in food supply, but the cattlepost-dwelling mothers may balance the caloric demands of lactation by being more sedentary and increasing the food supply.

Figure 10.9, the weights of bush-living mothers, shows a lower mean and less variance in weight at each stage of the reproductive process. The bush-living women seem to gain about the same amount of weight during pregnancy, but lose more after childbirth and continue losing weight during the first postpartum year. If these women are close to their own critical weights for ovulation at conception, it is reasonable to hypothesize that the weight gains of pregnancy are not gains in fatness, but rather the weight of the baby and the enlargement of the uterus and breasts that accompany childbirth, so that weight losses in the postpartum year may be depletion of fat deposits, bringing at least some of the women, some of the time, below the critical levels for ovulation. Long birth intervals, therefore, may be caused (in part) by failure to establish ovulation during the period of heavy lactation and continual carrying of the baby while the mother

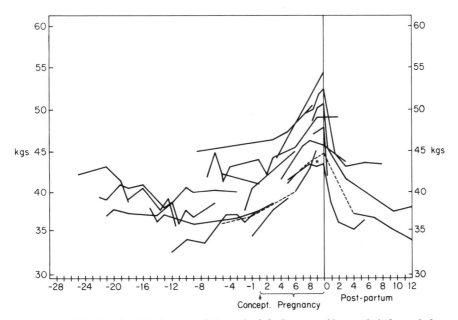

Figure 10.9. Weights of fertile women living on bush foods, arranged by months before and after a live birth.

goes about her work (providing, in large part, the increased demands for food of the family).

The hypothesis seems plausible. Although we cannot test it directly, we can test it indirectly by looking at the length of birth intervals for the groups of mothers, fat and thin, who live on cattlepost and bush foods, the same women shown in Figures 10.8 and 10.9.

Fatness and the Length of Birth Intervals

Utilizing the dividing line of 42 kg, all fertile women have been divided into two groups on the basis of their highest nonpregnant weight recorded, calling the two groups "fat" and "thin" respectively. We do not reclassify women when they move to or away from a cattlepost, or gain or lose weight, and of course we do not know what the critical level of fatness is for any particular woman. The categorization, then, is only rough. Following the Frisch hypothesis, we predict that the

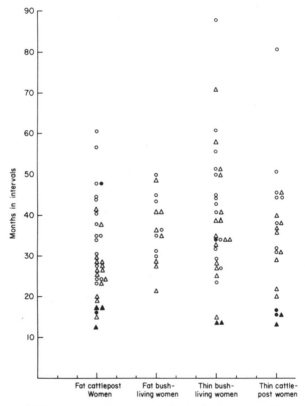

Figure 10.10. Length of birth intervals, by weight and source of diet.

order of the groups, from those having the highest proportion of short intervals to those having the lowest proportion, will be: (*a*) fat cattlepost women (because they are on the average fatter than "fat" bush-living women; (*b*) fat bush-living women; (*c*) thin bush-living women; and finally (*d*) thin cattlepost women (again, because they are on the average thinner than the bush-living women).

Figure 10.10 shows the scattergram of the length of birth intervals in months for the four groups and Figure 10.11 shows the probability of having closed the birth interval by a live birth *x* months after the first for the same groups. Both figures show that the fat cattlepost women have a higher proportion of the shortest birth intervals. The difference between the fat cattlepost women and the others is greatest at month 30. At that time, the probability is .48 that the fat cattlepost women will have had another child, but is less than .25 for the other three groups. Under 24 months, the differences between the groups are primarily due to the proportion of infant deaths to the first child within the groups (24% for the thin cattlepost women; 15% for the fat cattlepost women; 13% for the thin bush living women; and 0% for the fat bush-living women.) I do not want to make too much of these differences in infant death rates, since the numbers in the groups are small and the causes of infant death may be unrelated to the weight of mothers and the type of settlement. These infant deaths, however, increase the proportion of short intervals for the groups. Following surviving children, there seems to be no substantial differences in the proportion of com-

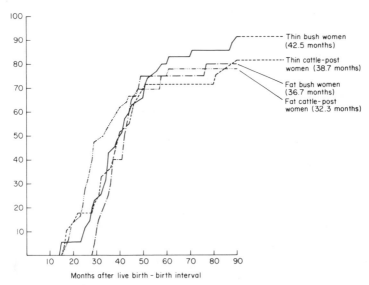

Figure 10.11. Birth intervals for fat and thin cattle-post and bush women. Probability of having had a birth by *x* months after a live birth. (Mean birth intervals calculated on only those in which first child survived.)

pleted birth intervals between months 24 and 48 for the thin cattlepost women and all bush-living women. Thin bush-living women completed the largest proportion of intervals and included a higher proportion of very long intervals (from 48 to 88 months).

The causal links between short birth intervals and fat cattlepost women are not entirely clear. It may be, as has been suggested before, that women who for some reason have a short birth interval are strongly motivated to move to a cattlepost in order to obtain the dietary supplements that will increase the probabilities of keeping both children alive. Being "forced" into the cattleposts by her high fertility, the woman might become more fat, so that the association could be produced by a selection process rather than the more obvious causation hypothesis that points to fatness causing the high fertility. The Frisch hypothesis suggests that the food supplements obtained by living on a cattlepost would increase the fertility of the women, no matter what factors led them to settle there originally.

The arrival of the Bantu in the Dobe area, therefore, seems to have had two distinct and contradictory impacts on !Kung fertility performance. On the one hand, the Bantu brought an epidemic of venereal disease that reduced the fertility of a substantial minority of women, primarily through reducing the supply of fertile women. On the other hand, the availability of a way of life that provides rich caloric sources in the form of milk and grains and a reduction of work demands on women through sedentary life seems to have increased the fertility of a segment of the population by shortening the birth intervals on the average. The combined effect of these two trends has produced a slight decline in !Kung fertility during the 1960s.

The Status of the Critical Fatness Hypothesis

Frisch's critical fatness hypothesis is relatively new and untested. It does not have the theoretical standing of a "fact" about human reproductive biology such that we can safely assume that it is true and go on to explore its implications through work loads and diet for hunting and gathering peoples. Certainly the data presented here can not be interpreted as a test of the hypothesis, since the weight measurements used are too distant from the central concepts of the hypothesis and the results found can be equally well explained by alternative hypotheses (such as selective migration of highly fertile women to cattleposts).

Research to evaluate the hypothesis is being actively pursued by Frisch and others. Some of the evaluation is focused on the details of measurement, evaluation of statistical techniques, and the logic of the hypothesis (Billewicz *et al.* 1976; Mosley 1977; Trussell 1978). Empirical investigations of the hypothesis are at an early stage, as most of the existing data collections do not include all of the data needed for a thorough investigation. Among preliminary investigations, the evidence looks good for explaining the age at menarche by fatness levels (Chowdhury et al. 1977; Mosley 1977), but the evidence on effects of fatness on postpartum amenorrhea is less convincing (Bongaards and Delgado 1977). Huffman et al. (1978), for example, found overlapping weights between women who had resumed menstruation and those still in postpartum amenorrhea 18 months after a birth in Bangladesh. Many of the amenorrheic women were found to be over an estimated "critical fatness" line. The test is not adequate, however, as Frisch's hypothesis does not claim that other factors in addition to thinness do not produce amenorrhea, so the issue is far from closed.

The hypothesis requires and deserves a full-scale test in populations of women who do not practice contraception, at least some of whom are sufficiently thin that they would be in the region at which critical fatness levels could be operative. A rigorous test will require regular monthly measurements and observations on a large number of women, over a period of time at least equal to the typical birth intervals for the population, collecting fatness indicators, calibrated for that population, in addition to the usual variables of birth interval studies such as coital frequencies and breastfeeding behavior. There are difficult ethical problems in carrying out a study of "natural" birth spacing, as it is probably important for the validity of the results that women and infants should not be treated for minor infections, should not be given food supplements by the investigators, and should not have their regular work activities interrupted, due to the likelihood that any of these changes will affect the fatness levels.

It is not realistic to recommend that the hypothesis should be tested rigorously on the !Kung women, as their numbers are too few and they are too difficult to locate regularly and measure accurately. Yet it is tempting to try to carry out tests of the critical fatness hypothesis on a hunting and gathering population, as the absence of supplies of stored food and the necessity of high caloric expenditure to obtain food are likely to have been general features of hunting and gathering life (outside of a few favored niches), precisely the conditions under which the critical fatness levels would be most important and most visible.

The mechanism proposed is a basic biological one, and if it can clearly be demonstrated to operate when fatness drops below critical levels in other populations, we can assume that the mechanism would also have restricted fertility without deliberate control in hunting and gathering populations. Such a conclusion will open the possibility of greatly increasing our understanding of the hunting and gathering adaptation, relating diet, climatic stress, work loads, and health problems to their implications for population structure. Since the hypothesis is amenable to empirical testing, and an empirical answer will no doubt become available within the next decade, we should properly hold off on speculation.

11

Population Size, Growth Rates, and the Age Distribution: Simulations of Fertility and Mortality

We concluded Chapter 5 by noting that a major source of confidence in our mortality estimates is derived from the observation that when they are combined with our best fertility estimates, they produce a population that matches the observable !Kung growth rate and age distribution. We could not demonstrate that this was true until we had established our best estimates of fertility. In Chapters 6–10 we explored the fertility of women and are now ready to return to the question of the interaction of mortality and fertility rates.

This chapter will show the calculations of the intrinsic rate of population growth and age distribution for the !Kung data and supplement that calculation by looking at simulations based on the !Kung fertility and mortality parameters, in order to learn about the expected range of stochastic fluctuations of populations with these parameters. Simulations will also permit us to assess the extent of the errors introduced in the empirical analysis by the need to estimate the ages of the !Kung. After extracting as much useful information as we can from these simulations, we will consider how the simulations must be modified in order to represent adequately the internal features of household and kinship relationships, in addition to the external features of size, growth, and age distribution.

Population Growth in the !Kung Population

One approach to the measure of population growth is simply to subtract the crude death rate (deaths per 1000 persons per year) from the crude birth rate

213

(births per 1000 persons per year) to obtain the crude "*r*," a measure comparable to bank interest compounded annually. But we have already observed that the crude vital rates can fluctuate wildly over years, as any annual rate is unstable in a small population. Furthermore, these rates fail to take advantage of the valuable information we have developed on age and sex patterns of birth and death. In addition, the crude rates can only be calculated for the years of the most recent decade, when the population appears to have changed rather substantially.

A more useful measure for our purposes is the net reproduction rate, a calculation of population growth per generation. To make this calculation, we need only the age-specific fertility rates and the life table as inputs. Table 11.1 shows the calculation for the best and most robust indicators of both, those for the pre-1950 period.

We start the analysis by multiplying the age-specific fertility rates (from Table 6.1) by a constant, .488, that represents the proportion of all births that are female (when the sex ratio at birth is 105 males per 100 females, as observed in the !Kung). The sum of these rates, multiplied by 5 (the length of the age intervals), is the gross reproduction rate, the number of daughters born to women who survive to the end of the reproductive period. Table 11.1 shows that the gross reproduction rate of the !Kung women is 2.29.

TABLE 11.1
Gross and Net Reproduction Rates for the Pre-1950 !Kung[a]

Age interval	Midpoint	Birth rates[b]	Person-years $_5L_x/l_0$	Daughters per newborn woman[c]	R_1[d]
15–19	17.5	.066	2.721	.1796	3.1430
20–24	22.5	.118	2.565	.3027	6.8108
25–29	27.5	.099	2.391	.2367	6.5093
30–34	32.5	.074	2.210	.1635	5.3138
35–39	37.5	.058	2.024	.1174	4.4025
40–44	42.5	.035	1.839	.0644	2.7370
45–49	47.5	.008	1.658	.0133	.6318

Gross reproduction rate = 2.290
Net reproduction rate = 1.0776
Mean age at childbearing = 29.5482
T = mean length of a generation = R_1/net reproduction rate = 27.42
r = intrinsic rate of natural increase = net reproduction rate − $1/R_1$ = .0026

[a]For further discussion of the methods used in the construction of this table, see Barclay 1958: 212–222.
[b]Daughters only.
[c]Column 3 multiplied by column 4.
[d]Mean age at childbirth; Column 2 multiplied by column 5.

The next step in calculating the net reproduction rate is to take into account the effects of mortality on the reproduction of women. Column 4 of Table 11.1 shows the average number of person-years lived in each 5-year age interval by the cohort of newborn women, calculated as $_5L_x/l_0$. If each newborn woman survived, each would contribute 5 years to the count of person-years lived in each age interval, but instead we see that each newborn contributes between 2.7 years (during the 15–19 age interval) and 1.6 years (for the 45–49 interval). When we multiply the person-years lived (in column 4) by the probability per year of having a daughter (column 3), we obtain "expected daughters per newborn woman," shown in column 5. The sum of these entries, 1.0776, is the net reproduction rate, which can be interpreted as the ratio of the size of successive generations: For 100 women in generation 1 there will be 107.76 women in generation 2, 116.12 in generation 3, and so on.

If we want to compare that rate with annual growth rates derived from the study of other populations, we must determine the length of the generation. Column 6 in Table 11.1 shows the intermediate calculation for determining this quantity, by multiplying the expected daughters born to newborn women by the midpoint of each of the age intervals. The sum of these is the mean age at the birth of daughters to mothers. Dividing by the net reproduction rate gives T, the mean length of a generation, which is the number of years required for the production by generation 1 of an equal number of members of generation 2. For the !Kung data, $T = 27.42$. The annual rate of population increase, r, the intrinsic rate of natural increase (this measure is equivalent to bank interest *continuously* compounded) is .00263, a growth rate sufficient to double the population approximately every 300 years. Such a growth rate would be unnoticeable to the members of the population.

By computing this rate for the !Kung data available, I do not mean to suggest that it has been a constant feature of the !Kung population over long periods of time. We have already seen that current fertility and mortality are somewhat lower than the figures calculated here. These differences are a substantial shift in the few decades since the women 45 and over were in the prime years of their childbearing. The actual !Kung population has had a history of fluctuations in their growth rate over the centuries, as the components of the growth rate, fertility, and mortality rates have varied from one period to another. The details of these fluctuations have left no traces that allow us to reconstruct them.

If, however, we think about the wider category of the type of populations like the !Kung, by which we mean groups of a few hundred to a few thousand people, living in the kind of environment that the !Kung have, with the same technological, ideological, and social resources for coping with that environment, we can pursue the question of variability in population growth rates somewhat further. As we noted in Chapter 5 when discussing variability in mortality rates over time, there can be two rather different but always intertwined sources of observed variation: (a) systematic variations, caused by fluctuations in the environment and the population's response to environmental variation, and (b) stochastic variability, caused by randomly distributed numbers of events in small categories, which can cumulate to substantial fluctuations over time. Although we lack a theory and a method for exploring systematic sources of variation in population fluctuations, the AMBUSH program provides a convenient tool for exploring the stochastic ("meaningless") sources of variation.

AMBUSH Simulations of Population Size and Growth

We have already looked at some aspects of the mortality process as simulated by AMBUSH. Those simulations naturally included a fertility component as well. This chapter will concentrate on the simulation of fertility and the interaction of mortality and fertility in producing the population size trajectory, indices of population growth, and the age distribution. We will show later in this chapter that the method of simulation of fertility used here is not entirely adequate as a means of distributing children to mothers. The method does, however, produce the correct number of children per year, and hence introduces no distortions in the estimates of size, growth, and age distribution.

To simulate fertility, AMBUSH requires a minimum of three parameters to be specified. The first of these is the age distribution of births to women, which were provided as age-specific fertility rates in Table 6.1. The level of fertility is a related but independent parameter, given by the total fertility rate of 4.69. The third parameter is the number of attempts at childbirth, corresponding to the maximum number of births observed to any particular woman. For the !Kung women, and for these simulations, the parameter is 9. AMBUSH generates the births that will occur in the future to a newborn girl by drawing 9 random numbers. The probability of a "success" (a birth) on any draw is .521 (4.69/9) and the age of the mother at that birth is determined by dividing the area of "successes" into segments proportional to age-specific fertility at that age. These births are scheduled for years in the future and activated when that time arrives. If a birth happens to be scheduled after the woman's year of death, it is disallowed. If a birth is assigned to a year in which another birth has been scheduled, it is disallowed and another random number is drawn to mimic the absence of twins in the !Kung society. Marriages occur in these simulations, but have no influence on the fertility of women. Parity (the number of children ever born) and the spacing of births are simple outcomes of the manner of generating births. Women who go through their reproductive years without bearing a child are not "sterile" in the sense of having no probability of conception; they are merely unlucky in the sense that they have been dealt zero successes in nine trials when their probability of a success was the same as everyone else's.

All of the simulations start with the 1968 !Kung resident population, but the events that occur in "year 100" and later are entirely fictional and will be different for each simulation. To avoid mixing real events with simulated events in the tabulations, we allow the members of the real population to pass through the fertile years before counting events, starting in "year 150," and continuing until "year 500," a period of 350 years, or a shorter time if the computer space allocated to hold records of the population is exceeded. In Chapter 5 we showed the contrasting results of simulations of varying periods of time. The principle established there that short runs can display irregular distributions and high variance is an important one for understanding simulations—and indeed small

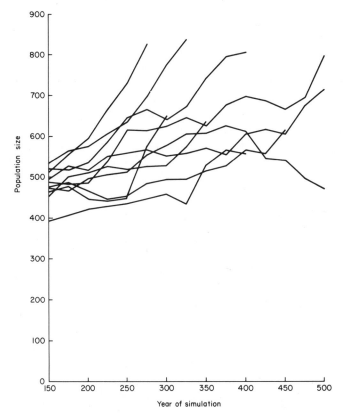

Figure 11.1. Size of simulated populations over time, 10 simulations which start at 455 people in year 100.

populations in general—but it is not necessary to demonstrate the same point in this section. Here we are interested in the macrodimensions of the populations and will be looking at changes of cross-sectional properties over time.

Figure 11.1 shows the absolute population size at 25-year intervals for 10 identical simulations. We see that the simulated populations grow, on the average, over time. They may sharply increase in size at a particular time (without any change in the underlying probabilities of birth and death) and they may or may not later decrease in size. One conclusion we are entitled to draw from the results in Figure 11.1 is that this set of population parameters provides a viable basis for the maintenance of populations over time. We note that none of the simulated populations reached size zero, or extinction, during the period observed, although we would not necessarily conclude that the input parameters were impossible or implausible if some of the simulated populations did become extinct. The probability of extinction at any time is a product both of the rate of growth implied by the input probability schedules and the size of the population in the recent past. With a very small population, say 50 people, the probability of extinction during the near future is very great even if on balance the fertility and mortality schedules have a positive intrinsic rate of natural increase (Dyke and MacCluer 1976). Although much of the danger to extremely small populations operates through the difficulties of finding proper marriage partners (a danger avoided in these simulations by making fertility independent of marital status), the smaller the population the more likely it is that random fluctuations in the number of births and deaths alone will finish the population. Since there is always some probability of extinction in a small population, and since a population cannot recover from extinction, we are forced to the logically correct but intuitively implausible conclusion that all small populations are certain to arrive at extinction eventually.

Escape from this paradox comes by noting that populations can also cease being small. The larger the population grows, the more the Monte Carlo method of generating events for individuals becomes irrelevant to the future of the population, so that eventually large populations come to have very regular fertility and mortality rates, with low variance from year to year, given constant probabilities. Steiger (1973) proposed that a small population might be defined as one in which stochastic variation from constant probabilities is detectable. With the probabilities of fertility and mortality used in these simulations, however, and with a starting population of 455, extinction is not likely to be observed. Since we cut off information about these populations when they reach a size of something over 800 people (for purposes of economy of computer use), none of these populations have grown sufficiently to count as a "large" population by Steiger's definition.

We can measure population growth in these simulations for the period we observe. Table 11.2 shows the mean net growth rates range between .0036 and .0001, with a mean rate for the 10 simulations of .0016, compared to the

TABLE 11.2
Growth of 10 Simulated Populations[a]

Simulation	Final year	Size in final year	Growth in period $(P_2 - P_1/P_1)$[b]	Mean net growth per year (r)[c]
1	405	574	.2615	.0008
2	465	641	.4088	.0009
3	310	689	.5143	.0020
4	500	795	.7472	.0014
5	500	477	.0484	.0001
6	335	838	.8418	.0026
7	275	827	.8175	.0034
8	405	823	.8088	.0019
9	500	710	.5604	.0011
10	360	657	.4440	.0014

[a] From 455 Persons in Year 100 to Year 500 or earlier termination by overflow of computer storage (data in Figure 11.1).
[b] P_1 = initial size (455) and P_2 = final size.
[c] $r = \dfrac{\log_e(P_2/P_1)}{\text{number of years}}$

intrinsic rate of .0026 calculated in Table 11.1. Note that by limiting the size of the populations, we are in effect oversampling the years of low growth rates. Nevertheless, differences between runs are rather substantial, even though all of these rates of growth are low by the standards of the twentieth century, when we see rates as high as .03 or even .04 per year in high-fertility populations with low mortality.

Imagine that we looked through the time machine postulated in Chapter 5 and observed these 10 populations with the artificial time and size limits imposed on the simulations removed. We have noted that the intrinsic rates cause doubling of the populations every 300 years, although particular populations might be growing or declining for random reasons at any moment. If we watched for 1000 years, we would likely see that some of the initial populations would climb into the size range where random fluctuations are no longer important. With time for more than three doublings, we would expect about half of the groups to exceed 4000 persons in cross-section by the end of the millenium. But other initial groups, with identical parameters, might still be in the hundreds or even extinct after 1000 years.

Surely if we observed such differences between populations we would wonder why some of these populations grow while others remain stationary or decline in size over time. If we had some way to carry out demographic studies in the groups, we would find that the observable indicators of fertility and mortality reflect their different fates, so that we would be sorely tempted, indeed forced, to infer different underlying probabilities of birth and death in these populations.

To understand the causes of the apparently differing fertility and mortality schedules, we might investigate the climate, the food supply, the social structure, and cultural practices that might be causing the differences. Similarly we might expect that the people who live in these populations (if one's imagination can accept such a notion) would ask the same questions in a somewhat different framework, asking why some groups in their environment are favored and thriving while others barely manage to exist. One can imagine that people might adopt the religious rituals or customs of their thriving neighbors, or, less peacefully, attempt to take by force the territory, food supply, or people of the competing groups.

The postulated situation has its absurd aspects, but it does help to clarify the problems of interpretation of empirical observations. We assume that variation has meaningfulness when we observe it, even though we can see in these simulations that variation can also appear without causal differences between populations. If merely random differences can play such a large role in creating differences between populations in size and growth rates, it behooves us to be cautious about attributing causal significance to differences in ecology or social structure. Indeed, I would argue that population size, which sometimes seems to be the simplest and most readily observed feature of a population, is frequently one of the most difficult to interpret. Size is stochastically unstable, heavily influenced by migration and other boundary problems, and difficult to define. A given set of population parameters can eventually produce a population of any size. Although changes in size over defined periods of time are more illuminating than absolute size, it is still true that a particular growth rate can be produced by a large number—if not an infinite set—of combinations of population parameters. Fortunately other population features, especially age distributions of vital events, are less variable and more illuminative of the underlying population dynamics.

Age Distributions in the Simulated Populations

We note in Figure 11.1 that although population sizes can move either up or down over time, they seem to be somewhat more likely to continue to move in the same direction, either up or down, that they were moving in the previous interval, so that from a cluster of population sizes in year 150, the simulations spread out over time. The mechanism by which this feedback operates, such that growth in the future is influenced by the history of growth in the recent past, is the age distribution. A run of "luck" that results in the birth of an unusually large number of children during a period of time automatically affects the age distribution by increasing the proportion of infants and children and hence reducing the proportions in the older age groups. Similarly an unusual number of deaths to older people at a point in time will also increase the proportions at the younger ages, as the total must sum to 100%. The populations "age" in the sense of having a lower proportion of the total population in the young age groups by a run of events that either reduces the number of children produced *or* increases the number of older people surviving by a run of few deaths at the older ages. The feedback mechanism operates in addition to the adjustment of proportions through the fact that surviving children arrive at the adult ages, when they are at risk of producing yet more children. Unexpected survivorship of postreproductive adults has only an additive effect on the size and age distribution of a population, but survivorship of children into young adulthood can have a multiplicative effect as well.

This feedback effect of the age distribution on future chances for population growth is not a special feature of the simulated populations, but is a generally well understood property of any population (Coale 1957; 1972). The essence of stable population theory (Lotka 1920) is that the age distribution of a population is produced by the history of fertility and mortality rates in the recent past and is unaffected by the initial age distribution in the remote past, where the growth rate determines the relative size of initial cohorts and the mortality rate determines the removal of individuals from their initial cohort over the life span. The age distribution of a population tends to "forget" its past and conforms to the underlying probabilities of fertility and mortality. Hence the age distribution, unlike

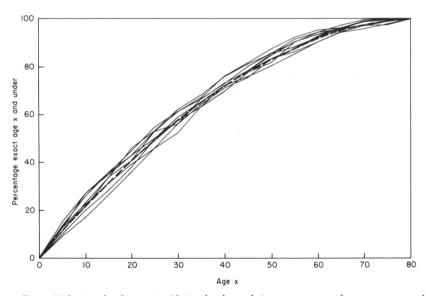

Figure 11.2. Age distributions in 10 simulated populations: percentage of women age *x* and younger.

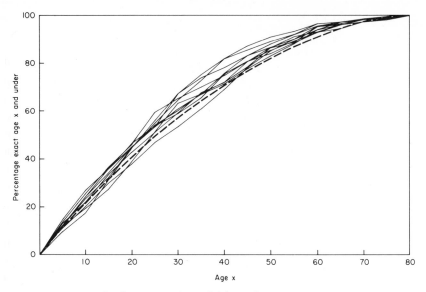

Figure 11.3. Age distributions in 10 simulated populations: percentage of men age *x* and younger.

the size of the population, tends to return to its intrinsic form over time, even though there is scope for stochastic fluctuations in small populations.

Figures 11.2 and 11.3 show the age distributions of the 10 simulated populations in the form of the proportion at age *x* and younger for females and males. Since age distribution is a property of a population seen in cross-section, we plot only one point in time for each simulation; the final year of the simulation run. If we had averaged the age distributions over the course of the run, they would be less variable, although it would still be true that those simulations that happened to grow more than others would be somewhat younger populations, with a higher proportion in the younger ages.

The age distribution of the stable population model from which the !Kung age estimates were made has also been plotted on Figures 11.2 and 11.3 (dashed lines). It is reassuring to see it centered among the simulated populations, even though the distribution (which can be seen in Table 2.1) was based on the assumption of a somewhat larger growth rate (.0076, as opposed to .0026) and hence is a slightly younger age distribution than the intrinsic age distribution of the simulations. This agreement of the stable population model age distribution with those of the simulated populations does not demonstrate that the correct stable population model was chosen, but does demonstrate that the simulated populations successfully mimic the processes that we have inferred as characteristic of the !Kung population.

Assessing Errors in Age Estimation

These simulations provide an opportunity to clarify the extent of errors in age estimation imposed on the !Kung population through the need to estimate ages,

TABLE 11.3
Errors of Age Estimation Procedure, Explored by Simulation[a]

Years	Simulation 1 Male	Simulation 1 Female	Simulation 2 Male	Simulation 2 Female	Simulation 3 Male	Simulation 3 Female	Simulation 4 Male	Simulation 4 Female	Simulation 5 Male	Simulation 5 Female
+10										
9	2									
8	14	1						1		
7	21	2			1	1	4	3		
6	18	3			3	8	9	9	3	1
5	23	6			11	16	20	17	4	5
4	18	17			10	27	39	34	42	49
3	10	45			78	83	54	45	75	69
2	8	48		10	75	81	60	55	55	51
+ 1	23	27	32	61	26	37	30	42	8	20
0	48	27	79	141	26	40	8	8	12	26
− 1	24	31	72	38	2	5			14	9
2	25	41	60	5						
3		10	19	6						
4		1		5						
5				2						
6										
7										
8										
9										
−10										
Totals	234	259	262	268	232	298	224	214	213	230
Average error										
Mean years	3.06	.96	−.83	−.06	2.28	2.30	2.90	2.76	2.51	2.38
Variance	7.22	5.34	1.28	1.28	1.82	2.37	2.30	2.14	2.14	2.18
SD	2.69	2.31	1.13	1.13	1.35	1.54	1.52	1.46	1.45	1.48
Absolute error										
Mean years	3.06	2.10	1.07	.66	2.29	2.34	2.90	2.76	2.64	2.46
Variance	7.22	1.96	3.05	.85	1.74	2.21	2.30	2.14	1.46	1.80
SD	2.69	1.40	1.75	.92	1.32	1.49	1.52	1.46	1.21	1.34

[a] Applying the method of Chapter 2 to AMBUSH simulations (body of table shows number of years that estimated age is older or younger than age given by AMBUSH).

as described in Chapter 2, by rank ordering the individuals and fitting a stable population model age distribution to those ranks. AMBUSH provides us with the number of individuals, males and females separately, at each single year of age from 0 to 80, in cross-sections of the population, given for these simulations at 25-year intervals.

For any age distribution, we can use the AMBUSH-provided ages simply as a rank order, and estimate an age for each living person by the methods of Chapter 2, as though the simulations were like the real population in having unknown ages. For each individual, then, we can count the number of years of difference between the estimated age and that person's age as provided by AMBUSH. Table 11.3 shows the distributions of the errors of estimated ages, in number of years older or younger than the "real" age, for the members of 5 simulated populations during year 150. Only 5 distributions are provided, although our 10 simulations provide more than 100 age distributions, because each is time-consuming and tedious to carry out.

Table 11.3 shows that the mean absolute error is about 2.5 years per person, with a standard deviation of about 1.5 years. Errors as large as 9 years in the estimation of the age of a particular person have been observed in the simulations. On the average the estimation procedure tends to make people appear older than they really are, according to these tabulations, a result produced in part by the fact that we selected the proportion under exact age 10, observed to be 21.87% in the !Kung 1968 population, as one of the crucial parameters in selecting the model stable population used. The proportion at age 10 and under is slightly but systematically higher in these simulations. Small number fluctuations also play a part. In other words, if we carried out this procedure on much larger numbers of age tabulations, I would expect to find more in which the estimation procedure makes people appear younger as well as older than their real ages, but that on the average I would expect a large number of tabulations to show some tendency to make people older. If we had estimated the ages for each cross-section by using the life table and the proportion under age 10, as we did for the !Kung, I would expect to find a symmetrical distribution of years of error, as often making people too young as too old. Note, however, that the symmetry would only be observed when a large number of tabulations were averaged. Within particular runs, errors will tend to cluster either on the positive side or the negative side of zero, reflecting the recent history of the populations. Errors in age estimation do not, unfortunately, tend to cancel out to zero over the course of the life span in a particular cross-section.

This analysis does not permit us to state with any particular level of confidence how great the errors in age estimation have been in the !Kung population. We can only say that if there are no errors in rank order of the population, the mean error per person is likely to be approximately 2–3 years.

Inadequacies of This Simple Simulation

We have seen that a simulation that produces births for all women in the 15–49 age group (without reference to their marital status), combined with a mortality schedule, is adequate to provide information on the stochastic variation and central tendencies of a number of important properties of populations, such as size (even if size tells us little about the population), age distribution, and the growth rate. Such a simulation also provides as output the stochastic fluctuations in sex and age probabilities of death (as we saw in Chapter 5) and in age probabilities of fertility for the women, via age-specific fertility rates and total fertility rate (not shown).

If we wish to exploit our simulations to tell us in addition about the internal structure of the populations, properties such as the composition of nuclear families and households and the kinship connections between individuals and groups, however, we find that this kind of a simulation is not adequate. A major deficiency of the logic of simulation used here is that half of the population, the men, are playing no role in the production of children. Children have no fathers in these simulations, contrary to reality, and all of the kinship ties formed through paternity cannot be made.

Even among the links of women and their children, however, the present form of simulation does not produce a reasonable approximation to reality. The consequences of this can be seen in many of the outputs produced by AMBUSH on internal connections within the population, but we can understand the difficulty most clearly if we look at the parity distribution, the numbers of children ever born to women who survive to age 50.

The parity distribution in the simulations is a stochastic version of the classical binomial distribution, treated as the number of successes in nine trials when the probability of a success on an individual trial is constant. The parity distribution for the !Kung women, however, has the same mean but a very different shape of distribution, illustrated in Figure 11.4, which plots the parity distributions of these simulations and that of the !Kung women. There is much more variability between women in achieved parity in the !Kung population than this form of simulation allows for. Nor is the !Kung population unusual in this regard: In most populations studied, the variance of the parity distribution is at least equal to the mean (suggesting a Poisson distribution) and the variance may be considerably greater than the mean, an observation which has led Cavalli-Sforza and Bodmer (1971:310–316) to suggest that parity distributions are best regarded as instances of the negative binomial distribution. Generating births by a binomial probability process, we conclude, is adequate to represent the external features of a population, but is not adequate to represent the human reproductive process descriptively. This method produces a systematic distortion of internal

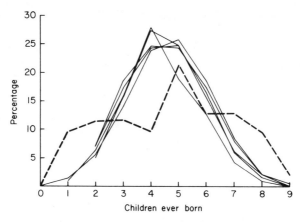

Figure 11.4. Parity distributions, from 5 simulated populations with !Kung parity.

features of connectivity by producing sibling groups that vary too little in size.

AMBUSH includes a feature designed to mechanically inflate the variance of the parity distribution by generating a distribution of differential fertility between women. Rather than resort to that mechanism, however, we can usefully explore observable sources of variation in the reproductive opportunities of women. The main one is marriages, including differences between women in the proportion of the childbearing years during which they are married. If we simulate the production of children within marriage, we will come considerably closer to a realistic model of the internal connections between individuals in the population. In order to simulate marriage and the male role in reproduction, however, we have to return to our empirical task of exploring the !Kung patterns.

The next chapter will examine the evidence on marriage from the !Kung population, looking at the ages of entrance to marriage for the two sexes, the durations and rates of marriage termination and remarriage, and patterns of age differences between husband and wife. The following chapter will look at the evidence on the fertility of men. With these empirically derived parameters in hand, we will return to the task of constructing an adequate simulation of the !Kung population and explore some of the results of those simulations.

12

Marriage and Remarriage Among the !Kung

There is a danger of ethnocentrism in the study of marriage—which we do not face when studying the unambiguous events of birth and death—the danger of mistaking what another people call marriage with what we call marriage in our own or other societies. Some societies have been reported to perceive a child born of a marriage as entirely the product of either the mother or the father, or to see the father of the child as necessarily the mother's husband, with no concept of biological as opposed to social paternity. In other societies, marriage serves important functions in determination of corporate group memberships, whereby adults may be formally severed from their place in the social structure at marriage, joining the group of the spouse. Marriage may also serve functions relating to the distribution of property and questions of inheritance may be crucial to marriage practices. In order to understand the !Kung system of marriage and the behavior of individuals in marriage, it is necessary to be clear what they mean by the term marriage, in distinction to what other people mean by it.

!Kung marriage relations are defined and expressed by making a house and living in it together, acting as a married couple within the village. Marshall (1976) describes the exceedingly simple ritual aspects of marriage for the !Kung. There are no formal or legal procedures aside from gaining the agreement of all interested parties and the adoption of the behavior of marriage. In this sense, all unions are consensual for the !Kung. The marriages that I saw established were marked primarily by a change in the use of kinship forms of address to others in the living group and changes in sleeping arrangements. Informants suggest elements of a "marriage by capture" ideology (Marshall 1976), but the only suggestion of "capture" that I observed were the angry responses of previous spouses in a few cases, who wanted to stop the marriage and bring the wandering spouse back home. Talking about the past, people were usually definite about whether a particular marriage had been established, even if briefly, but contemporary events sometimes generated a certain amount of disagreement. The criterion of a "real" marriage seems to be social acceptance. The term "divorce" is used here to describe the ending of a marriage other than through death, even though there is no formal or legal channel of divorce, in order to distinguish the end of a marriage from temporary visits of spouses to other places. The !Kung term for the voluntary end of a marriage, *sa sarakwe*, translates clearly as "separation."

What the !Kung gain by marriage is a set of kinship obligations and services, primarily from the spouse but also from the spouse's family. Married people share the production and consumption of food, water, and shelter, regular opportunities for sexual relations, and the use of whatever possessions the two parties have. There is less material advantage or disadvantage in marriage for the !Kung than for most people of the world, because the !Kung typically own very little. There is no usual or expected transfer of property at marriage and children typically inherit no material goods from their parents. Both parties to the marriage may expect to receive reproductive, sexual, and economic services from the other, and the marriage may end in divorce if these services are not provided. Daily subsistence is provided by the adults of a living group for all of the members of the living group, their own families first with any surplus distributed to other families. There is a special obligation to provide for the needs of one's own spouse, but food is shared so routinely throughout the living group that temporarily unmarried adults do not appear to be particularly handicapped. Land rights, or "ownership" of a *n!ori* (named place), are vested in both men and women through their parents' rights to exploit these places. Rights are extended to a spouse as long as the marriage persists, and to children through birthright, so that a parent may claim rights to a place through his or her living children even though the original marriage has ended. In fact, these land rights offer little material advantage to an individual and do not seem to be a major factor in marriage choices.

Prohibited Spouses

The prohibited spouses are identified on two criteria: (*a*) consanguinity, and (*b*) the name taboo. The consanguinity prohibition extends only to first cousins, that is, one may not marry anyone who is descended from one of his or her grandparents. Descendents of a grandparent's siblings are allowed but not preferred spouses. The name taboo is based upon the important fictional kinship relationships that the !Kung use to establish kin-like relations to all those to whom they cannot trace a direct consanguinal or affinal tie. The naming rules for children state that parents cannot name a child for themselves, but should name their children for their own parents, parents' siblings, or their own siblings, giving preference to any kinsman who has not yet had a child named for him. The child and the person for whom he or she is named have a special relationship throughout life. Fictive kinship is then established for a pair of unrelated persons by allowing the older of the pair to use the kinship term he or she uses for another person of the same name; the other uses the reciprocal of that term. The name taboo states that one may not marry anyone who has the same name as one's own parent or sibling. The fictive kinship rule states that two people of the same name may be equivalent; the marriage prohibition states that people with the same name as those for whom marriage would be incest cannot marry. The prohibitions hold for both men and women. An otherwise desirable marriage would be improper if either the woman has the same name as the potential husband's mother or sister or if he has the same name as her father or brother. There are only 40 male names and 42 female names in use among the approximately 1000 people known; some of these are very common in the Dobe area. A person with a common name is somewhat handicapped in arranging marriage, since it is likely that many potential spouses will have an "incest" relative with that name. A person who comes from a nuclear family comprising many persons (and therefore many names) of the opposite sex is also handicapped. Even these forms of prohibited marriages can occur under some circumstances however. Couples who are determined to marry but are prohibited by the name taboo have been known to change the name of the offending spouse and first cousins have been accepted as properly married people after producing a child.

Preferential Criteria for Selection of Spouses, and the "Marriage Market"

The preferential criteria for selection of spouses are harder to describe, at least in part because sometimes it is the parents and other interested kin of spouses who do the selecting and sometimes it is the spouses themselves. For either set of parties, there may be a big difference between the abstract process of describing an ideal husband or wife and the actual process of choosing among the available candidates. No doubt one would find wide agreement that a husband ought to be a good hunter and provider, sexually attractive and faithful, mild-mannered and pleasant, and so forth, with a similar list of desirable traits for wives. Since the !Kung population appears to vary widely on such characteristics, and since nearly all adults marry eventually, it is probably not useful to explore marriage choices through such lists.

When parents or other kin select a husband for a young woman around the age of menarche, they are likely to scan a wide range of potential husbands, some of whom they may not know personally. During the years before marriage, visiting kin from distant places may be asked if they know of good candidates and the parents may use their usual visits to other groups to look around. It is considered desirable to marry into a family that is already distantly linked to one's own or into a family into which some member has already married, so that the marriage transaction can be conducted with acquaintances rather than strangers. On the other hand, it is desirable to marry someone who does not have strong kin ties that will draw the married couple away from the family. Parents are likely to choose a husband for their young daughter who is old enough that his capacities as an adult, especially hunting ability and personality, have been demonstrated. More than a third of the husbands in women's first marriages had been married before, so their qualities as a husband could be judged. Some of those men will be currently married, so that the new wife is added as a second wife in a polygamous family. Polygamy is permitted by the !Kung, but is not a preferred marriage pattern. When the other wife is a sister or close relative of the new bride, the polygamous marriage may be seen as advantageous, but, among the younger women especially, polygamy is often a temporary state until one or another of the wives leaves.

When the spouses themselves are active or dominant in making the choice, their criteria are likely to be somewhat different from those of their parents. Parents may scan the candidates in distantly related families spread over a large territory, but the spouses tend to choose from the immediately available partners. Marriages in which the participants are active in the selection process often involve small age differences between spouses, or the wife may actually be older than the husband. The youngest ages at marriage for men, in the low twenties, most often involve couples who decided on marriage for themselves, since parents tend to select older men as husbands for their daughters. Only a minority of first marriages for women are formed by active participation of the couple, but second and later marriages, especially those of mature people, are most often made by the spouses themselves.

Our usual model of a "marriage market" is predicated on the idea that there is a minority of the adult population who are unmarried and searching for a spouse at any one time. In fact, the real situation for the !Kung is more complex than this. We frequently see married people becoming involved in a sexual relationship with someone outside the marriage, and divorcing and remarrying the new partner simultaneously. This suggests that there is a sense in which married people are "on the market" for new spouses as well as unmarried people. In a population so small that only a few young women arrive at the age of first marriage in each year, and in which the rate of divorce and remarriage is high, one has the impression that more of the testing of the qualities of the spouse takes place after marriage than before.

Marital and Non-Marital Sexual Behavior

The !Kung have two rather different modalities for coitus, within the village, at night, and out in the bush, during the daytime. Sexual relations are not confined to married people, but sleeping together in the village at night is. Since the whole village sleeps around a circle of fires within easy earshot of one another, with married couples and their children sharing their few blankets or animal hides and their body heat for warmth, coitus in the village tends to be very restrained. Couples who are obviously having coitus in the village can expect to be teased about it later by their "joking" partners, but since some of the members of the village are likely to be "respect" relatives, in whose presence no sexual jokes should be made, it is not easy to integrate coitus into village life. The most important "respect" relations are the couples' own parents and own children, who are precisely the people who are likely to be closest to them in the sleeping arrangements of the village (Shostak 1976). It may occasionally happen that an unmarried couple will quietly get together within the village while others are asleep, but this is unlikely to be entirely unobserved. If the observer happens to be a relative of an absent spouse, for instance, a great fuss would surely be made.

Premarital coitus and a range of sexual experiences after marriage take place outside of the village, in some quiet spot out in the bush where the couple is unlikely to be observed. The couple may leave the village together, ostensibly to gather food or go visiting another village, or may meet by prearrangement or chance out in the bush, always in the daytime. Since the !Kung are excellent trackers, recognize the footprints of other !Kung, and are usually interested in the location and activities of others, these discrete meetings often come to be public knowledge. Married couples who want a more uninhibited opportunity for sexual relations than the village offers may go to the bush together. While the couple has a nursing child (who accompanies the mother everywhere), these opportunities are limited for the mother. Couples who have not yet had a child, and those whose children are old enough to be left in the village, may have sexual relations in the bush as often as they wish. Unmarried couples (including couples who are both married, but not to each other) have intercourse out in the bush; if they decide that they like each other on the basis of these experiences, they may marry. "Affairs" are unlikely to be long-lasting, because someone is likely to learn of it and object, especially if one or both of the parties is already married. When members of the same living group risk sexual jealousy by having nonmarital sexual relations, the group as a whole may split into warring factions. It is more common for "affairs" to be conducted with members of other living groups, nearby, or those to which one comes as a visitor.

Legitimacy and Custody of Children

Despite the ever-present possibility of premarital and extramarital sex, it is striking that few children are born out of marriage or confuse their social father with their biological father. Only 4 babies out of the 500 born to interviewed women were said to have been born outside of marriage; in each of these cases the whole community knew who the biological father was. Harpending's (1971) genetic studies confirm that the named father was in fact the biological father in almost all cases. The "paternity exclusions" identified by lack of congruence of blood types of fathers and offspring were no more frequent than "maternity exclusions"—a few of each—and should probably be attributed to the small amount of error in labeling samples that inevitably creeps into a study of this kind rather than mistaken paternity. The congruence of marriage and paternity is extraordinarily high, I suppose, not because the nonmarital conception rate is low, but because the people are highly effective in adjusting marriage to match the *fait accompli* of pregnancy. Premarital pregnancy rates are kept low by early marriage and the arrangement of marriages is almost surely influenced by the parents' perception that a given young woman is maturing quickly and needs a marriage to prevent the possibility of premarital pregnancy. When premarital or extramarital pregnancy does occur, the identification of the father seems to be accurately made and a marriage to the father almost always contracted. !Kung women do not acknowledge pregnancy until it shows, around the third or fourth month, but marital rearrangements before that time provide evidence that the woman is quite aware of her condition.

Nearly all children know their father and have the parents married to each other at the time of birth. Nearly a quarter of the children, however, have the experience of the remarriage of their mother to someone else during their dependent life. The "custody" arrangements for children in cases of divorce and death of father are simple: In virtually all cases, unmarried children continue to live with the mother. If she remarries, her new husband will be called "father" by the children of previous marriages, but they continue to identify the biological father as the "real" father, if asked. The child is likely to retain a strong tie to the biological father and to his kin throughout life and may make claims to land rights, for instance, through the mother and the father rather than the mother's husbands. The mother's new husband must accept the mother and her dependent children as a group and provide for all of them in addition to the children that may be born to the new marriage. Since fathers do not ordinarily play an important role in the teaching or disciplining of their children in any case, there is little occasion for strain between stepfathers and children, though the father may show more affection and attachment to his own child. Men, then, may practice what the sociobiologists call "true altruism" in the raising of children who are not their own, while women are rarely called upon to do so.

If the mother dies, the maternal orphans may be cared for by the father with the help of his female relatives (in one case, his mother, the children's paternal grandmother) or by adoption by relatives of the dead wife. If the child is young enough to require breastfeeding, the chances of the child's survival are very slight, although the chances have improved since cattle were brought to the area. There were no cases in the population of a woman being called upon to "altruistically" raise a child of her husband and his previous wife. In each of the few cases where a mother abandoned a child, the father was Bantu and the child was being raised by Bantu relatives. Older children are frequently left with other relatives for care for a period of months or years, without being abandoned by !Kung standards.

Marital Status of Adults in 1968

Tables 12.1 and 12.2 show the marital status of !Kung women and men, respectively, as of the end of 1968, comparable to a census or a survey of marital status in other populations. We show seven categories of marital status for women in Table 12.1, three for unmarried women (single, divorced, and widowed) and four for types of marriages (monogamous and polygamous marriages to !Kung men, and monogamous and polygamous marriages to Bantu men). In the case of polygamous marriages to Bantu men, the other wife is likely to be a Bantu woman rather than a !Kung; in polygamous marriages to !Kung men both wives are likely to be tabulated in Table 12.1. In fact there are six polygamous marriages represented, involving 11 women: One wife had not appeared in the Dobe area to be included in this study. The number of !Kung husbands implied by the marital categories of Table 12.1 is 116.

Table 12.2 shows a parallel tabulation for the !Kung men, collected and tabulated by R. B. Lee. Lee included 151 men in his interviewing, almost all of the residents over age 18 and 12 under age 18. Lee organized his age categories by decade of birth, so that the age classes in Table 12.2 are not the same as those for the women. Nevertheless the pattern is clear. Table 12.2 shows 112 husbands, 7 of whom are polygamously married during 1968, implying the existence of 119 !Kung wives. No !Kung men have married Bantu women in the Dobe area as of 1968. The proportion currently married among the men 39- to 58-years old is about 90%, although all men over the age of 40 have been married at least once.

TABLE 12.1
Current Marital Status by Age[a]

| | | Unmarried | | | Married to !Kung | | Married to Bantu | | Percentage |
Age	N	Single	Divorced	Widowed	M	P	M	P	married
15–19	16	[b]	2	0	8	4	2	0	56
20–24	21	0	2	0	18	0	1	0	90
25–29	16	0	0	0	15	0	1	0	100
30–34	18	0	1	0	12	1	4	0	94
35–39	19	1	3	0	10	3	0	2	79
40–44	13	0	0	0	12	0	1	0	100
45–49	15	0	1	0	12	0	1	1	93
50–54	12	0	0	3	9	0	0	0	75
55–59	9	0	0	3	3	1	2	0	66
60–64	12	0	0	5	6	1	0	0	58
65+	14	0	0	6	5	1	1	1	57
Totals	165	1[b]	9	17	110	11	13	4	
Percentage of total	100	.6	5.5	10.3	66.6	6.6	7.8	2.4	
				16.3%			83.7%		

[a] As of December 1968 for 165 women (M = monogamous; P = polygamous).
[b] Single women in the 15–19 year age group were not interviewed. There were 9 such women in December 1968.

TABLE 12.2
Current Marital Status by Age (at End of 1968) for 139 !Kung Men Age 19 and Over[a]

| | | | | | Married | | Percentage |
Age	N	Single	Divorced	Widowed	M	P	married
19–28	28	11	3	0	14	0	50
29–38	42	2	4	0	35	1	86
39–48	31	0	1	1	26	3	94
49–58	23	0	0	3	19	1	87
59–68	8	0	0	1	5	2	88
69+	7	0	0	1	6	0	86
Totals	139	13	8	6	105	7	
Percentage		9.4	5.8	4.3	75.5	5.0	80.6

[a] Data courtesy of R. B. Lee; M = monogamous; P = polygamous.

At a point in time, Table 12.2 shows that 6% of the married men are married polygamously, each of them to two wives. Since polygamous marriages to old people have no reproductive significance, we note that 5% of married men under age 58 are polygamous.

Marital Histories

When we ask the same people shown in Tables 12.1 and 12.2 how many different people they have ever been married to, we see evidence for instability in !Kung marriages. Table 12.3 shows the numbers of marriages to the 165 informants by the age of the woman in 1968. This tabulation includes the 132 current marriages included in Table 12.1 plus 199 terminated marriages. Table 12.4 shows the comparable information for the !Kung men interviewed by Lee, again arranged in decades. The women report marriage to 331 husbands; 132 of these are current husbands, 65 died during the marriage, and the remainder are ex-husbands, most of whom are in the population and many of whom are included in Lee's tabulation. Clearly not all of these husbands are distinct individuals, as some of the men have been married to several women in the population. Similarly the men report on 254 wives, many of whom are women in the study population.

In order to understand the role of marriage in reproductive life and in the connections of individuals through kinship, we have to look more closely at the process of ending marriages.

TABLE 12.3
Number of Marriages to Women Age 15 and Over by Age in 1968

Age	Number of marriages						Total N
	0	1	2	3	4	5	
15–19	9	12	1	1	1		25
20–24		12	8	1			21
25–29		8	5	3			16
30–34		6	10	3			19
35–39	1	6	5	3	2	2	18
40–44		7	4	1	1		13
45–49		2	3	4	5	1	15
50–54		2	5	2	3		12
55–59		1	4	2	2		9
60–64		5	5	2			12
65+		2	6	5	1		14
Totals	10	63	56	27	15	3	174
Number of marriages		63	112	81	60	15	331

TABLE 12.4
Number of Marriages to Men Age 19 and Over by Age in 1968[a]

| Age | \multicolumn{8}{c}{Number of marriages} |
	0	1	2	3	4	5	6	Total N
19–28	11	14	2	1	0	0	0	28
29–38	2	17	15	7	1	0	0	42
39–48	0	11	9	10	1	0	0	31
49–58	0	5	9	6	0	2	1	23
59–68	0	1	2	4	1	0	0	8
69+	0	1	1	3	2	0	0	7
Totals	13	49	38	31	5	2	1	139
Number of marriages		49	76	93	20	10	6	254

[a] Data courtesy of R. B. Lee.

Probabilities of Marriage Termination

The majority of the marriages reported by women are terminated, 199 out of 331. Sixty-five of these terminated marriages ended with the death of the husband, an event that can be understood in terms of the probabilities of death to men by age and the difference in age between husbands and wives. Most of the marriages that ended in the death of the husband are reported by older women; many lasted a long time and were reproductively important. The rate of widowhood is not surprising, it is the rate of divorce that sets the !Kung marriage system apart from others.

Marriages that end in divorce are frequent (134), but shorter than other marriages. Seventy-five (56%) of the marriages that ended with divorce lasted less than a year, and some of these were as short as a week or two. Eighty-six percent of the divorces occurred within the first 5 years of marriage (approximately—it is difficult to date the length of a marriage that occurred long ago). When you combine the briefness of the marriages ending in divorce with the tendency for young, often prefertile women to have such marriages, it is clear that the demographic importance of divorce, while significant, is overestimated by the sheer number of cases.

In order to estimate the probabilities of marriage termination by divorce and by death of husband, we need to have an estimate of the number of events and the number of marriages at risk of those events. The number of deaths and divorces over time are derived from the data in Table 12.5, which presents the coded answers to the question "For each terminated marriage, approximately how long did this marriage last?". The women could not, of course, answer this

TABLE 12.5
Length of Terminated Marriages
(for 199 Marriages That Ended in Death of Husband or Divorce)

		Widowhood		Divorce	
	N	N	Cumulative percentage	N	Cumulative percentage
1 year or less	78	3	4.6	75	56.0
1–5 years	52	12	23.1	40	85.9
6–10 years	21	10	38.5	11	94.1
11–15 years	12	9	52.3	3	96.3
16–20 years	9	6	61.5	3	98.5
21–25 years	11	11	78.4	0	98.5
26–30 years	10	9	92.2	1	99.2
31 or more years	6	5	100.0	1	100.0
Totals	199	65		134	

question directly and it was not asked of them in this form. The periods of time that the marriages persisted are guesses on my part, based on what the respondent said about the season of the year in which the events took place (for short periods of time), the ages of the children of the marriage or other related children at the beginning and end of the marriage, and so on. Some of these events occurred during the period of observation and can be dated exactly, while others took place as long ago as 50 years, in some cases leaving little or no trace.

Table 12.5 shows the frequency distribution of length of marriages by cause of termination. In order to translate these frequencies into probabilities, we have to estimate the number of marriages that were at risk of termination in that duration. To do this, we combine the current marriages and the terminated marriages that survived long enough to have been at risk of termination in that duration, as has been done in life table analyses before.

Table 12.6 shows the calculations of the life table for marriages. In the first year of the marriages, called "year zero," there were 331 marriages that started the interval. Eight current marriages were still in the interval, so we subtract them from the total to obtain 232 as the number of marriages exposed to the risk of termination by divorce and widowhood during the first year. We calculate two q_x measures: q_{x1} for the probability of divorce during the interval and q_{x2} for the probability of the death of the husband. The joint probability of termination of marriage during the interval is $(q_{x1} + q_{x2} - (q_{x1} \cdot q_{x2}))$.

Table 12.6 shows that the probability of divorce is high at the beginning of the marriage, but declines to a minute quantity by the time the marriage has

TABLE 12.6
Probabilities of Marriage Termination Caused by Death of Husband and Divorce, by Duration of Marriage (for 331 Marriages Reported by !Kung Women)

Duration of marriage (years)	N starting interval	N in interval	N exposed to risk	Divorces			Death to husband		
				N	q_{x_1}	p	N	q_{x_2}	p
Year 0	331	8	323	75	.232	.232	3	.009	.009
1–4	245	26	219	40	.183	.046	12	.055	.014
5–9	167	17	150	11	.073	.015	10	.067	.013
10–14	129	21	108	3	.028	.006	9	.083	.017
15–19	96	18	78	3	.038	.008	6	.077	.015
20–24	69	16	53	0	.000	.000	11	.208	.042
25–29	42	11	31	1	.032	.006	9	.290	.058
30+	21	15	—	1			5		

Duration (years)	Survivorship of marriages[a]		
	l_x	$q_x{}^b$	d_x
0	1000	.239	239
1	761	.228	174
5	586	.135	79
10	508	.109	55
15	453	.112	51
20	402	.208	84
25	318	.313	100
30	218		

[a] Given survival of wife.
[b] q_x in the survivorship curve is $q_{x_1} + q_{x_2} - (q_{x_1} \cdot q_{x_2})$.

survived 10 years, whereas the probability of the death of the husband starts very low but continuously increases as the marriage and the marriage partners age together. Figure 12.1 graphs these probabilities for single years of marriage, showing that together the competing risks form a U-shaped curve.

Table 12.6 shows that the probability of survival of a marriage over a period of 30 years, approximately equal to a full reproductive span, is only about .22. At least a few marriages, however, endure much longer than 30 years: During 1968, one of the central Dobe waterhole families was headed by a couple who had been married nearly 50 years (see Biesele and Howell forthcoming) and at /Xai/xai there was a couple who had been married about 55 years, the first and only marriage for both of them. The !Kung seem to accord a special regard and respect to these old people who have maintained proper marriages over long periods of time.

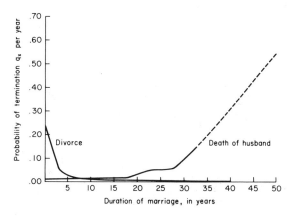

Figure 12.1. Marriage termination probabilities by divorce and by death of husband, by years of duration of marriage.

Remarriage Probabilities

Much of the demographic significance of terminated marriages depends upon the amount of time spent in the unmarried state between the end of one marriage and the start of another.

!Kung women are not forced by cultural prescription or by economic necessity to remarry immediately. If the woman has kin ties to members of her living group, she is likely to remain in the same group, continuing to receive a share of the meat brought into the camp by the hunters. If the woman's ties to the living group were through her husband, she is likely to move to another group, generally that of her parents if they are still living. There are several cases in the population of women who were widowed in their thirties who did not remarry for long periods of time, relying upon primary kin and their own efforts to provide for themselves and their children while the children were young, and shifting group membership to live with married children at least part of the year when the children were grown.

An alternative for a woman who has few or no primary kin to draw her into other groups is to remarry a brother of her ex-husband. Eight cases of levirate remarriage are reported by the women, six of which followed the death of the husband, one of which followed the desertion by the husband to live with another woman, and one of which represented *ja* (stealing) by the younger brother. The wife reports, many years after the event, "my husband said 'I like my brother more than I like my wife, so I will give her to him rather than kill my brother.'" It is interesting to see levirate remarriage occur in a society in which it has no effect on the concentration of property.

TABLE 12.7
Length of Time from Termination of Marriage to Remarriage for Divorced and Widowed Women

Time since termination	N				Probability of marriage in interval (q_x)	(l_x)	(d_x)
	Beginning interval	Still in interval	Finished interval	Married in interval			
Divorced women							
At termination	134	0	134	26	.194	100,000	19,400
1 month	108	1	107	54	.505	80,600	40,703
1 year	53	3	50	30	.600	39,897	23,938
2 years	20	2	18	11	.611	15,959	9,751
5 years	7	3	4	4	—	6,208	—
Widowed women							
At termination	65	0	65	2	.031	100,000	3,100
1 month	63	0	63	26	.413	96,900	56,880
1 year	37	1	36	7	.194	40,020	7,764
2 years	29	4	25	9	.360	32,256	11,612
5 years	16	12	4	4	—	20,644	—

Table 12.7 shows the data on the length of time that elapsed from the termination of marriage until the formation of the next marriage, if any. Some of the periods are extremely short, essentially simultaneous events, and the majority of those who will remarry do so within a year of termination. Table 12.7 shows that the pattern of remarriage is somewhat different for marriages that end in divorce and those that end in widowhood: Divorced women remarry more quickly. In many of the cases in which a divorced woman remarries within a month of termination, the cause of the divorce was that her husband objected to her sexual relations with another man, who in turn becomes the new husband.

Not shown in Table 12.7 is the age pattern of remarriage. The widowed women, who remarry more slowly and more often do not remarry, tend to be older than the divorced women. After the reproductive period is ended it seems to be a matter of convenience whether women remarry at all. One woman in her sixties reports that she went directly from her husband's burial site to join her sister in a polygamous marriage as a junior wife; it is not clear, in this particular case, whether the new husband was consulted.

Reproductively able women, however, generally have no difficulty in attracting a new husband. Typically the new marriage is arranged by the partners themselves rather than their parents, and typically it is preceded by sexual relations as a stage in forming the new marriage. A woman who is pregnant or lactating with a child of the previous marriage may find it difficult to attract a new husband temporarily, even though her need for a new husband to help with

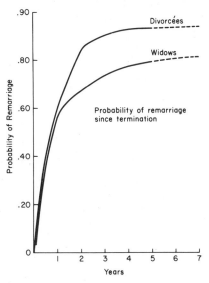

Figure 12.2. Probability of remarriage following termination of marriage by divorce or widowhood, time since termination.

the support of her other children may be acute. One of the cases of infanticide reported was by a woman who was pregnant when her husband died. She felt that she would be unable to marry for several years if the child survived, so she killed the baby at birth without apparently having already selected a new husband. She did remarry within a year or so of her husband's death, and later had two more children in addition to the three she had by the first husband.

Differences in Age Between Wife and Husband

Another important dimension of the marital behavior of a population is the distribution of differences in age between husbands and wives. This distribution of differences is important for social structure in that it determines the age patterns of affinal kinship relationship, ultimately determines the length of generations through influence on the difference in age of children and their parents, and may be important psychologically in determining the typical forms of marital attitudes and behaviors of the partners toward one another. We will examine the evidence from the contemporary !Kung on the differences in age of spouses as seen in 1968.

Although we are limited to only the relatively few recent marriages for purposes that require knowing the date of the marriage (such as the age at first marriage for the two sexes), we can learn about the differences in ages of spouses from the much larger group of marriages in which both parties are in the population and have had their ages estimated. The data collection is biased, however, by the requirement that both parties be in the 1968 population. Almost all of the husbands in the marriages ended by death (exceptions being those who died after 1963)—and many of the husbands in marriages ended by divorce—cannot be placed in the age sequence, so we cannot learn anything about age differences in these marriages. This is unfortunate, because it would be useful to know if the age difference of spouses is related to the probability of success or failure of marriage. Older women have had longer exposure to the risk of losing their husbands by death or divorce than younger women, so a smaller proportion of the marriages reported by older women enter into the analysis. The selection process is consistently biased toward loss of information for the marriages in which the husband was much older than the wife. The only woman who can be as much as 50 years younger than her husband, to take an extreme example, is a young woman, and an older woman who once made such a marriage will not be represented in the data presented here. These biases require that we continually question our interpretations of the raw data to ask what effects they are likely to have had.

Figure 12.3 shows the scattergram of difference in age of spouses by the current age of the wife (in 1968) for the 174 marriages reported by the women for which the ages of both parties could be determined. The central features of

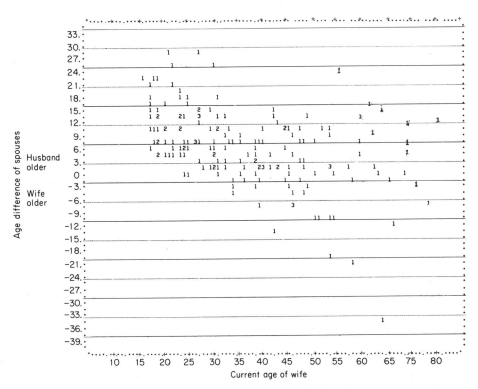

Figure 12.3. Age difference of spouses, by current age of wife, all marriages.

Figure 12.3 are clear: Husbands are more frequently older than their wives, 5.88 years older on the average. The largest differences in age tend to be seen among the youngest wives: Under age 30, it is not uncommon to find husbands 20 years and more older. Among older women these extreme differences are not seen, probably in part, as suggested above, because the husbands at those ages would be at high risk of death and perhaps also because marriages with large age differences have a higher probability of divorce than other marriages.

To understand how these patterns of age differences vary over the life cycle, we look at a subset of the data in Fig. 12.3, those marriages that were the first marriages for women. As we have seen before, women tend to marry for the first time during the teenage years and have virtually all been married by age 21. Some of the first marriages reported in Figure 12.4, therefore, have occurred long ago. Again the pattern is clear: Husbands are older than their wives at the women's first marriages. Only two women were tabulated as slightly older than their husbands, a finding that is likely to be due to errors in the age estimation procedure. Indeed, as we have described the marriage procedure, the husbands have to be older than the wives at first marriage because the men do not start to

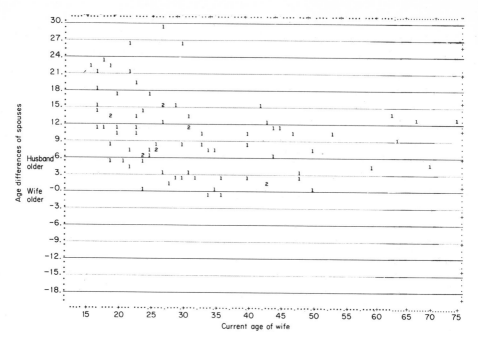

Figure 12.4. Age difference between spouses, first marriage for women only.

form marriages until the age when the women are all married. The mean difference in age of spouses for first marriages for women is 9.3 years, with a standard deviation of 7.6 years. The absence of marriages in which the husband is more than 15 years older than the wife for women over 30 is probably due to the likelihood that such marriages have ended with the death of the husband, rather than a real absence of such marriages when the older women were young.

When men marry for the first time, slightly more than half marry girls who are also marrying for the first time. In this culturally preferred form of first marriage, which is generally arranged by the parents of the two spouses, the bride will invariably be young and the husband will typically be between 22 and 30, about 9 years older than the girl.

As we can see in Figure 12.5, however, the men who marry women who have previously been married when they marry for the first time select wives who are closer to their own age, or who, in some cases, are considerably older. The mean difference in age of spouses for first marriages for men is only 3.43 years, although the standard deviation is still large (8.57 years). Clearly large differences in age of the spouses with the husband much older would imply that the man had to wait until a very advanced age for his first marriage. The extreme case in Figure 12.5—in which a man of 41 is 23 years older than his first wife—

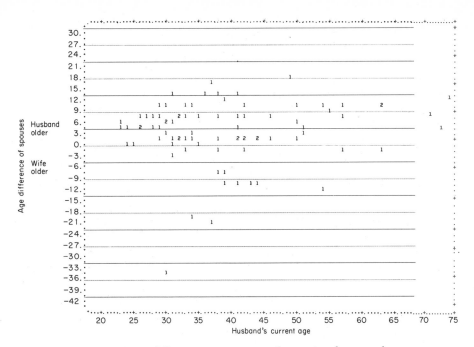

Figure 12.5. Age difference between spouses, first marriage for men only.

represents an unsuccessful man who has lived out much of his adult life without a wife.

A few young men have married women much older than themselves, in the extreme case a man of 30 married a vital and capable woman of 65. Several other men have married women 20 years their senior. Although these marriages are not likely to be reproductively successful and are very likely to be followed by marriages to younger women (either polygamously or after a divorce or death of the older wife), the marriage may offer a man who is unable to attract a younger woman some of the advantages of marriages, the "comforts of home." That there are no such marriages recorded for the men over 40 does not imply that the men did not make such marriages when they were young, as a woman who was 20 years older than him is unlikely to have survived to report the event.

We can see, therefore, that the differing ages of entrance into first marriage for the sexes builds in a tendency to what might be interpreted as a gerontocracy, without there being any ideological or behavioral predisposition to practice gerontocracy in marriage. When we look at the marriages to women past age 20, we see that there are 82 represented in Figure 12.3. Of these, in 47% of the marriages the wife is older or the same age as the husband, in 53% the husband is older. If we could follow cohorts of !Kung men and women as they experience

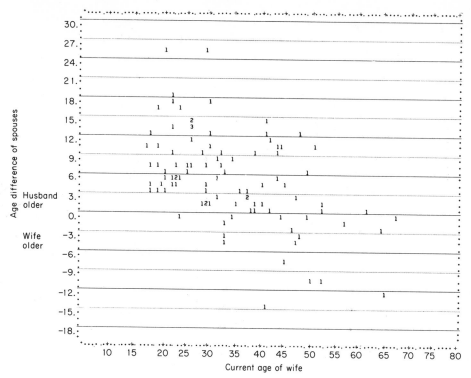

Figure 12.6. Age difference of spouses for reproductively successful marriages.

their marital histories, retaining all of the age differences of spouses in our tabulations, it seems likely that we could see a normal distribution of age differences with a mean of about 5 years older for the husbands.

From the point of view of the society and the population, the most important marriages are those that produce children, whereas the many marriages that are sterile are only important to the participants and to the families they link. Figure 12.6 presents the difference in age of spouses for the 99 marriages that produced at least one child. The mean difference in age of spouses is 6 years.

The impression formed from looking at Figure 12.6—that younger women have reproductively successful marriages with much older men but older women succeed primarily with men younger than themselves—is deceptive. Younger women cannot have had reproductively successful marriages with men younger than themselves because those men are not yet old enough to marry by !Kung cultural standards. Many of the older women who once had reproductively successful marriages with older men have seen those husbands die (and removed from possible inclusion in this body of data), but husbands younger than themselves are likely to still be available.

The "Two-Sex Problem" in Marriage

Every marriage implies the existence of a husband and a wife, and any statement made about the universe of marriages must apply to the husbands and wives equally. In a monogamous, endogamous group, the number of husbands and wives must be equal, and the number of each available forms a limitation on the number of the other sex who can be married. In small-scale populations, it can easily be shown by simulation that any rigid rules for matching spouses will regularly produce a situation in which substantial proportions of one or the other sex will be unable to marry due to random fluctuations in the sex ratio at birth and the sex ratio of mortality. Small-scale populations adjust to the supply of spouses by flexibility of the relative age of spouses, the extent of polygamy (or polyandry) and marriage outside the population, differences for the sexes in age at entrance to the marriage pool and age at leaving it, and by simply leaving some of the adults unmarried. How the society arranges the adjustment of numbers of available wives and husbands can be called the "two-sex problem" of marriage, although it need not be perceived as a problem by the people of the society.

The relative number of people of each sex is determined overall by the slightly greater number of males born (106 males per 100 females at birth is the mean for a large number of well-studied populations, 105 males per 100 females were observed among the 500 children born to interviewed !Kung women) and the slightly greater mortality of males from birth to old age. Strictly on the basis of the sex ratio in the population as a whole, then, we would expect to see a deficit in the number of males above any age. The ratio of males to females over the age of 10, for instance, is 91 males per 100 females for the stationary population formed by the life table of the !Kung. If the goal in such a society was to have all of the people over age 10 married all of the time, we would expect 9% of the females to fail to find a spouse or about 10% of the marriages to be polygamous.

Another way of adjusting the relative number of the sexes would be to permit the males to marry slightly younger than the females. The !Kung pattern, how-ever, is to permit women to marry at a younger age, 9 years younger than the men on the average, and with less variance in age at first marriage. Naturally, this greatly increases the expected deficit of potential husbands to potential wives over a given age. If we multiply the person-years lived at each age (the L_x column of the life table) by the cumulative percentage ever married at that age, the sex ratio of "potential husband-years" is only 68 for each 100 "potential wife-years." A relative scarcity of husbands, then, is a regular and expected part of the !Kung marriage system.

The later entrance of men into marriage is partially balanced by an earlier age of exit from marriage for women, at least an earlier age of exit from potentially fertile marriages. Women are fertile between the ages of 15 and 49, 35 years at the maximum. For most women the period is much shorter—16 years as we saw in Chapter 6. The fertility of men, however, is much less definitely limited by age, and men as old as 55 have been observed to become fathers. The supply of husbands for fertile marriages, then, is expanded by the older age of exit of men from such marriages.

Marriage Success Rates for Men and Women

We noted that almost all !Kung adults eventually marry, but we have also noted that individuals differ in their age at marriage and that some of the individuals may change marital partners once or more, and may spend some period of their adult lives as single, widowed, or divorced persons. Some individuals, then, may be said to have a high rate of "marital success" as measured by the proportion of their adult years during which they are married, whereas others have a low rate, spending relatively little of their adult life in the married state. Note that marital success does not mean here obtaining an attractive spouse, a happy marriage, or even a reproductively successful marriage.

For women, we can measure marital success by the time during the fertile years (15–49) that she is married. A woman who is continuously married during this period can be considered 100% maritally successful with a score of 35 years. A woman who marries by age 15 but divorces in the middle of the period and takes 6 months to remarry is 98.5% successful, with a score of 34.5 years. This measure is not entirely satisfactory, as there is on the average a much smaller loss of potential fertility at the beginning and ending of the fertile years than in the middle, when fertility is at its maximum, but it gives us a uniform method for computation. Note that Coale's I_m index, shown for the !Kung and other populations in Table 8.1, is a computation of the mean proportion of women in the fertile years who are married, weighted by fertility potential in each age group. Here we are interested not so much in the mean of that distribution, but in the differences between individuals.

We have no rigorous data on the exact numbers of years and months that women past reproductive age spent married, but we have fragmentary evidence from the marital status of women by age during the most recent decade and approximate reconstructions of the marital histories of the older women. Analysis of this information has been combined into a summary of the probable distribution of marital success rates for women at the end of the reproductive period, as shown in Figure 12.7. This figure shows that only about 25% of the women who survive to age 50 will have been continuously married throughout the reproductive years. A majority of the women have lost small amounts of time to marriage after age 15 and to the "waiting" periods between marriages when they change partners. A large proportion of the time lost to marriage, however, is contributed

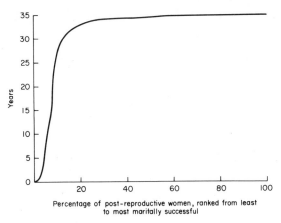

Figure 12.7. Distribution of years of marital success for women.

by a small proportion of the women, those who have been notably "unsuccessful" in marriage.

There is only one exception to the universality of marriage for women in the current population, a woman who had menarche many years later than other girls her age and was simply not chosen for marriage by any of the local men. She went on living with her parents well into her twenties, and went to live at a Bantu cattlepost when her sister married a man there. A !Kung man reports that when his wife died, he was asked to marry this woman, but as he reported it, "when I saw that she had no wits, I took her back to her people." She has demonstrated fertility by conceiving with a Bantu visitor, who never actually lived with her, and her son has survived. The explanation of her decisive rejection by !Kung men seems to be that she is mentally retarded.

Another woman, in her late thirties, is classified as divorced rather than single, but her marital success rate is hardly any higher than the mentally retarded woman. The divorced woman married around the time of her menarche, but stayed with her husband for only a few months before she asked to be returned to her relatives. As we have seen, this is a common situation among young women. In this case, however, the original marriage was not followed by a second. In 1968 she was somewhat crippled, and chronically withdrawn and angry in style. The crippling was said to have resulted from an accident that occurred well into her adult life, so it is unlikely that this alone is the cause of her lack of marital success. Like the first woman, she has demonstrated fertility by giving birth to a child with a Bantu father to whom she was not married. Long-standing mental illness is the probable cause of her lack of marital success. !Kung informants described both of these women as "lacking wits" and as *zu dole* (strange people, the term for non-!Kung). It is striking that both women derive most of their subsistence from Bantu families rather than !Kung, and do not follow the usual pattern of spending part of the time living by hunting and gathering out in the bush. It is doubtful whether either of these women could have survived long under completely bush-living conditions, as the same definition of them as "non-!Kung" (except to their close kin) may cause the withholding of essential support in the bush.

These women represent the extreme cases. There are, in addition, about 10–20% of the women who have spent some substantial period, on the order of 5–15 years, unmarried during their reproductive period of life. Some of these seem to have been selected more by their reproductive status at the time than by permanent characteristics. A woman who loses her husband through death or divorce soon after the birth of a new baby may remain unmarried for some years, providing that she has ties to kindred who will give her a place to live and a share of the meat hunters bring in, until she is ready to engage in the sexual relations that usually precede marriage for mature adults. Other women who lose their husband when they have an infant may marry a brother of the ex-husband, or may marry an otherwise undesirable spouse, one who is very old, sick, blind, or crippled.

Another category of women who may remain unmarried for relatively long periods of time during the reproductive years is made up of women who are known or believed to be infertile or reluctant to engage in sexual relations. One woman who is now past reproductive age told me that she didn't like men, and remained unmarried for a long period after the death of her first husband. Eventually she married a crippled man.

Marriages serve so many functions for the !Kung—love and parenthood, the formation of kinship ties, and simple economic services such as the provision of food, water, and firewood—that a woman who is undesirable as a sexual or reproductive partner may still be valued by a husband, albeit a relatively undesirable husband.

Now consider the distribution of marital success rates for men. We measure men's success not through the number of years of their own lives during which they are married, but by the number of years they are married to women in the reproductive period. Men's marital success is less constrained by biological factors than women's success, as a man can be simultaneously "pregnant," "lactating," and prefertile, through his links to different women, but a woman can be in only one of these states at a time. The possibility of polygamous marriage increases the possibility of marital success for the men far in excess of that of the women.

Detailed data on the number of woman-years of marriage for men have not been collected, but we can infer something about the shape of the marital success distribution from extreme cases and from the "two-sex" problem. Figure 12.8 shows an impressionistic version of the distribution of marital success for men. A few men are vastly more successful than others, achieving as much as 70 years of

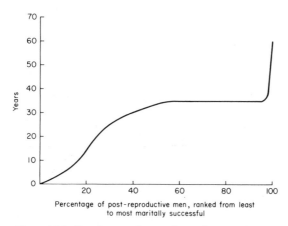

Figure 12.8. Distribution of years of marital success for men.

reproductively relevant woman-years by the time they are old through being married to several women throughout their reproductive lives. The largest group of men achieve a reproductive success of approximately 30–35 years, the duration of a single woman's fertile period. The group of relatively unsuccessful men is somewhat larger than the comparable group of women, as is implied by the greater success of a few. There were no men over age 40 in the 1968 Dobe population who had never been married, but there were several men in their late thirties who had not managed to get a wife yet. Marshall (1976:131) reports that there was one man in the Nyae Nyae region who had never been married by old age, a man with vision problems that prevented him from hunting. Among the relatively unsuccessful men in the Dobe area are several who have had a number of brief marriages terminated by divorce about which the wife complains, "he had a bad temper," or "he hit me." Sickness or physical handicap does not seem to be associated with low marital success for men, although these men may get relatively undesirable wives. It seems plausible, though it cannot be proven by data available here, that marital status is more closely associated with the probabilities of survivorship for men than for women, as the products of women's labor, the vegetable foods, are essential to the !Kung and are typically not widely shared beyond the nuclear family household, whereas unmarried women would routinely receive a share of meat brought into camp by hunters. Nevertheless, unmarried men can be observed, both at cattleposts and in bush camps, making their own huts and gathering and cooking their own vegetable foods.

Relating the person-years married implied in Figures 12.7 and 12.8 to one another is a complex task, made more difficult by the need to include the marriage participation of persons who die before the end of the reproductive span. Yet the "two-sex problem" reminds us that the two distributions must correspond. The form of the correspondence has rather important implications.

To the extent that some women are unmarried because they cannot obtain a husband, the women are effectively competing against one another for reproductive opportunities; to the extent to which some men are polygamously married in excess of the amount of polygamy needed to provide each marriageable woman with a husband, the men are competing against one another. The methodology of simulation happens to be a useful one for exploring "matching" problems of this kind, and AMBUSH will permit us to assess the need for polygamy, for example, in this population. AMBUSH cannot, however, mimic the marriage system of the !Kung perfectly, and it is not designed to take into account some factors that have introduced change into the !Kung marriage system recently.

Sources of Recent Change in Marriage

In recent decades there have been at least two processes of consequence for the !Kung marriage system, processes that represent changes from the pattern that must have existed when the !Kung were entirely engaged in a hunting and gathering life. The first of these is the possibility of marriage for !Kung women to Bantu men, an arrangement that has many attractions for the !Kung, who can thereby gain a kinsman far richer than any !Kung. The age pattern of marriages to Bantu can be seen in Table 12.1 for the 17 cases currently married at the end of the research period. These marriages, and 30 other marriages to Bantu or other non-!Kung that had been terminated by 1968, affect the sex ratio of marriages for the !Kung because the opportunity to marry out is not reciprocal for men and women. No !Kung man married a Bantu woman and the !Kung say that there is little or no sexual contact between !Kung men and Bantu women.

The second factor that may disturb current marital patterns from the traditional hunting and gathering pattern is the new possibility of employment of !Kung men (and sometimes women) in wage work. Some of the men are undoubtedly delaying marriage until after completion of a term of work as a cowboy, within or outside the study area, and some men have taken wage contracts at the Johannesburg gold mines. This factor may have raised the average age at marriage for men in the recent past and may do so increasingly in the decades to come.

In earlier chapters we have proceeded as though the analysis of fertility were simply a property of the supply of available mothers and their variations in fecundity over age and across individuals. But the "two-sex problem" directs our attention to the fact that every child born is equally a function of the supply of available fathers and their differences in fecundity over age groups and across individuals. The next chapter will show the evidence on the physical and social maturation of men, their age-specific fertility and differences between individuals in parity achieved, attempting to understand marriage and fertility as the intersection of properties of both the wife and the husband.

13

Fertility Performance of !Kung Men

!Kung men have received scant attention in the preceeding chapters, since we focused—as most demographic studies do—on fertility process as a function of the women. This chapter will attempt to repair the neglect, showing parallel data for men for some of the issues raised for the women, issues such as the timing of growth and maturation, entrance into marriage, and fertility. Some of the data in this chapter comes from direct observation of the !Kung men during 1967–1969, some comes from the women's reports on their husbands, and some has been provided by R. B. Lee, who carried out an interviewing study of the men at the time I was studying the women.

We begin with data on physical development. Frisch does not suggest that men have a critical level of fatness needed before they can become parents. On the contrary, it is known that during the adolescent growth period when the girls are depositing fat on their bodies the similar weight gains in young men are largely made up of lean muscle mass increases. Nevertheless, it is plausible that there are advantages in preventing parenthood by young men before the time they have completed their full growth, whether these restrictions are social or biological. We seek evidence, therefore, whether there is any relationship between fatherhood and completed growth in the males.

Growth and Development of !Kung Men

The methods for making height and weight measurements of the !Kung have been detailed in Chapter 7. As for the women, measurements for small children

TABLE 13.1
Weights of Five Male Infants in the Dobe Area, 1967–1969

I.D. number	Age in days	Weight in kg
561[a]	1	3.23
562	1	3.32
767	4	3.11
662	5	2.95
577	14	3.91

Mean weight for males = 3.30 kg.
SD = .366

Mean weight for all infants = 3.08 kg.
SD = .458

[a] At 10 days, kase (561) weighed 3.74 kg.

are probably skewed toward the older ones, those who were able and willing to cooperate in measurements. The weights of five !Kung male infants are shown in Table 13.1. All had !Kung fathers as well as mothers, and all survived the first year of life.

Figure 13.1 shows the height of individual men plotted by the age estimates made by the procedure described in Chapter 2. Use of a stable population model to estimate ages guarantees that the ages are not simply another perception based upon height. When we note irregularities in the number of people at a specific age (for example, four 17-year-olds and no 18-year-olds), we can be confident that the explanation of the irregularities of the age distribution can not be that the writer had an unconscious preference for calling adolescents 17 rather than 18. All it means is that on this particular occasion most of the boys estimated as 17-year-olds showed up to be measured while none of the 18-year-olds did. There may be a systematic reason for this, having to do with the work obligations of older boys, for instance, or it may well be simply due to a random fluctuation in the small numbers.

The pattern of height by age shown in Figure 13.1 is one of continuous increases in mean height to the age of 22. After 22, there is continued variability in height, but no further mean increase. The single sharpest increase in height is at 15-years old. Between 15 and 19, the boys gain over 25 cm of mean height. It is striking that the tallest men in the population are in their early twenties and all those over 170 cm are under age 40, so that their growth could have been affected by the changes in diet introduced by the arrival of cattle-keeping Bantu. The tallest (and heaviest) men are more likely than others to be currently employed in a regular capacity to work as cowboys for Bantu, or to have had work experience out of the area, but it is not clear whether this is due to the selective

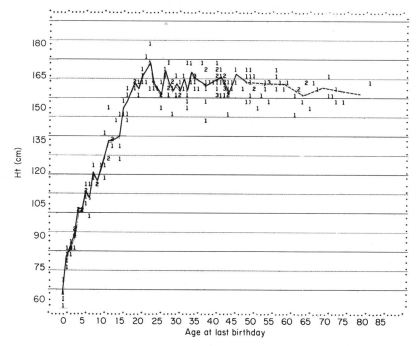

Figure 13.1. Scattergram and mean height by age, 191 men and boys.

factor that larger men find it easier to get these jobs or whether the diet changes associated with the jobs have actually made them bigger. The two tallest men, both in their early twenties, have relatively tall fathers *and* have grown up with a regular diet of milk by living on a cattlepost. The mean heights for men decrease somewhat in older ages, no doubt as a combination of differences in the diets they had as children and of changes in vertebrae and posture with old age.

The shortest adult men, the eight at 150 cm or less, all have "short" (*!oma*) as a nickname attached to their regular name, used as a term of address and reference. These short men are not necessarily handicapped by their stature: The group includes Kasupe, the successful father used to illustrate age estimates in Chapter 2 and several men well known and respected for their hunting ability.

Figure 13.2 shows the weights for these same men, by age. Clearly there is more variability in weight than in height, although it is striking that there is no obesity among these men. Some of the men are extremely thin: The 32-year-old who weighed 38 kg, for instance, was acutely ill with TB. In general, the lightest men tend also to be the shortest, as Fig. 13.3, clearly shows. The oldest men tend to be light and part of this trend is due to the previously noted tendency for them to be short. There is also a noticeable loss of muscle mass among the older men, who are often relatively strong and vigorous late into life, as the way of life

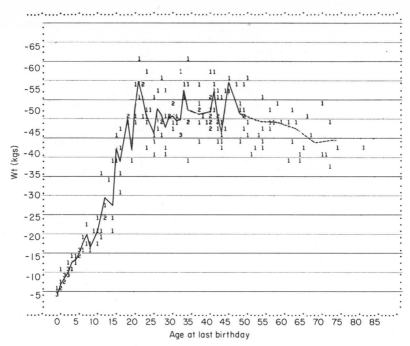

Figure 13.2. Scattergram and mean weight by age, 191 men and boys.

demands of them, but do lose weight and often have wrinkled skin that marks the process.

Figure 13.3 shows the scattergram of height and weight measures. It is striking how clearly the relationship of both height and weight to age can be seen in Figure 13.3, where no ages are given, as the correlation of height and weight for growing boys is a strong one. For the whole table, the Pearson product–moment correlation, $r = .9481$, suggests that about 90% of the variance in weight can be explained by height. The correlation is not so high, however, when computed only on the fully grown men. The short heavy boy who stands out on Fig. 13.3 at 99 cm and 20 kg has a Bantu father and is being cared for by both !Kung and Bantu relatives.

In Figure 13.4 the mean heights of the small numbers of people at a single year of age are plotted for both men and women, showing a jagged pattern from year to year, but a clear pattern over the life span. The boys tend to be only slightly taller than the girls of the same age throughout childhood. The means diverge significantly only after the age of about 15, when the girls approach their adult stature (reached by age 18) but the boys go on growing rapidly to age 20, reaching their full adult stature only around the age of 22. It is striking that in the

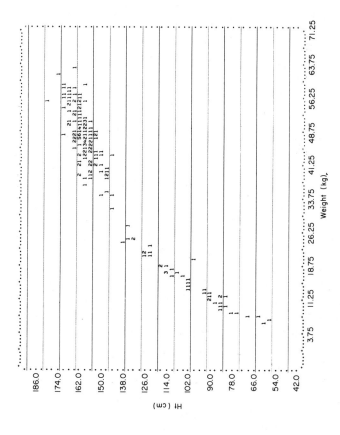

Figure 13.3. Height by weight, 191 men and boys. (r = 0.9481.)

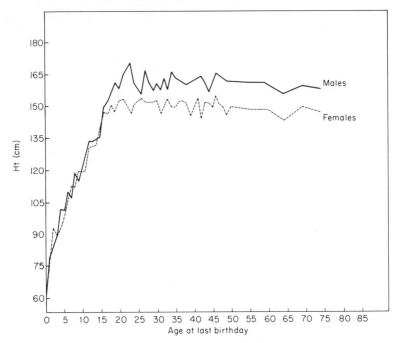

Figure 13.4. Mean height by age, for !Kung males and females.

field the teen-age boys appear to be considerably younger in facial features and mannerisms than the girls of the same age, even if they are taller.

Figure 13.5 shows the comparable data on mean weights for men and women, showing a divergence between the sexes in the late teens and early twenties that is maintained throughout adult life.

It is tempting to interpret the peaks and valleys in mean height for single years of age, where these coincide for the men and the women at that age, as evidence of environmental fluctuations at critical periods of their growth. The numbers at each age are too small to justify this interpretation, however, as individual variation is considerable.

Age at First Marriage

Part of the perception of immaturity of young men no doubt derives from their social status among the !Kung. At the ages when young women are having their first marriages, the !Kung would consider it impossible for a boy to marry, he is *šinaha dama !ko* ('still an infant') in the !Kung categories. Young men are supposed to have killed their first large animal and have been given the ritual

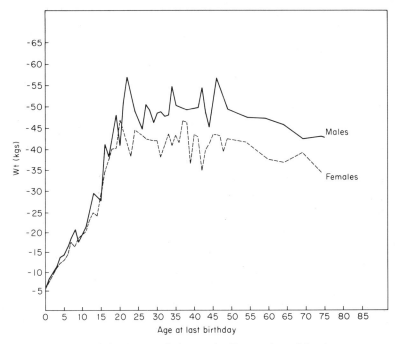

Figure 13.5. Mean weight by age, for !Kung males and females.

scars of the "first buck ceremony" from the accomplished hunters of the group before the women consider them adults. In fact, it is my impression that the young men attempt with varying degrees of success to be accepted as lovers by the young women, both married and single, for years before they are considered ready for marriage by themselves or by others. It is possible that the average age at marriage for men is somewhat older now than it was under traditional conditions, as some of the young men take up terms of work with cattle and put off both hunting and marriage until after the term is finished. Indeed, some young men show no interest in hunting and no interest in receiving the ritual of the "first buck" ceremony in the Dobe area today (though Marshall reports that such nonchalance about hunting was unknown in the Nyae Nyae area during the 1950s).

Young men who succeed in having sexual relations before their first marriage may obtain a wife if the woman becomes pregnant during the affair, as the woman is likely to divorce her husband and marry the father of her child. There is some evidence that young men are not always anxious to obtain a wife in this way. Wiessner's field assistant, a single man about 25-years old, lost enthusiasm about visiting a certain camp where Wiessner knew that he had an affair in progress. Asked about it, he said that her youngest child was getting big, and that

AGE AT FIRST MARRIAGE   **259**

TABLE 13.2
First Marriage Frequencies by Age for 18 Men Married for the First Time Between 1963–1968

Age (x)	N	Total (%)	N at risk at age x	Probability of marriage at age x (q_x)	At risk of marriage at age x (l_x)	Number of marriages at age x (d_x)	Proportion already married at exact age x
21	0	0	18				
22	4	22.2	18	.222	100,000	22,200	0.
23	4	22.2	14	.286	77,800	22,251	22.20
24	0	0	10		55,549		
25	1	5.5	10	.100	55,549	5555	44.45
26	1	5.5	9	.111	49,994	5549	50.01
27	2	11.1	8	.250	44,445	11,111	55.56
28	2	11.1	6	.333	33,334	11,110	66.67
29	1	5.5	4	.250	22,234	5558	77.77
30	0				16,676		
31	0						
32	0						
33	0						
34	1	5.5	3	.333	16,676	5553	83.32
35	0				11,123		
36	0						
37	1	5.5	2	.500	11,123	5561	88.88
38	0				5562		
39	1	5.5	1	1.000	5562	5562	94.44
40+	0				0		100.00

Mean age at first marriage = 26.67 years
SD = 5.24 years
Median age at first marriage = 25.5 years

she would probably get pregnant again soon. "It is her husband's turn now," he said (Wiessner personal communication 1976).

Compared with women, the pace of entrance into first marriage for men is slower and the absolute ages are higher, according to the data in Table 13.2, which presents age at first marriage for 18 men married between 1963 and 1969. The number of first marriages for men and women happened to be the same for both sexes, but these individuals did not necessarily marry each other. Some of the first marriages for both men and women were to people who had already been married before. In the whole population of 165 women, 65% of first marriages for women were to men marrying for the first time.

Table 13.2 shows that the beginning of risk of marriage comes at age 22 for men, with a rapid rise in proportion ever married to the mean at 26, differing from the distribution for women by the slower rate of approach to unity in the second half of the distribution. Clearly the distribution for men is not the same

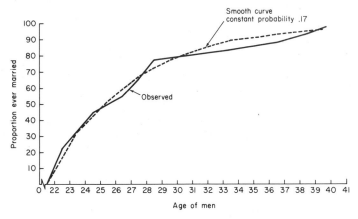

Figure 13.6. Proportion of men ever-married by age.

kind of a curve as the Coale series (shown in Figure 9.2), which is not claimed to fit the age distribution for men. The data for men can be described as a situation in which the probability of first marriage during the next year is a constant, estimated as .17 (for the ages 22–30). The cumulative proportion ever married grows at a decreasing rate because fewer men are still unmarried at increasing ages. Figure 13.6 shows the cumulative proportion married by age, the observed proportion based upon the data in Table 13.2, and the expected curve based on a constant probability of first marriage per year of .17.

Although the data collected on male reproductive performance is not as detailed as that collected for women, we can nevertheless explore some of the issues of men's fertility through the analysis of the same data collected for women. Each of the children reported has two parents, so whatever we learn about childbearing from the women can be examined from the male perspective as well.

From this data we will examine the age pattern of fatherhood and ask to what extent the men have a distinctive pattern of age-specific fertility apart from that of the women who were the mothers of their children. We will also look at the differential rates of reproductive success for men, though their parity distribution, and ask to what extent that distribution is different from that of the women due to polygamy and other factors.

Men's Age-Specific Fertility Rates

During the 1963–1973 period there were 241 births to !Kung mothers, 179 of which were allocated to mothers who were resident in the Dobe area and for

TABLE 13.3
**Men's Age-Specific Fertility Rates, 1963–1973
(Based on 142 Births to 147 Resident Dobe Men)**

Age	Single-year age groups			5-year age groups		
	Births	Man years	A.S.F.	Births	Man years	A.S.F.
20	0	33	.000			
21	2	32	.063			
22	2	31	.065	9	162	.056
23	2	31	.065			
24	3	35	.086			
25	3	34	.088			
26	6	38	.158			
27	4	38	.105	21	193	.109
28	6	42	.143			
29	2	41	.049			
30	13	44	.295			
31	3	43	.070			
32	5	41	.122	33	218	.151
33	7	46	.152			
34	5	44	.114			
35	4	41	.098			
36	5	46	.109			
37	6	46	.130	32	227	.141
38	11	48	.229			
39	6	46	.130			
40	7	46	.152			
41	3	42	.071			
42	9	41	.220	29	208	.139
43	6	42	.143			
44	4	37	.108			
45	4	39	.103			
46	5	39	.128			
47	4	30	.133	14	157	.089
48	0	25	.000			
49	1	24	.042			
50	2	24	.083			
51	0	23	.000			

(*continued*)

13. FERTILITY PERFORMANCE OF !KUNG MEN

TABLE 13.3 (*cont.*)

Age	Single-year age groups			5-year age groups		
	Births	Man years	A.S.F.	Births	Man years	A.S.F.
52	0	23	.000	4	115	.035
53	1	23	.043			
54	1	22	.045			
Totals	142	1,280	3.542	142	1,280	.720

Total fertility rate = 3.6
Mean age at birth of all children = 35.80 years
SD = 7.44 years
Median age = 36

whom I could be quite certain that all the births they had were known. Naturally all of the 241 births had fathers as well, but again many of these are better eliminated from the detailed analysis due to lack of certainty that all of the children born during the period, and all of the relevant characteristics of the men at risk of being those fathers, are known. Children with Bantu fathers (16 of the 241) are not tabulated. Another 85 fathers lived in the /du/da area rather than Dobe, or lived in Nyae Nyae, the east, or other areas, only known from temporary visits to Dobe or, in some cases, never seen at all.

During the 1963–1973 period, there were 147 resident Dobe men between the ages of 20 and 59 who were closely observed. These men were fathers to 142 children born during the same period. Table 13.3 shows the age-specific fertility rates for these men, calculated by the same methods as used for Table 7.1.

As we see in Table 13.3, the fertility of the resident Dobe men during the period seems to be lower than that of the Dobe women that we examined in Chapter 9. Part of this lower level of performance is due to Bantu men competing with !Kung men for the reproductive capacity of the !Kung women, occupying about 7% of the reproductive opportunities. Some of the lower level, however, is likely to be due to underrecording of births to men, since the link between father and child, although known to the !Kung and ascertainable through careful questioning, is not so obvious as that of the women, who can be seen pregnant and carrying the child. Many of the births to women in the Dobe area were fathered by men from outside the area and it is entirely possible that a similar study carried out in the man's district of residence would miss the Dobe births. Similarly, Dobe men may have children born outside the area which they genuinely do not know about for some period of time, or, more likely, that they know about but I do not.

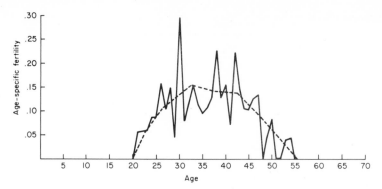

Figure 13.7. Age-specific fertility rates for !Kung men, 1963–1973.

This problem was illustrated by the man who we observed (in Chapter 3) beating his wife with a donkey whip over a fight about whether he should take their sole blanket on a visit to another woman. The wife had two births during the 11-year period of observation; the second woman (who is not in our group of residents) had at least one by him. And during the last days of the field work, in 1969, he had a surprise visit from a third woman and her family, who brought a 4-year-old who also turned out to be his child, much to the chagrin of his long-suffering first wife. We tabulate this man as having four births during the period; whether there are more yet to be discovered, we cannot be sure. The extent of this man's extramarital breeding seems to be unusual among the !Kung, but there may be other undetected cases.

Despite the possibility of underrecording of births, we can learn something of male reproductive patterns from Table 13.3. The age pattern of male fertility differs from that of women in that it is an older pattern, from ages 20 to 54 rather than 15–49; and it is a flatter pattern, with a plateau of fertility between ages 30 and 44 rather than the peak during the twenties observed from the data on

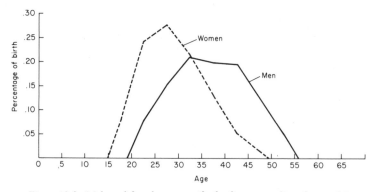

Figure 13.8. Male and female age-specific fertility rates, adjusted to total 1.

13. FERTILITY PERFORMANCE OF !KUNG MEN

women. Figure 13.7 shows the single-year and the 5-year rates for men, and Figure 13.8 shows the 5-year rate for men and for women, adjusted to a common base of 1.00. The mean age of fathers at the birth of their children was 35.80 with a standard deviation of 7.44 years. The youngest father was 21 (a young man who was not permitted to marry until after the birth of his child) and the oldest was 54 during the period.

Men's Fertility by Age and Age of Wife

We generally assume that the scarce resource in fertility is the women's reproductive capacity, since men's capacity for fertility generally appears to be biologically simpler and more dependent upon social and cultural rather than biological sources of variation. Men begin to produce viable sperm sometime around the time of full growth, probably somewhat sooner. Reproductive capacity seems to decline only very gradually over time.

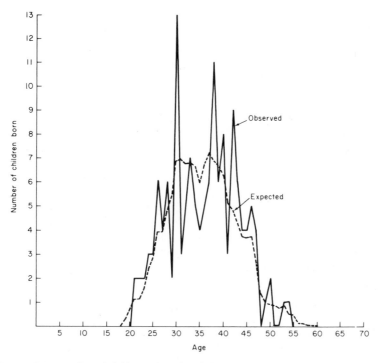

Figure 13.9. Number of children expected and observed to be born to men at age x (note—"expected" calculated from the age-specific fertility rates of their wives).

We can explore the question of whether the men have an age-specific fertility pattern distinct from that of the women they are married to by comparing the observed numbers of children to men in age groups with the number of births we would expect to see in a group of men of that size if their annual probabilities of birth were merely that of the women at the ages of their wives.

This calculation has been performed, for the men included in Table 13.3, summing the probabilities of birth to women at the age of each of their wives over the time period (if there are three men age 25 in 1963, for instance, and one is married to a woman 22, one is married to a woman 18, and one is unmarried, we sum .208, .063, and 0, the probabilities for women of giving birth at those ages). Polygamously married men have the sum of their wives' probabilities; unmarried men have zero probability. The age-specific fertility rate for the wife is used even if that woman is known to be sterile. Figure 13.9 presents the conclusions of those calculations and shows that there is a remarkably close agreement between the numbers expected on the basis of the wives' characteristics and the observed numbers, a finding that suggests that underreporting of births is not significant in this data collection, and that indicates that there is no evidence in the men's reproductive performance that they are unable to produce children, either at the young ages or at the older ages, but merely that they are unable to obtain wives who are in the peak reproductive years at those ages.

During the late teens and early twenties, the explanation for low male fertility seems to be simply that many of the women whom these men will ultimately marry are still children, or are in the 15–19 age group, when age-specific fertility for women is low. The restraint on male fertility seems to be exercised by the society as a whole through not allowing these men to marry.

At the other extreme, the declining fertility of men over age 45 reflects the declining fertility of their aging wives: Whether their own fertility is also declining we cannot know without sperm counts or observing them attempting to conceive with young women. It is interesting to note, when you go through the material case by case, that the oldest men who are married to the youngest girls are conspicuously *not* the most successful and dominant men of that age group, but are quiet, inconspicuous men who are marrying for the first time at an advanced age. The women in these marriages have not demonstrated much reproductive success, in part, I suspect, because they are semi-handicapped women who were not highly valued on the marriage market, due to sterility, unconventional behavior, or a low level of intelligence. One of the largest age differences between spouses in a marriage involving a young woman and a man about 50 varies from this generalization in the other direction: The man is a popular and dominant individual who has never had a child despite five marriages, each of which lasted several years. The first four of his wives had children before or after marriage to him. He is probably infertile and has been given this young wife as a gesture of support and sympathy in his problem.

TABLE 13.4
Number of Births During 11-year Period for Men (by Age in 1963)

Age in 1963	Number of men	Number of births					
		0	1	2	3	4	5
10–14	19	15	4				
15–19	12	6	4	2			
20–24	17	6	6	2	2	1	
25–29	20	5	6	2	6	1	
30–34	19	11	2	2	4		
35–39	25	8	3	4	3	5	2
40–44	9	7	1	0	1		
45–49	11	8	1	2			
50–54	9	8	1				
55–59	6	6					
Total men	147	80	28	14	16	7	2
Total children	142	0	28	28	48	28	10

Differential Success

Table 13.3 shows the age pattern of reproductive success, but does not provide information about differences in success between individuals. We explore this question by asking how many children were born to particular men during the same 11-year period used for the women. Table 13.4 shows the results of this tabulation, with the number of births during the period cross-tabulated by the age of the men in 1963. As was seen with the women (Table 7.4), there is a triangular pattern in Table 13.4, with men who are just entering the reproductive period and men who are in the process of leaving it during the period achieving lower numbers of births. The men 25–39 in 1963 have the greatest reproductive success in the subsequent 11 years, with the men 35–39 most successful.

The 147 men father 142 children, producing a mean number per parent very similar to the women's distribution. To compare the differential success among the members of the two sexes, Figure 13.10 shows a Lorenz curve of the inequality distributions for the sexes separately. Only those of each sex who have one or more children during the period are included, showing that $x\%$ of the parents (those who had only one child during the period) have $y\%$ of the children, and so on. Figure 13.10 shows that there is very little difference in differential reproductive success between the sexes over a set period of time.

This conclusion is not an obvious one. One would think that men, via polygamous marriages, would have the opportunity to have much more reproductive success than women. If we look at the nine most successful men, those

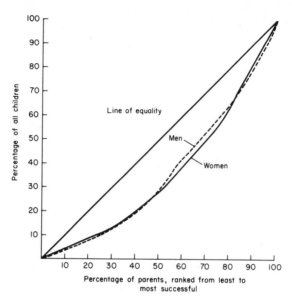

Figure 13.10. Lorenz curve of reproductive success of men and women, 1963–1973.

who had four or five children during the period, we see that polygamy plays some role in men's reproductive success, but not an overwhelming one. One of the men who had five children is polygamously married to sisters, one of whom is in her early thirties and had two children between 1963 and 1969; her younger sister was still prefertile. By 1973, when Lee made another census, the older wife had one more child and the younger sister had two. Since this man had two children by a wife who died prior to this polygamous marriage, and two children by the senior wife prior to 1963, he had altogether nine children by the age of 46, and his younger wife still has many childbearing years ahead of her. It seems likely that this man will be the "champion" father of his generation. Since he lives on a cattlepost, and is a responsible employee with access to milk, meat, and grains, he is not likely to have difficulty providing for his large family.

The other man who had five children during the 11-year period lives in the bush, and is monogamously married to a woman at the height of her fertile years.

Among the men who had four children during the period, one is the man mentioned above who had four children by three women, not forming a polygamous household in the usual !Kung way, but attempting to deceive and conceal each of the women from the others. This man's "reproductive strategy" seems to be refusal to play by the rules of the game. It is not at all clear, of course, that reproductive success is the goal of his behavior. The other six men who had four children each during the period are all monogamously married.

13. FERTILITY PERFORMANCE OF !KUNG MEN

TABLE 13.5

Parity Distribution (Number of Children Ever Born), by Number of Times Married (Polygamously and Monogamously) for 35 Men Age 50 and Over

Number of children ever born	Number of times married								
	0	1	2	3	4	5	6	7	Total
0	0	1	1			1			3
1	0	1							1
2	0	2	1	1					4
3	0	0	1	2					3
4	0	0	1	1					2
5	0	0	1	4					5
6	0	1	0	1	0	1	1		4
7	0	1	2	1	2				6
8	0	1	0	1	1				3
9	0	1	2						3
10	0								0
11	0								0
12	0	0	0	1					1
Total	0	8	9	12	3	2	1		35
$\bar{X}$		4.38	5.11	5.42	7.33	3.00	6.00		5.14

Variance = 8.60
SD = 2.93

The topic of differential reproductive success can be further explored from another source of information, the completed reproductive careers of 35 men age 50 and over interviewed by Lee. These men had between 0 and 12 children apiece over their lifetimes, with a mean of 5.14 (compared to the women's mean of 4.69) and a variance of 8.60 (compared to the women's variance of 4.87). Clearly reproductive success is more unequally distributed among men than it is among women, when whole lifetimes are examined. Table 13.5 shows the parity distribution of the men past 50 in 1968.

Men's Parity Distributions

On the average a group of newborn males will have the same number of children ever born as a group of newborn females from the same population, but the distribution of reproductive success can be much more unequal among the males than it is for the females.

One of the reasons why this is true is that prereproductive mortality is heavier on males than it is on females. As was seen in Chapter 4, infant and childhood mortality rates are usually higher for males; the available evidence for the !Kung, from the mortality to children born to 165 mothers, suggests that the !Kung are no exception to this generalization. For females, the probability of surviving to age 15, which may be taken as the beginning of the reproductive period, is .550. For males the probability of surviving to the same age is .534. The difference between those probabilities represents the component due to higher mortality for males. As we have seen, however, men do not actually begin to be at risk of birth until age 20, and the probability of surviving to that age for men is only .509. Higher prereproductive mortality for males means that there are fewer potential fathers available and so some men will have to have more children to make up for those who have none.

Mortality continues to skew the male parity distribution throughout the life span more for men than for women, in small part because of higher probabilities of death at each age, in greater part due to the older age at which men have their children. The mean age of women at the birth of all their children is about 27.5 and the probability of women surviving from birth to that age is .478, but the mean age of men at the birth of their children is about 35 and the probability of men surviving to that age is only .405. When we compare postreproductive men and women (Table 13.5 and Table 6.2), we note that a smaller proportion of the men survive to the end of the reproductive period to report their success.

Table 13.5 shows the number of children ever born to men age 50 and over. Note that we include men in the last few years of the childbearing period, just as we included women in the age group 45–49, in order to increase the numerical base as much as possible, recognizing that these people will have very few additional children, if any.

Table 13.5 includes an additional source of variance in men's parity distribution: the possibility that men can be married to several fertile women, simultaneously (through polygamy) or in sequence, thereby vastly increasing their chances for reproduction.

The data comparing reproductive success for men and women is shown in two ways. Figure 13.11 is a Lorenz curve, parallel to that of Figure 13.10, which compares reproductive success of men and women over the 11-year period, but computed on reproductive careers as a whole for people past reproductive age. Figure 13.12 shows the parity progression ratios (see Chapter 8, pp. 156–158) of !Kung men and women. Both forms of data presentation agree in the conclusion that reproductive success is significantly more unequal for men than for women.

Ten of the men past 50 had been married polygamously, yet a careful examination of the data case by case reveals that polygamy is the crucial feature of the most successful men but plays a minor role in differential reproductive success overall. Most of the polygamous marriages, even if established for a while, are unsuccessful in the sense that one of the wives "refuses," in the characteristic !Kung term, and leaves, so that polygamy is no different from a

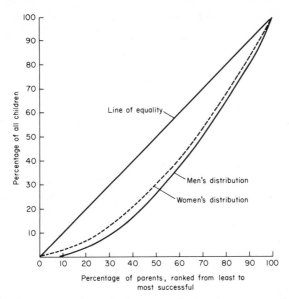

Figure 13.11. Lorenz curve of reproductive success of men and women, completed reproductive careers.

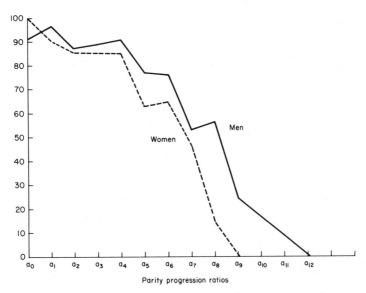

Figure 13.12. Parity progression ratios: !Kung men and women past reproductive age.

MEN'S PARITY DISTRIBUTIONS   **271**

divorce and change of marital partners. Perhaps the example of the history of a much-married man will illustrate the issues. In his youth, this man married a woman who was both fertile and willing to tolerate polygamy. Over the years she had five children, during which time her husband married three young girls, one after the other, each of whom was premenarchial and each of whom left after some weeks or months. Whether the senior wife deliberately made things difficult for the young girls, I do not know, as she has died and was not interviewed. In his forties, the man finally succeeded in obtaining a mature second wife, by marrying the widow of his older brother, who must have been about 35 at the time. They had one child, and this marriage persisted until after the death of his first wife, although the junior wife was described as independent, and spent a fair amount of time away from the husband and the first wife, visiting her own relatives. Lee observed in 1964 that he had three wives at that time, the main wife, who was getting old and sick, the second wife, who spent much of her time away, and a third wife, a widow who was postmenopausal when he married her. Since that time he has been reduced to only the third wife, and he is old and blind but still a vital and active member of his group, well-known for his trance performances and curing. Clearly this man has been dominant and active all of his life, but we note that the number of children that have resulted from these six marriages is only six, a level of reproductive success matched by many of the men who had only one or a few wives.

The most successful man, the one who had 12 children, was polygamously married to two women, but the second fell to him by the chance of his older brother's death rather than being actively sought. The first wife had 9 children, (she is among the most successful !Kung women) and the second wife had 3 by him.

Some of the other men's histories demonstrate that polygamy is a risky strategy for increasing one's number of children, as there is a substantial risk that one of the women will refuse the marriage and opt for divorce instead; if this woman has substantial reproductive opportunities ahead, the man may be less well off than before the attempt at polygamy. A safer strategy is to have a family with one woman and then, at the age when her fertility is declining and his is still high, marry for a second time and have a second family. This strategy, however, requires an early first marriage for the man. Serial monogamy is as effective as polygamy in increasing reproductive success for men, while having two families simultaneously is difficult to manage, both economically (in providing for a large number of dependents) and socially (in avoiding the conflicts and irritations of polygamous marriage). The chances of managing the interpersonal problems seem to be improved when the two wives are sisters, and, interestingly enough, when one is the widow of the husband's brother.

Many of the polygamous marriages observed are postmenopausal for one or both women, or involve a sterile woman as one of the wives, so that polygamy has little reproductive significance.

TABLE 13.6
Parity Distribution by Number of Reproductively Successful Marriages for 35 Men Age 50 and Over

Number of children ever born	Number of reproductively successful marriages			
	1	2	3	Total
1	1			1
2	3	1		4
3	1	1	1	3
4	2			2
5	4	1		5
6	3	1		4
7	5	1		6
8	2	1		3
9+	1	3		4
Total	22	9	1	32 [a]
$\bar{X}$	5.27	6.44		5.14
Variance	4.97	7.03		8.60

[a] Three men had no reproductively successful marriages.

Table 13.6 shows the effective contribution of multiple marriages on the reproductive success of men, in contrast to Table 13.5, which showed the gross numbers. The men who have had only one reproductively successful marriage have an average of 5.36 children, whereas those who have two or more reproductively successful marriages (only one man had three) have an average of 6.6 children. Multiple marriages among the !Kung, then, add to but do not multiply men's reproductive success.

Population Growth as Measured Through the Male Generation

We earlier calculated a !Kung net reproduction rate of 1.0776 (see Table 11.1, p. 214), implying an annual rate of growth of .0026, from the data on women. Since the males and females are two halves of the same population structure, the men should show the same rate, even though they have slightly higher mortality, a different age structure of fertility, and a longer generation length. Table 13.7, which shows the computation of the gross and net reproduction rates for the men, shows a net reproduction rate less than unity, and an annual rate of population growth estimated as −.0113 per year. According to

TABLE 13.7
Gross and Net Reproduction Rates Calculated on Males

Age interval	Midpoint	Birth rates (sons only)	Person-years $_5L_x/l_0$	Sons per newborn male[a]	R_1[b]
20–24	22.5	.0287	2.4639	.0707	1.5908
25–29	27.5	.0558	2.2943	.1280	3.5200
30–34	32.5	.0773	2.1151	.1635	5.3138
35–39	37.5	.0722	1.9232	.1389	5.2088
40–44	42.5	.0712	1.7166	.1222	5.1935
45–49	47.5	.0456	1.4995	.0684	3.2490
50–54	52.5	.0179	1.2714	.0228	1.1970

Gross reproduction rate =		.8438			
Net reproduction rate =				.7145	
Mean age at childbirth =					25.2729

T = mean length of a generation = R_1/net reproductive rate = 35.37
r = intrinsic rate of natural increase = net reproductive rate − $1/R_1$ = −.0113

[a] Column 3 multiplied by column 4.
[b] Mean age at childbirth; column 2 multiplied by column 5.

these calculations, the female population is growing and the male population is declining in size.

Part of the explanation of this unlikely situation is artifactual. We used estimates of both fertility and mortality from the pre-1950 period for the women, but we combined pre-1950 mortality with fertility estimates for the 1963–1973 period for the men. Another part of the explanation is derived from the real recent changes in !Kung marriage and parenthood. !Kung men are now competing with Bantu men for reproductive opportunities and are losing a substantial proportion of the woman-years available. Both sexes are suffering the results of sterility induced by venereal disease, whether the sterility is primarily affecting the wife or the husband.

This unlikely conclusion directs our attention again to the pitfalls of empirical study of small populations and the usefulness of simulation methods as an adjunct to empirical studies. Internal inconsistencies in population structure, such as this one, can and do occur as a result of small number fluctuations and the loss of data that results from migration in real populations. By artificially closing the population to migration and by accurately keeping track of the events for individuals as they vary stochastically over time, simulation allows us to explore the internal consistency and interactions of the various parameters that we observe empirically. A schedule of age at entrance to marriage and proportions married in the various age groups determines the supply of available spouses and hence the supply of potential parents; and the supply of parents and their age-specific fertility rates determine the absolute numbers and the distributions across families of children ever born. These distributions, in turn, determine the properties of the kinship system, in ways that will be discussed later. Simulation, then, is a tool that permits us to explore whether it is possible for a population to function in the way we have described it. This is probably the most valuable property of simulation studies.

Simulation can provide an answer to the question of whether it is possible for a large number of statements about a population to all be true at the same time, in a way that formalized theory can not. The value of the answer, of course, depends in large part upon the degree of realism built into the simulation procedures. The method of simulation used here, AMBUSH, is not entirely successful in providing a realistic model of the population structure of the !Kung, but nevertheless provides some insights into the !Kung population structure that we could not obtain without it. In the next chapter, we turn to the task of construction of our most realistic simulation model for the !Kung, and examine its limitations.

14

The Simulation of
Fertility Within Marriage

We return now to the task of constructing a more realistic simulation of populations like the !Kung, so that we can exploit these simulations to tell us about aspects of the population structure that are otherwise invisible. The model constructed in this chapter will be the best version of simulation used in this work, although I would not, of course, argue that it is the best and most realistic simulation that could possibly be constructed to mimic the !Kung. All simulations are simplifications, since in model construction there is a trade-off between theoretical clarity, generally achieved by making the model as simple as possible, and precision in tailoring the model to the target population, which usually requires introducing complexity. In general, AMBUSH has been constructed to operate as simply as possible, so that the outputs can be understood in terms of the interactions of a few processes. Nevertheless, the procedures used must be understood in order to interpret the outputs; these procedures are sufficiently complex that this chapter is devoted to explaining them. The first section of this chapter will explain how AMBUSH arranges marriages and generates fertility within those marriages. We will then look at the input probabilities to the simulations and the outputs of those variables (as they interact) and others produced directly by the input. Along the way, we see some of the implications of the solution of the "two-sex" problem for men's fertility and the growth rate of the population as measured for the two sexes.

The AMBUSH Method for
Generating Marriages

The units of analysis in AMBUSH are, of course, computer records, not people, although we call them people for convenience. Each has an age and a sex, a birth and a death, and eventually a marital and reproductive history.

At the time of birth of one of these "people," the sex, the future age at death and the future age of eligibility for marriage is generated from probability schedules and stored for future activation. When the age of eligibility for marriage arrives, assuming that the person has survived to this age, he or she enters the pool of potential spouses after the processing of births and deaths for that year has been completed.

The pool consists of a list of people mixed in sex and ranked in age from oldest to youngest. To form marriages, each year AMBUSH starts with the oldest man in the pool and begins the search for an appropriate spouse with the oldest woman younger than him. We simplify the marriage choice process by ignoring the !Kung rules for avoiding marriage with anyone who has the same name as a close relative. In order to make the kinship structure realistic, however, we mimic the !Kung incest rule, which forbids marriage with first cousins and closer kin. AMBUSH checks the kinship connection between the pair of potential spouses by access to a map of ties; if the two share a common grandparent, the match is rejected and the next oldest woman on the list is tried. When AMBUSH finds a proper match, the two are marked married and removed from the pool. Their subsequent joint fertility history is generated (explained below) and the kinship map is updated to include their marriage. AMBUSH moves on to the next oldest man and repeats the search process, continuing through the list until all men have found or failed to find wives among the women in the current pool. Since matches are symmetrical, we would have the same number of marriages if we started with the women and sought a husband for each, although the identity of some of the partners might be different. The number of marriages formed will be limited by the supply of the scarcer sex and the availability of non-incestuous partners.

We have seen that !Kung men and women have characteristic and rather different rates of entrance to first marriage by age. We can mimic that feature of the simulated populations by adjustment of the eligibility schedule for men and women. We note, however, that in attempting to mimic the real !Kung population in the simulations, it is the output of these simulations, not the input, that we wish to match. Input variables may interact in unpredictable ways, so we resort to "fine tuning" the inputs to maximize the fit to the real population. Since outputs are stochastic, this sometimes requires a considerable amount of experimentation.

Results of this experimentation show that when we admit the women to the marriage eligibility pool with a probability of .33 at ages 14, 15, and 16, we obtain a reasonably close approximation to the age at first marriage for the simulated women among those who succeed in getting a husband.

Experimentation with men's eligibility schedules demonstrate that the current ages at first marriage for men introduce too great a difference between the ages of husbands and wives (in part because we do not permit simulated men to marry women older than themselves) and leave too many women unable to obtain husbands. The input eligibility schedule for men in the simulations, therefore, has been adjusted by speeding up the rate of entrance of men into the marriageable category. The minimum age at marriage in the simulations is kept at age 22, as observed, but we increase the rate of entrance into the pool to 15% of the cohort for each age from 22 to 27, with 5% entering the pool at ages 28 and 29.

Even after increasing the supply of available husbands in this way, the men are still much scarcer in the marriage pool. About 95% of the men succeed in marrying during the first year they are in the pool and less than 1% fail to marry after 5 years. Among the women, however, only about half of the eventually successful marry during their first year in the pool, with about 15% successful in each of the following 4 years. After attempting marriage in 5 successive years, we regularly see that about 10% of the young women who are trying to marry for the first time still have no husband. If we leave these women in the pool longer, their presence distorts the age distribution of first marriages for women, as these necessarily older women have preference over those just entering the pool under the marriage rules of AMBUSH. Rather than allow this to happen, we remove any person, male or female, who has been in the pool 5 years without success, mark them "never married," and give them no opportunity to have children.

This procedure is admittedly a distortion of events in the !Kung population, in which the equivalent women would obtain husbands by polygamy, and would therefore not be deprived of all opportunity for reproduction. By coincidence, the proportion of "never married" women is approximately equal to the expected number of involuntarily sterile women we would expect to see in a population like the !Kung (discussed in Chapter 6, pp. 123–127). We could, of course, institute a procedure in AMBUSH for assigning these "never married" women to be second wives of married men, but this change would complicate the marriage process enormously, as the formation of polygamous marriages influences the future supply of husbands and wives in complex ways. Rather than complicate the simulation process in this way, we restrict AMBUSH to forming monogamous marriages and we tolerate the small but systematic distortions in the population structure that this procedure implies.

Differences in the age of spouses are produced mechanically in the simulations by the matching procedure, which searches for the wife closest in age but younger than the man, and hence is a product of the supply of available partners. It is interesting to see that the simulations duplicate the age differences between spouses in the !Kung population quite closely, if we look only at the couples in which the man is older. The mean age difference is somewhat greater in the simulations and the variance is considerably less, because we do not allow men to marry women older than themselves.

In AMBUSH, as in the real world, marriages can end in three ways, by the death of the wife, by the death of the husband, or by divorce. The probability of the end of the marriage through death is merely the probability associated with the ages of the two spouses, respectively.

We saw in Table 12.6 that the probability of divorce in !Kung marriages is quite high: Approximately 45% of the marriages end in divorce during the first 10 years of marriage. We also noted in Chapter 12, however, that many of these marriages that end in divorce are of little demographic consequence, since they are extremely short marriages, sometimes lasting only a few days or weeks, and the participants may remarry very quickly. Since in the AMBUSH simulations a change of marital partners frequently costs the woman some opportunities for fertility, we would be exaggerating the importance of divorce to simulate them all. Hence the divorce rate used in these simulations is a fraction of the observed divorce rate: Of all marriages formed, 20% of them are slated for divorce, if the marriage does not end by the death of one of the participants first. Concretely, a random number is drawn for each new marriage to determine if and when it will end in divorce. In 80% of the cases, the marriage is not slated for divorce, and will continue until the first death of one of the partners; for the 20% for whom divorce is scheduled, the timing is .50 during the first year of the marriage; .22 during the second year; .065 during the third year; .043 for each year from the fourth to the seventh year of marriage; and .022 for the eighth and ninth years of marriage. No divorces occur during or after the tenth year of marriage. This distribution is a reduction and truncation of the distribution of divorce shown in Table 12.6. The achieved percentage of marriages that end in divorce is somewhat higher than the initial probability, as marriages that end in divorce are shorter than other marriages.

When marriages end by the death of one of the spouses, the other is put back into the marriage pool during the same year and allowed to search for a spouse along with those marrying for the first time. At divorce, both parties are put back into the pool and allowed to find a new spouse and there is no procedure to prevent them remarrying each other. At the time of all marriages, first or remarriages, a fertility history for that marriage and a risk of divorce will be generated and stored for future activation. Only the "never married" and persons over age 55 are not returned to the marriage pool at the end of a marriage.

The AMBUSH Method for
Generating Births for Marriages

The birth generation process in AMBUSH has been discussed in Chapter 11 for the case in which fertility is generated for women regardless of marital status. The method used when fertility is generated only within marriages is the same, except that the procedure occurs at the time of her marriage instead of her birth and only those births generated that fall within the years of the current marriage are utilized, others are discarded. If a woman married at age 22, for example, and a divorce is scheduled for 3 years later, a fertility history for the marriage is produced by drawing nine random numbers, each of which can result in no birth or a birth at an age between 15 and 49. Only those births that fall on her ages 23–25 will be incorporated into the population as the fertility of this marriage; those that fall on younger and older ages will be disregarded. If she remarries at age 27, again she will have nine tries at birth, out of which all that fall on ages below age 28 and past the date of termination of this marriage will be ignored.

Generating fertility only within marriages clearly increases the variance in reproductive success between individuals. Since a woman has a birth history generated as many times as she is married, it is possible that some may ultimately have more than nine births during a reproductive career (although we will see that this is rare). Because a considerable number of woman-years are lost to the fertility process through nonmarriage, both years in the group of "never married" and some years prior to and between marriages, the probability of success in each trial for the women who are married must be raised in order to prevent the population as a whole from declining in size. We want to mimic the !Kung age-specific fertility rates for the total population. To do so, experimentation shows that our parameter B (which was equal to the total fertility rate in the simulations of Chapter 11) must be raised to 5.80 under these marriage conditions, so that the probability of a success on each trial (B/C) in these simulations is .644. In addition, the input probability of birth is raised slightly at the young ages, when relatively few women are married, in order to produce a !Kung-like age-specific fertility schedule for the total population.

What we are doing in modifying the simulations by raising the fertility of married women to compensate for the loss of fertility to women for whom we are unable to arrange a marriage might be best understood by looking at the simulated populations in terms of Coale's measures of total fertility (I_f), marital fertility (I_g) and proportion married (I_m), which we examined for the !Kung and a range of other populations in Chapter 8. The average of five long simulations have an I_f of .36 in comparison to the rate computed for the 1968 !Kung population of .34. The rate is slightly higher in the simulations because we are mimicking the pre-1950 !Kung population. The measure I_g is .44 in the simula-

TABLE 14.1
Input to AMBUSH: Individual Probabilities of Vital Events by Age and Sex

Age	Males Death (d_x)	Males Eligibility for marriage	Females Death	Females Eligibility for marriage	Fertility
0	29546		25573		
1	3119		3305		
2	3119		3305		
3	3119		3305		
4	3119		3305		
5	543		614		
6	543		614		
7	543		614		
8	543		614		
9	543		614		
10	373		455		
11	373		455		
12	373		455		
13	373		455		
14	373		455	33	
15	491		571	33	1
16	491		571	33	15
17	491		571		30
18	491		571		43
19	491		571		47
20	663		677		47
21	663		677		49
22	663	15	677		51
23	663	15	677		48
24	663	15	677		47
25	693	15	710		46
26	693	15	710		43
27	693	15	710		40
28	693	5	710		38
29	693	5	710		36
30	741		743		34
31	741		743		32
32	741		743		31
33	741		743		29
34	741		743		27
35	793		748		26
36	793		748		25
37	793		748		24
38	793		748		23
39	793		748		21

(*continued*)

TABLE 14.1 (*cont.*)

| Age | Males | | Females | | |
	Death (d_x)	Eligibility for marriage	Death	Eligibility for marriage	Fertility
40	860		731		20
41	860		731		17
42	860		731		14
43	860		731		12
44	860		731		8
45	876		713		8
46	876		713		7
47	876		713		1
48	876		713		
49	876		713		
50	948		823		
51	948		823		
52	948		823		
53	948		823		
54	948		823		
55	950		903		
56	950		903		
57	950		903		
58	950		903		
59	950		903		
60	1001		1075		
61	1001		1075		
62	1001		1075		
63	1001		1075		
64	1001		1075		
65	936		1070		
66	936		1070		
67	936		1070		
68	936		1070		
69	936		1070		
70	791		1017		
71	791		1017		
72	791		1017		
73	791		1017		
74	791		1017		
75	559		771		
76	559		771		
77	559		771		
78	559		771		
79	559		771		
80	1863		3067		

THE AMBUSH METHOD FOR GENERATING BIRTHS FOR MARRIAGES **283**

tions (in contrast to .40 for the 1968 !Kung) and I_m is .82 (in contrast to the observed rate of .86). In other words, we achieve the desired level of fertility (slightly higher than the 1968 rate) by a pattern that has a slightly lower proportion married and a slightly higher level of fertility within marriage. Examination of these indices for the range of populations shown in Table 8.1 shows that the differences between the !Kung and the simulations are quite small. Certainly the simulated populations would still fall into the "type" of populations characterized by early and near-universal marriage and low marital fertility discussed in Chapter 8.

Male age-specific fertility rates in AMBUSH are simply a function of the fertility of their wives. AMBUSH "solves" the "two-sex" problem by allocating each birth both to the father and to the mother. We will see the relationship of those curves later.

Input Parameters for Simulations

The input parameters used to generate this batch of simulations can be classified as three types. One of these is the rules of simulation, as just discussed (and also discussed in Chapters 5 and 11).[1] The second set of input parameters consists of the probabilities of events (deaths, births, and eligibility for marriage) by age and sex of individuals. These probabilities are summarized in Table 14.1. The third source is those probabilities for which marriages are the unit of analysis rather than individuals. These probabilities—really only those of the end of the marriage by divorce, since termination of the marriage by death and births to the marriage are given by individual probabilities—are given on p. 280. These inputs, fluctuating stochastically and interacting with one another, produce all of the output presented in the remainder of this chapter and in subsequent chapters.

Output Parameters of Simulations

To explore the implications of these input parameters, we present the results of a series of 10 simulations made with these parameters. If the purpose of this exercise were further refinements of the model, we might want to make many more runs, and analyze the output statistically. Our goal here, however, is illumination of the properties of !Kung-like populations and we want to get an idea of the central tendencies and variability among runs in particular variables. For these purposes, examination of the features of a small number of individual runs is more useful.

Each of these simulations is a "long run," continuing to year 500, so that we can look at implications that are only clear over a substantial period of time and

[1] For a full account of the rules of AMBUSH, see Lehotay and Howell (1978).

we can cumulate sufficient events so that the central tendencies and variance become clear. As we saw in Chapter 5 (p. 103), variance between runs is inflated when results are based on small numbers of cases, whether the small numbers result from a small population or from observing a larger population over a brief period of time. We will look at variability among runs as it appears in cross-section or when cumulated over a brief period of time for a few variables in which this aspect is important.

As in Chapter 11, we begin cumulating results from these simulations in year 150 rather than year 100, when the simulations begin, in order to avoid combining events that occurred to the real !Kung population with those produced by simulation. In these simulations, we have in addition a short-term problem that did not arise in the full fertility simulations of Chapter 11. This can be called the "start up problem," which results from features of the initial population.

All of the simulations shown here start with the resident Dobe population of 1968, 455 persons. This initial population has an age–sex composition that was formed by processes, including migration and polygamous marriage, that we do not take into account in the simulations. There were 244 women in the 1968 populations and only 211 men. Some of the adult women in the population were married to men who are not included in the initial population, because they were away from the Dobe area or because they are Bantu rather than !Kung. During the processing of the population for the initial year of the simulation, AMBUSH goes through the list of people and marks as unmarried all of those women who do not have a husband in the list. When AMBUSH comes to a second wife for a man, she is classified as unmarried and put into the marriage pool. During the first year of simulation, AMBUSH regularly puts 38 women, but only eight men, into the marriage pool, only a few of whom are young people eligible for a first marriage. A maximum of eight marriages can be formed, so 30 women remain in the pool for the next year, when a smaller group of newly eligible men and women enter the pool. Men search for wives only among women younger than themselves, so the older women in the group have little chance of obtaining a spouse. The problem of surplus women in the marriage pool cannot be solved by the simulation in the short run, so after spending 5 years in the pool most of these women are marked "never married" and the population loses their reproductive potential. This loss of population is merely an artifact of simulation and does not correspond to any predicted crisis in the real population. It regularly has the effect of producing a population "crash" of 50–100 people in the short run. Most of the people lost are births foregone during the first decade of simulation, with a smaller "echo" effect centered 30 years later when the children who were not born would have contributed to the production of the next generation. We avoid most of this disturbance by waiting until year 150 to begin tabulating features of the population. The size of these populations start at a lower level than those of the simulations of Chapter 11, and

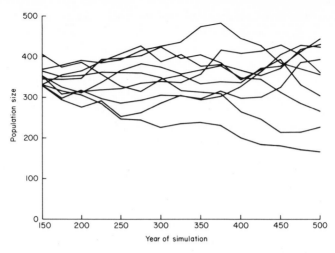

Figure 14.1. Size in cross-section of 10-simulated populations.

none of them have outgrown the computer size allocated to hold them by year 500.

Viability of the Simulated Populations

A crucial criterion for judging the "success" of simulation is the viability of the populations: The population must be able to produce enough births and sufficient survivorship to maintain the population size over time. Figure 14.1 shows the size of the 10 long simulations at 25-year intervals. The populations are smaller than those shown in Figure 11.1, due to the start up problem. Growth in population size over short periods of time tends to be less abrupt in these simulations, because there are more interactions between variables that prevent a short run of "luck" (such as the birth of an unusual number of babies) from being translated into an automatic increase in population when those babies mature to become potential parents. Irregularities in the sex ratio of births, for instance, may lead to a "marriage squeeze" that reduces fertility in the long run. In any case, Figure 14.1 shows that the input parameters used here clearly provide a basis for viable populations.

Age Distribution

Figures 14.2 and 14.3 show the percentage of the population at each age and younger, for the two sexes, in cross-sections of the simulated populations, during

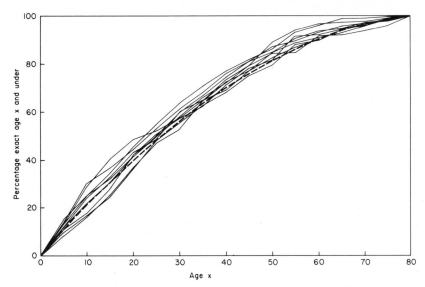

Figure 14.2. Age distribution in the final year of simulation: percentage of males exact age x and younger.

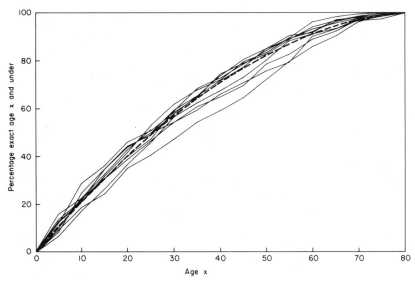

Figure 14.3. Age distribution in the final year of simulation: percentage of females exact age x and younger.

AGE DISTRIBUTION 287

the final year of the run. The age distribution used to estimate !Kung ages is centered among the distributions for simulated populations, as we expect. Variability in age distribution between runs tends to be increased in smaller size populations, but this tendency is counteracted to some extent by the trend toward smoother rates of population growth in these simulations. On balance, these age distributions are only slightly more variable than those of Chapter 11. The recently growing populations are systematically the "younger" populations compared with those that have been stationary or declining in the recent past, as expected (Coale 1972), with an additional component of "noise" (unsystematic variability in the proportion in age categories) caused by randomly generated events in small categories.

We see, therefore, that these simulations meet the criteria of producing simulated populations with the proper "external" features of population composition. Let us now have a closer look at the internal features of the simulted populations.

Marital Status in the Simulated Populations

Table 14.2 shows the central tendency and variance in marriage parameters in the first 5 of our 10 simulations. The marriage parameters are close to, but not identical with, the !Kung rates. The age at first marriage for women in the simulations is very close to that of the real population, but the mean age of men at first marriage is about a year and a half younger in the simulations.

The age difference between spouses is about 7.5 years in the simulations and not substantially different for first marriages and all marriages, whereas the !Kung show a mean difference of about 9 years for first marriages (for women) and about 6 years for all marriages. The difference in age between spouses is important in any simulation that generates fertility for women, as it is a determinant of the age pattern of fertility for men and the length of a male generation and enters into all of the kinship ties that involve marriage and paternity. The difference in age between spouses in the simulations (but not in the real population) coincides with the mean difference in age of parents at the birth of their children, confirming our assertion that the population structure of the simulations is simpler than that of the real population.

A crucial parameter of simulations in which fertility is only produced for married couples is the proportion of persons in each age group who are married. Figures 14.4 and 14.5 show the proportion married in 5-year age groups in the five simulations detailed in Table 14.2, along with the !Kung proportions observed in 1968. Since proportions married are a population feature that shows up in cross-section, we plot the proportions married for only the final year of each run. Figure 14.4 shows that there is little variability among runs in proportions of

TABLE 14.2
Marriage Parameters (Outcomes) in Five Simulated Populations

Parameters:						Simulation number						
	1		2		3		4		5			
	M	F	M	F	M	F	M	F	M	F		
N marriages	1925		2147		1523		1846		2032			
Age at first marriage												
$\bar{X}$	24.95	16.62	24.93	17.15	24.68	17.16	24.88	17.03	25.09	16.70		
Variance	3.70	2.24	4.06	1.98	3.83	2.11	4.06	2.33	3.99	2.38		
Age at all marriages												
$\bar{X}$	29.27	21.64	29.47	22.27	29.48	22.36	29.60	22.13	29.44	21.65		
Variance	63.69	83.75	65.58	81.34	73.34	87.99	70.53	86.69	62.62	79.63		
Age difference in first												
$\bar{X}$	8.03		7.43		7.21		7.56		8.02			
Variance	5.35		5.11		4.95		6.08		6.45			
Age difference in all												
$\bar{X}$	7.62		7.43		7.21		7.46		7.78			
Variance	14.51		14.91		13.97		15.91		16.62			

(continued)

TABLE 14.2 (*cont.*)

Parameters:	Simulation number									
	1		2		3		4		5	
	M	F	M	F	M	F	M	F	M	F
N marriages	1925		2147		1523		1846		2032	
Tries at marriage—percentage successful in										
year 1	93.0	52.6	97.1	45.1	97.5	43.4	94.6	47.0	92.8	53.1
year 2	3.3	14.0	1.1	11.9	1.7	14.1	3.0	10.7	3.0	12.2
year 3	1.9	14.7	1.1	16.6	.3	15.8	.9	14.2	2.4	13.2
year 4	.9	9.4	.3	13.6	.2	13.4	.8	14.2	1.0	12.4
year 5	.6	9.1	.2	12.6	.1	13.0	.4	13.2	.6	8.9
Never married										
N	2	84	5	135	0	117	11	123	20	97
Percentage of population at risk	.2	7.5	.4	10.2	0	12.0	1.1	10.6	1.7	7.9
Divorces										
N	437		473		329		430		465	
Percentage of marriages	22.7		22.0		21.6		23.3		22.9	
Age at divorce										
Mean	31.10	23.59	31.22	23.94	32.12	24.63	31.28	23.87	31.46	23.94
Variance	65.85	87.22	64.04	71.66	80.73	99.96	68.19	85.61	60.70	82.09

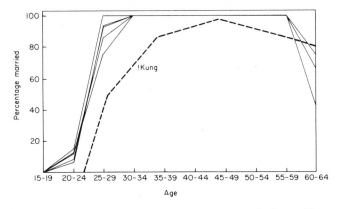

Figure 14.4. Proportion of men married, in 5-year age groups, in final year of five simulations.

men married by age, as all men 30–55, those passed the age of eligibility, have a wife or get a new one during their first year in the pool. Figure 14.5 shows that the marital status of women is less predictable, as their success is limited by the fluctuating supply of men. Note that the numbers in these categories are very small, which exaggerates variability among runs.

Fertility Performance in the Simulated Populations

We concluded in Chapter 11 that the full fertility procedures could not qualify as adequate mimicry of the !Kung population because the binomial

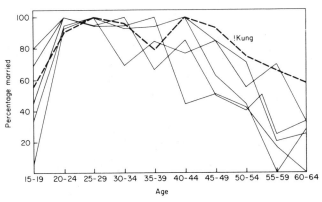

Figure 14.5. Proportion of women married, in 5-year age groups, in final year of five simulations.

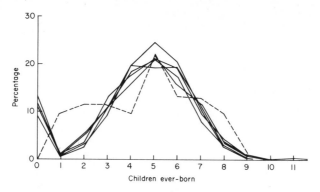

Figure 14.6. Parity distribution: five simulations and !Kung distribution.

probability process that allocates children to mothers consistently produces far too little variance between women in the number of children ever born to those who survive to the end of the reproductive period. Restricting fertility to married people and restricting marriages to monogamous ones inflates the variance in parity for women to the desired degree. Figure 14.6 shows, however, that the shape of the parity distribution is somewhat different in the simulations from what was observed in the !Kung population. The major difference is a reversal in proportions at parities zero and one. The simulations have a substantial proportion at parity zero, most of whom are those "never married" women who had no opportunity for childbearing, while in the observed population we expressed concern earlier about the unexpected absence of any women at parity zero, suspecting that some 5–10% of the total population had been missed from the data collection through some combination of small number fluctuations and migration out of the area.

Some of the irregularities in the observed !Kung parity distribution must be due to small number fluctuations. The simulations in Figure 14.6 are based on as many as a thousand completed reproductive careers in each simulation, but these are only 62 cases from the !Kung. Figure 14.7 compares simulations based on a comparable number (50–60) of completed reproductive careers with the !Kung distribution, confirming the suspicion that the simulated distributions are also irregular in shape when based on so few cases. We note, however, that the reversal in proportions at parities zero and one remains. We accept this distortion as one within the margin of tolerance for simulation. In the kinship analyses that follow, we will have to keep in mind that our method of simulation is producing slightly fewer and slightly larger (on the average) sibling groups than our observation of the !Kung patterns justifies.

The fertility parameters are made up of a number of distinct variables: age-specific fertility rates, ages of parents at birth, and a number of measures of reproductive performance. Table 14.3 presents these variables for the first five

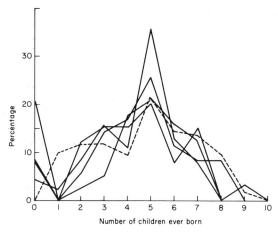

Figure 14.7. Parity distribution, five simulations of only 20 years, and observed !Kung distribution.

simulations, showing the central tendency and variance of each variable.

We note in Table 14.3 that alternative measures of fertility performance, computed in different ways, produce somewhat different indices, even within the same simulation. The mean of the total fertility rates computed on cross-sections of the population at 25-year intervals, for example, is not identical to the sum of the age-specific fertility rates computed by cumulation over the whole course of the run and neither of these is identical to the mean of the parity distribution, which is computed on only those women who completed a full reproductive career by surviving to age 50 or later. In addition, each of these indicators varies among runs, although all are produced by the same input probability schedules. Both kinds of fluctuations can be interpreted as a warning not to take small differences in indicators between populations—especially if computed by somewhat different methods or different periods of observation—too seriously in empirical studies of small populations.

Table 14.3 also gives age-specific fertility rates and total fertility rates for both men and women and provides our first basis for the solution of the "two-sex" problem: What fertility level and pattern for men is implied by the fertility of women in the same population?

Male age-specific fertility rates in AMBUSH are simply a function of the fertility of their wives. We argued in Chapter 13 that this was apparently true of the observed population as well, as we could obtain the expected age-specific fertility rates of men as accurately by tabulating the probability of birth to a woman the age of the man's wife as by counting births and man-years at risk. Table 14.3 shows the male age-specific fertility rates and total fertility and directs our attention to several differences between the results of simulations and the

TABLE 14.3
Fertility Parameters (Outcomes) in Five Simulated Populations

	Simulation number									
	1		2		3		4		5	
Parameter:	M	F	M	F	M	F	M	F	M	F
N births	4511		5210		3754		4443		4879	
Annual rates [a]										
Crude birth rate	37.24		34.82		30.18		33.22		38.45	
Variance	64.13		88.00		75.60		111.40		101.66	
Total fertility		5.00		4.42		3.81		4.20		4.71
Variance		2.60		2.33		1.20		2.00		1.86
Cumulative rates [b]										
Age-specific fertility rates [c]										
15–19	76	448	84	384	98	358	99	380	83	449
20–24	838	1196	921	1200	963	1160	904	1206	857	1237
25–29		1082		1055		1034		1048		1093

30–34	1220	811	1281	780	1207	765	1248	753	1176	799
35–39	1067	583	1044	599	1097	513	999	576	1021	609
40–44	844	331	808	338	771	339	821	306	869	366
45–49	576	84	561	82	579	59	583	60	592	94
50–54	300		276		287		238		335	
55–59	96		72		67		71		95	
60+	47		30		18		31		30	
Total fertility	5.06	4.53	5.08	4.43	5.09	4.28	4.98	4.32	5.06	4.64
Mean age	35.95	27.46	35.48	27.65	35.57	27.84	35.67	27.54	35.99	27.56
Variance	56.64	49.37	54.18	48.57	55.43	48.43	55.88	48.19	57.98	50.52
Mean parity		4.36		4.37		4.17		4.35		4.61
Variance		4.80		4.88		4.94		4.49		3.95

[a]Calculated for single years at 25-year intervals; variance is interyear.

[b]Calculated on all events during the run.

[c]These rates are the sum, rather than the average, of the 5 single-year rates. To compare with age-specific fertility rates elsewhere (as in Tables 6.1 and 7.1), divide these by 5.

actual fertility performance of men in the Dobe population during 1963–1973. These differences are plotted in Figure 14.8. Most strikingly, the age-specific fertility rates for men in the simulations are higher than those observed in 1963–1973, as they must be in a closed population in order to provide a father for each child. The difference between the curves of observed and simulated in Figure 14.8 represents the extent to which Dobe men have been losing out in competition with Bantu men and !Kung men from outside the Dobe area. Note that Figure 14.8 presents two forms of age-specific fertility, the usual one, calculated on all men at that age, and a marital rate, which calculates the rate only on married men at that age. During the twenties, marital age-specific fertility is much higher than the measure for the whole male population at that age, as the minority of married men are fathering all of the children, but after age 30 there is virtually no difference between the measures, as almost all men are married.

On the question whether men have biological limits to their fertility, independent of the age of their wives, the simulations provide a perspective that we were unable to perceive in the examination of the real population. The simulations show that although death rates and the declining fertility of older wives explains most of the decline in fertility for men, we should expect to find a small but significant proportion of births to men over 55 if the men's own fecundity were constant over a wide range of age. In the simulations, about 2.5% of all births occur to men over age 55. The absence of any such cases in the observed population could be due to small number fluctuations, but is more likely due to systematic action on the part of the !Kung that prevents such situations from arising. Men past age 55 are valued members of groups among the !Kung, but such men usually do not hunt and are not proper fathers of young families. It is likely that when a man of 40 marries a girl of 15, he will find that a younger man steals his wife before he reaches age 55.

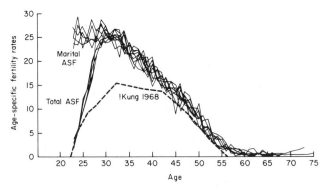

Figure 14.8. Male age-specific fertility rates and marital age-specific fertility rates, for single years of age, from simulations. !Kung 1968 rates plotted for comparison.

TABLE 14.4
Marital Fertility Parameters (Outcomes) in Five Simulated Populations

	Simulation number									
	6		7		8		9		10	
	M	F	M	F	M	F	M	F	M	F
Parameters:										
N births	3859		4066		2727		4484		5156	
Annual rates [a]										
Crude birth rate	34.82		35.22		31.43		30.77		38.62	
Variance	115.86		103.53		47.66		99.53		88.73	
Marital total fertility rate		4.39		4.81		3.63		4.10		5.20
Variance		2.00		3.20		0.86		2.33		1.06
Cumulative rates [b]										
Marital age-specific fertility rates [c]										
15–19		941		834		739		837		810
20–24	526	1400	472	1407	544	1303	503	1359	491	1373
25–29	1354	1162	1307	1085	1197	1169	1271	1129	1214	1152

(continued)

TABLE 14.4 (*cont.*)

| | | | | | Simulation number | | | | | |
| | 6 | | 7 | | 8 | | 9 | | 10 | |
	M	F	M	F	M	F	M	F	M	F
Parameters:										
N births	3859		4066		2727		4484		5156	
30–34	1259	897	1240	932	1233	894	1265	867	1285	900
35–39	1103	723	997	732	1052	668	959	706	1054	770
40–44	769	480	836	477	762	410	654	373	838	437
45–49	586	98	557	98	510	85	569	79	607	107
50–54	310		276		250		297		323	
55–59	73		79		99		61		113	
60+	15		27		125		29		70	
Marital total fertility rate	5.99	5.70	5.79	5.56	5.77	5.26	5.60	5.45	5.99	5.55
Mean age	35.47	27.68	35.48	27.79	35.66	27.88	35.51	27.66	36.05	27.61
Variance	55.11	49.60	55.46	49.96	60.75	47.14	55.71	48.89	58.99	49.63

[a]Calculated for single years at 25 year intervals; variance is interyear.
[b]Calculated on all events during the run.
[c]See Footnote *c*, Table 14.3.

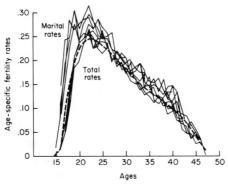

Figure 14.9. Female age-specific fertility rates and marital age-specific fertility rates, from simulations. !Kung rates plotted.

The marital age-specific fertility rates plotted in Figure 14.8 differ from the "total" rates presented in Table 14.3 by being calculated on only the married persons in each age group. AMBUSH can calculate the fertility measures either as total or marital rates, but not both in the same run. Table 14.4 presents the marital fertility measures for runs 6–10. We note that marital total fertility (which can be interpreted as the number of children born to persons who are continuously married during ages 15–49 for women, ages 22–80 for men) is between five and six for both sexes. Differences between the usual measure of total fertility and the marital total fertility rates shown here are greater for women than for men because women are more frequently unmarried than men during the reproductive years in these simulations.

Figure 14.9 shows the regular age-specific fertility rates in single years of age for women and the marital age-specific fertility rates, which parallel the same distributions for the men shown in Figure 14.8. We note that the fit of the (total) age-specific fertility rates to the smoothed !Kung rates for women is satisfyingly close. It is interesting to note that the distributions from the simulations are not smooth from one year of age to the next, even though the input rates have been smoothed. This result is caused by the stochastic fluctuations in the births to the small numbers of women in each age group, a parameter that does not "settle down" to its expected number even in the rather long period of time over which results are cumulated here.

Parity of Newborns and Generational Growth

We have seen that the simulated populations display distributions of the conventional demographic parameters that are plausible for populations of their type and comparable, within margins of tolerance, to the observed !Kung population. One of the beauties of simulation as an adjunct to empirical study is that in addition to providing distributions for variables that are observable in the real population, it permits examination of some variables that are invisible in the field but must be operating. One of the most interesting and useful variables is the distribution of parity to newborn women.

We have discussed parity distributions at a number of points in this work and have always meant by that term the number of children ever born to women who survive to the end of the reproductive period. AMBUSH counts parity in this way; its distribution for these simulations was plotted in Figure 14.6 and the means and variances in Table 14.3.

AMBUSH also counts "parity," the number of children ever born, to women who survive to age 15 (whether or not they die before age 50), at the time of their death or at age 50, whichever comes first, providing the full distribution of completed reproductive careers. Summing the number of women who die prior to age 15 and adding them to the group who have no children, we obtain the distribution of number of children ever born to a cohort of newborn women. This distribution is rarely available for empirical studies except for village or family reconstitution studies from historical demography, as its tabulation requires long periods of cumulated observation on completed reproductive careers. In cross-sectional studies, the reproductive histories of the women who die between ages 15 and 49 (a substantial proportion of the initial cohort in a population like the !Kung) cannot be reliably studied because we do not know that a woman will be in this group until she has died, when she is no longer present to be studied. I cannot give the comparable distribution for the Dobe !Kung, for example.

This valuable if elusive distribution is the nexus for connection of several aspects of population structure. On one hand, it provides the components for analysis of what the geneticists calls "selection intensity" (we will discuss the meaning of the distribution in that context in Chapter 16). At the same time, it is closely related to the demographic concept of the net reproduction rate, differing by providing the distribution for all children, not just those of one sex and in providing the whole distribution so that measures of variance can be computed, instead of simply the mean. The mean of the parity distribution for newborns, reduced by the sex ratio at birth, *is* the net reproduction rate, and hence the distribution can be interpreted not only in terms of events to individuals, but also in terms of population growth per generation, and, with the addition of information on the length of generation, as a measure of population growth per year. The same distribution can provide the distribution of sibling group sizes by multiplying the parity by the proportion of women at that parity and calculating the percentage.

TABLE 14.5
Simulated Parity of Newborn Women and Measures of Generational Growth

Parameters	Simulation number				
	1	2	3	4	5
Percentage dead by age 15	45	44	45	44	46
Parity of newborns					
0	53.82	53.46	55.59	53.18	53.69
1	3.25	2.63	2.59	3.19	2.97
2	4.24	4.09	4.18	4.54	4.21
3	7.76	7.50	6.44	6.16	6.25
4	8.58	8.74	9.08	9.80	9.67
5	9.19	9.97	9.85	9.63	9.88
6	6.77	7.84	7.48	8.12	7.99
7	4.90	3.98	2.97	4.09	3.89
8	1.21	1.51	1.43	1.23	1.13
9	.28	.28	.39	.06	.32
Mean parity	2.024	2.076	1.965	2.058	2.053
Variance	6.38	6.64	6.27	6.33	6.39
Children per 100 newborns	202.40	207.68	196.63	206.03	205.49
Daughters per 100 newborns	98.77	101.31	95.87	100.45	100.19
Sons per 100 newborns	103.63	106.37	100.67	105.47	105.12
Net reproduction rate (daughters per newborn)	.9877	1.0131	.9587	1.0045	1.0019
R_1 (mean age at childbirth)	27.48	27.65	27.84	27.54	27.56
T (mean length of generation = R_1/net reproduction rate)	27.82	27.30	29.04	27.42	27.51
r(intrinsic rate of natural increase = net reproduction rate − $1/R_1$)	−.00045	.00047	−.00148	.00016	.00007
Calculation check: net reproduction rate = e^{rT}	.9875	1.0130	.9586	1.0045	1.0019

Table 14.5 shows the distribution of parity to newborns for the women in five simulations. Note that we use the results of simulation rather than the life table or stable population model for all parameters shown in Table 14.5 except the sex ratio at birth, which is the input rate—105 males per 100 females—rather than the output for that simulation.

Note in Table 14.5 that the annual rate of population growth, r, is very low for these simulation, as could be seen from a glance at Figure 14.1, which shows their size over time. Although their birth and death rates would limit a population of any size to a small rate of growth, these simulated populations are losing some of their potential for growth to stochastic fluctuations in the supply of spouses due to their small sizes.

Whatever rate of population growth is achieved within a particular simulation, on the average the same rate will characterize the male and female halves of the same population, since differing rates would lead to changes in the sex ratio over time and other implausibilities. Given that this is true, we can utilize the rate of growth, r,—derived from the study of the newborn parity distribution for females—to estimate the net reproduction rates achieved in these simulations by males, which implies the mean numbers of sons and daughters born to newborn males. Since a simulation program like AMBUSH is capable of counting any definable series of events in the population, it is unfortunate that we cannot show the parity distribution for newborn males. AMBUSH does not count these events for males, simply because parity is so uniformly defined as a property of females that I failed to anticipate its usefulness and did not request the count. Nevertheless, Table 14.6 shows the results of computation of the net reproduction rate, mean length of a generation, and numbers of children of each sex born to newborn males. The final rows in Table 14.6 reconcile our statements about reproductive performance of males and females. Differences between the number of children ever born to 100 newborn women and 105 newborn men are merely the result of rounding error.

TABLE 14.6
Simulated Male Generational Growth and the Reconciliation of Male and Female Replacement

Parameters	Simulation number				
	1	2	3	4	5
r (annual growth, from Table 14.5)	−.00045	.00047	−.00148	.00016	.00007
Male mean age at children's birth (R_1)	35.95	35.48	35.57	35.67	35.99
Net reproduction rate'[a]	.99322	1.01597	.94736	1.00570	1.00252
T (mean length of a male generation)	36.19	34.92	37.55	35.47	35.90
Net reproduction rate $= e^{rT}$	.9836	1.0165	.9472	1.0057	1.0025
Sons per newborn man	.9836	1.0165	.9472	1.0057	1.0025
Daughters per newborn man (sons × .9534)	.9377	.9691	.9031	.9588	.9558
Children per newborn man	1.9213	1.9856	1.8503	1.9645	1.9583
Children per 105 newborn men	201.74	208.49	194.28	206.27	205.62
Children per 100 newborn women	202.40	207.68	196.63	206.03	205.31

[a] Net reproduction rate' calculated as $rR_1 + 1$.

A Review and Overview of the Simulations

We have seen in this chapter that artificial populations with demographic parameters tailored to mimic the Dobe !Kung, under the simplified but generally realistic processing procedures of AMBUSH, are viable stable populations that maintain their age distribution, proportions of persons married, differences in age between spouses, and fertility performance of the two sexes over time despite random fluctuations within and among simulations.

Having constructed such a simulation, we are not prevented from taking a critical attitude toward the results. Depending upon one's theoretical and empirical purposes, one might decide that the fit of the simulations presented here is not adequate to represent the !Kung population and resort to additional "fine-tuning" of input parameters or modification of the processing procedures of AMBUSH in order to improve the fit. For some purposes, for example, one might decide that it is necessary to simulate polygamous as well as monogamous marriages, or feel the need to increase the complexity of the marriage selection procedures to include the prohibitions on marriage to persons who have the same name as a close relative.

On a more metaphysical level, one might be critical of the results of the simulations on the grounds that the "people" in the simulations, really computer records, fail to behave as real people do. Real individuals, of course, have goals of various sorts, perceive their situation relative to their goals, and take action to improve their situations. By modeling the !Kung population by the generation of events by Monte Carlo simulation, I do not intend to imply that the !Kung people are equally helpless to influence their fate. Like people everywhere, the !Kung have some, but not unlimited, power to influence their lives. The environment, through the populations of microorganisms and other risks to life and health, through the food supply, and through the availability of other people who make up the social universe of each person, sets up constraints within which individuals attempt to control their fate. These constraints may be seen as parallel to the probability schedules that the computer program imposes on simulated "persons." It has been an important insight of sociology that many complex processes that result from the sum of large numbers of individual decisions and actions can be described collectively as simple probability processes. These simulations may be seen as another version of that hypothesis, in which it is postulated that marriage, fertility, and survivorship operate *as if* individuals were at the mercy of their probability schedules.

The acceptability of the simulations, then, may differ by research tasks and perhaps by the style of the investigator as well. For the present purposes, the simulations presented here are adequate to justify going beyond the reporting of the demographic outputs to look at the implications of these demographic parameters for questions of social structure (such as the probabilities of kinship ties and the composition of kinship groups and households) and for the transmission of genetic material from generation to generation. These tasks will be taken up in the following two chapters. In each, we will use concrete outputs of the simulations to suggest the range of expected outcomes in populations of this type. We will also try to understand the interrelations between variables in a population like that of the !Kung for processes that are invisible or difficult to study in the real population, without (I trust) becoming confused about the locus of reality. The simulations are hypothesis-generating tools, focusing our attention on aspects of population functioning we might otherwise miss. Just because a particular result is produced in the simulations does not imply that real populations will necessarily show the same result. But they may and the simulations will have served their purpose if they direct our attention to features of real populations that might provide testable hypotheses.

15

Social Structural Implications of Demographic Parameters: Kinship Ties and Kinship Groups

We have seen in the last chapter that a set of processing rules and a set of input probabilities imply a rather large set of features of the populations produced by simulation. Some features, like size, are unpredictable, but others, including the age distribution, proportions married, difference in age between spouses and between parents and children, even such a nonobvious feature as the variance in the male age-specific fertility schedule, are predictable within narrow ranges because they are produced—however complex and indirect the pathway—by the input probabilities and the rules of simulation.

The numbers of kin that individuals will have at the various stages of life is also predictable, being formed, as are the demographic distributions, by the creation (through the birth process) of individuals and the removal of those individuals (through death) at individually unknown but collectively predictable times. The probability of having one or more kin, for a given ego, depends upon the joint probability that (*a*) someone was ever born into that relationship and (*b*) survives to ego's current age.

By asserting that demographic processes are the generators of kinship ties in a population we need not take the reductionistic stand that demography is the only important determinant. Real people may create kinship ties by adoption, may terminate them by choice, and may treat some kin as far more important than others. Nevertheless, there is a basic kinship inventory generated by demographic processes before it is modified by choice, and simulation allows us to count ties in that basic inventory, to compare the numbers for the two sexes and different age groups, and to experiment with the amount of fluctuation expected in populations of given size. The ability to make such counts, indeed, allows us to quantify the extent to which the demographic processes—as opposed to cultural rules—are the determinants of features of social structure by comparing the results of simulations that use only demographic determinants with data from real societies that may operate in more complex ways. Wachter *et al.* (1978), in their explorations of household composition, demonstrate that the mechanical simulation of kinship structures is most useful in exploring specific social structural hypotheses, where the relevant results of simulation can be presented concisely. Here we are interested in demonstrating the general features of kinship as generated by this particular set of demographic parameters. The presentation of results will necessarily be rather extensive, even if not exhaustive of the kinship results provided by AMBUSH, and will necessarily be somewhat unfocused, seeking the general features of the production of kinship by demographic parameters and noting some of the more interesting results of the simulations for !Kung-like populations.

The Cultural Definitions of Kinship

The !Kung, like people everywhere, have a system for organizing the facts of biological relatedness (and fictional relationships) into categories of terminology that imply obligations and responsibilities between pairs of people. This system is well described by Marshall (1976:201) for the Nyae Nyae !Kung; it generally applies to the Dobe !Kung as well. The kinship system of the !Kung is bilateral (rather than lineal) and is based on a shallow depth, which means that relationships that would be traced through common ancestors long dead tend to be ignored, or forgotten. It is rare for !Kung to trace relationships beyond that of the generation of the oldest living people (although deceased members of that generation will often be evoked to trace a relationship). Coincidentally, the !Kung kin terms correspond quite closely to the familiar kin terminology of American society (aunts, uncles, cousins, nephews, etc.), differing from these categories primarily by the !Kung addition of a relative age term in each, and the addition of categories of "joking" and "avoidance" to the meanings of the terms. Since we are using an unfamiliar methodology in this chapter, it will increase clarity to report the results in the familiar categories, which we can do without commiting real violence to the social reality of the !Kung. All of the categories used here are important ones for the !Kung, and there are few strong ties (mostly based on the name relationships) that are excluded from this category system.

The AMBUSH Method for Counting Kin

We mentioned in the discussion of marriage choices that AMBUSH consults a map of kinship ties to determine whether potential spouses are related as first cousins or closer kin in order to avoid incestuous marriages. This continuously updated map, which is really a list of lines with pointers to other lines, allows us to count the numbers of kin in particular types of relationship to ego, for all egos, and to tabulate those distributions classified by age and sex.

The units on the kinship maps are sibling groups rather than individuals, because siblings have the same relationship to many others and this form reduces redundancy in information. A sibling group consists of the children born to a particular marriage, with pointers to the two parents. As members of the sibling group marry and have children, pointers are added to other groups, so that one person in another sibling group is the spouse of ego and the additional members become the brothers and sisters-in-law. When individuals die, they are retained on the kinship maps (so that kin ties can be traced through them) until the youngest member of the sibling group reaches age 81 (no matter what age he or she died prior to age 81), when the group as a whole is removed from the kinship map and all of the ties that were made through those individuals are disconnected. New groups are continually being added and old groups removed. The space previously occupied can be reused (the list "wraps around" in computer jargon), so that the accuracy of the connections counted is smoothly maintained over time. It can be shown that the level of connectivity of the population by kinship ties is on the average steady in the simulations shown here, although this would not necessarily be the case in rapidly growing groups or in groups where the genealogical depth being maintained (the age of removal of sibling groups) were much greater than that used here.

AMBUSH actually counts the numbers of ties between living individuals at a point in time. Note that this is a more restricted question than the geneticists' concept of average relatedness (kinship) in a closed population, where, since everyone is descended from the original group of founders, and since they have to marry each other, they would all eventually come to trace kinship with others in the same population, often in a number of distinct ways simultaneously. Even though we are using a shallow genealogical depth in tracing relationships, it still happens that individuals may be related in several ways in the simulated populations. For counts of individual ties, we will count each type of tie, although for the summary measure of all ties, we will eliminate double counting.

Variability in Kin Ties

There are several kinds of variability in distributions of kin ties and the data presentation figures of this chapter are designed to display each of them.

One of these is the distribution from zero to N of the number of kin in a particular category that a given person can be expected to have. For many purposes, for instance, it may not be important that the mean number of brothers is one: we want to know in addition whether that mean is achieved by nearly everyone having exactly one, or whether many people have none but a minority have quite a few. Indeed, if we were satisfied to know the mean number expected, there would be no advantage to simulation, as analytic methods developed by Goodman, Keyfitz, and Pullum (1974) permit calculation of the mean from fertility and mortality schedules for persons of particular age and sex groups. For presentation of the distribution of the expected number of kin, we are primarily interested in the stable form of this distribution, hence we wish to base the distribution on a large number of egos in each age and sex group. For this purpose, AMBUSH has counted the kin ties for each living ego every 25 years during the 350-year run of Simulation 1 and has cumulated those counts for a distribution that minimizes stochastic fluctuations. These distributions are plotted in the figures of this chapter, connected by a dashed line for the males and a solid line for the females. These points represent our best estimate of the long-run expectations of the distribution.

Another form of variability that we are interested in is the fluctuation around the expected values that are observed in cross-sections of the population, comparable to what would be observed if we counted kin ties at a point in time in a real population. For this purpose, AMBUSH counted the kin ties for only the final year in simulations 2–5. These results have been plotted on the same figures with a "+" for males and a dot for females. It should be stressed that some of the age–sex categories have only a few members in the cross-sections, particularly at the oldest ages. Age groups of egos have been increased to 10-year from our usual 5-year groups to reduce this problem.

Looking at the results for any particular kind of relationship, we might want to ask many questions. Do males have more kin than females?, Do the number of persons having kin increase or decrease with age? Do people have more grandmothers than grandfathers? Most of these questions can be answered from inspection of the figures; we will note some of the more striking observations as we go along.

Proportions of Persons Having a Living Mother, by Age

We start with the distribution of frequency of having a living mother, both because it is one of the most important relationships among kin and because it is conceptually the simplest.

All children have a living mother at their birth and the probability of having a living mother is a function of the age of the mother at the birth and the duration

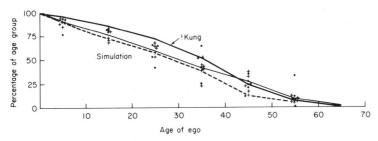

Figure 15.1. Proportions of egos who have a living mother, in 10-year age groups, from simulations, and proportion of !Kung in 1968 who have a living mother.

from birth to the current age of ego. Figure 15.1 shows the proportion of egos in each age group who have a surviving mother. Males and females are plotted separately in Figure 15.1, but there are no systematic differences between the sexes in this probability, as on the average brothers and sisters have the same age difference between themselves and their mothers. The two curves, therefore, should be interpreted as two estimates of the same distribution.

The proportion of !Kung residents of the Dobe area in 1968 who have a surviving mother (whether or not the mother is a Dobe resident) is also plotted for each age group in Figure 15.1. The two sexes are combined to increase the base number of cases, since there are no substantial differences in the !Kung proportions by sex.

It is clear from Figure 15.1 that the !Kung people have a higher proportion with living mothers at each age than the simple probabilities of death that we have estimated would suggest. This finding could be interpreted as evidence that the mortality probabilities of the !Kung are not as high as we have used in the simulations. Indeed, we have seen evidence that mortality rates have improved somewhat during the 18 years preceeding the data collection, which would tend to increase the proportions with living relatives in all classes, especially for the younger people. But a more important source of the difference between the simulations and the observed population is likely to lie in the lack of independence of the probability of death of mothers and their children. AMBUSH treats the probability of death for a person and his or her mother as independent. In the real population, though not in the simulations, there is likely to be an association between the probability of survival of the child and the mother. A young maternal orphan among the !Kung is unlikely to survive, which tends to inflate the proportion of living children with living mothers. The direction of the cause of the association is likely to shift at the older ages, when the probability of survival of the mother may be increased by the presence of her living children. In any case, we see that about 40% of the people in the 30–39 age group can expect to have a living mother, but only a few will still have a living mother by the time they are in the 50–59 group. The oldest person with a surviving mother in the 1968 !Kung population is Kasupe, the 56-year-old man whose family was used to illustrate the age estimation procedure in Chapter 2.

Proportion of Persons Having a Living Father, by Age

Figure 15.2 shows the parallel distribution for the proportion of persons, male and female, who have a surviving father. The probability of having a living father is somewhat lower than that of having a living mother at each age. A trivial source of the difference is that the fathers have been at risk of death for 9 months longer than the mothers, since it is necessary for fathers to be alive at the conception but not at the birth of their children. A more substantial source is that fathers tend to be older than mothers, and hence have higher probabilities of death for equal durations. The proportions for the two sexes have again been plotted separately from the simulation, but there is no systematic difference between them. The observed proportion of !Kung in 1968 who have a living father is closer to the predictions of the simulations than was the case for mothers, due to some combination of small number fluctuations and the likely fact that fathers are less essential to the survival of their children than mothers are. Over the age of 40, there is quite a substantially higher proportion of !Kung with a living father than expected, in part due to the survival of a particular old man with eight surviving middle-aged children, all of whom are reporting on his survival, an example of small number fluctuations.

The survival of fathers, and indeed of any particular relatives other than the mother, probably does not have a strong influence on the probability of survival of children. It is interesting to consider customs of the !Kung, such as the principle that meat provided by the hunters of a group is shared widely among all of the members of the group rather than going exclusively to the families of the hunters and the ease of remarriage for widowed women, in their implications for the interactions between survival probabilities for the various parties. It is also

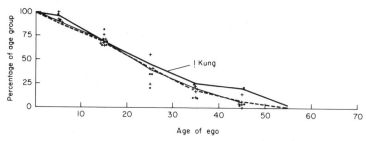

Figure 15.2. Proportions of egos who have a living father, from simulations, and proportion of !Kung in 1968 who have a living father.

15. KINSHIP TIES AND KINSHIP GROUPS

interesting to relate these figures to the extent to which the culture requires the existence and participation of parents or other specified relatives in the lives of their descendents. About 65% of the women, but only about 40% of the men, for example, can expect to have a living father at the time of their first marriage. If there were a rigid rule that the father has to participate in the marriage rituals, a substantial proportion of young people would have a problem. Instead, the !Kung culture tends to be very flexible about specifying which relatives take the responsibility and initiative in managing life-crisis rituals.

The distribution of living parents is easier to present than the distributions for other groups, in that persons can only have zero or one, so that a single graph can show all of the information.

We turn now to other members of the parental generation, the aunts and uncles. Because it is possible to have more than one relative of the type, the

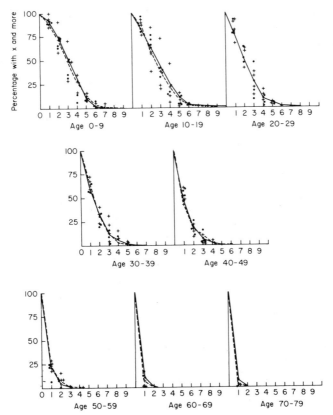

Figure 15.3. Proportions of age group who have x and more living aunts (parent's sisters or spouse of parents' brothers), from simulations.

distribution from zero to nine and more will be shown for each 10-year age group.

Proportions Having Living Aunts, by Age

The category labeled "aunts" includes sisters of both mother and father and the wives of parents' brothers. The sisters, of course, can be either younger or older than the parents, but are on the average the same age as the connecting parents. Husbands, however, are on the average about 7.5 years older than their wives. Among the four possible types of aunts, therefore, the type most likely to survive to any age of ego is mother's brother's wife (on the average 7.5 years younger than mother), then mother's sister and father's brother's wife (who are, on the average, the same age as the mother), and finally father's sister (who is on the average the same age as the father, 7.5 years older than mother). When we

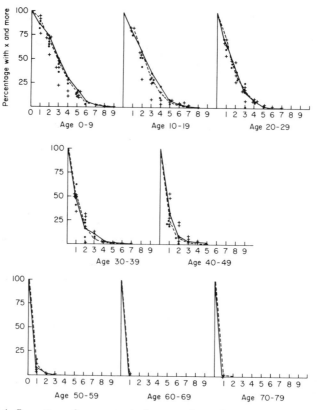

Figure 15.4. Proportions of age group who have *x* and more living uncles, from simulation.

combine these four groups into a single category, we find the distributions by age shown in Figure 15.3. It is very rare for an aunt (of any kind) to be younger than ego, hence people 0–9 have the largest number of aunts that they will have over their life span, with the lowered proportions in all succeeding age groups due to the continuing risk of death of the aunts over time. There are no differences between the two sexes in the probability of having x and more living aunts at any age. By age 40–49, about half have no living aunts; by age 60–69, only a few have any.

Proportions Having Living Uncles, by Age

Figure 15.4 shows the parallel distributions for living uncles, by age, where uncles are defined, as aunts, as parent's sibling of the same sex plus spouses of opposite-sexed siblings. The proportions for each age group are identical to those for aunts, the four distributions (aunts and uncles, male and female egos) differing simply as estimates of the same quantity.

Proportions with Living Grandparents, by Age

Grandparental ties are like parental ties in being constrained in number. A person can have only 0, 1, or 2 living grandmothers and 0, 1, or 2 living

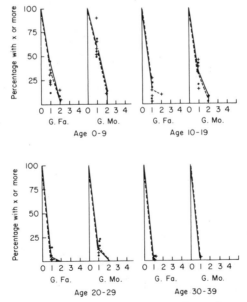

Figure 15.5. Proportions of age group who have x and more living grandparents.

grandfathers. All of the potential ties are created before ego's birth, so the depletion over age groups is simply a function of the probability of death of the old people. Grandmothers are more likely to be alive than grandfathers, for each age group, because they are on the average 7.5 years younger. We do not tabulate maternal grandparents separately from paternal here, but if we did we would find that maternal grandmothers are more likely to be alive than paternal ones and maternal grandfathers more likely than paternal ones. No one over age 40 has a living grandparent, in either the simulations or among the real !Kung population. Figure 15.5 shows the distributions.

We have seen the major categories for the older generations. We now turn to close relatives in the subject's own generation.

Proportions Having Living Siblings

Changes over the life span in the number of living siblings differs from the relationships we have already considered in that new members can be added to the group during ego's lifetime. Figure 15.6 shows the proportions who have x and more living siblings. Clearly the proportions are higher for age 10–19 than they are for 0–9, when only some of the members of the sibling group have already been born. During that 10-year period of life, the probability is greater that additional members will be added by birth than that members will be removed by death. By the 20–29 age group, it is still possible that additional members will be added, but only in the case where ego is one of the oldest and the mother has children over a long period of time. (We saw in Chapter 6 that the mean difference in age between first-born and last-born children is about 16 years.) Death is the only process changing the number of living siblings from one age group to the next past age 20–29, when the groups are gradually reduced in size. Up to age 50–59, chances are better than 50% that ego will have at least one living sibling and even in the age group 70–79 he or she has a probability of about .25 of having at least one. On the other hand, at least 15% of people will not have a living sibling during the 10–19 age group, when it is most likely, and so the !Kung culture, which prescribes how siblings are to be treated if one has them (distinguishing older brothers and older sisters, but lumping younger siblings of both sexes together), but which does not require the participation of a sibling in any important life event, is realistic.

There are no important differences between males and females in the probabilities of having living siblings.

Probabilities of Having Living Cousins

AMBUSH lumps together relatives traced through several chains as "cousins," defined as the children of one's parents' siblings (not counting their spouses). Cousins are one of the largest kinship categories tabulated, in large part

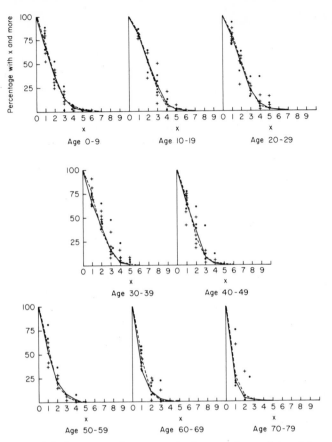

Figure 15.6. Proportions of age group who have *x* and more living siblings.

because we do not distinguish the sex of the cousin. Figure 15.7 shows the distribution of *x* and more cousins over the life span, where we see that the number of cousins goes on increasing for egos up to the age group 20–29 as younger siblings of parents complete their families, but declines regularly after that age. There are no differences in expected numbers for the two sexes.

According to Lee (1972c) and Marshall (1976:184) cousin ties among adults supplement sibling ties in forming the core links between the nuclear families that make up a village or camp. We can see in Figure 15.7 that the probability of having an available relative with whom to form the core of a camp is greatly increased by the inclusion of cousins, whereas the requirement of having an available sibling is quite a restrictive one for the age groups 30–60.

AMBUSH severs cousin links during old age, when the linking sibling group, that of the parents and parents' siblings, is removed from the kinship maps as the

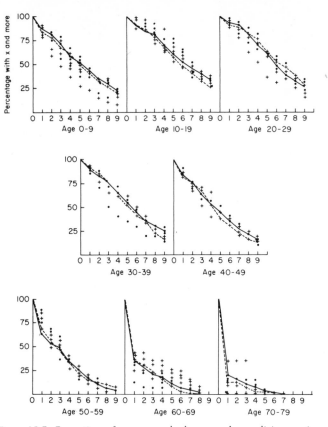

Figure 15.7. Proportions of age group who have *x* and more living cousins.

youngest member of that group (living or dead) reaches age 81. People in the 60–69 and 70–79 age groups, therefore, could expect to have more living cousins than Figure 15.7 shows, assuming that they, unlike AMBUSH, do not "forget" the relationship in the absence of the linking relatives. This artifact of simulation does not distort the counts of other ties presented here.

Proportions Having Living Children

Sons and daughters are distinguished terminologically, but there are only very minor differences in the probabilities of having *x* and more of the categories by age, the minor differences being caused by the slightly greater probability that a given birth will be male (.512) rather than female, and the slightly greater probability that a female will survive to each age. Figure 15.8 plots the propor-

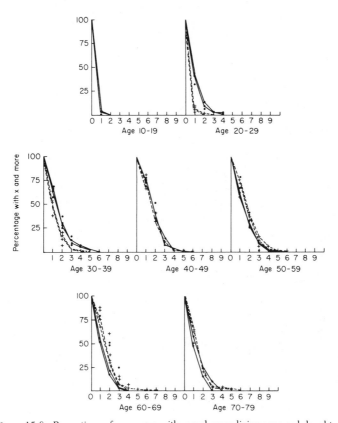

Figure 15.8. Proportions of age group with x and more living sons and daughters.

tion with x or more living sons and daughters separately, but the differences are very small, hardly exceeding the differences due to sampling fluctuation.

The probabilities are substantially different, however, for males and females as egos, and the pattern of difference changes over the life span, reflecting the reproductive careers of men and women. No one has a child in the age group 0–9, so it is omitted in Figure 15.8. During the 10–19 age group, a very small proportion of women have a living son or daughter, but no men do. During the 20–29 age group, the probability of a woman having one or more living sons is about .40, a living daughter about the same, while less than 10% of the men have either of these ties. The proportion with x and more living offspring increases throughout the thirties and the forties for both sexes, with men "catching up" with the women as they have their children at an older age. By age 50–59 the patterns have reversed and the men are substantially more likely to have one or more living sons and living daughters than the women their own age, an advantage they maintain throughout the rest of their lives. In the age group 70–79 more than 70% of the men have at least one living daughter and about 65% have a living son, but only about 40% of the women in that age group have at least one living son and 40% have at least one living daughter. Because women have their children at an earlier age, there is more time during which they are at risk of losing those children through death before they die. The monogamous marriage requirement of the way fertility is generated in AMBUSH means that about 10% of the women are "never married" and have no opportunity to have children. In a polygamous marriage system, the women would increase their advantage in the proportion having one and more living children during the 20–50 period (by about 10% of the observed frequency) and would decline below the men's level more slowly after 50. Most of the difference between the sexes, however, is due to the difference in timing of the reproductive careers rather than to this artifact of simulation.

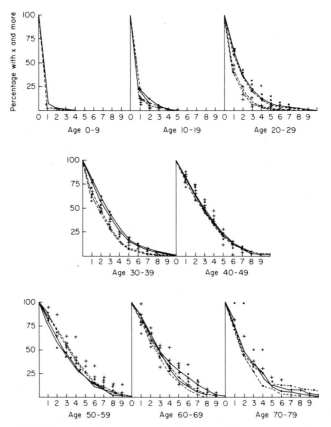

Figure 15.9. Proportions of age group with x and more living nephews and nieces.

Proportions with Living Nephews and Nieces

The wider circle of primary kin on the generation of ego's children, comparable to that of aunts and uncles on the generation of ego's parents, and to cousins on ego's own generation, is the group of nephews and nieces, defined as the children of ego's siblings and spouse's siblings. A married couple, then, shares a pool of nephews and nieces, just as they share the group of children, and this pool is counted for each of them. We do not include the spouses of nephews and nieces in the count.

Figure 15.9 shows the distributions for numbers of nephews and nieces over the life span. We see that it is rare to have any during the 0–9 and the 10–19 age group, as it requires that one have siblings old enough to be bearing children. The proportion with one and more becomes substantial only during the 20–29 age group, and increases, for both sexes, in each age group up to 50–59.

We note that during the 20–29 year age group the curves for the sexes diverge and women are substantially more likely than men their own age to have living nephews and nieces. The reason has nothing to do with the woman's own reproductive success being higher at this age, as it is the offspring of the siblings that we are counting here. Nor is the cause that the siblings of women tend to be older and hence further along their reproductive career: the siblings of both sexes are, on the average, the same age as ego and are equally likely to be either sisters or brothers for the two sexes. Women's advantage comes from the second route

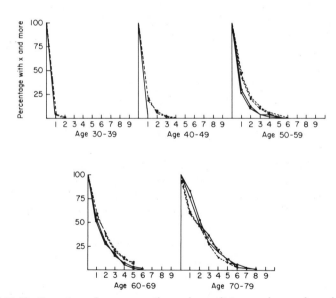

Figure 15.10. Proportions of age group with *x* and more living grandsons and granddaughters.

to obtaining nephews and nieces: the offspring of the spouse's siblings. Since women marry at a younger age and a higher proportion of them are married at each age and older, and since they marry men who are on the average 7.5 years older and hence have siblings who are also on the average 7.5 years older than the woman, the women have more opportunity to be linked to nephews and nieces than men their own age. The men "catch up" during the 40–49 age group and pass the women during the 50–59 age group, retaining their advantage throughout the rest of life. Again we see that because the women obtain their relatives earlier in life, they are at risk of losing those ties for a longer period and hence are somewhat more likely not to have any in old age.

Proportion with Living Grandchildren

When we look two generations down from ego, to the children of his or her children, we obtain the distributions of grandchildren. Note that grandsons and granddaughters are presented separately in this distribution, although the probabilities of having them differ only slightly, from the sex ratio at birth and differential survival.

No one has a grandchild at less than 30 years of age, and only a very small percentage of the women 30–39 have any. The proportion with x and more grandchildren of both sexes increases steadily from age group to age group and is still rising at age 70–79, which signifies that the probability of an addition to the group, through birth, is larger than the probability of a reduction of the group through death. By age 70 the women's daughters have largely completed childbearing, though their sons are still having children, whereas men at this age may have both sons and daughters who are still producing new grandchildren for them.

The difference between the sexes is that women have more grandchildren than the men of their age group for some decades, with the men catching up later and passing the women by age 70–79. It is interesting to note that in this society, which places a certain amount of stress upon the grandparent–grandchild relationship and in which a sort of immortality is achieved by having one's name given to grandchildren in the *!ku n!a–!ku ma* ("old name"–"young name") relationship, approximately 50% of the people in the 60–69 age group will not have a living grandchild of their own sex, and about 25% of the males and 40% of the females in the 70–79 age group will lack the relationship.

Affinal Ties

Affinal (in-law) ties differ from consanguinal ties by being generated not by the birth of the other but by the marriage of the linking relative. The numbers of affinal ties increase greatly at the time of ego's marriage, when he or she forms all of the ties generated by that marriage. Even before marriage people have affinal ties to those who have married their consanguinal kin. Affinal ties can predate ego's birth, especially for "aunts" and "uncles" who are affines. These ties can be severed by the death of the other, as in the case of consanguinal ties, but can in addition be severed by the termination of the marriage that links the pair, either through divorce or through the death of the spouse. On the other hand, affinal ties are replaceable, through a new marriage, in a way that consanguinal ties are not. AMBUSH counts only the affinal ties generated by current marriages.

The same probabilities of birth and death that generate and sever consanguinal ties apply to affinal ties, but the pattern of age difference between the pair differs from consanguinal ties by the distribution of difference in age between husbands and wives, as we have already seen in examining some of the other relative categories. All of these differences between affinal and consanguinal ties can be illustrated by the examination of one kind of tie, that to parents-in-law.

We have already seen the probability of having a living wife or husband (in Chapter 14) and the distribution of differences in age between husbands and wives, which determine the probability of survival of the spouse and other relatives to whom he or she is connected. One gets a mother-in-law, for example, by marrying a person who has a living mother; the probability is the joint probability of marrying a person of a given age and the probability that a person of that age has a living mother. No one can have a mother-in-law below the age of marriage and the proportion who have one will increase during the period of life that many new marriages are being made and will decrease over the life span as the mothers-in-law die. Figure 15.11 summarizes the distribution over the life span for males and females. A substantial proportion of teenage girls (about 15%) have a living mother-in-law; women 20–29 have the highest proportion (about 40%) and the proportion declines over the rest of the life span as the mothers-in-law die. At no age are the women as likely to have a living mother-in-law as they are to have a living mother. The men, on the other hand, start acquiring mothers-

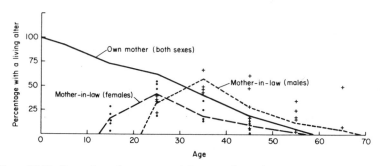

Figure 15.11. Proportions of age group with living mother-in-laws, compared with proportions with a living mother, by age and sex, from simulations.

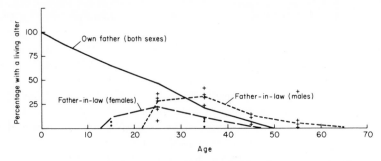

Figure 15.12. Proportions of age group with a living father-in-law, compared with proportions with a living father, by age and sex, from simulations.

in-law at a later age (20–29) and by 30–39 a majority of men have a living mother-in-law. Throughout the rest of their lives, men are more likely to have a living mother-in-law than a living mother, because their mother-in-law is younger (on the average 7.5 years younger) than their own mother.

Figure 15.12 shows the parallel distributions for the proportion who have a living father-in-law and father for the two sexes. The principles are the same except that both are less likely to survive to any given age of ego, because they were older at ego's birth. A maximum of one-third of adult men will ever have the experience of having a living father-in-law under the demographic conditions of the !Kung.

The Total Inventory of Kin

AMBUSH makes a summary of all of the relatives counted, including all those discussed above plus one's spouses, and their siblings, and children, checking to see whether the same individuals are counted twice by being related in multiple ways (for instance both cousin and aunt, by marriage). In this summary count (but not in the counts for individual relations) individuals appear only once. Table 15.1 shows the computer-produced cross-tabulation of the number of relatives by the age of ego (the two sexes are combined). The marginal totals for numbers of relatives show that the distribution is smooth and unimodal, with a mean number of relatives per person in all age groups of 16.07 in this simulation (confirmed to be approximately 16 in replicated simulations). Almost no one has no living relatives in these simulations, and almost no one has more than 40 living relatives in these close categories. Clearly the simulations confirm that there is a need for weaker forms of kinship, handled by the !Kung through the name relationships, to provide a basis for association of most of the pairs of people in this kinship-based society.

TABLE 15.1
Cross-Tabulation of Number of Relatives by Age (from Simulation)[a]

									Number of relatives															More than 45	Total
Age	1	3	5	7	9	11	13	15	17	19	21	23	25	27	29	31	33	35	37	39	41	43	45	More than 45	Total
4	0	11	20	19	17	20	14	10	11	6	10	8	5	5	2	3	5	2	0	0	0	0	0	0	11
9	2	13	13	13	10	12	13	11	8	9	6	8	8	7	1	3	10	2	0	0	0	0	16	0	9
14	5	16	16	10	10	10	11	9	8	7	4	9	9	5	6	5	10	0	0	0	0	0	0	4	9
19	13	14	6	6	10	9	6	12	10	11	8	10	9	6	6	3	5	2	0	8	0	0	16	17	9
24	2	5	7	8	9	6	9	9	9	11	9	7	5	11	12	13	8	18	11	16	27	9	16	17	8
29	5	2	4	8	5	5	6	6	10	13	8	11	11	12	15	14	12	15	13	16	0	0	0	17	8
34	2	2	3	3	4	6	7	7	7	6	9	9	10	12	15	10	10	10	8	8	36	27	8	0	7
39	0	0	3	4	4	3	3	7	6	7	9	8	9	11	8	14	8	7	19	8	9	9	8	4	6
44	0	3	2	4	5	3	5	5	5	5	9	4	8	8	8	14	5	5	16	8	0	45	0	13	5
49	5	3	3	5	3	4	5	6	5	6	7	8	6	6	10	4	3	13	11	25	0	0	0	17	5
54	10	3	2	4	4	4	5	3	6	4	6	7	5	4	3	1	8	10	8	8	18	0	8	8	4
59	18	3	3	3	4	4	3	4	4	3	5	3	3	5	3	5	1	5	11	8	0	0	8	0	4
64	8	1	4	2	2	2	2	2	2	2	2	0	2	0	3	0	1	5	0	0	0	0	8	0	2
69	5	8	3	2	4	2	3	2	2	2	1	1	1	0	0	2	1	0	0	0	9	9	8	0	2
74	10	5	2	2	2	1	0	0	1	1	1	1	0	0	0	0	1	0	0	0	0	0	0	0	1
HI	8	1	1	1	1	1	0	0	0	0	1	0	0	0	0	1	0	0	0	0	0	0	0	0	0
Number of persons	37	106	240	323	417	532	551	611	542	469	410	311	272	204	132	84	58	38	36	12	11	11	12	23	5442

[a] Entries in cells other than *Total* are percentages of columns. *Totals* give the *Ns* in rows and columns.

There is not a strong age pattern of the total numbers of ties to others in Table 15.1. Young children and old people tend to have somewhat fewer ties than middle-aged people. Examination of other simulations in which the sex of ego is distinguished confirms, as we have seen for individual ties, that women tend to reach their maximum kinship count somewhat earlier in life than men, but overall the changes are not great, as ties to members of younger generations tend to replace the diminishing number of ties to members of the older generations over the life span.

Households and Kinship Groups

To this point, we have discussed the formation and maintenance of kin ties simply as pairs of related people, summing them as though they are all equally important. Kinship ties are, in addition, clustered into groups that for some purposes serve as the basic building blocks of the social organization. One kind of group that is very important to !Kung life is the household, the units that live together, move together, and make up the bands or camps of people who carry out the economic organization of life.

TABLE 15.2[a]
Household Size by Age (from Simulation)

Age	1	2	3	4	5	6	7	8	9	More than 9	Total
4	0	0	15	22	19	21	25	27	55	0	11
9	0	1	10	16	22	20	26	27	11	0	9
14	2	4	9	11	18	25	19	20	11	0	9
19	30	9	2	0	0	0	0	0	0	0	9
24	19	12	6	4	0	0	1	0	11	0	9
29	5	14	11	7	5	4	3	5	0	0	8
34	2	6	9	10	9	5	7	7	0	0	7
39	1	3	8	9	8	9	3	5	0	0	6
44	2	4	7	7	8	6	8	7	11	0	5
49	3	7	8	5	4	4	4	0	0	0	5
54	3	10	6	3	2	1	0	0	0	0	4
59	5	11	3	1	1	0	0	0	0	0	4
64	4	5	1	0	0	0	0	0	0	0	2
69	7	4	0	0	0	0	0	0	0	0	2
74	4	2	0	0	0	0	0	0	0	0	1
HI	3	0	0	0	0	0	0	0	0	0	0
Total	1205	958	1239	1096	600	204	91	40	9	0	5442

[a]See footnote a, Table 15.1.

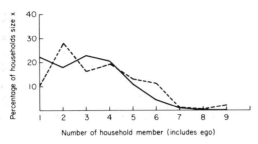

Figure 15.13. Household size distribution, from a long simulation (N = 5442) and from the !Kung population of 1968 (N = 569).

AMBUSH counts the members of households by applying a few simple rules. Married couples are always counted as being in the same household, along with their children under 15-years old, if any. In cases of divorce, children are counted in the household of the mother, whether or not she remarried. Orphaned children remain with their surviving parent, if any, and are counted as a sibling group if both parents are dead. Orphans, like other children, leave the household one by one to form households of one member from age 15 until their marriage.

Table 15.2 shows the computer-produced cross-tabulation of household size and age of egos, and Figure 15.13 shows the household size distributions from this simulation and from the !Kung population in 1968 (see Table 2.3). We note in Figure 15.13 that the simulation, following these simple rules of allocation, produces a distribution that agrees with the observed one in that household sizes of six and greater are rarely observed and ten and greater are never observed. The simulations lead us to expect more households of size one than observed, but as we have noted people find such households inconvenient and form temporarily larger households of several unmarried young adults or a grandmother and one or more of her adolescent grandchildren.

The age pattern of household composition is a strong one, even if it is somewhat stronger in the simulations than in the real population. Children tend to be located in large households, young adults tend to be in small ones, mature adults again have large ones, and old people are in small ones. The causes of this oscillation over the life cycle can be found in the composition of the two kinds of relative groups that, over the course of each person's life, serve as the basis for household formation. These groups are the natal family (or family of orientation) and the conjugal family (or family of procreation).

Natal Families

The first type of group we will look at is the natal family, that made up of ego's living parents (whether or not they remain married to one another) and living full

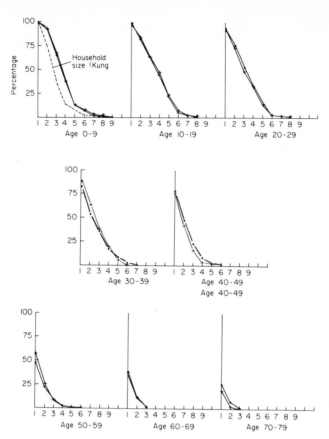

Figure 15.14. Proportions of age group who have *x* and more living members of their natal family, from simulation.

siblings. Individuals may have from 0 to 10 living members of their natal family, counting two parents and up to eight siblings (in addition to themselves). But, in fact, few groups larger than 6 members are observed for egos of any age.

Figure 15.14 shows the cumulative percentage of egos in 10-year age groups who have *x* and more living members of their natal family. For persons 0–9 (of both sexes), for instance, about 99% have at least one living parent or sibling, 92% have two or more, 67% have three or more, and so on. Household composition is based entirely upon the natal family only for the persons age 0–9 and even at that age the household size is consistently lower than the size of the natal family, as parents may be divorced and older siblings may have left the household. Household size is plotted by dashed lines in the 0–9 segment of Figure 15.14.

It is clear in Figure 15.14 that the probability of having x living members of the natal family decreases steadily with age. There are no systematic differences between males and females in their probabilities of having x living members of the natal family.

Conjugal Families

The distribution of conjugal family membership (the family formed by marriage, consisting of spouse and children) is, on the other hand, quite different over the life span for men and women. People age 0–9 never have a conjugal family, so they are omitted in Figure 15.15. Among the 10- to 19-year-olds, only women have conjugal families and most of these are small, consisting of self and husband, and rarely one child.

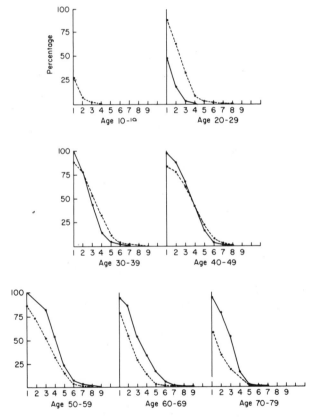

Figure 15.15. Proportions of age who have x and more living members of their conjugal family, from simulation.

Among the 20- to 29-year olds, there are conjugal families for both men and women, but women have a higher frequency of families at each size and larger. Because women marry younger than men, they are further along the process of family formation at each age compared to men their own age. Compared to their husbands, however, who are on the average 7.5-years older, women are at the same stage, except that a certain percentage of women do not ever marry. By age 30–39, all of the men have at least one member of a conjugal family (the wife) and about 80% have one or more living children. In the 30–39 age group, the distribution of conjugal family size is almost identical to household size for both men and women.

By age 50–59 men have higher conjugal family sizes in general than women of the same age, in large part because their wives are younger and hence are less likely to have died than the women's husbands. This trend continues throughout the rest of the lifespan, with women more likely than men to have no or few surviving members of their conjugal family. By age 70, over 40% of the women, but less than 10% of the men, will have no surviving members of their conjugal family.

Household size, then, is a function of the probabilities of having x number of living members of one of two groups, natal families from ages 0–14 and conjugal family from ages 15 on, reduced by the probability that living members will not be in the household due to divorce or by having reached maturity. The families called "natal" for the children, are, of course, the same family units that are called "conjugal" from the point of view of the parents of those families, which causes the similar distributions for the young and the middle-aged.

Number of Simultaneously Living Generations

One of the general observations brought out by the simulations is the frequency of simultaneously living generations in a population like the !Kung. We have seen in Figures 15.5 and 15.10 that three simultaneously living generations are commonly observed, even though a majority of the living people at any time will not be a part of one of them. The ties between the generations can be broken by failure of connections in either direction: Many of the younger people will fail to have living parents and grandparents, and many of those who survive to old age will fail to have living children and grandchildren.

The existence of four simultaneous generations is not counted by AMBUSH, but can be estimated by calculation of the joint probability of people in particular age groups having *both* living grandparents and children or *both* living parents and grandchildren. For the 20- to 29-year old group, for instance, about 10% of the women and about 2% of the men will be members of a four-generation family. Four simultaneous generations, then, should be an infrequent but regular occurrence among the !Kung. There were several four-generation families observed in 1968, including the one used for illustration of the age estimation procedure in Chapter 2.

Five-generation families can only occur when a person in the 30–39 group has both a living grandparent *and* a living grandchild. The 30- to 39-year-old would necessarily have to be a woman, as none of the men in that age group have any grandchildren yet. This would be an extremely rare event, underestimated by AMBUSH because we cut off life span at age 80, but very rare in the real world as well. There were no cases of five generations simultaneously living in 1968, although several of the four generation families had teenagers in the youngest generation. The probability of achieving five generations simultaneously is of course increased when the generations are traced through women, as their generation length is shorter, both for the minimum and for the average.

Kinship Relations as Resources

There is a sense in which having kinship ties of all kinds, even ties to dependent kin, is a source of social strength for people like the !Kung. The results of these simulations of the frequency of such ties underscores the fact that the inventory of relatives is created and maintained for particular egos in part before his or her birth (for ascending generations), in part at a considerable distance from ego (for aunts, uncles, cousins, nieces, and nephews) and only in part through events over which he or she has any immediate control, such as marriage and the creation of one's own group of offspring. A particular demographic regime will produce regular distributions of individuals who have few and many kin. These distributions are characteristics of individuals, influencing their life chances and their social position, just as characteristics such as personality and skill do. Individuals have very little control over their position in the kinship group.

The Early Social Prominence of Women

We have seen in this chapter that there are typical differences between men and women of the same age in their kin resources over the life cycle. Women are equal to their male peers in connectivity to the two older generations and to their own generations, but are equal to their older husbands in the two descending generations of kin. The tendency for women to have more kin than men of the same age is even more pronounced among the affinal kin during the twenties and thirties than among the consanguinal kin that we have concentrated upon here.

The consequences of these differences between men and women over the life cycle, at least for a group like the !Kung, who maintain a bilateral and symmetrical kinship system, is that women tend to be socially more important than men earlier in life, particularly during their childbearing years, whereas men take a more dominant position in the social structure of kinship later in life, especially after age 50. A number of observers have commented on the relative sexual equality of the !Kung (Lee 1972a; Draper 1975). If we interpret the status of the sexes not as a cultural category but as the sum of the social resources of the members of the two groups, we can see some of the reasons why this should be true. Women not only contribute substantial amounts of food by gathering, but their kinship connections are important in the social structure. On the other hand it is also clearly true that men who survive into old age are far more likely than women to be the central members of kinship clusters, whereas a substantial proportion of old women will become isolated by their failure to have surviving children and grandchildren, so that isolated old women will be more often seen than isolated old men.

Kinship and Demography: Review and Overview

We have seen in this chapter that simulation is a useful tool for spelling out in some detail the implications of a set of demographic rates for the kinship ties between individuals in a given population. Once we have seen that it is possible to generate the expected distributions of numbers of ties of particular types from the demographic parameters, it is natural to go back to ask how accurate and how useful these distributions are likely to be.

The accuracy of the results might be judged on criteria of internal consistency, of agreement with other methods of estimation, or, perhaps most importantly, with the observed distributions counted in the real population from which the demographic parameters have been computed. On this last criteria, we see that there are several reasons why one might find disagreement between empirical populations and the simulations. The simulation model represents a simplification of the structure of a real population and deviations from these simplications might well lead to a difference in kinship structure between real and simulated populations. One important source of difference is the assumption in simulation that the underlying probabilities of births and deaths are constant over long periods of time, despite stochastic fluctuations in measurable rates per year, whereas the underlying probabilities of events may vary over time in any real population. Particularly if these rates are correlated in complex ways—perhaps by the alternation of "good years" in which fertility tends to be above average and mortality less than average with "bad years"—the variance in numbers of kin per category in the real population might be inflated over that of the simulations. Another assumption built into the simulations that may not be an accurate representation of events in real populations is the independence of probabilities of fertility and mortality from the number of kin. Having large numbers of kin may actually increase the probability of survival and reproduction for some individuals, perhaps through improvements in the diet of those who are central in the kinship system compared to those who are marginal. Conversely, it could be that having a large number of kin implies that one will have a large number of dependents and competitors for scarce resources, so that the fertility and survival of those with large numbers of kin might be lower than average, which would reduce the variance of the distributions. Complicating interrelationships of this sort can only be explored and quantified by large amounts of what promises to be difficult research.

The usefulness of the simulated distributions derives in part from the ease of obtaining them in comparison with the substantial cost of counting kin in a real population. We plotted the proportions of !Kung with living kin only for the simplest relationships, those of mother and father, because of the substantial investment in labor required to take each individual in turn as ego, and go through the geneologies counting the number of ties to others. This laborious job can be reduced by use of computer programs such as Collier's (1974) KIN-PROGRAM. This method may prove useful in the future for the purpose of exploring the accuracy of simulated results. As a method for formulating the null hypothesis of the relationship of kinship and demography, a simulation program like AMBUSH is clearly very useful.

One might ask in addition whether it is possible to use the method in reverse, estimating demographic parameters for a population in which direct information is no longer available from information on the genealogical connections of a population from which the distributions of living relatives in certain types can be obtained. There are, for instance, some very detailed genealogies collected at early stages of contact by explorers, missionaries, or anthropologists. Can these lists be "mined" for demographic data with the use of these new computer tools? Ideally, the answer would seem to be that, yes, these valuables sources of information could be used in this way. Yet we can anticipate some difficult and perhaps fatal problems that will necessarily be encountered along the way.

One issue is the availability of age information on the living persons mentioned in the genealogies. It is unfortunately true that most of the peoples we might want to study in this way are among those who have no ability to provide information on their own ages. Making reasonable age estimates will be difficult without the cooperation of living people. A second problem has to do with the completeness and accuracy of the data collection: Underreporting of ties will lead us to overestimate mortality, whereas including fictive ties along with biological relationships will lead us to underestimate mortality (or overestimate fertility through the size of sibling groups). A third problem is inherent in the size of the population covered by the genealogies. We have seen in this chapter that cross-sections of populations as small as 300–400 persons display considerable irregularity in size distributions, and the long run that cumulated information on the size distributions of kin groups from observations every 25 years and displayed such smooth and potentially useful distributions was based on more than 5000 egos. This size represents an unrealistic goal for those early investigators. Although theoretically it should be possible to "work backwards" from the kinship to the demography, then, practically it may not be possible, at least at our current level of understanding of the relationships.

16

Genetic Implications of !Kung Demography

We started this book by discussing, in Chapter 1, the reasons why the Dobe !Kung are of more than ordinary interest to scientists and why it is worthwhile to pursue demographic studies of them despite handicaps such as their inability to provide information on their ages and the small total numbers available for study. The main reason, we argued there, is that the !Kung provide an "ethnographic analogy" for increasing our understanding of the very long, and evolutionarily crucial, hunting and gathering stage of human adaptation. Having described the demographic processes of the Dobe !Kung that have been observed, it is appropriate to go on to consider explicitly what these parameters imply for studies of human evolution.

When we mention human evolution we think immediately of the dramatic events of the transformation from prior forms of our genus (*Homo*) or our species (*sapiens*), events that geneticists refer to as macroevolution. The !Kung cannot, unfortunately, provide us with any clearer perspective on those important events than any other people living today, since, as was noted in Chapter 1, they cannot serve as a satisfactory proxy for "early man." The !Kung are separated from the speciation event by approximately the same number of generations as all other contemporary peoples and their gene pool has been "at risk" of modification by microevolutionary processes over this whole period of time.

It is microevolutionary questions—those of the continuous maintenance and modification of the gene pool as one generation follows another—that we can ask and attempt to answer on the basis of knowledge of the demographic processes of the !Kung. The !Kung have been living as hunters and gatherers in the Kalahari for many generations. The microevolutionary events that have molded their particular gene pool, then, are influenced by their particular environment, their way of life, the size of their breeding group, and other features of their lives, some of which we may hope to know on the basis of the current series of studies.

We know that the real San population is distinctive from other groups in a number of apparently genetically determined traits, such as their small stature, peppercorn hair, and epicanthic folds. Although such surface features can be recognized at a glance, geneticists find that blood types and other biochemical traits of individuals are more useful in exploring the processes of microevolution in a particular population. But the adaptive significance of any particular trait is difficult to evaluate and the demographic information available is not particularly helpful in answering the question. We will not, therefore, attempt to tabulate features of genetic distinctiveness of the !Kung or attempt to incorporate Harpending's (1971) data on gene frequencies of the !Kung into the discussion. Instead we will concentrate on using the demographic information available to explore the mechanics of genetic transmission across the generations implied by those demographic parameters, mechanisms that can, in principle, lead to distinctness of populations.

Microevolutionary changes occur primarily from some individuals having more viable offspring than others, so that the genes of the successful parents come to make up a larger proportion of the gene pool of the population in the next generation. When this occurs because the probability of survival or reproduction for individuals of a particular genotype is consistently greater in a given environment than that of individuals of an alternative genotype, we speak of natural selection. When the proportion of alleles of one type shifts from that of the previous generation simply through chance factors, such as the stochastic fluctuations in population structure that we have seen operating in AMBUSH simulations, we have a case of random drift. Both processes tend toward the elimination of some allele forms and tend to make the population distinctive from others. These are the processes we explore in this chapter, using the data on the !Kung demography.

We have already established the facts of !Kung demography we need for this analysis. Here we will merely rearrange some of the facts to put them into a convenient form for the consideration of genetic and evolutionary implications.

The Demographic Facts of !Kung Women's Lives

The distribution that expresses all of the facts we need to know in order to understand genetic transmission is that of the eventual parity of newborns, a

TABLE 16.1
Reproductive Success of a Cohort of !Kung Women[a]

Parity distribution	Age 0 ($N = 100$)		Age 15 ($N = 56$)		Age 50 ($N = 31$)	
	"Mothers"	Children	Mothers	Children	Mothers	Children
0	52	0	8	0	2	0
1	3	3	3	3	1	1
2	4	8	4	8	2	4
3	7	21	7	21	3	9
4	10	40	10	40	6	24
5	10	50	10	50	7	35
6	8	48	8	48	6	36
7	4	28	4	28	3	21
8	2	16	2	16	1	8
9	0.+	0	0.+	0	0.+	0
Totals	100	214	56	214	31	141
$\bar{X}$		2.14		3.86		4.52
Variance (V_r)		6.52		5.14		4.38

Net reproduction rate = 1.044
T (mean length of a generation) = 27.5
r (intrinsic rate of natural increase) = .0016

[a] Pre-1950 rates used for fertility and mortality. Parity distributions are prospective (*i.e.*, the number of children who will eventually be born to survivors at age x).

distribution that was shown for some simulated populations in Chapter 15. Table 16.1 shows a single, roughly rounded version of the eventual parity of cohorts of !Kung women we will use in this chapter to represent the central tendencies of what we have learned about !Kung demography. Table 16.1 shows the eventual parity to survivors at three points in the lifespan: birth, the beginning of the child-bearing period (age 15), and the end of the childbearing period (age 50). The distributions for later points in the lifespan are shown for comparison with other populations, where only the later information may be available.

Note that Table 16.1 shows the fate of a cohort, a group of people born at the same time and moving through the lifespan together. The table is "size-free": we merely assert that there are 100 members of the initial cohort, which can be interpreted as 100% of an unknown number. The net reproduction rate is implied by the distribution of parity to newborns, 1.0444, slightly lower than other estimates due to the rough rounding used here. With a mean length of a generation of 27.5 years for the women (again rounded for simplicity), we have an intrinsic rate of natural increase of .0016 per year, a low but plausible estimate

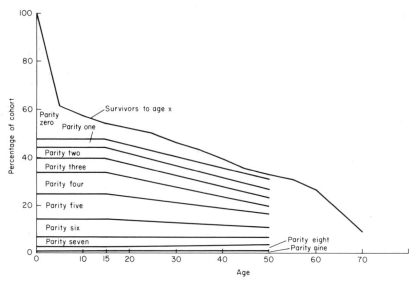

Figure 16.1. Eventual parity of survivors to age x, based on !Kung women.

for a population like the !Kung. Figure 16.1 shows the same information as Table 16.1, in the form of a graph of eventual parity.

Numbers of Descendents in Successive Generations

By extention from Table 16.1 we can also calculate the expected numbers of grandchildren and great-grandchildren for the members of the initial cohort. The calculations can be carried out for any number of generations, provided that we are willing to make the assumption that the eventual parity of newborns is independent of that of their ancestors. This is a very interesting assumption, of the sort made routinely by demographers and by mathematicians in branching theory (of which the question of numbers of descendents in successive generations is a part). Note however that the assumption requires us to assert that there is no heritable component to reproductive success, that the offspring of the most successful parents will be just as successful and unsuccessful as the children of any parents. Since this is a central issue in the study of the effects of demography and evolution, it would be a mistake to accept that assumption too readily and plunge into the detailed calculation of the number of descendents in successive generations as though those calculations answered all of the questions we wish to raise. Nevertheless, it is interesting to look briefly at the results of this kind of calculation, just to establish the null hypothesis (what we would expect to observe if the assumption were true).

One issue is the probability of failing to have any descendents in each generation. We have seen that 52% of a cohort of 100 women will fail to have any children. Some will have children, but will fail to have any grandchildren. We calculate this proportion by summing the probability of having no grandchildren for each of the parities, which is .52 for the 3% who had one child, $.52^2 = .27$ for the 4% of the initial cohort who had two children, $.52^3 = .14$ for the 7% who had three children, and so on. These probabilities sum to 4.94%, which we can interpret as saying that roughly 52% will fail to have any children and an additional 5% will fail to have grandchildren, so 57% will fail to have descendents born after two generations. By the third generation the probability of joining the group who have no descendents becomes very small, as the mean number of descendents for those who have any moves away from the low frequencies, where the probability of failing is high.

Among those who have any descendents, the mean number more than doubles in each generation, and the distribution as a whole "flattens out" to form, after a few generations, an L-shaped distribution with a substantial proportion at zero descendents and a very small proportion at each of the frequencies. Both the mean and the maximum number of descendents per generation increases swiftly, so that at least a few members of our initial cohort can have very large numbers of descendents born in late generations (64 grandchildren if each of 8 children had 8 children, 512 great-grandchildren if each of those grandchildren had 8, and so forth. This sequence of events would be extremely unlikely (indeed, the probability is vanishingly small), but it illustrates one of the

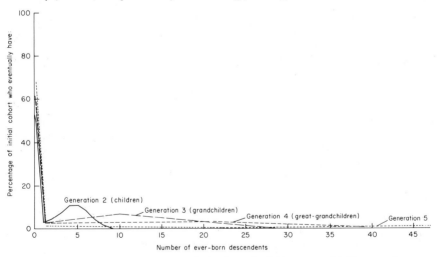

Figure 16.2. Expected distribution of number of children, grandchildren, and great-grandchildren, to a cohort of !Kung women.

many pathways to the number of descendents in future generations. Figure 16.2 illustrates the shape of the distributions for the number of descendents born in successive generations to the initial cohort. There is no point in attempting to illustrate more than three generations, as the distributions only become flatter, closer to zero frequency at each number, and spread out further. Illustrating this process with the example of a small closed population demonstrates vividly that the route to having a large number of descendents in successive generations necessarily requires that some individuals will occupy multiple slots in the genealogies of their descendents as the expected number of descendents soon exceeds the size of the whole population. !Kung incest rules prohibit the same person from appearing in more than one place within two generations of any person, but successful members of older generations can and will be multiply related to their descendents. It is also true, of course, that the contributions of ancestors to their descendents' gene inventory along each pathway of descent is diluted, approximately halved, for each generation we count.

Table 16.1 and Figure 16.2 provide the basic facts we need to interpret genetic transmission in a population like the !Kung women. Before we consider what they tell us, let us look at the similar distribution for the !Kung men, so that we can compare the two sexes.

Demographic Facts of Genetic Transmission: Men's Rates

As we noted before, AMBUSH does not count men's parity, either at the beginning or at the end of the reproductive ages, but we have the facts needed to estimate the distribution directly. In any case, the simulations do not permit polygamy, which tends to inflate individual variance in reproductive success for men, so we will obtain a more accurate distribution by working with the observed parity distribution for men 55 and over (found in Table 13.5). We start by plotting the number of survivors to each age out of the initial cohort, the l_x column of the male life table. We note that 23.05 (rounded to 23) of an original 100 newborns survive to age 55. From the distribution of parity to real !Kung men age 55 and older, we calculate the proportion of those 23 survivors who would have x offspring. There are so few men with 10 and more children that they are grouped and coded at parity 11. We know from the study of real !Kung men that there is no fertility below age 20, so we count the beginning of the reproductive period for men at that age. The life table tells us to expect 50.93 (rounded to 51) survivors to age 20 out of each 100 newborns. This group must have all the children ever born to the cohort, including those reported for men 55 and over. If 100 women have 214 children, 100 men must have 204 children (allowing for the extra 5 men implied by the sex ratio at birth). The mean of the

TABLE 16.2
Reproductive Success of a Cohort of !Kung Men [a]

Parity	Age 0 (N = 100)		Age 20 (N = 51)		Age 55 (N = 23)	
	"Fathers"	Children	Fathers	Children	Fathers	Children
0	62	0	13	0	2	0
1	3	3	3	3	1	1
2	3	6	3	6	2	4
3	4	12	4	12	2	6
4	4	16	4	16	1	4
5	5	25	5	25	3	15
6	5	30	5	30	3	18
7	6	42	6	42	4	28
8	4	32	4	32	2	16
9	3	27	3	27	2	18
11 (10–12)	1	11	1	11	1	11
Totals	100	204	51	204	23	121
$\bar{X}$		2.04		4.00		5.26
Variance (V_f)		9.27		10.36		8.93

Net reproduction rate = 1.045
T (mean length of a generation) = 35.0
r (intrinsic rate of natural increase) = .0013

[a] Parity distributions are prospective (number of children who will eventually be born to survivors at age x).

parity distribution for survivors to age 20, then, must be exactly 4. The upper tail of the parity distribution for men at age 20 is given by the distribution for men at age 55: If one survivor at age 55 had 11 children, at least one of those at age 20 must also have had 11. At each parity we start with the number of those at age 55 who had that number and consider how many of those who died between ages 20 and 55 must have had that number in addition. The distributions at age 20 and at birth (found in Table 16.2), then, are fictional but plausible. Use of the known parameters—survivors to each age, the mean number of children produced, and the minimum frequencies at each parity given by the experience of older men— reduces the range of error introduced by guessing to such a degree that it is likely that errors introduced by rough rounding exceed the errors introduced by guessing at the form of the distribution. In any case, the men must have some distribution of this form; we will explore the implications of the one given. Figure 16.3 shows the same information as Table 16.2, in graphical form.

An examination of Table 16.2 shows that the distribution of reproductive success for men in the !Kung population is flatter, with a higher variance, than

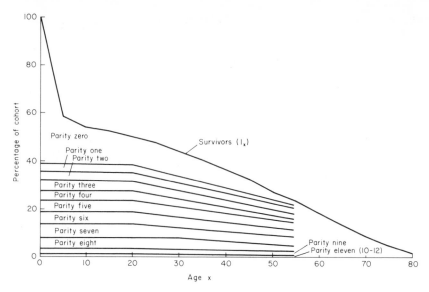

Figure 16.3. Eventual parity of survivors to age x, based on !Kung men.

that of the !Kung women. The maximum number of children born to the most successful man is higher, 11 children, than the maximum born to the most successful woman, 8. Higher proportions of men have 0 children, because the men's rate of prereproductive mortality is slightly higher at each age and because the men do not start their reproductive careers until age 20. The older age schedule of fertility for the men insures that there are fewer men available to be fathers than women available to be mothers, so the successful fathers must be more successful, on the average, to provide a father for each child.

If we plotted the number of descendents in each generation for men, as we did for women in Figure 16.2, we would see that the distribution is even flatter for men than it is for the women at each generation.

The Opportunity for Natural Selection

Each generation is produced by only the successful reproducers of the previous generation, so that microevolution occurs through the mechanics of differential reproductive success. When the rate of microevolution is measured by demographic performance rather than from measures of the frequency distributions of alleles, it represents a ceiling, a maximum rate of speed of change in gene frequencies. This rate is called the opportunity for natural selection.

Consider what it would mean if a population had no opportunity for natural selection. Imagine a population in which all infants born are certain to survive to

16. GENETIC IMPLICATIONS OF !KUNG DEMOGRAPHY

maturity, in which the sex ratio is equal, in which all adults mate and have exactly two children (one boy and one girl, at least on the average), who in turn will be certain to survive long enough to do the same. The opportunity for natural selection as measured by their demographic performance is zero: There is no possibility that the gene pool will change from one generation to the next because some people have more offspring than others.

These conditions do not hold in any known population. Some people always have more offspring than others, hence changes in the gene pool can occur in this way between generations. We can rank populations in the degree of difference in reproductive success between members of initial cohorts, from those in which reproductive success is distributed quite equally to those in which a small minority produce all of the subsequent generation.

We will look at the opportunity for natural selection among the !Kung, as shown for the females in Table 16.1 and for the males in Table 16.2, in two ways. The first is a Lorenz curve of the distributions, a visual method that spells out the differences between individuals quite clearly. The second is the computation of Crow's indices of the opportunity for natural selection, a more precise algebraically manipulatable measure that permits comparison with other populations.

Figure 16.4 shows the Lorenz curve for !Kung women and men, per generation. To plot the curve, we rank order the groups by parity and plot the cumula-

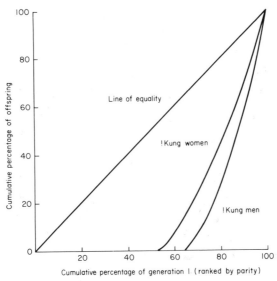

Figure 16.4. Lorenz curve of the distribution of reproductive success (eventual parity) to !Kung men and women.

tive proportion of groups of parents by the proportion of offspring which they have. One hundred percent of the parents necessarily produce 100% of the offspring, so the end point of the graph is fixed. In our example of a population that had no opportunity for natural selection because all parents have exactly two children, it would be true that 10% of the parents would produce 10% of the children, 50% produce 50% of the children, and so on. The plot for such a group would be that marked "line of equality" in Figure 16.4. For the !Kung women, however, Table 16.1 tells us that 52% of the potential parents in a cohort of newborns (those at parity zero) will produce 0% of the children, the least successful 55% (those at parities zero and one) produce 1% of the children, and so on. We read from Figure 16.4 that 50% of the children are produced by the most successful 18% of the women and the most successful 10% of the women produce about 30% of the children in each generation.

Among the men, the distribution is more unequal. About 50% of the children are produced by the most successful 12% of the men and the most successful 10% of the men produce 45% of the children. Clearly the level of opportunity for natural selection implied by these demographic parameters is very high in an absolute sense. If the genes of the successful minority are different from those of the unsuccessful members of their cohort, we would expect to see radical changes in the gene pool of the population over a period of time as short as a

TABLE 16.3
Crow's Index of the Opportunity for Natural Selection for !Kung Men and Women

!Kung women	Age 0	Age 15	Age 50
I_f, index of selection intensity due to fertility $(= V_f/\bar{X}^2)$	1.424	.345	.214
I_m, index of selection intensity due to mortality $(= p_d/p_s)$	—	.786	.786
I, total index $(= I_m + (1/p_s) I_f)$	1.424	1.402	1.168

!Kung men	Age 0	Age 20	Age 55
I_f	2.228	.648	.323
I_m	—	.961	.961
I	2.228	2.232	1.594

where

V_f = variance of the fertility (parity) distribution
$\bar{X}$ = mean parity
p_d = the probability of death from birth to the beginning of the reproductive age
$p_s = 1 - p_d$.

generation, as nearly everyone would come to be descended from the successful minority.

Crow's index of the opportunity for natural selection represents an alternative way of understanding the implications of the same distributions. Crow's index consists of two subcomponents, one of which measures the effect of prereproductive mortality on differential reproductive success, the other of which measures the differences in childbearing among the parents who survive long enough to reproduce. Table 16.3 shows the formulae and the computation of these indices for the !Kung. Due to limitations of available data, Crow's indices are usually computed only for the women of a population by combining the mean and variance of parity for women at the end of the reproductive period with the rates of prereproductive mortality, a form of computation that, as we can see in Table 16.3, rather substantially underestimates opportunity for natural selection for any population that has a substantial proportion of the cohort dying between the beginning and the end of the reproductive years. It is acknowledged in population genetics that this form of computation underestimates opportunity for natural selection, but since it is the usual form in which data are available, it is the one that should be used to compare the !Kung with other populations. Kobayashi (1969) has proposed an alternative method for correcting the error introduced.

We ask two questions about the results shown in Table 16.3. First, is the index of opportunity for natural selection for the !Kung high or low in comparison to other populations observed?

Table 16.4 presents data on Crow's indices as computed for a range of populations and collated by Spuhler (1976). We see that the !Kung rates (for women at the end of the reproductive period) are not particularly high among populations with premodern levels of mortality and expectation of life at birth of less than 50 years. In general, it is easy to see from the form of the computation of Crow's index that the higher the mortality, the greater the opportunity for natural selection. Similarly, when we look at the fertility component, we see that opportunity for natural selection is at a maximum when the variance of the parity distribution is high and the mean low. The !Kung women have both a low mean and variance in parity, compared to other populations. Natural fertility high-parity populations, like the Hutterites, have a high variance and a high mean, which together minimize the opportunity for natural selection. Indeed, it is interesting to note that the fertility component is maximized in modern populations practicing contraception, in which the mean is low and the variance is inflated by subgroups that do not practice contraception, or practice it ineffectively. It is true, however, that the availability of effective medical care and contraceptives give a population the technological capacity to approach the extreme model described above in which there is no opportunity for natural selection. Each couple can control their fertility and limit it to the "ideal" size, which

TABLE 16.4
Crow's Index of the Opportunity for Natural Selection in Selected Populations and the !Kung Rates[a]

	I	I_m	I_f
Natural fertility populations			
1. Hutterites (around 1950)	.229	.053	.167
2. Khana, Punjab (1959)	.646	.440	.143
3. New South Wales (1900)	.753	.253	.399
4. Nyasaland (1957)	.793	.320	.358
5. Ashanti (1945)	1.159	.280	.687
6. !Kung women (1950)	1.168	.786	.214
7. San Carlos Apache (1905)	1.227	.919	.161
8. Oglala Sioux (1900)	1.446	1.112	.158
9. !Kung men (1950)	1.594	.961	.323
10. Sioux-Ojibwa (1890)	2.193	1.173	.469
11. Yanamamo (1970)	2.573	1.22	.61
Contracepting populations			
1. U.S. Whites (1964)	.950	.030	.920
2. Japan (1965)	1.040	.280	.760

[a] All data from Spuhler, 1976, except !Kung (present study) and Yanamamo (Weiss personal communication 1977).

in many modern societies is close to two children, and under the low mortality schedules characteristic of these populations the children are very likely to survive to maturity. Yet most modern populations have indices comparable to the !Kung's: Cavalli-Sforza and Bodmer (1971:320) give an index of 1.38 for U.S. women age 45–49 in 1950. We must keep in mind that any cause of failure to reproduce, whether due to celibacy, homosexuality, fear of overpopulation, or the "child-free" ideology developing among some young adults, is equivalent to prereproductive death in its effects on the opportunity for natural selection.

Our second question about the opportunity for natural selection is that of its interpretation: What do the indices mean for the study of microevolution? Crow's index (1958:2) was derived from Fisher's formulation of the "fundamental theorem of natural selection," which states that "The rate of increase in fitness of any organism at any time is equal to its genetic variance in fitness at that time" (Fisher 1958:37). To the extent that differences between individuals in eventual parity are due to genetically determined causes that can be inherited by the offspring of the successful parents, Crow's index (I, the total index) is the instantaneous geometric rate of increase in the mean fitness of the next generation.

Yet geneticists also stress that the index represents a ceiling. The effects of natural selection make up some part of the index, but random and environmental causes of differential reproductive success make up another component of the measure, one which cannot be distinguished from that of natural selection on the basis of the information that goes into the computation. Let us assume for a moment that the opportunity for natural selection of a population is very great at a moment in time and that the random component is small, so that the measure of the opportunity of natural selection is a good indicator of the rate of natural selection. If each offspring had the mean fitness (eventual parity) of his or her parents and the determinants of that fitness are genetic and inherited by the offspring, the parity distribution for the children's generation should shift toward the higher parities, with the inevitable implication that natural selection would produce a population explosion of impressive magnitude over only a few generations. This may occur sometimes, and may be very important in the evolutionary history of a population, but it would be an inherently short-lived phenomena, ending when all the members of the population have the more successful genotype and competition between equals for reproductive opportunity resumes. Rather than rapid change, what we find from the long-term study of undisturbed populations is a regular replication of the probabilities of survivorship and reproduction, generation after generation, which suggests that random and environmental determinants make up the largest part of the opportunity for natural selection.

In order to detect ongoing natural selection in a population, then, we have to go beyond data on the demographic parameters to look at the intergenerational correlation of reproductive success between parents and children. Elsewhere I have explored this question for the !Kung (Howell 1976c). Following the model of Fisher's (1958:214) study of intergenerational correlation of children born to members of the British peerage, the numbers of children born to !Kung women past reproductive age have been tabulated by the number of children born to their mothers. It was only possible to locate 90 cases where the eventual parity of daughters could be correlated with that of their mothers. The 95% confidence limits for rejecting the hypothesis that the true correlation coefficient is zero on a sample of this size are $\pm .21$. The observed correlation coefficient was .028. We are forced to conclude, therefore, that there is no empirical evidence that natural selection is currently occurring in the !Kung population, despite the considerable opportunity for it to occur as measured by differential reproductive success.

The unsuccessful search for empirical evidence of natural selection directs our attention rather forcefully to several theoretical conclusions previously known but underscored here. Attempting to understand the genetic consequences of demographic rates subjects us to the risk of confusing levels of analysis and the units proper to them. It is a population in a particular environment that has as a property a mortality schedule, a fertility schedule, a rate of growth, and a Crow's index of the opportunity for natural selection. Individuals in that population have an age at death and an eventual parity. It is they and their phenotypes that are acted upon by natural selection. The units of analysis of the gene pool of the population, however, are the alternative alleles of the genes. The alleles are transmitted to offspring in a process slightly more complicated than the process of producing offspring. Each individual can be seen as the collection of large numbers of pairs of alleles of genes, each of which contributes to, or subtracts from, the capacity of that individual to survive and reproduce in a given environment. It is probably counterproductive to speak of the eventual parity of individuals as their "fitness," as this formulation seems to imply that there is some one gene—or small set of genes—that ultimately determines reproductive success and can be inherited by the offspring. Instead it is probably more realistic to consider fitness a property of the particular alleles of genes, as geneticists do when making proband studies of the reproductive success of groups of people who do or do not have some particular genetic trait. This perspective makes it clear that the fitness of some particular genotype can only be measured on individuals by assuming that all of the genotypes at other loci that an individual holds are equal in their contributions to fitness. To explore microevolution in the !Kung population, then, we need to shift our attention from the individual level to that of the alleles in the gene pool.

Microevolution on the Allelic Level

Ernst Mayr, whose work on evolution has stressed the integration of the entire genome, has referred to genetic studies that focus upon single genes considered one at a time as "beanbag genetics." Mayr (1963) stresses, with the concurrence of modern geneticists, that it is a mistake to equate one gene with one trait. Genes code for complex molecules, not physical features such as blue eyes, and the pathways between the complex molecules and their consequences for the phenotype are (fortunately) not part of our concern here. It is important to note, however, that a single gene can affect many phenotypic traits; conversely a single trait can be influenced by the actions of many genes. The more that is learned about the redundancy of the genetic code and the regulatory genes, the clearer it becomes that we will not be able to thoroughly understand evolution as the sum of the events at single loci.

Nevertheless, "beanbag genetics" is the classic model in the field, and it is within this framework that the demographic information we have developed can be brought to bear on the evolutionary process. We begin the task of looking for the implications of demographic rates on allelic transmission by defining some terms and drawing on some of the basic facts of genetics for the background which we need.

Each person's genetic material consists of two matching segments of DNA at each of a large number of loci. The two matching segments are called alleles; the pair is called a "gene" or a locus, referring to the fact that the pairs are organized into locations along particular chromosomes. The number of chromosomes for each person is a species-specific constant (with certain exceptions caused by chromosomal abnormalities). The mapping of the chromosomes is proceeding rapidly at the present time, but has not yet been accomplished. The number of gene pairs for each person lies in the range of tens of thousands to perhaps millions, with the number 100,000 serving as a useful estimate of the order of magnitude (Cavalli-Sforza and Bodmer 1971:35).

Most of the gene pairs, in human beings as in other species, are believed to have only one form of alleles, so that the genes are monomorphic. Lewontin (1967) estimated that 70% of human genes are of this form, although the estimate is far from precise with current knowledge. Naturally all individuals are homozygous (having two identical alleles) for those loci. Genetic investigations of human populations are confined to the approximately 30% of the loci that are known to be polymorphic. While there must be some 30,000 such polymorphisms, only about 50 of these can be identified in individuals by examination of blood samples or other bodily secretions with current techniques. Most of these polymorphic genes have been found to have 2 alleles, but 3 alternatives alleles for the same locus are known (as in the ABO blood group) and higher numbers, up to about 10 alleles for a single locus, are known. Individuals can only hold a maximum of 2 alleles for a given locus, either the same (so that the person is homozygous, for any of the possible alleles) or different (heterozygous), no matter how many forms the alleles are known to take.

Genetic studies of particular populations, then, take the form of obtaining the frequency distribution in cross-section of the proportion of the population that displays each of the homozygous and heterozygous forms of the alleles at each of a small number of loci. Populations are characterized by their frequency distributions of individuals within types, and populations that are close to one another on criteria like distance are generally found to be similar in their frequency distributions. Search for "marker genes," found in all members of a given population and absent from all persons who are not part of that population, have so far been unsuccessful. It is not possible by bioassay to identify positively the group from which a person was drawn, as each individual will have some allelic form that is known to appear in other groups.

When it comes time to reproduce, then, each potential parent forms haploid gametes (ova or sperm) made up of a random sample of one from each pair of chromosomes held, the combination of the two haploid cells making up the full genetic inventory of the offspring. When the reproductive process works perfectly, the child can have no genetic material that was not a part of the inventory of one of the parents, although the combination of alleles over the large number of loci will necessarily be different than that of either of the parents. To understand microevolution on the allelic level of analysis, then, our primary task is to determine the number of copies of parental alleles that will be passed on to the next generation.

Genetic variability can in addition be created and increased over time. In a closed population, this can only occur by mutation. Mutations are random changes in the DNA of an allele during the replication process that forms the haploid cells. Through mutation, a child can start life with a uniquely different allele than those of either parent. It is a rare event, estimated by Cavalli-Sforza and Bodmer (1971:80–110) to be on the order of 10^{-4} to 10^{-8} per gene per generation, but since we have a large number of loci at risk of mutation (10^5), it is not a rare event when individuals are the unit of analysis. It has been estimated that the average person has several mutations in their genetic inventory. When an individual who has received a mutant allele survives and reproduces, that allele enters into the reproductive process like any other, with a .5 probability of inclusion in each haploid cell formed.

The Distribution of Number of Allelic Copies Transmitted per Parent

Each parent has two alleles at each locus and will transmit one of these to each child. Let us pick a locus at random and focus on one of the alleles (say the "left" one, even though they are not spatially arranged as right and left). The

TABLE 16.5
Distribution of Expected Number of Allelic Copies, !Kung Women's Rates (See Text for Method of Calculation)

Parity	Number of copies produced									Totals
	0	1	2	3	4	5	6	7	8	
0	52.000									52.000
1	1.500	1.500								3.000
2	1.000	2.000	1.000							4.000
3	.875	2.625	2.625	.875						7.000
4	.625	2.500	3.750	2.500	.625					10.000
5	.313	1.563	3.125	3.125	1.563	.313				10.000
6	.125	.750	1.875	2.500	1.875	.750	.125			8.000
7	.031	.219	.656	1.094	1.094	.656	.219	.031		4.000
8	.008	.063	.219	.438	.547	.438	.219	.063	.008	2.000
Totals	56.477	11.227	13.250	10.532	5.704	2.157	.563	.094	.008	100.000

Mean transmissions per mother = 1.07
Variance = 2.172
SD = 1.47

TABLE 16.6
Distribution of Expected Number of Allelic Copies for !Kung Men

Parity	Number of copies produced											Totals
	0	1	2	3	4	5	6	7	8	9	10	
0	62.000											62.000
1	1.500	1.500										3.000
2	.750	1.500	.750									3.000
3	.500	1.500	1.500	.500								4.000
4	.250	1.000	1.500	1.000	.250							4.000
5	.155	.780	1.565	1.565	.780	.155						5.000
6	.080	.470	1.170	1.563	1.170	.470	.080					5.000
7	.048	.330	.984	1.638	1.638	.984	.330	.048				6.000
8	.016	.124	.436	.876	1.094	.876	.436	.124	.016			4.000
9	.006	.054	.210	.492	.738	.738	.492	.210	.054	.006		3.000
11	.000	.005	.027	.081	.161	.226	.226	.161	.081	.027	.005	1.000
Totals	65.305	7.263	8.142	7.715	5.831	3.449	1.564	.543	.151	.033	.005	100.000

Mean transmissions per father = 1.02
Variance = 2.822
SD = 1.68

probability of transmission of that allele is .5 at each birth and the number transmitted over the lifetime is a function of the number of children eventually born. If the parent has zero children, the probability of transmission of the allele is zero. For one child the probability is .5, for two the probability of transmission at least once is .75 (the independent probability of transmitting it to each of two children).

Given a population for which we know the eventual parity distribution, as shown for the !Kung in Tables 16.1 and 16.2, we can calculate the whole distribution of number of allelic copies transmitted per parent. Tables 16.5 and 16.6 show these distributions for the !Kung women and men, respectively. A parent cannot transmit more copies of a particular allele than he or she had children, so the form of the table is triangular: from 0 to 8 copies for women, from 0 to 11 for men. The shape of the distribution on each row is that of Pascal's triangle, with each row multiplied by its frequency in the distribution of eventual parity. The mean number of transmissions per parent is uninteresting, since the mean will be very close to one in a stationary population, and greater than one when the population is growing. The mean, in fact, is closely related to the net reproduction rate, as the proportion of births that are female (.488 here) is very close to the probability of transmission per birth (.5). The variance of this distribution, on the other hand, will differ between populations and is inherent in a set of demographic rates.

Changes in the Allelic Proportions per Generation: Microevolution

The distributions shown in Tables 16.5 and 16.6 must be accurate, on the average, for all alleles in a population, no matter what microevolutionary events are occurring at any time, with the exception of the possibility that mutation will occasionally cause a parent to pass on neither of his or her alleles at the given locus. Since the probability of mutation at any particular locus is very low, the errors of prediction caused by creation of new mutations will not approach those introduced by rough rounding in the eventual parity distributions.

Let us step back from our focus on only a single allele to consider the implications of this process on the whole gene pool of the population. We can limit our task considerably by first eliminating from our consideration the large number of loci that are monomorphic, that have only one allelic form. All parents are homozygous for these loci, and it makes no difference at all to the gene pool that some 56% of women fail to transmit any copies of their "lefthand" allele but other women transmit multiple copies of it and similarly 56% of the women fail to transmit the "righthand" copy. For monomorphic genes 100% of the children and 100% of the parents will hold the given alleles and there is no possibility of microevolution unless mutation (or migration) changes the locus into a polymorphism. With that simple observation we solve an estimated 70% of the problems.

A large task remains: There are something on the order of 30,000 polymorphisms that can shift in frequency from one generation to the next, and four processes needed to describe the fate of any particular allele as it is transmitted from one generation to the next. These processes are (a) mutation, (b) natural selection, (c) random drift, and (d) equilibrium, the expected distributions, which provides the background within which change processes occur. Our demographic perspective does not permit us to describe exactly what the results of these processes will be in a population like the !Kung, but does allow us to clarify how various demographic parameters interact with the processes.

Mutation

The mutation process is crucially important in evolution, as it is the only means by which totally new possibilities can enter into a gene pool. Our demographic understanding of the !Kung, however, does not provide any particular insight into the mutation process in such a population, as the probability of mutation of each locus seems to be a variable dependent upon the chemical and radiation environment of the cells, unaffected by the demographic rates. There are just a few observations about mutation that might be useful.

We known that mutation is a rare event and that it occurs within a single cell ready to be passed on to an offspring. Geneticists are quite confident that most mutations are harmful to their possessors. If the mutation is so deleterious that the zygote cannot develop, the mutation is called lethal and it enters into our demographically based analysis of the number of alleles transmitted by parents only by being an event that tends to increase the length of birth intervals and hence limit total births. It is very unlikely that the *cause* of low fertility in a population like !Kung could be the extremely high rate of lethal mutations causing spontaneous abortions, because such mutations cannot be inherited, but must arise anew in each generation. (It is, however, possible that a population could be plagued with a high abortion rate if a genotype is lethal in the homozygous form but the heterozygous form is successful. A sublethal example of this is found in populations with high rates of the abnormal hemoglobin that produces the sickle cell trait; this is not a mutation process, but natural selection). Lethal and extremely harmful sublethal mutations may have tragic consequences for individuals, but have little effect on gene pools.

If the mutation does not eliminate itself, there are several possibilities that can happen. It may, by chance, take the form of an allele that already exists in the population. The substitution of a single nucleotide is the most common form of mutation (Cavalli-Sforza and Bodmer 1971:18) and such an event, if it happens not be harmful to the organism, is likely to have occurred previously. Such a mutation would affect the gene frequencies of the population only trivially.

The crucial kind of mutation is one that transforms an allele into a new and unique alternative. The new allele then competes with the alternative alleles at that locus for the survival and reproduction of its carriers. If there are differences in fitness between the alternative alleles in all or some portion of the environmental range experienced by the population, the natural selection model predicts its fate. If the alternative alleles happen to be equal in fitness, the equilibrium plus random drift model is needed. In other words, once an allele is in the genetic inventory of a member of the population, it is not important whether that allele arose by mutation in the current generation or many generations back, with the crucial exception of the fact that a newly formed allele is, by definition, a rare allele in the early stages of its introduction into a population, subject to all of the special influences on rare alleles to be discussed later.

Natural Selection

We have already explored the usefulness of demographic information for understanding natural selection through the concept of the opportunity for natural selection and found that analysis disappointing. Tables 16.5 and 16.6, which show the expected numbers of alleles transmitted by parents, permit some increase in conceptual clarity, though they do not permit us to predict the rate or direction of natural selection operating on the !Kung.

Let us go back to the focus on the "lefthand" allele at some particular locus and consider what happens if there is natural selection at that locus. The locus must be a polymorphism, and to keep the task as simple as possible, let us assume that there are only two alleles that parents can transmit to their offspring. The children receive genotypes formed by the contributions of their two parents; let us assume that there are only two genotypes relevant to the natural selection (in other words, one allele is dominant over the other in cases of heterozygosity). If we knew the frequency distribution of the alleles in the parents, we could calculate the expected number of offspring of the two genotypes.

Now when we look back at the reproductive success of the offspring, we know that the combined distribution for the two genotypes will be that of Tables 16.5 and 16.6. To see the effects of natural selection, we should divide up the total population into groups composed of only those with the two relevant genotypes and look at the eventual parity distribution of the two groups (dividing the variability in reproductive success into that component that can be attributed to the effects of this particular genotype and that due to all other causes). To believe in the results of this analysis, we have to be willing to assume that the environment is equal for the two groups. Of course, the measurement of the opportunity for natural selection is only valid for that particular environment, not for all possible environments.

Clearly the empirical task would be difficult and the results would be complex to interpret. We shall make no attempt to carry it out for the !Kung. The imaginary experiment, however, provides one useful conclusion. There are something like 30,000 polymorphisms in the gene pools of human populations; to test whether natural selection is operating on each of these polymorphisms it would be necessary to test them all. Clearly we would exhaust the variance in eventual parity to be allocated over such a large number of causes and would expect to find that—even with perfect information on a large population—most of the genotype differences could not be distinguished from zero (or neutrality of fitness of the alternative genotypes). It would be astonishing if there were not complex interaction effects and multiple chains of causation leading to the same result. From this perspective, Mayr's point about the limitation of the additive model of "beanbag genetics" is impressive.

Equilibrium and Random Drift

In an infinitely large population in which mating choices are made at random, the proportion of each generation that will have a particular allele will not change from one generation to the next (in the absence of mutation and natural selection), as the failure to transmit that allele by some parents will be balanced by the multiple transmission of it by others. This is the Hardy-Weinberg law, a cornerstone of population genetics, which gives in addition the method of calculating the proportions of homozygotes and heterozygotes of the various types formed by the alleles at a locus.

Real populations, however, are not infinitely large and potential parents do not mate at random. Deviations from the "ideal" assumptions can produce changes in the frequency distributions of the allelic proportions in successive generations without any natural selection being involved. The mechanism of change is sampling error, the kind of stochastic fluctuation that AMBUSH has demonstrated can play such a large role in the dynamics of small populations. These processes are called the Sewall Wright effect, or random drift.

Equilibrium and drift are closely related processes. The proportion of a population holding a particular allele in a generation is a random variable with the mean of that of the previous generation and a variance that depends upon two factors: the size of the variance in the number of allelic copies transmitted, as shown in Tables 16.5 and 16.6 for the !Kung, and the size of the total population. The proportion holding a particular allelle, then, can shift between generations and the size of the shift expected is a function of these two factors, which are both constant for a particular population at a given time. For neutral alleles, the jump is equally likely to occur in either direction, the proportion can increase or decrease. There is no mechanism that tends to return the frequency to some initial or most probable value. The two end points of the proportional distribution (zero and one), however, are absorbing states: Once the frequency of a particular allele reaches one of these extremes, random drift ceases and the population is fixed on the remaining allele. Once the gene is fixed (becomes monomorphic) it no longer matters that some 56% of the individuals (according to the women's rates) fail to transmit one of their alleles, whereas identical copies have been multiply transmitted.

Microevolution by random drift, then, can be observed in two ways, by shifts in frequency distributions of allelic forms between generations, a continuous, unpredictable, and generally small effect in each generation, and by the elimination of allelic forms from a gene pool, a reduction in genetic variability of a gene pool. Note that these effects operate on all loci, including those that are influenced by mutation or natural selection. Drift might accelerate or retard the influence of natural selection at a point in time, and it would rarely be possible to tell in any particular instance whether an allele was "finished off" by natural selection or by drift.

We already know the probability that some particular allele will fail to be transmitted to any offspring: This distribution is given in the first columns of Tables 16.5 and 16.6. We saw there that the probability of failure to transmit a given allele is about .56 for the !Kung women and about .65 for the !Kung men. This observation is important for the maintenance of genetic diversity in the gene pool only in the case of rare alleles. If only one member of a population has a particular allele, even if it is a perfectly good allele with neutral fitness in the particular environment, that allele is very likely to be lost from the genetic inventory of the population in the present generation. When more than one person has the allele, the probability of loss of it from the group in the present generation declines swiftly (.31 for two holders, .18 for three, .10 for four, .06 for five, and .0001 for 16 holders of some particular allele). These rates are computed from the women's data, in Table 16.5, with the assumption that the reproductive success of the individuals who hold the allele is independent. The probability of loss is slightly higher for each number of holders using the men's rates from Table 16.6: It takes 21 holders of the allele to bring the probability of loss in the generation down to .0001 at the men's rates.

The central importance of the eventual parity distribution, then, lies in its effects in reducing genetic variability when the number of such alleles in the total population is a very small number. Note that this is a property of numbers, not proportions of the total. Population size becomes important in this formulation only because in a small population even a rather substantial proportion of the total will be made up of a few people, each of whom is at high risk of failing to transmit particular genes, and hence even the usually unimportant fluctuations in frequency distributions of alleles between generations can permit large numbers of alleles to have relatively few holders and be at high risk of extinction in each generation. In order to understand the force of random drift as an evolutionary process in the !Kung population, then, we must know how large the !Kung population really is.

Population Size, Isolation, and Random Drift

Population size is a difficult topic. Although it is easy to count people, it is sometimes difficult to know which ones to count and when to stop counting. Census size means all those alive and present within a defined geographical area on a particular date: Chapter 2 gives census sizes for the resident !Kung of Dobe at several dates. Geneticists add two other concepts that are needed to understand how large a role drift plays in the evolution of groups of people like the !Kung; effective population size and the breeding group. Effective population size, N_e, takes into account that when we observe a number of people living in a space, they will ordinarily be members of different and overlapping generations. Some adults will not reproduce and there is variance in the family size of those who do reproduce. One formulation (Harrison *et al.* 1977:168) is

$$N_e = \frac{4N' - 2}{2 + \sigma^2}$$

where N' is the number of individuals per generation who have 1 or more offspring and σ^2 is the variance in number of gametes contributed by parents.

Tables 16.1 and 16.2 allow us to use this formula to calculate the effective population size for the !Kung. If the whole population size is composed of only 100 women in cross-section, for instance, N', the number who eventually have one or more children, is 48. The variance of the number of offspring, calculated on only those who have 1 or more, is 3.36. The effective population size for 100 women then, is 35.4. For 100 men, the effective population size is 28.6. The rate of drift would be extremely high in such a small population, as it would frequently occur that only a few individuals held one of the alleles of a polymorphism. Other aspects of the concept of effective population size cope with situations of fluctuating population size, differences in the sex ratio through polygamy, and so forth (Cavalli-Sforza and Bodmer 1971:416).

The difficulty with using the concept of effective population size to delineate the rate of random drift is that all of the formulae require knowing the "real" population size as an input. Although we know census size for the Dobe residents at various dates, these data are not an adequate input. The ideal input is the size of an isolated group that provides mates for its members, so that the ancestors and the descendents of the group are a continuously maintained population. The group has to have boundaries if we are to speak meaningfully about the elimination of a particular allele from the gene pool. The theory of random drift makes it clear that any small population that is totally isolated over a long period of time, say on the order of 10 generations (about 300 years), should be detectably more invariant than other human groups, with a smaller proportion of polymorphisms in all loci. Are they? And are the !Kung one of these groups?

There are several instances of very small human groups who are believed to have been totally isolated from contact with outsiders for a period of some centuries in remote areas of the world. The Thule Eskimo of northern Canada (Sutter and Tabah 1956) and the Tiwi Islanders of Australia (Hart and Pilling 1960:10) are examples. Benoist (1973) has reviewed the evidence on the influence of random drift on isolates, showing that the evidence is inconclusive. Unfortunately both groups ended their isolation at a time when bioassay techniques and blood storage techniques were not adequate for full empirical investigation. It is probable that these groups did lose some of their polymorphisms; it is also probable that this kind of situation is the relevant model for macroevolutionary models of the dramatic changes in a gene pool that occur during speciation. It may well be that extreme isolation of small groups has occurred more often among hunter–gatherers than among people organized in more complex ways. We naturally wonder whether there are special features of the gene pools of hunter–gatherer peoples, such as high rates of monomorphism, that might reflect their special adaptations and generally small observed population sizes.

Genetic investigations have been carried out on the !Kung by Harpending (1971), on the Australian aborigines by Birdsell (1975), and on the Pygmies by Cavalli-Sforza et al. (1969). The evidence, valuable as it is for many purposes, cannot settle the question of the proportion of all loci that are monomorphic for the whole population, as one would have to include all members of the population in the study and survey all (or a random sample) of the polymorphisms, but there are always some uncooperative or unavailable individuals. Techniques for genetic bioassay are currently available only for some 50 loci, a small proportion of the total. Furthermore, some of these techniques are prohibitatively expensive to carry out. In any case, none of these populations are claimed by their investigaters to be bounded, endogamous groups. Birdsell (1968:247), in arguing that the Australian populations are clearly bounded, notes that only 85% of marriages occur within the groups.

Without the existence of natural boundaries that prevent intermarriage, it is difficult to know how to count a breeding population. We have seen that the Dobe residents number about 500, but when we start with that group to try to identify the group from which they draw their spouses, the task becomes very complex. People who were born at Dobe have parents, spouses, and children who come from both inside and outside the district. People identify with many places, and there is no clear way to say where they "really" belong.

The evidence on the "real" size of the breeding population of the Dobe area comes more from Harpending's (1971) studies than from my own. In the course of collecting genetic information over a much larger area than Dobe, Harpending (1976:160) found large distances between the birthplaces of spouses (mean about 66 km) and between the birth places of parents and their children, implying long-distance movements over the lifetime of individuals. He found polymorphisms among the !Kung on all loci studied and a low coefficient of Wahlund's F measure (a characteristic of populations with low inbreeding). He also found an elevated rate of homozygosity in individuals in the Dobe area and in some of the other !Kung groups that are believed to have been relatively isolated, but this is not the same as finding a high rate of monomorphic loci, which would imply random drift. Harpending's results converge on the conclusion that the !Kung breeding group size is much larger than the number of individuals physically present in the Dobe area.

We can interpret Harpending's results in either of two ways: by saying that there are a number of small populations among the !Kung with migration between them or that the !Kung population is much larger than the group studied for purposes of estimating demographic parameters, in the thousands rather than the hundreds. The usefulness of these formulations depends upon the aspects of group functioning in question. For purposes of management and exploitation of food and water resources, the traditional !Kung group size might best be considered that of the local camp, averaging 20–50 people. For purposes of spreading out risks of resource failure, the group is much larger, perhaps like that of the Dobe area, around 500 people. This is the "magic number" that seems to correspond to the dialect tribe (Lee & DeVore 1968) and what Adams and Kasakoff (1975) call the "80% breeding group," referring to the individuals within a definable geographical area who provide most of the spouses for the members of the group. Whether such population units are geocentric and relatively clearly bounded or egocentric and overlapping probably depends a great deal on the distribution of resources within the territory. To obtain the whole breeding group, however, which is the unit for which any boundary effects such as those explored for random drift are applicable, we must look further afield to the entire population from which spouses are drawn. In practice it will rarely be possible to put a number on the size of this group.

Let us adopt the terminology of distinct small populations with migration between them and consider the consequences. The 10 small populations simulated and shown in Figure 11.1 can serve as examples. Each of these populations is around 500, effective population size about 150, and each would be at risk of losing a fraction of their polymorphisms in each generation. The groups are likely, however, to lose different polymorphisms or to become fixed on different alleles at the same locus. The tendency to loss of genetic variability could be readily overcome if they exchanged only a few individuals as mates in each generation.

Bringing even one new mate into a small and isolated population is more effective than hundreds of mutations in increasing the variability in the gene pool of that group. Because the new person is likely to be an adult, the high probabilities of loss of alleles due to prereproductive mortality are avoided. We know from the existence of the individual that the allelic forms being introduced to the gene pool are not disasterously detrimental. And the means of introduction is efficient: The individual's alleles might differ from those already in the gene pool at not just one but at large numbers of loci.

We are forced to conclude, then, that the Dobe !Kung are not a small population for purposes of modeling the effects of genetic drift on their gene pools. Both drift and natural selection as an adaptation to specific local conditions, two processes that tend to differentiate the gene pools of local populations, are swamped by the human capacity for long-distance mobility and flexibility in marriage choices.

Implications of !Kung Demography for Genetic Transmission: Review and Overview

We have seen in this chapter that knowing something of the demographic parameters of a population allows us to spell out in some detail the concrete mechanics of the genetic transmission process from generation to generation on issues such as the number of children ever born to cohorts, the expected numbers of descendents in successive generations, the degree of opportunity for natural selection and drift for the two sexes, and so on, but does not allow us to conclude anything very concrete on issues of the direction and intensity of natural selection and drift in such a population. Exploration of these questions require knowledge not only of the demographic performance of a total population, but of the performance of individuals identified by their genotypes and the statistical study of the reproductive performance of genotypes in a range of environmental circumstances.

Such research is the province of genetics; demography will never be more than an adjunct to these investigations. Empirical study of fitness of genotypes is likely to become both far more complicated and more interesting with the impact of advances in molecular genetics, by which the mapping of chromosomes and the identification of the specific action of particular genes and their alternative alleles is progressing. One naturally hopes that the results of this research will become available while there are still at least some groups like the !Kung who are direct descendents of people who lived by hunting and gathering over long periods of time, in case the structure of the genetic information itself suggests some hypotheses about how hunting and gathering groups may differ from larger and more sedentary populations. In the meantime, investigators like Harpending and Cavalli-Sforza are collecting and storing blood samples of the surviving hunter–gatherers, in anticipation of the time when more complex questions may be asked of the data. Similarly, demographic studies, such as the present one on the Dobe !Kung, represent a storage of data to provide answers to questions that have not yet been asked.

17

The Demographic Prospects
for the Future of
the Dobe !Kung

Since Chapter 13 we have been making increasingly general statements on the basis of models of the Dobe area !Kung people, using the rates which seem to have characterized the population prior to 1950. We do not want to end this work without returning to some consideration of the real people on whom those models were based, people who are facing a future in which the constraints on their lives are already changed greatly and will, no doubt, for better or for worse, be changing more in the future.

Social and Economic Changes

We discussed in Chapter 1 some of the changes in the Dobe area that had occurred during the period 1950–1968, including the construction of a store and a school, the fencing of the border, the increased truck traffic in the area, and so on.

Since 1968 there has been another round of social change in the Dobe area (Lee 1976). A major source of change has been generated by the activities of the South African police and army, who have instituted regular patrols along the border, sparked by the war in Angola, and increasing concern about guerrilla fighters entering Namibia. The South African police have hired a number of !Kung, for cash payments and food rations, to live in camps along the border to serve as trackers, informants on local conditions, and laborers for the South Africans. Whole camps—men, women, and children—live next to the border road, remaining in villages established for the convenience of others, inconveniently far from water and overexploiting the local food resources. Wilmsen (personal communication 1976) reports that !Kung who live in other villages as well as those in the border camps have established the custom of sending requests and money with the police when they go into town. The police bring them back supplies of food, cloth, and other consumer goods. Whether this is done informally through sympathetic policemen or whether it is now governmental policy to maintain good relations with the indigenous peoples in case of war is not at all clear.

But the relations with the border police are only one source of social change in the area since 1968, when the present study was finished. It has become easier to earn cash incomes in several ways. Botswanacraft, a national marketing board for curios, has established relations with the !Kung of the area, sending a truck into the area for regular collections to buy beadwork and traditional implements, many of which are now being made for that purpose (Wiessner personal communication 1976). Wilmsen (1976) estimated that 30% of the cash income of the /Xai/Xai people in 1975 came from the sale of crafts.

Wage labor is also increasing, in employment taking care of cattle, and, more ominously for the !Kung, in digging wells. The well digging issue could easily be the major one in determining the future state of the Dobe !Kung.

The nation of Botswana as a whole has been in the process of changing the nature of land holding from a tribal basis to one of individual rights and control. The government has passed a law that allows anyone who improves a well or digs a water source in previously unclaimed territory, and registers that well with the government, to hold title to the land surrounding the well. With the new law, Hereros and Tswanas who can raise the capital for blasting equipment and labor, ironically often !Kung labor, can transform minor water sources into major ones and thereby claim ownership of vast tracts of land, transforming it from hunting and gathering territory to grazing land for cattle. The !Kung could, if they had the legal skill and the capital for well improvement, use the same laws to obtain permanent title and control to much of their traditional lands. In the interest of helping them to do this, anthropologists, a missionary who has taken up residence in the area, and the newly established Botswana Office of Masarwa Development have contributed time, energy, and money. The difficulties are great, in part because the !Kung culture does not encourage the identification of particular individuals to serve as the nominal "owners" of a resource, but several wells have been dug and the registration process begun. The legal situation is still far from clear.

And, during the period, the amount of agriculture and livestock keeping, both by immigrants and among !Kung, has expanded considerably, and every expansion of food production tends to make the hunting and gathering way of life more difficult. The social and economic future of the !Kung people is very uncertain. It is fruitless to wish that they could preserve their hunting and gathering way of life into the twenty-first century, however much we might admire and respect its strengths. The !Kung, although they have no formal decision-making system, seem on the whole to want the advantages of modern life—at least donkeys to ride if not yet trucks to drive, things from the store, and certainly injections of penicillin to save lives. The conditions under which they will ultimately join the larger society, whether under optimal conditions of equal opportunity and control over their own land, or the less attractive alternatives of being rural proletariat, as most of the !Kung have already done, remains to be seen. Yet their demographic future is readily predictable within narrow limits.

Demographic Changes

We have seen that since 1950 the mortality and fertility schedules of the !Kung have changed with increasing contact with outsiders in their area. The mortality seems to have improved somewhat in the period of 1950–1968 and we know that the area will increasingly come under the care of the Botswana public health and medical services. A medical team visited the Dobe area to carry out an intensive vaccination and curative treatment plan in 1972 (Fleming Larsen personal communication 1974) and the !Kung people are increasingly becoming more aware and more able (due to increased truck traffic in the area) to visit hospitals and medical stations within a radius of 50 km of Dobe. Plans to establish a medical dispensary in the Xangwa area were started in the early 1970s, which may, for all I know, already be functioning. Since we saw in Chapter 3 that most of the causes of death that keep mortality high in the Dobe area are infectitous and parasitic disease, the conditions that Western medical practice is best able to treat and to control, we can predict with little fear of contradiction that mortality levels will increasingly decline in the future in the Dobe area for !Kung as well as other peoples.

We have seen that one of the costs of modernization and contact with outsiders for the Dobe !Kung has been an epidemic of venereal disease that reduced fertility. Increased modernization and contact, however, is more likely to lead to a rise in fertility than a further decline. Venereal disease can be controlled by modern medical practice and its sterilizing effects can be reversed by prompt treatment in most cases. The effects on !Kung fertility of access to medical care are likely to be complex: Reductions of venereal disease will increase it, reductions of infant mortality will decrease it (as birth intervals tend to be longer after surviving children), improvements of caloric availability and fatness will tend to increase it. On balance, we expect fertility to change less than mortality in the period before birth control is adopted by the people.

Combining these two trends, we have as an automatic consequence that the Dobe !Kung population is going to grow, that the age distribution is going to become younger, and that the dependency burden of children and old people on the productive adults is going to increase within the next few decades.

We have no crystal ball which will allow us to predict the size of each of these trends at specified times in the future, but it is an easy task to project the population forward under guessed assumptions. Detailed results of these projections will not be shown here, as the general trends are equally clear from all projections, and extraneous factors, such as the development of a source of wage labor outside the area open to !Kung could easily make nonsense of the projections by a wave of emigration.

Under the assumption of a modest and gradual decrease in mortality and no increase in fertility, the size of the Dobe !Kung will increase by about 40% by the year 2000. More rapid improvements in mortality and a slight increase in fertility will produce a doubling of the population in the same time.

We live in a world in which these kinds of rapid population growth are commonly seen. Many thoughtful people, including most demographers, feel that problems of population growth have reached crisis proportions and the need for birth control programs is very great. It is one of the ironies of the twentieth century that population growth, which was probably a very reasonable indicator of well-being and "good luck" under traditional conditions, is now found in both prosperous and impoverished communities and occurs even in periods of social turmoil, deprivation, and virtual starvation. Is the anticipated population growth of the Dobe !Kung an indicator of their improved life chances, one which should be welcomed by those who wish them well, or is it merely another indicator of the worldwide "population explosion"?

I suppose the answer is that it is both. In the short run the Dobe !Kung will be delighted to have a higher proportion of their children surviving and a higher proportion of adults managing to produce a number of adult children to provide them with grandchildren. I observed no ambivalence among the !Kung on the issue of saving lives (with the possible exception of those of deformed infants). They need, want, and ask for "death control," which is the primary and irresistable reward of civilization for them.

In the longer run, however, the adoption of death control extracts its prices from any population. On the individual and family level, the survival of more children will necessarily require increases in the productivity of working adults to avoid reduced subsistence for each family member. On a larger scale, population growth makes it difficult for a country like Botswana, which has a scarcity of capital, to provide the services—medical, educational, and other—that constitute such an important part of a rising standard of living. It is in the hope of reducing these costs for the !Kung that it would seem to be wise and humane for the medical people to offer birth control services to the population through the same channels and in the same voluntary way death control is offered. Certainly one needn't argue for the provision of birth control services on the grounds of a threat to the "spaceship Earth" from 1,000, 2,000 or even 4,000 Dobe !Kung within the next century: They would still have one of the lowest levels of population density on the planet. By the adoption of more intensive agricultural and stockkeeping techniques, it is entirely possible that the standard of living could be maintained or significantly improved through several doublings of population size.

The costs of population growth can be more forcefully seen through the computation of the dependency burden than through the projections of population size itself. Traditionally, the !Kung adults (men and women 15 to 64) have supported about .57 dependents (children under 15 and persons 65 and over) per adult. During the recent past that dependency burden seems to have eased somewhat, to about .52, by the migration of families with a large number of dependents to cattleposts, where the living is easier. That burden will necessarily increase in the future as mortality declines and fertility remains steady or increases, to as little as .66 for modest improvements, to as much as .94 for the projections with the greatest and swiftest improvements in mortality (figures for year 2000; both indicators continue to increase past that time if the conditions are maintained). If birth control is adopted by the fastest growing population, starting in 1980, and used only to the extent of reducing total fertility by .2 births in each 5-year period, so that fertility is down to 3.6 by 2000, the effects on the size of the population are slight, but the effects on the dependency burden are substantial. The dependency burden decreases from .68 in 1985 to .53 in the year 2000. The short run advantage of birth control to a population, then, is not so much in preventing population growth and crowding, but in the more immediate advantages to parents in decreasing their work load and increasing their options to continue hunting and gathering, to do wage work on cattleposts, or to attempt to invest in stock and set up their own cattle (or goat) economies, as they see best. If birth control is available to those parents who have had all of the surviving children they feel they can raise, to tailor the means and ends available to individual families, it can only help the !Kung as they move through this necessarily turbulent period of social change. And if, in the future, the Kalahari desert comes to be crowded with people on some criteria, it can only help the people to have developed a gradual familiarity with these techniques.

Social and cultural changes of the sort needed to adopt contraception can be amazingly swift when conditions are right. It is difficult for me to imagine the !Kung women, who told me over and over again, "God has been stingy with children," seeking contraception, but both Konner and Wiessner, who were in the field in the early 1970s, report that considerable interest was expressed by some of the heavily burdened young mothers.

Personally, I like the !Kung people and value their beauty, charm, the practical flexibility of their culture, and the humor and exuberance that has persisted through centuries of hardship in the Kalahari. If the future of these people involves a doubling, or several doublings, of their population size, I can only think that the world will be better off for it.

References

Adams, J. W. and A. B. Kasakoff
  1975   Factors underlying endogamous group size. In *Population and social organization*,
            edited by Nag, M. The Hague: Mouton.
Barclay, G.
  1958   *Techniques of population analysis*. New York: Wiley.
Barclay, G., A. J. Coale, M. A. Stoto, and T. J. Trussell
  1976   A reassessment of the demography of traditional rural China. *Population Index* 42 (No.
            4: October 1976):606–635.
Benoist, J.
  1973   Genetics of isolate populations. In *Methods and theories of anthropological genetics*,
            edited by Crawford, M. and Workman, P. Albuquerque: Univ. of New Mexico Press.
Biesele, M. and N. Howell
  In press "The old people give you life": Aging among the !Kung San. In *Other ways of growing
            old*, edited by Amoss, P. and Harrell, S. Stanford: Stanford Univ. Press.
Billewicz, W. Z., H. M. Fellowes and C. A. Hytten
  1976   Comments on the critical metabolic mass and the age of menarche. *Annals of Human
            Biology* 3 (1):51–59.
Birdsell, J. B.
  1968   Some predictions for the pleistocene based on equilibrium systems among recent
            hunter-gatherers. In *Man the hunter*, edited by Lee, R. and DeVore, I. Chicago:
            Aldine.
  1975   *Human evolution: An introduction to the new physical anthropology*. Chicago: Rand
            McNally.
Blacker, J.
  1965   Use of sample surveys to obtain data on age structure of the population where respon-

dents in a regular census enumeration cannot give accurate data. In *World Population Conference III:* 126–130.

Bleek, D.
1928   *The Naron, a bushman tribe of the central Kalahari.* Cambridge: Cambridge Univ. Press.

Bongaards, J. and H. Delgado
1977   Effects of nutritional status on fertility in rural Guatemala. Center for Policy Studies working paper. New York: The Population Council.

Brass, W.
1975   *Methods for estimating fertility and mortality from limited and defective data.* Laboratory for Population Statistics (occasional publication), Chapel Hill, Carolina Population Center.

Brass, W., A. J. Coale, P. Demeny, D. F. Helsel, F. Lorimer, A. Romaniuk, and E. van de Walle
1968   *The demography of tropical Africa.* Princeton: Princeton Univ. Press.

Buck, J. L. (Editor)
1937   *Land utilization in China.* (3 vols.) Nanking: University of Nanking. (Distributed in the United States by the Univ. of Chicago Press.)

Carrier, N. and J. Hobcraft
1971   *Demographic estimation for developing countries.* London: Population Investigation Committee.

Carroll, V. (Ed.)
1975   *Pacific Atoll populations.* Honolulu: Univ. of Hawaii Press.

Cavalli-Sfortza, L. L., L. A. Zonta, L. Bernini, F. Nyzzo, W. DeJong, P. Meera Kyan, A. K. Ray, L. N. Went, M. Siniscalco, L. E. Nijenhius, E. van Loghem, and G. Modiano
1969   Studies on African Pygmies: I. A pilot investigation of Babinga Pygmies in the Central African Republic. *American Journal of Human Genetics* 21:252–274.

Cavalli-Sforza, L. L. and W. Bodmer
1971   *The genetics of human populations.* San Francisco: Freeman.

Chapman, J.
1868   *Travels in the interior of South Africa.* London: Bell and Daldy; Edward Stanford.

Chirenje, J. M.
1977   *A history of Northern Botswana 1850–1910.* Rutherford: Fairleigh Dickinson Univ. Press.

Chowdhury, A.
1977   Malnutrition, menarche, and marriage in rural Bangladesh, *Social Biology* 24: 316.

Clark, J. D.
1976   Prehistoric populations and pressures favoring plant domestication in Africa. In *Origins of African plant domestication,* edited by Harlan, J. R., J. M. deWet and A. Bh. Stemler. The Hague: Mouton.

Coale, A. J.
1956   Effects of changes in mortality and fertility on age composition. *Milbank Memorial Fund Quarterly* 34:79–114.
1957   How the age distribution of a human population is determined. *Cold Springs Harbor Symposium on Quantitative Biology* 22:83–89.
1965   Factors associated with the development of low fertility: An historical survey. Belgrade: United Nations World Population Conference Paper WPC/WP/194.
1971   Age patterns of marriage. *Population Studies* 25:193–214.
1972   *The growth and structure of human populations: A mathematical investigation,* Princeton: Princeton Univ. Press.

Coale, A. J. and P. Demeny
1966   *Regional model life tables and stable populations.* Princeton: Princeton Univ. Press.
Coale, A. J. and D. R. McNeil
1972   The distribution by age of the frequency of first marriage in a female cohort. *Journal of the American Statistical Association* 67:743–749.
Coale, A. J. and J. Trussell
1974   Model fertility schedules: variations in the age structure of childbearing in human populations. *Population Index* 40:185–257.
Collier, G.
1974   The impact of airphoto technology on the study of demography and ecology in Highland Chiapas. In *Aerial photography in anthropological field research*, edited by Vogt, E. Z. Cambridge: Harvard Univ. Press.
Crow, J. F.
1958   Some possibilities for measuring selection intensities in man. *Human Biology* 30:1–13.
Crow, J. F. and M. Kimura
1970   *An introduction to population genetics theory.* New York: Harper and Row.
Current Anthropology
1974   Review symposium on G. Acsadi and J. Nemeskeri, History of human life span and mortality. *Current Anthropology* 15.
Draper, P.
1972   *!Kung bushman childhood.* Ph.D. dissertation in Anthropology, Cambridge, Harvard University.
1975   !Kung women: contrasts in sexual egalitarianism in the foraging and sedentary contexts. In *Toward an anthropology of women*, edited by Reiter, R. New York: Monthly Review Press.
1976   Social and economic constraints on child life. In *Kalahari hunter–gatherers*, edited by Lee, R. B. and DeVore, I. Cambridge: Harvard Univ. Press.
Dyke, B.
1971   Potential mates in a small human population. *Social Biology* 18:28–39.
Dyke, B. and J. W. MacCluer
1973   *Computer simulation in human population studies.* New York: Academic Press.
Eaton, J. W. and A. J. Mayer
1953   The social biology of very high fertility among the Hutterites. *Human Biology* 25:206–264.
Elphick, R.
1977   *Kraal and castle: Khoikhoi and the founding of white South Africa.* New Haven: Yale Univ. Press.
Feeney, G.
1975   Demographic concepts and techniques for the study of small populations. In *Pacific Atoll populations*, edited by Carroll, V. Honolulu: Univ. of Hawaii Press.
Fisher, R. A.
1958   *The genetical theory of natural selection.* New York: Dover.
Friedlander, J. S. and D. L. Oliver
1976   Effects of aging and the secular trend in Bougainville males. In *The measures of man*, edited by Giles, E. and Friedlander, J. S. Cambridge: Peabody Museum Press.
Frisch, R. E.
1972   Weight at menarche: Similarity for well-nourished and undernourished girls at differing ages and evidence for historical constancy. *Pediatrics* 50:445–450.
1974a   A method of prediction of age at menarche from height and weight at ages 9 through 13 years. *Pediatrics* 53:384–390.

1974b   Critical weight at menarche, initiation of the adolescent growth spurt, and control of puberty. In *Control of onset of Puberty*, edited by Grumback, M. M., G. Grave, and F. Meyer. New York: Wiley.

1975   Demographic implications of the biological determinants of female fecundity. *Social Biology* 22:14.

1977   Critical weights, a critical body composition, menarche and the maintenance of menstrual cycles, In *Biosocial interrelations in population adaptation*, edited by Watts, E., F. Johnson, and G. Lasker, The Hague: Mouton.

1978   Population, food intake, and fertility. *Science* 199:22–30.

Frisch, R. E. and J. W. McArthur

1974   Menstrual cycles: Fatness as a determinant of minimum weight for height necessary for their maintenance or onset. *Science*, 185:949–951.

Frisch, R. E. and R. Revelle

1969   Variation in body weights and the age of the adolescent growth spurt among Latin American and Asian populations in relation to caloric supplies. *Human Biology* 41:185–212.

Frisch, R. E., R. Revelle and S. Cook

1971   Height, weight and age at menarche and the "critical weight" hypothesis. *Science* 194:1148.

Goodman, L. A., N. Keyfitz, and T. Pullum

1974   Family formation and the frequency of various kinship relationships. *Theoretical Population Biology* 5:1–27.

Graunt, J.

1662   Natural and political observations mentioned in a following index, and made upon the bills of mortality. Reprinted in *The economic writings of Sir William Petty, II*. New York: Cambridge University Press, 1899.

Guenther, M. G.

1976   From hunters to squatters: Social and cultural change among the farm San of Ghanzi, Botswana. In *Kalahari hunter-gatherers*, edited by Lee, R. and DeVore, I. Cambridge: Harvard Univ. Press.

Hansen, J. D., A. S. Truswell, C. Freesemann and B. MacHutchon

1969   The children of hunting and gathering bushmen. *South African Medical Journal* 43:1158.

Harpending, H. C.

1971   *!Kung hunter-gatherer population structure*. Ph.D. dissertation in Anthropology, Cambridge, Harvard University.

1974   Genetic structure of small populations. *Annual Review of Anthropology* 1974:229–243.

1976   Regional variation in !Kung populations. In *Kalahari hunter-gatherers*, edited by Lee, R. B. and DeVore, I. Cambridge: Harvard Univ. Press.

Harpending, H. C. and J. Bertram

1975   Human population dynamics in archeological time: Some simple models. *American Antiquity* 40:82–91.

Harpending, H. C. and T. Jenkins

1973   Genetic distance among Southern African populations. In *Methods and theories of anthropological genetics*, edited by M. Crawford and P. Workman. Albuquerque: Univ. of New Mexico Press.

Harrison, G. A., J. S. Weiner, J. M. Tanner and N. A. Barnicot

1977   *Human biology* (second edition). Oxford: Oxford Univ. Press.

Hart, C. W. and A. Pilling

1960   *The Tiwi*. New York: Holt.

Henripin, J.

1968 *Tendances et facteurs de la fecondité au Canada*, (Monographie sur le recensement de 1961), Ottawa: Bureau Fédéral de la Statistique.

Henry, L.

1961 Some data on natural fertility. *Eugenics Quarterly* 8:81–91.

1972 *On the measurement of human fertility*, New York: Elsevier.

1976 *Population analysis and models.* London: Arnold.

Howell, N.

1976a The population of the Dobe area !Kung, In *Kalahari hunter–gatherers*, edited by Lee, R. B. and DeVore, I. Cambridge: Harvard Univ. Press.

1976b Toward a uniformitarian theory of human paleodemography. *Journal of Human Evolution* 5:25–40. Reprinted in *Demographic evolution of human populations*, edited by Ward, R. and Weiss, K. New York: Academic Press, 1976.

1976c Selection intensity rates for the !Kung and other hunter-gatherer peoples. Paper presented at the American Anthropological Association annual meetings, Washington, D.C.

Howell, N. and V. A. Lehotay, Jr.

1978 AMBUSH: a computer program for stochastic microsimulation of small human populations. *American Anthropologist*.

Huffman, S. L.

1978 Postpartum amenorrhea: How is it affected by maternal nutritional status? *Science* 200:1155–1157.

Jorde, L. B. and H. C. Harpending

1976 Cross-spectral analysis of rainfall and human birth rate. An empirical test of a linear model, *Journal of Human Evolution* 5:129–138.

Kasakoff, A. B.

1974 How many relatives? In *Geneological Mathematics*, edited by Ballonoff, P. The Hague: Mouton.

Katz, R.

1976 Education for transcendence: !kia healing with the Kalahari !Kung. In *Kalahari hunter–gatherers*, edited by Lee, R. B. and DeVore, I. Cambridge: Harvard Univ. Press.

Kennelly, B., A. Truswell and V. Schrire

1972 A clinical and electrocardiographic study of !Kung bushmen. *South African Medical Journal* 46:1093–1097.

Keyfitz, N.

1968 *An introduction to the mathematics of population.* Reading: Addison-Wesley.

Kobayashi, K.

1969 Changing patterns of differential fertility in the population of Japan. In *Proceedings of the eighth international congress of anthropological and ethnological sciences.* Tokyo: Science Council of Japan.

Konner, M. J.

1972 Aspects of the developmental ethology of a foraging people. In *Ethological studies of child behavior*, edited by Blurton-Jones, N. G. Cambridge: Cambridge Univ. Press.

1973 *Infants of a Foraging People.* Ph.D. dissertation in Anthropology, Cambridge, Harvard University.

1976 Maternal care, infant behavior and development among the !Kung. In *Kalahari hunter–gatherers*, edited by Lee, R. B. and DeVore, I. Cambridge: Harvard Univ. Press.

Lee, R. B.

1965   Subsistence ecology of the !Kung bushmen. Ph.D. dissertation in Anthropology. Berkeley: University of California.

1967   Trance cure of the !Kung bushmen. *Natural History* (November, 1967):30–37.

1968   The sociology of !Kung bushmen trance performance. In *Trance and possession states*, edited by Prince, R. Montreal: R. M. Bucke Memorial Society.

1969a   Eating Christmas in the Kalahari. *Natural History* 78 (December, 1969):14–22; 60–63.

1969b   !Kung Bushmen subsistence: An input–output analysis. In *Environment and cultural behavior*, edited by Vayda, A. P. Garden City: Natural History Press.

1972a   Population growth and the beginnings of sedentary life among the !Kung Bushmen (and) the intensification of social life among the !Kung Bushmen. In *Population Growth: Anthropological implications.* edited by Spooner, B. Cambridge: M. I. T. Press.

1972b   !Kung spatial organization: An ecological and historical perspective. *Human Ecology* 1:125–147.

1972c   Work effort, group structure and land use in contemporary hunter–gatherers. In *Man, settlement, and urbanism*, edited by Ucko, P., R. Tringham, and G. W. Dimbleby. London: Duckworth.

1976   From foraging to farming. In *Science Year 1976*. Chicago: World Book Encyclopedia.

Forth-   *Ecology of the Dobe !Kung.* New York: Cambridge Univ. Press.
coming

Lee, R. B. and I. DeVore (Editors)

1968   *Man the Hunter.* Chicago: Aldine.

1976   *Kalahari hunter–gatherers.* Cambridge: Harvard Univ. Press.

Lehotay, V. and N. Howell

1976   User manual "AMBUSH": A stochastic microsimulation of demography and kinship for small human populations. Toronto: University of Toronto.

Lewontin, R. C.

1967   An estimate of average heterozygosity in man. *American Journal of Human Genetics* 19:681–685.

Livingston, D.

1851   Extracts of letters from the Rev. D. Livingston, 24 August, 1850. *Journal of the Royal Geographic Society* 21:18–24.

Lotka, A. J.

1907   Relation between birth rates and death rates. *Science* 26:21–22.

Marks, S.

1972   Khoisan resistance to the Dutch in the seventeenth and eighteenth centuries. *Journal of African History* 13:55–80.

Marshall, J. (Producer)

1956   *The hunters* Wilmette: Films Incorporated. (Film).

Marshall, L.

1976   *The !Kung of Nyae Nyae,* Cambridge: Harvard Univ. Press.

MacCluer, J. W.

1967   Monte Carlo methods in human population genetics. *American Journal of Human Genetics* 19 (3): 303–312.

MacCluer, J. W., J. V. Neel and N. A. Chagnon

1971   Demographic structure of a primitive population: a simulation. *American Journal of Physical Anthropology* 35 (2):193–207.

Mayr, E.

1963   *Animal species and evolution.* Cambridge: Harvard Univ. Press.

McArthur, J. W.
1976   Endocrine studies during the refeeding of young women with nutritional amenorrhea and infertility. *Mayo Clinic Proceedings* 51:607–616.

Mellits, E. D. and D. B. Cheek
1970   The assessment of body water and fatness from infancy to childhood. *Monographs in Social Research on Child Development* 35:12–26.

Menken, J. A.
1974   Biological determinants of demographic processes. *American Journal of Public Health* 64:657–661.
1975a   Biometric models of fertility. *Social Forces* 54:52–65.
1975b   Estimating fecundability, in sociology. Ph.D. Dissertation, Princeton University.

Montague, M. F. A.
1957   *The reproductive development of the female, with especial reference to the period of adolescent sterility.* New York: Julian.

Moore, F. D., K. H. Olesen, J. D. McMurrey, H. V. Parker, M. R. Ball, and C. M. Boyden
1963   *The body cell mass and its supporting environment.* Philadelphia: Saunders.

Mosley, W. H.
1977   The effects of nutrition on natural fertility. Paper in the seminar on Natural Fertility, Paris, National d'Etudes Demographiques.

Murdock, G. P.
1968   The current status of the world's hunting and gathering peoples. In *Man the Hunter*, edited by Lee, R. B. and DeVore, I. Chicago: Aldine.

Nei, M.
1973   Genetic distance between populations. In *Genetics of population structure*, edited by Morton, N. E. Honolulu: Univ. of Hawaii Press.

Perrin, E. B. and M. Sheps
1964   Human reproduction: A stochastic process. *Biometrics* 20:28–45.

Population Reference Bureau
1972   World population data sheet, Population Reference Bureau, Washington, D. C.

Potter, Jr., R. G.
1965   A case of birth interval dynamics. *Population Studies* 19:81–96.

Preston, S.
1976   *Mortality patterns in national populations, with special reference to recorded causes of death.* New York: Academic Press.

Preston, S., N. Keyfitz and R. Schoen
1972   *Causes of death: Life tables for national populations.* New York: Academic Press.

Preston, S. and V. E. Nelson
1974   Structure and change in causes of death: An international summary. *Population Studies* 28:19–51.

Romaniuk, A.
1974   Modernization and fertility: the case of the James Bay Indians. *Canadian Review of Sociology and Anthropology* 11 (4):344–359.

Romaniuk, A. and V. Piche
1972   Natality estimates for the Canadian Indians by stable population models, 1900–1969. *Canadian Review of Sociology and Anthropology* 9:1–20.

Rose, F. G. G.
1960   *Kinship, age structure and marriage of Groote Eylandt,* New York: Pergamon.

Schapera, I.
1930   *The Khoisan peoples of South Africa: Bushmen and Hottentots.* London: Routledge.

Sheps, M. C. and J. A. Menken
- 1972   Distributions of birth intervals according to the sampling frame. *Theoretical Population Biology* 3:1–26.
- 1973   *Mathematical models of conception and birth.* Chicago: Univ. of Chicago Press.

Shorter, F. C. (with the assistance of D. Pasta)
- 1974   *Computational methods for population projections.* New York: Population Council. Distributed by Key Book Service, Bridgeport Conn.

Shostak, M.
- 1976   A !Kung woman's memories of childhood. In *Kalahari hunter–gatherers,* edited by Lee, R. B. and DeVore, I. Cambridge: Harvard University Press.

Silberbauer, G.
- 1965   *Bushman survey report.* Gaberones: Bechuanaland Government Printer.

Spuhler, J. N.
- 1976   The maximum opportunity for natural selection in some human populations. In *Demographic anthropology quantitative approaches,* edited by Zubrow, E. Albuquerque: University of New Mexico Press.

Steiger, W. L. and C. Schrire
- 1974   The use of computer simulation to set limits to the frequency of infanticide among Inuit groups. Paper presented to Population Association of America, New York.

Sutter, H. E. and L. Tabah
- 1956   Méthode mécanographique pour Établir la généalogie d'une population: application a l'etude des Esquimaux polaires, *Population* 11:507–530.

Tanner, J. M.
- 1960   Genetics of human growth. In *Human growth,* edited by Tanner, J. M. London: Pergamon Press.
- 1962   *Growth at adolescence* (Second Edition). Oxford: Blackwell.

Thomas, E. M.
- 1959   *The harmless people.* New York: Knopf.

Tietze, C.
- 1957   Reproductive span and rate of reproduction among Hutterite women. *Fertility and Sterility* 8:89–97.

Trussell, J.
- 1978   Menarche and fatness: Reexamination of the critical body composition hypothesis. *Science* 200:1506–1509 (and reply 1509–1513.)

Truswell, A. S. and J. D. L. Hansen
- 1968   Medical and nutritional studies of !Kung Bushmen in northwest Botswana. *South African Medical Journal* 28:1338–1339.
- 1976   Medical research among the !Kung. In *Kalahari hunter–gatherers,* edited by Lee, R. B. and DeVore, I. Cambridge: Harvard Univ. Press.

Truswell, A. S., J. D. L. Hansen, P. Wannenburg, and E. Sellmeyer
- 1969   Nutritional status of adult Bushmen in the northern Kalahari, Botswana. *South African Medical Journal* 20:1157–1158.

United Nations, Department of Economic and Social Affairs
- 1955   Age and sex patterns of mortality: Model life tables for under-developed countries. Population studies No. 22. ST/SOA/Series A/22. New York, United Nations.
- 1967   *Manual four: Methods of estimating basic demographic measures from incomplete data* (U.N. Population Studies No. 42). New York: United Nations.
- 1968   *The concept of a stable population* (U. N. Population Studies No. 39). New York: United Nations.

Wachter, K. W., with E. A. Hammel and P. Laslett
1978   *Statistical Studies of historical social structure.* New York: Academic Press.
van de Walle, E.
1966   Some characteristic features of census age distributions in illiterate populations. *American Journal of Sociology* 71:549–555.
1968   Characteristics of African demographic data. In *The demography of tropical Africa*, Brass, W., A. J. Coale, P. Demeny, D. F. Heisel, F. Lorimer, A. Romaniuk and E. van de Walle. Princeton: Princeton Univ. Press.
van de Walle, E. and J. Knodel
1970   Teaching population dynamics with a simulation exercise. *Demography* 7 (4): 433–448.
Washburn, S.
1968   Discussion. In *Man the hunter,* edited by Lee, R. B. and DeVore, I. Chicago: Aldine.
Weiss, K. M.
1973   *Demographic models for anthropology.* (Memoirs of the Society for American Archeology, No. 27.) *American Antiquity* 38: No. 2, Part II.
Wiessner, P. W.
1977   Hxaro: A regional system of reciprocity for reducing risk among the !Kung San, Ph.D. dissertation, in Anthropology. Ann Arbor, University of Michigan.
Wilmsen, E. N.
1973   Interaction, spacing behavior and the organization of hunting bands, *Journal of Anthropological Research 29.*
1976   Subsistence hunting as a source of income for Bushmen at /ai/ai in northwestern Ngamiland. In *The Rural Income Distribution Survey in Botswana 1974–1975.* Appendix 23. Gaberones: The Government Printer.
World Health Organization
1961   *Public health aspects of low birth weight.* Geneva: Technical Report Service.
Yellen, J.
1976   Settlement patterns of the !Kung, an archaeological perspective. In *Kalahari hunter–gatherers,* edited by Lee, R. B. and DeVore, I. Cambridge: Harvard University Press.

Index

models, 79; of height–weight measures, 193; on menstrual cycles, 147; on mortality, 47–48, 80–92; size needed, 110–111

Death: from bush fires, 58; certificates, 47, 68; in childbirth, 58; to children of interviewed women, 80; control, 364; current period, 87; diagnosis of cause, 48; d_x measure, 75, 104, 107; expected in a simulated population, 106; from exposure, 58; extreme of morbidity process, 51; frequency of, 51; from lack of nursing care, 53; probabilities by age, 76; registration, 47; religious explanations, 48; from thirst, 8; by violence, 62

Deceased persons, data on, 18

De facto population, 17

Deficiency diseases, 50

Deformed children, 119–120

Degenerative diseases, 66–68; cases of, 67; incidence in comparative perspective, 68–69; rate of mortality, 69–70

De jure population, 17

Delousing, 49

Demography, 21; change, 70, 363–365; focus on women, 253; and genetics, 358–359; techniques, 99

Dependency, 5; on Bantu, 16; in future, 365; rate of, 54; ratio, 42–43, of villages, 43

Dependents, 54

Depression, during pregnancy, 118

DeVore, I., 56, 187

Diagnosis, of venereal disease, 64

Diarrhea, 65

Dias, B., 9

Diet, 50; changes, 363–364; cow's milk for infants, 121; and critical fatness levels, 192; and disease, 50; and fertility, 210; and growth in males, 254–255; and growth at menarche, 203; and health, 66; and mortality, 71; and sterility, 203–205; supplements in infancy, 121; and weights of women, 206–207.

Difference in age of spouses, see Age differences of spouses.

Differential success of men, 267–269; components caused by natural selection, 344

Digestive diseases, 65

Disciplining of children, 233

Distribution of birth intervals, smooth and rough, 134

Division of labor, 192

Divorce, 180; age of parties, 236–238; and assault, 60; cause of marriage termination, 236; defined, 228; failure to provide, 52–53; incidence of, 236–238; length of marriage, 236; and presence of woman's kin, 119; probabilities by duration, 237–238; and remarriage, 231; in simulation, 280

Divorced persons, see Marital status

Dobe area, 3, 5; physical features, 6–9

Dobe waterhole, 6

Dogs, dangers of, 55

Domesticated animals, 1

Dominance, in kinship, 330

Doubling rates of population growth, 219, 366

Draper, P., 58, 121, 330

Drift and natural selection as competing processes, 354

Drinking water, see Water

Drought, effects on fertility, 145

/Du/da (place), 18, 30–31, 97

Duration, of childbearing period, 131–133

Dutch East India Company, 10

Dust, as a sunscreen, 49

Dyke, B., 218

Dysentery, see Amoebic dysentery

E

Ears, condition in old age, 67

East (place), 60, 96

Eaton, J. W., 154

Effective population size, 355–357

Eighteenth-century conditions of !Kung, 11–13

Eligibility for marriage, in simulation, 278–279

Elimination, disposal problems, 48–49

Elphick, R., 10

Embarassment of husband by wife, 60

Emphysema, 65

Endogamy, 17, 247

Environmental fluctuations, 40, 100, 112, 216; and annual birth rates, 144–145; and differential reproductive success, 344; and fertility and mortality rates, 220, 330

Epidemics of contagious diseases, 63; and venereal disease, 65

Equilibrium process in genetic transmission, 353

Equilibrium and random drift, 353

Errors of age estimation, 23, 24, 25, 31–40, 107, 224, 242–246

Errors in age rankings, 26; in genealogies, 331; in mortality studies. 113; in observation, 22, 112; from sampling, 99; in skeletal data collections, 114; sources of, 124; of under-reporting parity, 125
Ethical problems of research, 211
Ethnocentrism in marriage, 227
Ethnographic analogy, 2, 333
European farmers, 5
European fertility pattern, 156
Europe, patterns of mortality, 77
Eventual parity of a cohort, 336, 345
Evolution, implications of !Kung demography, 333
Exhaustion of variance by natural selection, 353
Exercise, effects on health, 66
Expectation of life at birth, 95
Expected births, 265; expected deaths, 106
Experimentation by simulation, 278
Exposure, as a danger, 58
External features of populations, 218, 288
Extinction: of alleles, 354; of a genetic line, 337; in simulated populations, 218
Extra-marital births, 264
Extrapolations of mortality, 79
Extreme ages, in mortality analysis, 113
Eyes: diseases, 67; effects of flies, 49; incidence of handicaps, 67; injuries, 67

F
Falls, source of danger, 57
Fathers, 225, 232, 253
Fathers-in-law, and own fathers, 322
Fatherhood of Dobe men, 263–273
Family, 34–39. *See also* Natal families and Conjugal family
Fatalism, 51
Fatness, 190–191; and cattleposts, 210; defined operationally, 208; of fertile women, 206; of infants, 120; of infertile women, 203–204; of !Kung women, 192; and menarche, 190; after menarche, 191; of poorly nourished Americans, 192; proportions of body weight, 191. *See also* Critical fatness hypothesis
Fecundability, 146, 149
Fecundity, proportion fecund by age, 130, 162, 191
Feedback, of age distribution on population size, 220

Fertility: annual variations, 142–143; effects of Bantu, 210; biological maximum, 154; comparative data, 133, 151, 153, 189; data sources, 137, 261; differentials, 226; and kinship, 331; future rise, 363; limitation, 134; and marriage, 249–250, 277–303; maximum, 154; of men, 253–275, 296; measurement of, 122; and mortality, 189, 213; natural and controlled, 154; and population maintenance, 189; problems, 187; schedules, 345; in simulation, 281; and venereal disease, 65
Fetal wastage, 138, 146, 148. *See also* Abortion and Miscarriage
Feudal relations, 13
Fictive kinship, 229, 322, 331
Fieldwork, observation of births, 137
Fights, *see* Assault
Final birth, 130, 149–150
Firearms, introduction of, 12
Fires, 55, 57, 58, 65
First buck ceremony, 259
First birth, 172–173
First marriages for men and women, 244–245
Fisher, R. A., 345
Fitness and opportunity for natural selection, 344
Fixation of genes, 354. *See also* Extinction
Flat-face disease, *see* Lupus vulgaris.
Flies, 48–49
Food, 5, 52–53, 57. *See also* Diet
France, fertility in 1870, 155
Freedom of women, 57
Friedlander, J., 196
Frisch, R., 156, 190–192, 196, 208, 210, 253
Full fertility simulations, 216–226

G
Gaberones, 15
Gathering, dangers to women, 57
Genealogies, 331, 338
Generations: descendents per, 336–338, 340; and effective population size, 355; length of, 214, 335; number simultaneously alive, 328–329; overlapping of, 35
Genes, allele numbers, 347; flow, 11; frequency shifts, 351; monomorphic, 347; number of, 347; and phenotypes, 346; polymorphic, 347; pools, 11, 346
Genetic descent, 9

Genetic disposition to resist death, 66, 68, 97
Genetic distinctiveness, 334
Genetic implications of demography, 334
Genetic studies, 127, 347, 356, 358
Geographic analysis, 192; patterns in mortality, 83
Germ theory of disease, 49
Ghanzi district, 11, 63
Ghost, 56–57
Gift-giving, 11
Gonorrhea, 63, 135, 180, 185–187
Goodman, L., 308
Good years, correlations of fertility and mortality, 330
Grandparents, 46; counts of grandfathers, 314; of grandmothers, 314
Grass fires, 6
Gratitude, 57
Graunt, J., 47, 68
Graveyard, 88
Groote Eylandt aborigines, 26–27
Gross reproduction rate, 214, 273–274
Group fission, 52
Group moves, 192
Group sizes, 54
Growth rates of population, 215, 222, 345; in the male generation, 273–274; in simulations, 116, 218, 302. *See also* Crude rates; Intrinsic rate of natural increase; and Net reproduction rate
Growth in body size, of men, 253–258; of women, 192–196. *See also* Height and Weight
Guenther, M., 11, 63

H

Handicaps; and cattleposts, 50; and fertility, 266; and marital success, 249; mental, 54; and sterility, 205; types of, 54
Hansen, J., 63–67
Hardy-Weinberg law, 353
Harmless people, 39, 59
Harpending, H., 50, 100, 127, 232, 334, 356, 357, 359
Harrison, G. A., 355
Hart, C. W., 356
Head wound, 59
Headman, 14, 119
Hearing. *see* Ears

Heart disease, 65, 67
Height, 26, 193–197, 253–256
Helplessness, in real populations and simulations, 303
Henripin, J., 157
Henry, L., 134, 146, 154, 158, 160–161
Herbal contraceptives, 121
Hereros, 14–15. *See also* Bantu
Historical changes in !Kung population, 186
Historical demography, 79, 153
History: of Dobe, 6; of growth rates, 215; of ethnic groups, 9; of events, 101; of a much-married man, 272
Homicide, *see* Murder
Homozygosity, 347, 357
Hormones, 191
Hookworm (Necator americanus), 65
Hospitals, 55–56, 58, 63
Hottentots, *see* Khoi
Households, composition, 42–46, 306, 324–326
Houses, 48–49
Howell, D., 56
Howell, N., 101, 284, 345
Hudson, D., 95
Huffman, S., 121, 211
Human evolution, 2, 333–359
Humor of !Kung, 2, 366
Hunter-gatherers populations, 3; contemporary, 2; critical fatness hypothesis, 192, 205; diet, 51; gene pools, 358–359; geographical distribution, 2; growth rates, 116; polymorphisms, 356; proportions ever married, 176; typicality of !Kung, 3
Hunters: first buck ceremony, 259; marriage, 229, 230, 251; modesty, 118; in a world of hunters, 9, 11
Hunting accidents, 55; by Bantu, 54
Hunting and gathering: duration of adaptation, 2; in settled areas, 5; skills, 5, 16; trips, frequency and duration, 192
Hunting, with guns, 12; and marriage, 179, 230; in Nyae Nyae area, 259; and poison, 55; predators, 54; trips by Tswanas, 13; and village locations, 49
Husbands, 119, 229, 260
Hutterites, 154–156, 159; birth intervals, 163; infertility, 165–166; parity progression ratios, 157
Hypertension, 66

Hypothesis: alternative, 79; on mortality, 82; on numbers of descendents in successive generations, 336–337; testing, 79, 107; use of simulation for formulation of null, 331
Hypothetical "people", 101, 303
Hxaro (trading, gift-giving), 11–12, 187

I

Idle period, *see* Birth intervals
Illegitimacy, 232
Illness, need for care, 53
Immaturity, appearance of young men, 258
Incest: in AMBUSH, 278; brother–sister, 61; and geneological overlap, 338; and marriage, 229, and naming rules, 229
Income, loss in illness, 53
Independence: of age segments for d_x and l_x, 107; of observations, 140–142, 144
Index of marital fertility, 155, 156
Index of overall fertility, 155, 156
Index of proportion married, 155, 156
India, fertility in 1945, 155, 156
Industrialized populations, 79, 156, 192
Infant death, 80; and birth intervals, 121, 149, 150, 209; definition, 112; and diet of mothers, 209; underreporting, 112–113
Infant development, 121
Infants: naming of, 80; protected from sunlight, 49; weights, 196
Infanticide: controlled by women, 119; demographic effects, 120; and genetic defects, 67; incidence of, 62, 120; and murder, 62; reasons for, 120; and remarriage, 242
Infectious disease: rates of, 63, 66, 68–69; and rate of mortality, 69–78
Infertile women, 148, 187
Infertility: causes, 135; concern about, 179; of husband, 266; among men, 180; and venereal disease, 64; as unemployment, 187. *See also* Sterility, primary and secondary
Influenza, 65
Informants, data problems, 112, 121
Initial populations, in simulations, 217, 221
Injuries, 54, 55, 60
Innoculation: against a range of diseases, 363; against smallpox, 63
/inono (*see* Gonorrhea), 64
Interactions of variables in simulation, 278, 286
Intercourse, *see* Sexual intercourse
Intermarriage, 11, 17, 356

Insects, 48
Interest rates, 213, 215
Internal consistency of results, 20, 116, 274–275
Internal features of populations, 288
Intrinsic rate of natural increase, 213, 218–219, 301, 335
Ireland, fertility pattern, 156
Isolated populations, 356
Isolation: in bush, 58; in old age, 318, 330
Invisible population features, 277
Invisible variables in simulations, 300

J

Jails, 5, 53, 59
Japan, fertility of rural groups, 161
Johannesberg mines, 180
Joking relations: and errors in age ranking, 41; and sexual relations, 231
Jorde, L. B., 100

K

Kennelly, B., 66
Keyfitz, N., 68, 70
Kgalagadi, 12
Khoi, 5, 9
Khoisan peoples, 5, 9
Kin, in life-crisis rituals, 311; and news of death, 90, and marriage, 230
KINPROGRAM, 331
Kinship counts, affinal ties, 320–322; age and sex patterns, 324; AMBUSH method, 307; aunts, 312; children, 316–317; conjugal family, 327–328; cousins, 314–315; and environmental fluctuations, 330–331; of fathers, 310–312; fathers-in-law, 322; generations, 328–329; grandchildren, 319–320; grandparents, 313–314; mean numbers, 308; mothers, 308–309; mothers-in-law, 321; nephews and nieces, 318–320; probability of survival and reproduction, 331; siblings, 314–315; total inventory, 322–323; uncles, 312–313; variability between and within simulations, 307–308
Kinship: and food distribution, 53; generational depth, 306; isolation, 318; joking and avoidance, 306; map of ties, 278; name relationships, 306; nursing care, 52; and orphans, 233; and parity distributions, 292; polygamy, 230; relative age terms, 306; as a resource,

Physicians, 48, 50, 51, 62
Pioneer Tswanas, 13
Plato, 19
Pneumonia, 63, 65, 71
Poisoned arrows, 61
Poisonous snakes, 54
Poisson distribution of parity, 124, 225–226
Police, 362
Polygamy, 230, 235, 241, 247, 252, 270, 272, 279; and reproductive success, 235, 267–270
Polygamous marriages, 233. *See also* marital status.
Polymorphisms, 356–357
Population, definition, 17–18; growth, 213, 274, 288, 300, 301, 302, 345, 364; size, 286, 332, 357; register, 137
Population Reference Bureau, 95
Portugese explorers, 9
Postpartum amenorrhea, 121
Precontact period, 16, 70, 100
Predators, 54, 71
Preferred spouses, 229–231
Pregnancy, 52–53, 117. 118, 146, 206–207, 259–260
Pregnancy wastage, 80. *See also* Abortion and Miscarriage
Prehistory, 2, 9, 100
Premarital pregnancy, 174, 177, 229, 259
Preston, S., 68, 70, 77
Prevention of accidents, 55
Prey species, 55
Primary sterility, 125–129, 167–181
Privacy and sexual relations, 231
Probability, 18, 19, 74, 303
Prohibited marriages, 228–229
Protection, of women by men, 57
Proteins, 50
Public health programs, 63, 79
Puerpereal infections, 58
Punishment of children, 62
Punjab villagers, fertility, 163

Q
Quebec, fertility, 157

R
Rabies, 55
Radix of a life table, 75
Random drift, 334, 353, 356
Random fluctuations and meaning, 220

Rare alleles, 354
Reconstruction of events, 18
Redistribution of food through kinship, 53
Registration system, 18, 89
Relative age, 26. *See* Age estimation
Religion and vital events, 48, 51, 122
Remarriage, 51, 135, 230, 232, 239–242, 280
Removal age of sibling groups, 307
Reproductive histories, 18, 261–273
Reproductive span, 131–133, 162–164
Reproductive strategies, 242, 268, 272
Reproductive success, 132, 245–246, 335–336, 338–341, 345
Residence, post-marital, 239
Residents of Dobe area, 27
Resistance to disease, 50
Respect relationships, 231
Responsibility for sick and handicapped relatives, 52
Retarded child, 120
Rheumatic fever, 65
Rituals, 51–52
Rock paintings, 10
Rose, F., 26–27
Rubella (measles), 62

S
Salt, 50
Sampling error, 3, 99, 124, 353
Sampling frame, 18
San peoples, 5
Sand, 48
Sanitation, 48–49
Sarwa, 12. *See also* San peoples
Scarcity of men as spouses, 279
Scavengers, 54
Schapera, I., 10
Schistosomes, 65
Schoen, R., 68, 70
Schools, 5
Schrire, V., 66
Scorpion stings, 55
Seasons, 7–8; of birth, 29, 137; and nutritional status, 193; residence, 9
Secondary sterility, 129, 184–185
Selection intensity, 300–302
Sensory deprivation in old age, 67
Separation and divorce, 228
Septicemia, 97
Serum cholesterol, 66

Settlement, duration, 5; stations, 5, 15
Sewell Wright effects, 353
Sex differences: height, 256; in kinship, 317; in marital success, 248–251; in mortality, 77; in parity, 269–271; in weight, 259
Sex ratio at birth, 214, 247, 286
Sexual equality, 57, 330
Sexual jealousy, 60, 61, 231
Sexual play of children, 174
Sexual relations, 57, 60, 64, 117, 120, 174, 205, 231, 241, 259
Sexual selection, 252
Shame, 61
Sharing and marriage, 228
Sheps, M., 146
Short runs, in simulation, 217
Shortage of males in marriage market, 247
Shorter, F., 21
Shostak, M., 118, 231
Siblings, 314–315
Sibling groups, 225–226, 300, 307
Silberbauer, G., 24
Simulation, 40, 102, 218, 223–226, 274, 277–278, 284–285, 292, 299–300, 303–304, 330–331. *See also* AMBUSH
Single-sex rates, 214. *See also* Gross reproduction rates and Net reproduction rates
Single persons, way of life, 251. *See also* Marital status
Size, of population, 218–220
Skeletal mortality studies, 88, 114
Sleeping arrangements, 45, 48, 120, 228
Small populations, 18, 99, 218, 355; extinction probabilities, 218; genetic implications, 353–354, 358; and marriage frequency, 231; measurement problems, 23, 41, 79, 82, 92, 100, 102, 105, 111, 126, 177, 194, 214, 217–218, 274, 293; two-sex problem, 247
Smallpox, 63
Smoke, 65
Smoothing data into distributions. 25, 92, 144, 299
Snakes, 54–55
Social change, 5, 6, 15, 20, 84, 123, 210, 361–363
Social control, 60, 61
Sodium chloride, 50
Sororal polygamy, 241, 268, 272
Speciation, 333, 356
Split-halves test, 82

Stable population models, 20, 25, 28–29, 40, 221
Stable reproductive ability, 191
Standard errors, 106, 107, 111, 114
Standard of living, 365
Start-up problem, 285–286
Statistical tests, 107
Stationary population assumptions, 89, 102
Status of women, 329–330
Stealing, 53, 296
Steatopygia, 203
Steiger, W., 218
Sterility, 121, 125, 126, 161–162; of husband, 266; of Hutterites and !Kung, 165; and extra-marital sex, 180; primary, 125–129, 167–181; secondary, 181–184; in simulation, 216; venereal disease, 64–65; 180; and weights of women, 203–205
Stinginess, 52
Stochastic fluctuations, 21, 100, 103, 111, 216, 278, 302
Stress, 23, 77
Stomach (cause of death), 65
Stroke, 66
Subordination, of ethnic groups, 5; of women to men, 57
Success, 145; *see* Reproductive success and Marital success
Suicide, 61
Sunburn, 49
Serfdom, 12–13
Survivorship, 75, 83, 86, 89, 97, 113. *See also* Mortality
Sutter, H. E., 356
Syphilis, 63, 67, 180. *See also* Venereal disease

T
Tabah, L., 356
Taiwan, fertility in 1930, 155–156
Tallness, in men, 255; in women, 195
Tanner, J., 178
Tawana chieftainship, 12
TB, *see* Tuberculosis
Ten-year runs in simulation, 106, 110
Terminated marriages, 236–238
Thinness, 51, 66, 205, 208
Thomas, E., 13, 39, 55, 59
Thorns (injuries to feet), 55, 97
Thule Eskimo, 356
Time calibration, 23

Time limits on simulations, 102
Time machine, 100, 102, 219
Tiwi islanders, 356
Tobacco, 65
Tonsilitis, 65
Tooth decay and wear, 66–67
Total Fertility Rate, 122. *See also* Fertility
Toxemia of pregnancy, 58
Tracking, 54–55, 57–59, 231
Tracoma, 67
Trance dances, 51
Travel, 5, 8; prehistoric, 11
Tribe, 4. *See also* Size of population
Trussell, J., 210
Truswell, A., 48, 50, 63–67, 195
Tsausi chisi (women's business), 117, 119
Tswana peoples, 12–14
Tuberculosis, 61, 63, 67
Tsetse flies, 14
Twenty-year runs in simulation, 105, 109, 217
Twins, 120
Tuning simulation inputs, 278
Two-sex problem in marriage, 247–248, 251–252, 277

U

Uncles, counts of, 313
Unconscious preference for adults, 97
Underreporting of events, 22, 113, 125
United Nations, 25, 76, 78
United States, fertility in 1900 and 1960, 155, 191
Units of analysis, 345
Utuhile, I., 14

V

Vaccination, 63, 363
van de Walle. E., 21, 24
van Riebeeck, H., 10
van Zyl, H., 13
Variance: of allelic transmissions, 350; of parity distributions, 124, 132; over time, 21
Variation, interpretation of, 219–220
Venereal disease, 63–64, 135, 162, 179–180, 185–187, 203, 205, 274, 363
Viability of parameters, 218, 286

Villages, 42–45, 48–58, 315
Violence, as a cause of death, 59, 68–70
Virginity, 174
Vision, *see* Eyes
Vitamins, 49–50

W

Wachter, K., 306
Wage labor, 60, 180, 252, 364
Wahlund's F., 357
Washing, 49
Water, 6, 7, 49–50, 58
Waterholes, 8–9, 28
Weaning, 118
Weights, 193, 195–196; of children, 193; of men, 255; of women, 50, 190, 191, 196, 203–204, 206–207
Weiss, K., 78–79
Wells, 49, 362
West series model life tables, 77
Widowed, 233. *See also* Marital status
Wiessner, P., 12, 53, 58, 63, 118, 138, 259, 366
Wilmsen, E., 362
Witchcraft, 12, 51
Wits, 62, 118, 249, 251
Work loads, 52–53, 118, 259
World Health Organization, 196
Women, 18, 19, 57, 80, 117, 119, 187, 329–330
Wright, S., 353

X

/Xai/Xai (place), 8, 60
Xangwa (place), 6, 8, 14, 15

Y

Years, allocating events to, 29
Yei settlers in Dobe, 14
Yellen, J., 9

Z

Zero births, 146
Zero parity, 125–126, 292
Zu dole (strange people), 249